# INDEX ON CENSORSHIP

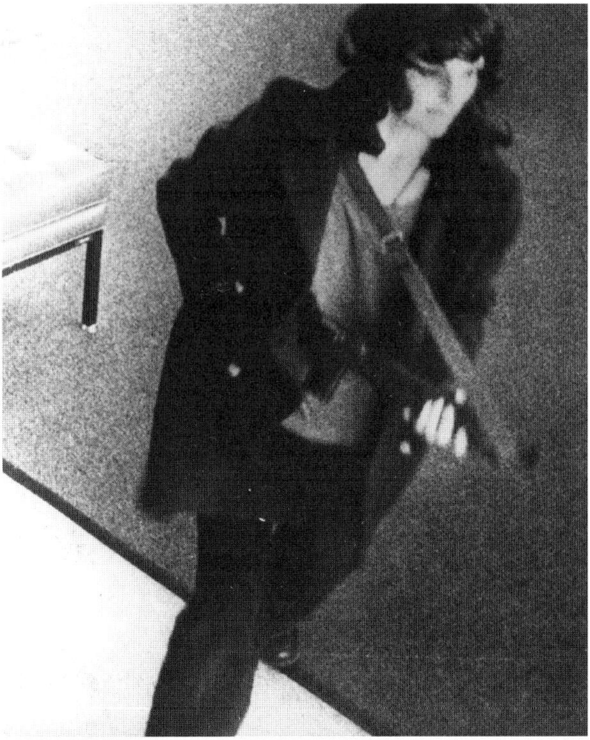

INDEX ON CENSORSHIP 6 1999

WEBSITE NEWS UPDATED WEEKLY

# INDEX ON CENSORSHIP

www.indexoncensorship.org
contact@indexoncensorship.org
tel: 0171-278 2313
fax: 0171-278 1878

Volume 28 No 6 November/December 1999 Issue 191



**Previous page:** Credit: Hulton Getty Picture Collection

***Index on Censorship*** (ISSN 0306-4220) is published bi-monthly by a non-profit-making company: Writers & Scholars International Ltd, Lancaster House, 33 Islington High Street, London N1 9LH. *Index on Censorship* is associated with Writers & Scholars Educational Trust, registered charity number 325003
***Periodicals postage***: (US subscribers only) paid at Newark, New Jersey. Postmaster: send US address changes to *Index on Censorship* c/o Mercury Airfreight International Ltd Inc, 365 Blair Road, Avenel, NJ 07001, USA


**Subscriptions (6 issues per annum)**
**Individuals: UK £39, US $52, rest of world £45**
**Institutions: UK £44, US $80, rest of world £50**
**Speak to Tony Callaghan on 0171 278 2313**

# EDITORIAL

## Camera obscura

There is something artificial about celebrating the end of a century – in some ways an arbitrary division of historical time. This one, minutely documented from its beginning by photography, has had its glories, but it is also the most genocidal century on record, haunted by the parallel tracks of fascism and communism.

Already we have been treated to a feast of visual reminiscence and recollection. But there is another, much less familiar history, and *Index* is offering a very different version of the past hundred years. For photography and censorship have always had a close relationship: here are photos that were banned and manipulated, photos blatantly used for propaganda, images of the body that disturb, records of events we're not supposed to know about, incidents we'd rather forget.

These photographs tell stories which range from the harrowing to the bizarre – from the banned picture of Ayatollah Khomeini's funeral to that of the newborn baby in the Benetton ad, from the airbrushing of Stalin's enemies to the Photoshopping of John Prescott's beer bottle. Even the unmanipulated images are not always what they seem. Just where *is* the woman with her hand raised in a Nazi salute (p97)?: or the war damaged buildings with armed soldiers passing by (118)? And what is Joan Crawford's companion up to (p26)?

Meanwhile, the photographs in 'Recovered Memory' and 'Unfinished Business' remind us of our ability to censor ourselves, dismissing the intolerable from our minds. But then what is intolerable? And who decides? 'Perhaps these daunting photographs are best seen as part of an attempt to get beyond shock', Adam Phillips suggests (p94).

In our century, photography, Alberto Manguel tells us 'conquered space and time, the present wittled down to a shared iconography.' News became 'real' and 'true' when it had a photo attached, an image that could be seen by millions of people, simultaneously, all over the world.

But photos can be cropped, retouched, manipulated, airbrushed, miscaptioned: digital cameras and computerised manipulation are, at the end of this spectacularly innovative century, putting more nails in the coffin of the photograph as the true version of events, as 'democratised reality'. The images in this issue of Index are immensely potent, but, as Philip Jones Griffiths says (p206) 'Photography will never be the same again, and we are probably the last generation that will accept the integrity of the photograph'. ❑

# contents

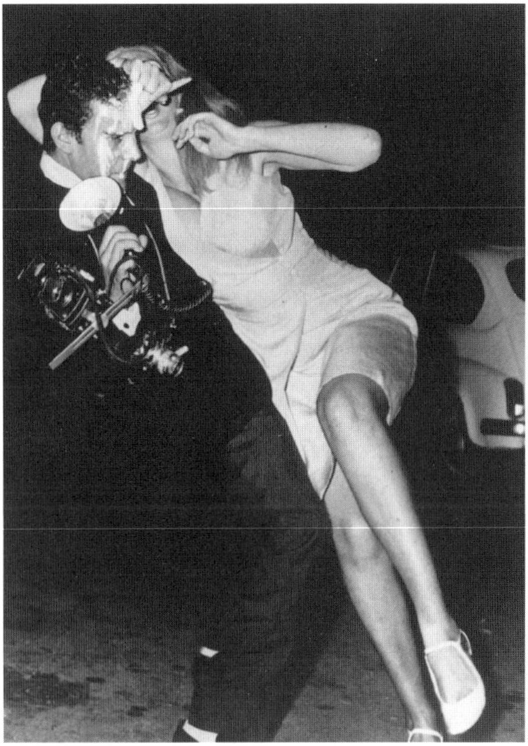

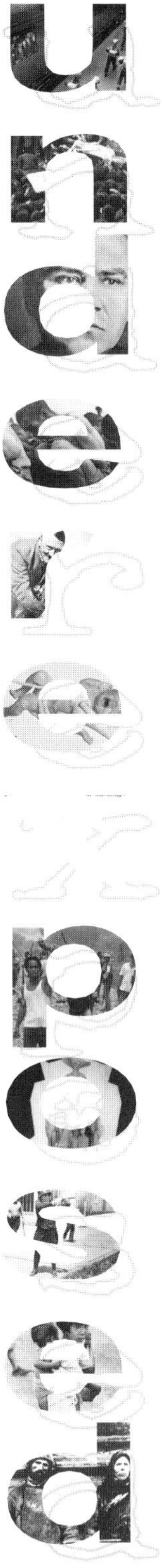
underexposed

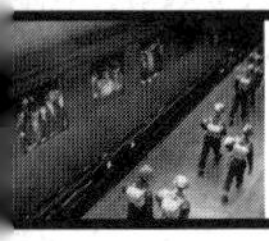

# Reading pictures

*Alberto Manguel*

'... to be only the lens of my camera, something fixed, rigid, incapable of intervention.' *Julio Cortázar,* Blow-Up

In the thirty-fifth book of his Natural History, the encyclopaedist Pliny the Elder wrote that, though the Egyptians claimed they had invented the art of painting before it crossed to Greece, and the Greeks argued that the invention had taken place in Sicyon or Corinth, there was universal agreement that painting had begun by the outlining of a man's shadow. To capture reality through the contrast between shadow and light seemed, to Pliny, the goal of art and he praised the *trompe-l'oeil* of the artist Zeuxis who produced such a successful representation of grapes that birds flew up to peck at them (Pliny notes that Zeuxis was outwitted by Parrhasius, who painted a curtain which Zeuxis asked be drawn aside, believing it hung in front of the real picture). The point of Pliny's story was that art could hold a faithful mirror to the world. Subjectivity, he thought, was detrimental.

Nineteen centuries later, in the late 1820s in Paris, the brothers Claude and Joseph Nicéphore Niepce, with the aid of a camera obscura and sensitised paper, developed a procedure for a hot-air, engine-powered lithography press that allowed them to produce pictures of reality that were, however, tonally reversed, that is to say, black for white, what we would today call negatives. Eventually this method produced a plate that could be etched to create a positive print. A few years later, Louis Jacques Mandé Daguerre perfected the Niepces' invention, which was then bought by the French government in 1839. The new technique, under the name of daguerreotype, became universally successful and barely a year later, in January of 1840, Edgar Allan Poe, after reminding his readers that the process itself was called photogeny ('from Greek words signifying sun-painting'), praised the French invention as 'the most important, and perhaps the most extraordinary triumph of modern science.'

Not everyone was convinced. Charles Baudelaire, in a letter published in the magazine *Le Boulevard* on 14 September 1862, derided this new art. Concerned that the pretension of photography – to portray reality accurately and objectively – would distract audiences from the artistic refusal to copy reality and 'confirm fools in their faith', Baudelaire wrote: 'In the domain of painting and statuary, the present day credo of the worldly wise, especially in France, ... is this: ... "I believe that art is, and can only be, the exact reproduction of nature." ... An avenging God has heard the prayers of this multitude; Daguerre was his messiah.'

In spite of Baudelaire's caveat, photography quickly became our society's

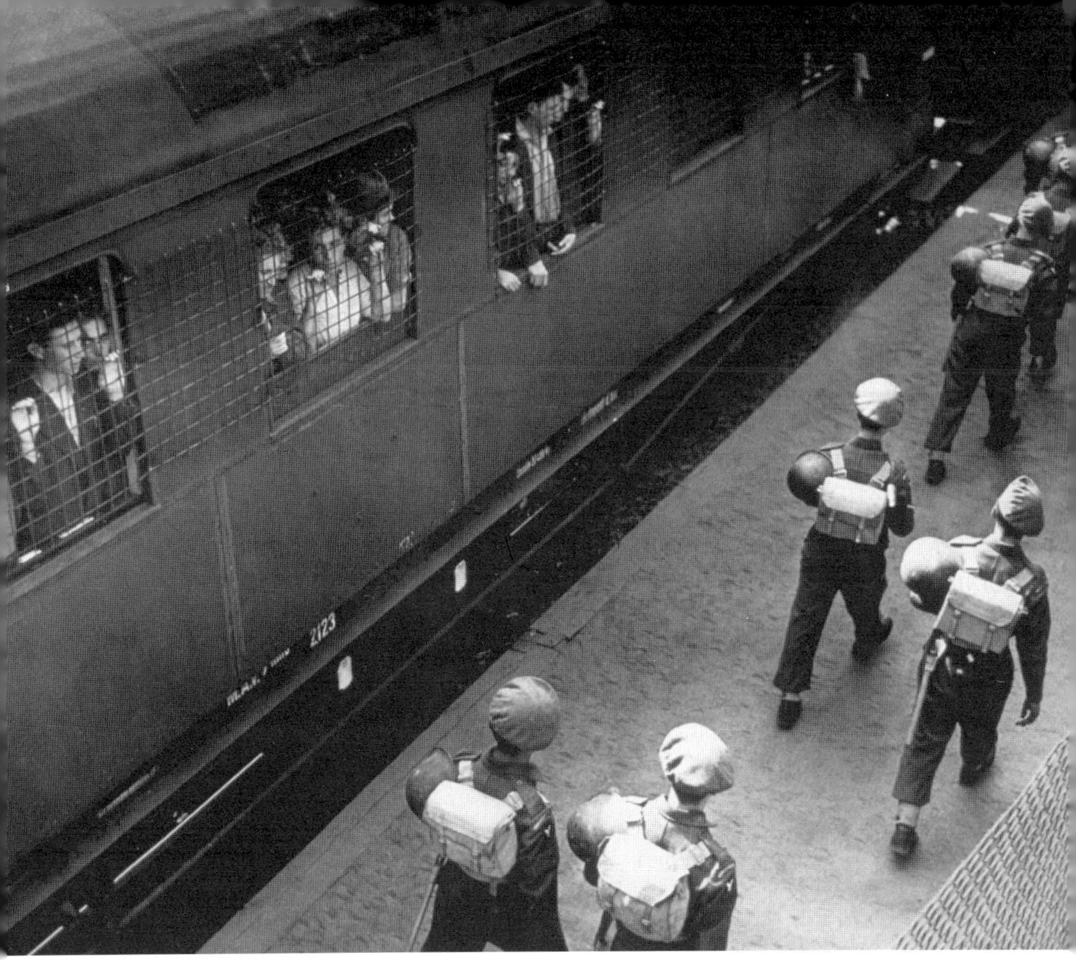

**What do you see?** German Jews on their way to the camps. But this is 1947, the war is over and the troops guarding the train are British. This was the exodus that failed as Jewish survivors of the Holocaust, hoping to set sail for Palestine in the first 'exodus' ship, Ocean Voyage, were rounded up and sent off to Poppendorf Camp by the British
*Credit: Hulton Getty Picture Collection*

purveyor of images. It conquered space and time and we became witnesses of what took place far away and long ago. War, momentous and private events, foreign places, the face our grandparents had in their childhood, were all offered by the camera for our inspection. Through the eye of the lens, the past became contemporary and the present whittled down to a shared iconography. For the first time in our long history, the same image (the burning of the Hindenburg or the tragic face of a migrant Californian worker), in all its exact details, could be seen by millions all over the world. News was not news unless there was a picture to back it. Photography democratised reality.

Or did it? 'A photograph,' writes John Berger, 'whilst recording what has been seen, always and by its nature refers to what is not seen.' Unlike a photograph, the world is not framed, the eye wanders and can take in what lies beyond the margins. We know the limits of a photographic document, we know that it shows only what the photographer has chosen to show and what a certain light and shade has allowed him to show, and yet the factual mirroring that Pliny claimed as a virtue overpowers such restrictions and hesitations. On the contrary: photography's claim to faithfulness has allowed (and allows still) for it to be manipulated without protest, a manipulation that electronic techniques have now made even more seamless. From Stalin's infamous removal of every *persona non grata* from the official pictures to the selective portrayal of war scenes in everyday reporting, from the dressed-up representation of celebrities to the doctored depiction of fashion models, from cropped documentary views to abstract or fantastical arrangements, photography allows, perhaps more than any other art, for the presence of censorship as an integral part of its own creative process. A text, a sculpture, a painting may suppress (does suppress) information from within the work itself, through the restrained hand of the artist, and also from without, through the restrictive hand of an official censor. But all these other art forms deliberately define themselves as subjective, accept their own fictions, require in order to exist (as Coleridge pointed out) the audience's willing suspension of disbelief. Photography, however, though acknowledging in its criticism and its manifestos the subjectivity of the camera, nevertheless relies on the conviction that what we, the viewers, see was actually once there, that it took place at a certain precise time, and that as reality it was captured by the eye of the beholder. Any photograph, whether deliberately censored or unconsciously manipulated, though it may offer itself as 'fixed, rigid, incapable of intervention' wholly depends on this necessary deception. ❑

***Alberto Manguel** won the Prix Médici for* A History of Reading. *His forthcoming book is* Reading Pictures *(Bloomsbury)*

INDEX ON CENSORSHIP

*Index on Censorship* would like to thank the following for their generous support for 'Underexposed'

The Hulton Getty Picture Collection
David King
Franziska Payer at Endeavour Group UK
Magnum
Liaison Agency
Associated Press
Sally Mann
Robin Tudge
John McFadden
Bloomberg News
The Economist Group
William Sieghart
The Esmée Fairbairn Charitable Trust
Ruthie Rogers
Thanet Press
Robert Fox Ltd

We would like in particular to thank Charles Merullo and Fiona Wilson of the Hulton Getty Picture Collection who have worked tirelessly with us, finding images, coming up with suggestions and having conversations about the concept and structure of this issue of *Index*. We are very grateful to them for their commitment and support – the project would not have been possible without them.

# Banned

*Kafka leaned his head toward his shoulder. 'Photography concentrates one's eye on the superficial. For that reason it obscures the hidden life which glimmers through the outlines of things like a play of light and shade.One can't catch that even with the sharpest lens. One has to grope for it by feeling... This automatic camera doesn't multiply men's eyes, but only gives a fantastically simplified fly eye's view'.*

Gustav Jounouch's Conversations
with Kafka

**Jungbauern Westerwald Germany 1914** In 1911, August Sander began a photographic catalogue of German 'archetypes' as he called them. In 1934, five years after its publication, the Nazis impounded the unsold copies of his book Antlitz der Zeit (The Face of our Time) and destroyed the printing blocks; they claimed it was 'anti-social'
*Credit: Die Photographische Sammlung/SK Stiftung Kultur-August Sander Archiv, Cologne, DACS, London, 2000*

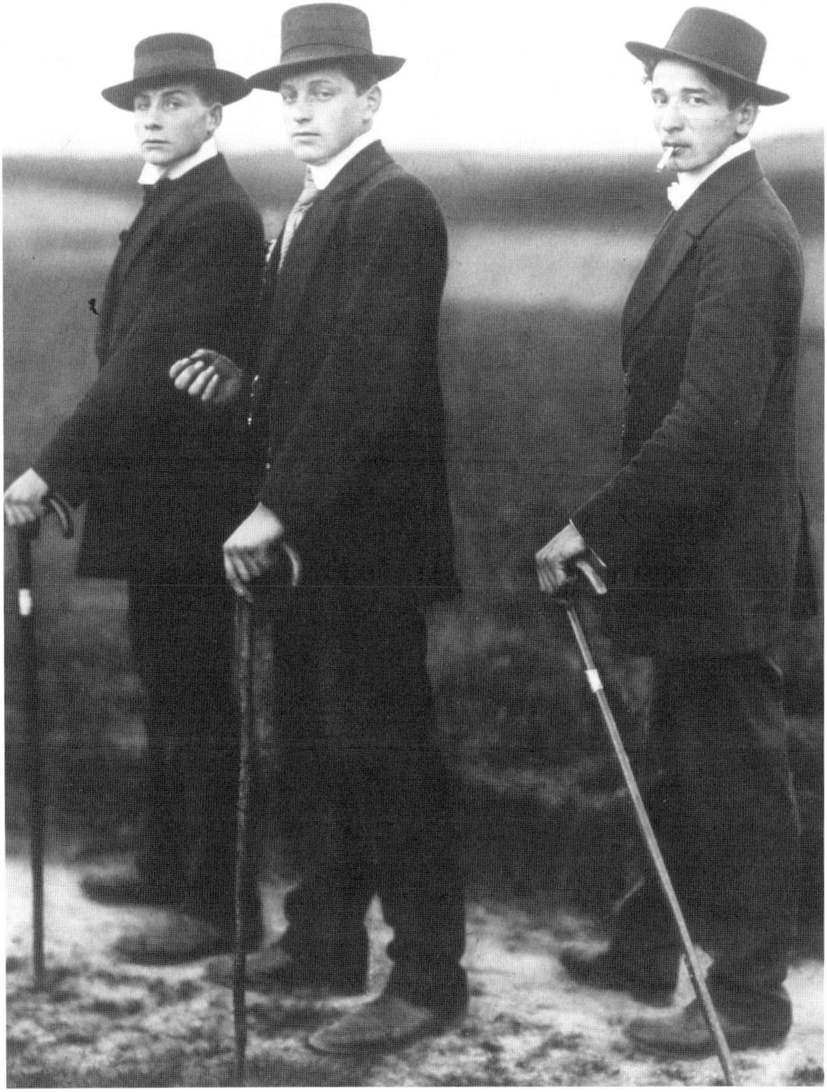

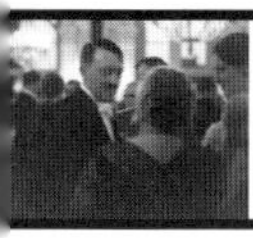

# Banned

*Harold Evans*

Big Brother is in good company. Many worthy people have joined the thought police in the suppression of images. Malcolm Browne's snapshot of a Buddhist priest immolating himself in a square in Saigon was considered unfit for America's breakfast tables by the editors of the *New York Times*.

That was a misjudgment on their part, even by the taste buds of the time. The event testified to the Buddhist sense of outrage at their persecution by the Saigon government. It was truly incredible. Many people could hardly believe the report that a priest had burned himself alive. The video was even more compelling; even if some thought the flames were a kind of circus magic.

There was an excuse for the caution of the *Times* editors. Violent images shock; readers make a fuss, cancel subscriptions. In the Gulf War, the *Observer* in London published a gruesome photograph of an incinerated Iraqi staring sightlessly from his truck. The editor was inundated with protests. Again, I think he was right to publish. The Gulf War had been presented as some kind of clean war where laser technology removed the pain. As a Syracuse editor said of the *Times'* suppression of the Saigon picture, an editor who would not use that picture would not have run one of the Crucifixion.

Are there any sensible limits? I think there are. I would not have published the photograph of Jayne Mansfield's head severed from her body in a car crash, nor the corpse of Lee Harvey Oswald stitched up after the autopsy. The test I applied as an editor was whether the violence or obscenity portrayed had social or historic significance and, if it did, whether the shocking detail was necessary for a proper understanding of the event or for its corroboration.

So I have occasionally been an unrepentant censor. What is the difference between this kind of censorship and government control? Well, in a pluralistic press it is not so much censorship as discrimination. One editor's decision does not amount to suppression. Another editor can take a different view. The *National Inquirer* had no hesitation in publishing Oswald on the pathologist's table. Editors have to decide whether the shock is worth the offence, and it is a useful calculus. A government edict is altogether a different matter. While the rules I have suggested are helpful, they leave room for discretion, for the special case that no legislator can envisage. A law of the kind the French government has proposed, banning photography at specific occasions, is inflexible. *Content* magazine recently canvassed opinions on the notion of banning photography at funerals in the light of intrusion on the Kennedy family following the death of John F Kennedy, Jr. As editors pointed out, if that prohibition had existed when his father was assassinated the world would never have seen the memorable image of John Junior giving a salute to his father.

In World War II, I might have hesitated to publish the images of charred bodies after the German bombing of Coventry out of deference to the relatives. Those pictures were suppressed by the government as damaging to morale and in a national crisis that is an argument that deserves some respect – but not too much. The people ought to have a clear idea of the sacrifices being made, of what is being done in their name. When authority moves to suppress it is usually an indication that they have little confidence in their actions – precisely the moment when a more informed debate can avert catastrophe. Governments were too ready to suppress pictures from the trenches in World War I. It was a stupid war, and the sooner everyone realised it the better it would have been. Both sides, busily suppressing, were, of course, only too ready to manipulate opinion by publicising the enemy's 'atrocities.'

Propaganda has to be met by propagation of the truth. Tom Hopkinson, the editor of *Picture Post*, was fired because he wanted to publish photographs during the Korean War that his ownership judged 'anti-western'. They showed North Korean prisoners, some only 12 years old, roped together and in obvious fear for their lives. It is true that these pictures were helpful to the North Koreans – but by caption or other photography an objective editor would have been entitled to remind readers that both sides were cruel. But a publication that strives always to be 'balanced' is treading dangerous ground. I remember the arguments advanced against publication of the photographs Ron Haeberle had taken at My Lai. It was 18 months before they became available. Viewing them with the editors of the *Sunday Times* colour magazine, I reached two conclusions: that we had to check out their authenticity and then, if satisfied, we not only had a right but a duty to publish. They were inconvenient for 'our side', but essential to corroborating an appalling story. We recognised that they would offend or upset, but the overwhelming necessity was to document the tragedy.

Today an even bigger problem for photography is the ease of manipulation with the computer. Senator Tydings, Joe McCarthy's main early critic, was famously killed in his reselection campaign by scissor work with two photographs that made him appear chummy with the leader of the American Communist Party. As David King and others have documented, the Stalinists, too, have always been expert at this kind of trick, especially in visual liquidation.

They all of them, censors and manipulators, testify to the power of the still image. ❑

***Harold Evans*** *is the author of* Pictures on a Page *and* The American Century. *He is vice-chairman and editorial director of the* Daily News *and* US News and World Report. *He is former editor of* the Sunday Times *and* The Times *of London*

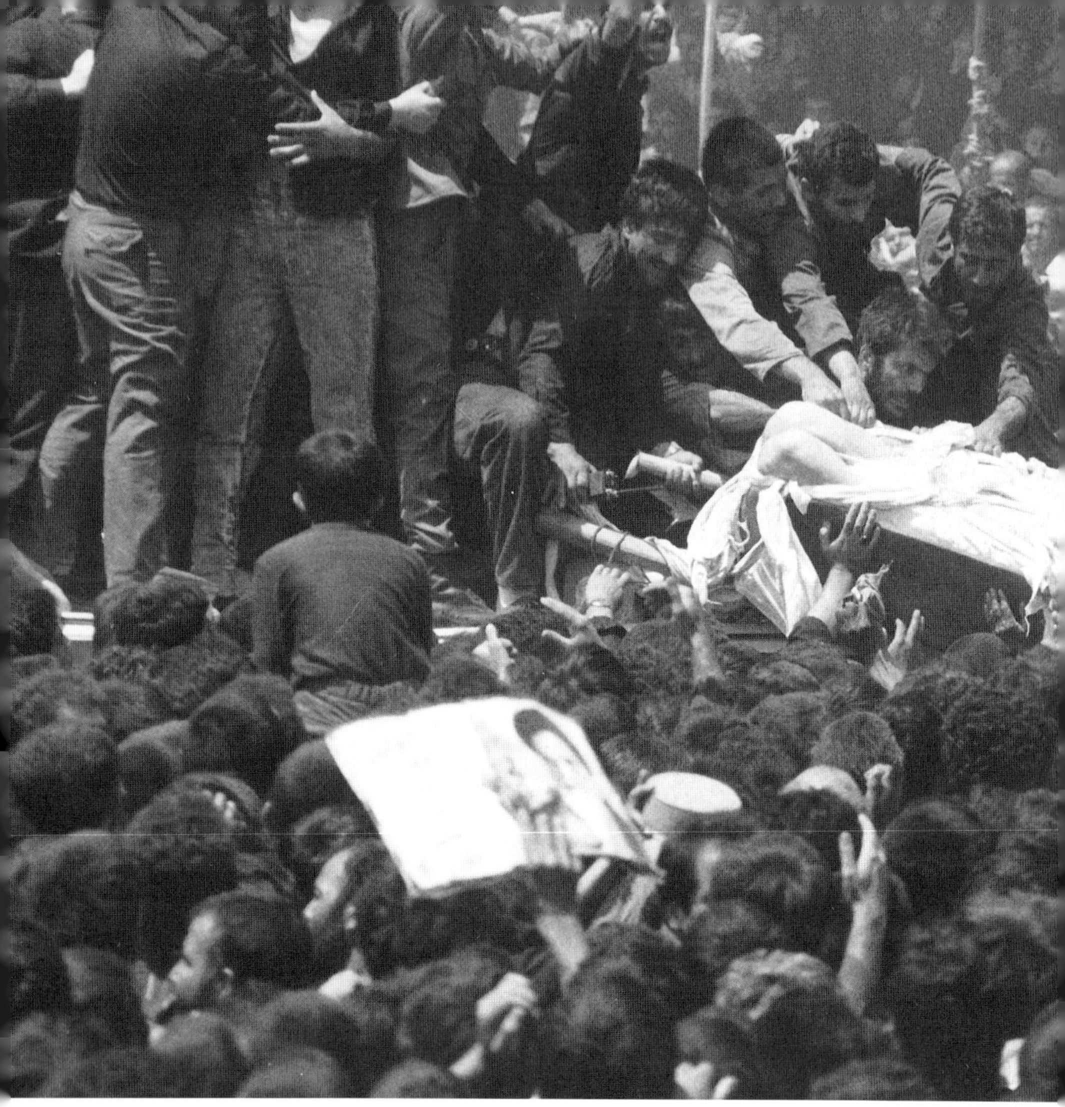

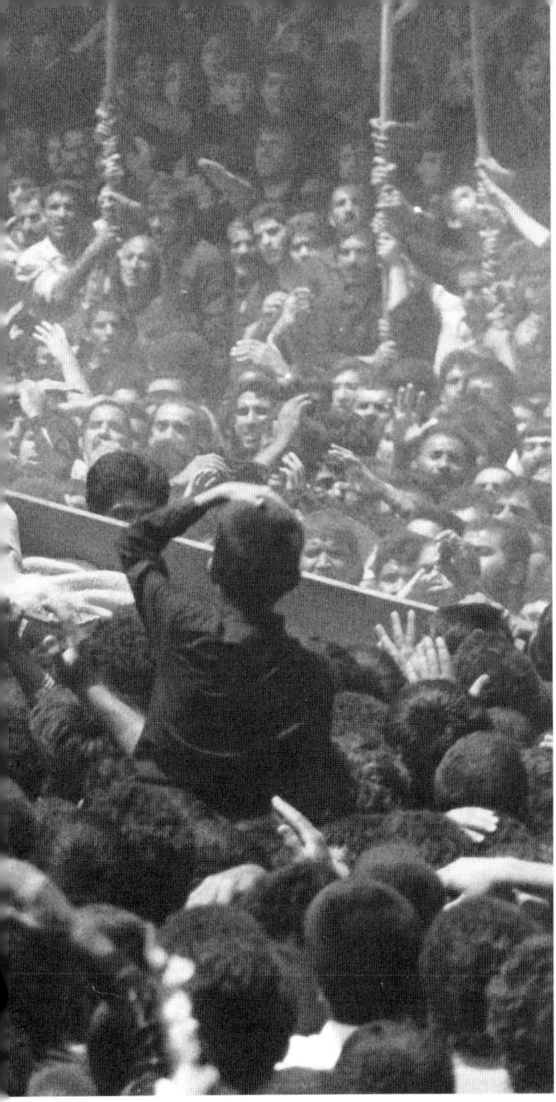

**Iran 1989** This was the only photograph showing the near-naked body of Ayatollah Khomeini to escape from Tehran following his funeral. The authorities confiscated and destroyed all other film of the scene at which the two million strong crowd stripped the body, anxious to secure a souvenir. *Credit: Anonymous*

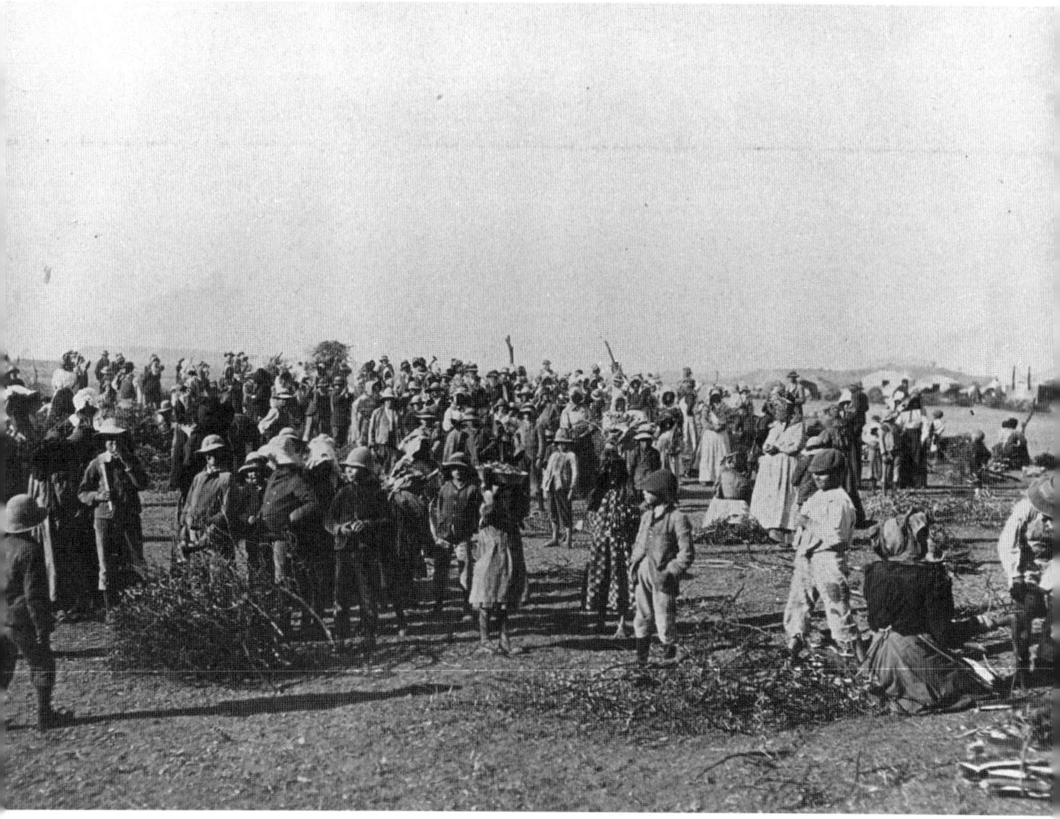

**Concentration camp South Africa 1899-1902** More than 120,000 Boer civilians, mainly women and children, were interned for security by the British forces during the second Boer War in what became known for the first time as 'concentration camps'. Many suffered malnutrition and disease and photographs of the camps were suppressed at the time in favour of more heroic images
*Credit: Hulton Getty Picture Collection*

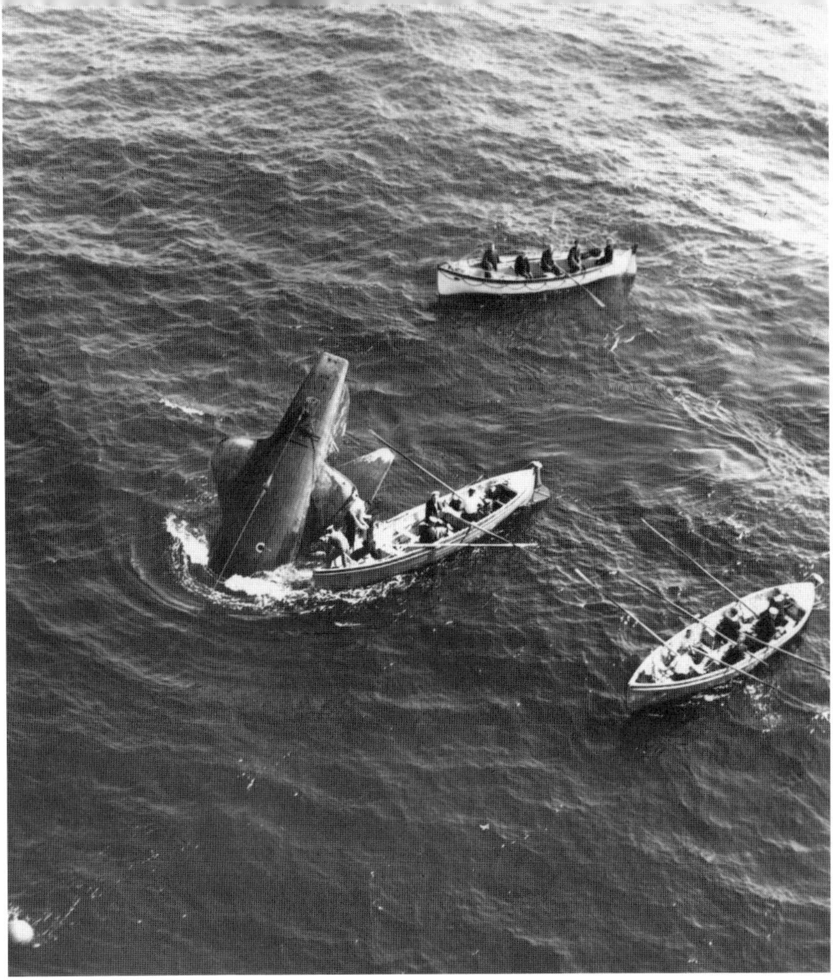

▲
**Liverpool Bay UK 1939** The Admiralty regrets ... the sinking of the Thetis, lost during sea trials with 99 of her crew – only four survived – shortly before the outbreak of WWII. Still the worst submarine disaster in UK history, photos were suppressed at the time as part of a general cover-up
*Hulton Getty Picture Collecton*

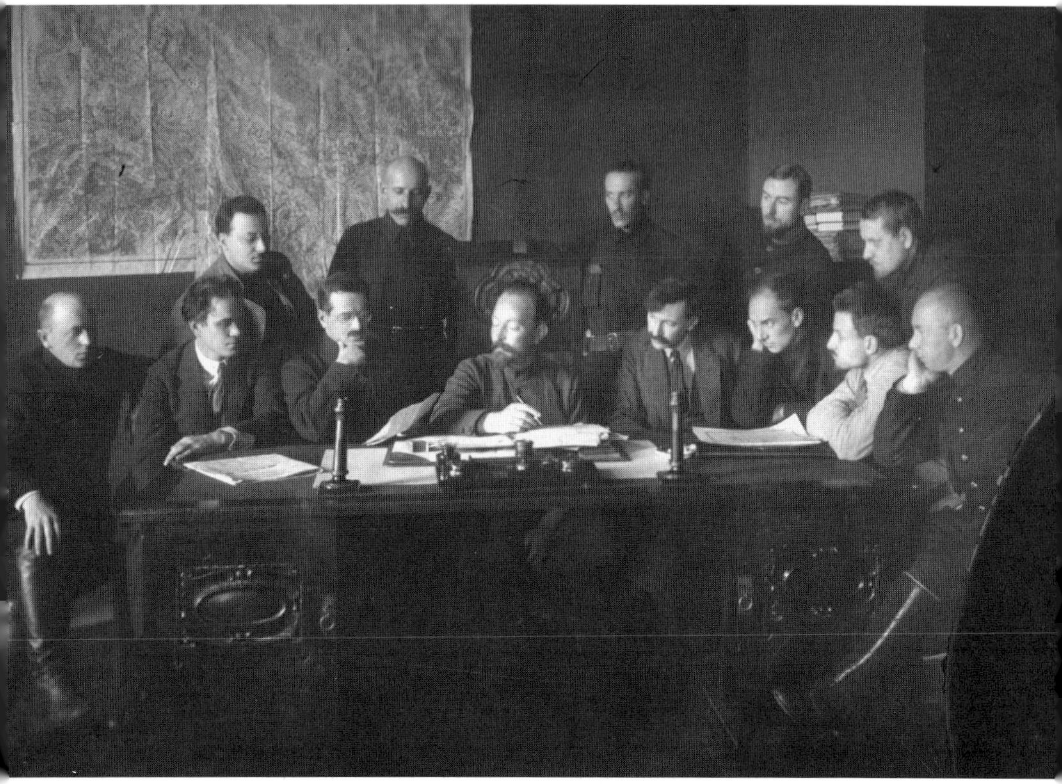

▲
**The Lubyanka Moscow 1922** Felix Dzerzhinsky, recently appointed head of the infamous *Cheka*, sits at his desk with his covert cronies in the Lubyanka, 1922. In the aftermath of the revolution, these men were the new leaders of Russia's secret services, dedicated, ruthless protectors of the Soviet state. The photo was stamped at the time 'not to be reproduced'. Most became victims of their own success: only Dzerzhinsky and his successor Menzhinsky died of natural causes; by 1941 most of those photographed had been liquidated
*Credit: David King Collection*

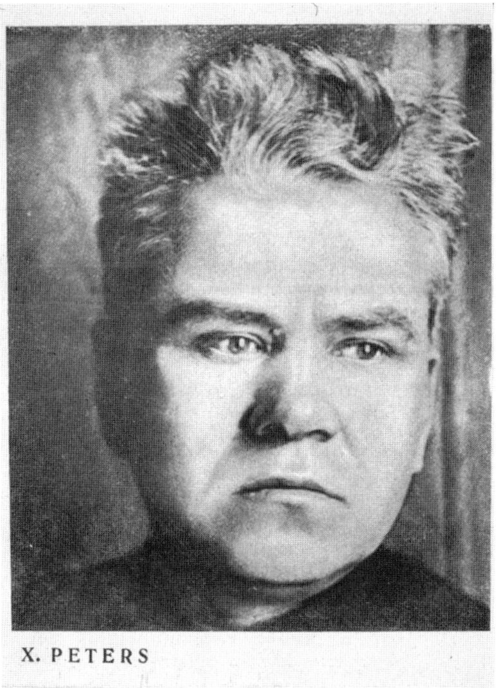


**USSR 1930s** Yakov Peters, deputy director of the *Cheka* and member of the Central Committee, before and after his fall from grace. Stalin had him arrested and executed in 1938 and, like so many more, all trace of him was dutifully erased from photos, publications and documents
*Credit: David King Collection*

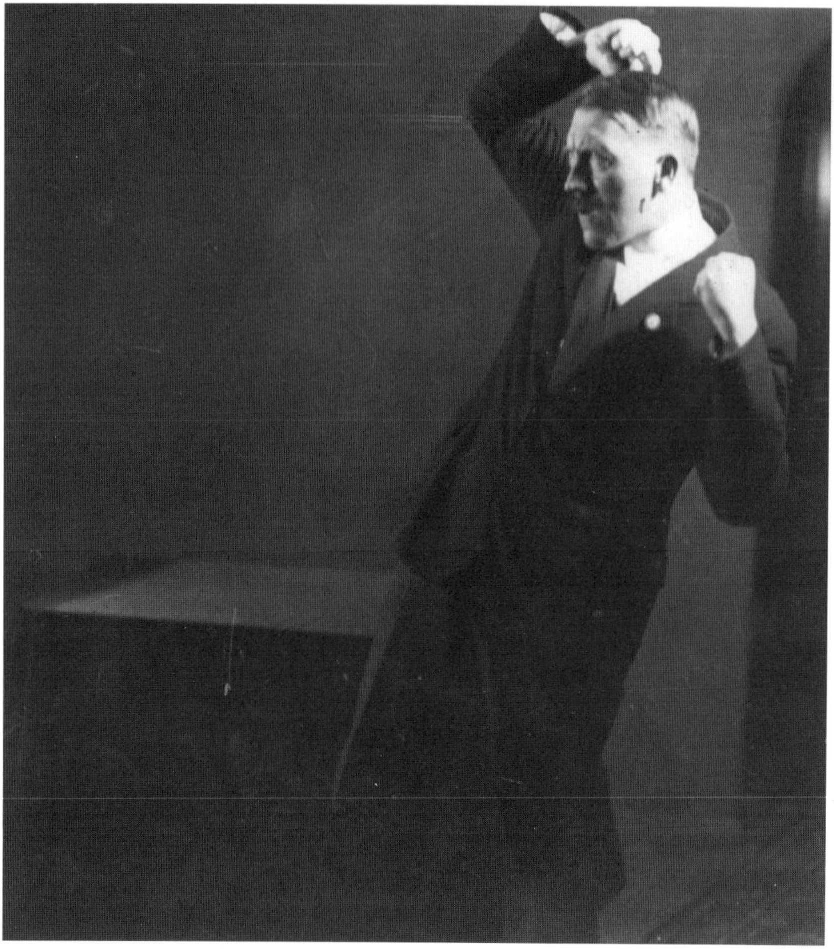

**Germany 1925** Hitler, gesticulating to a recording of an earlier speech, hones his supposedly 'natural' demagogic skills. Hitler ordered his official photographer Heinrich Hoffman to destroy the negatives. Hoffman disobeyed
*Credit: Hulton Getty Picture Collection*

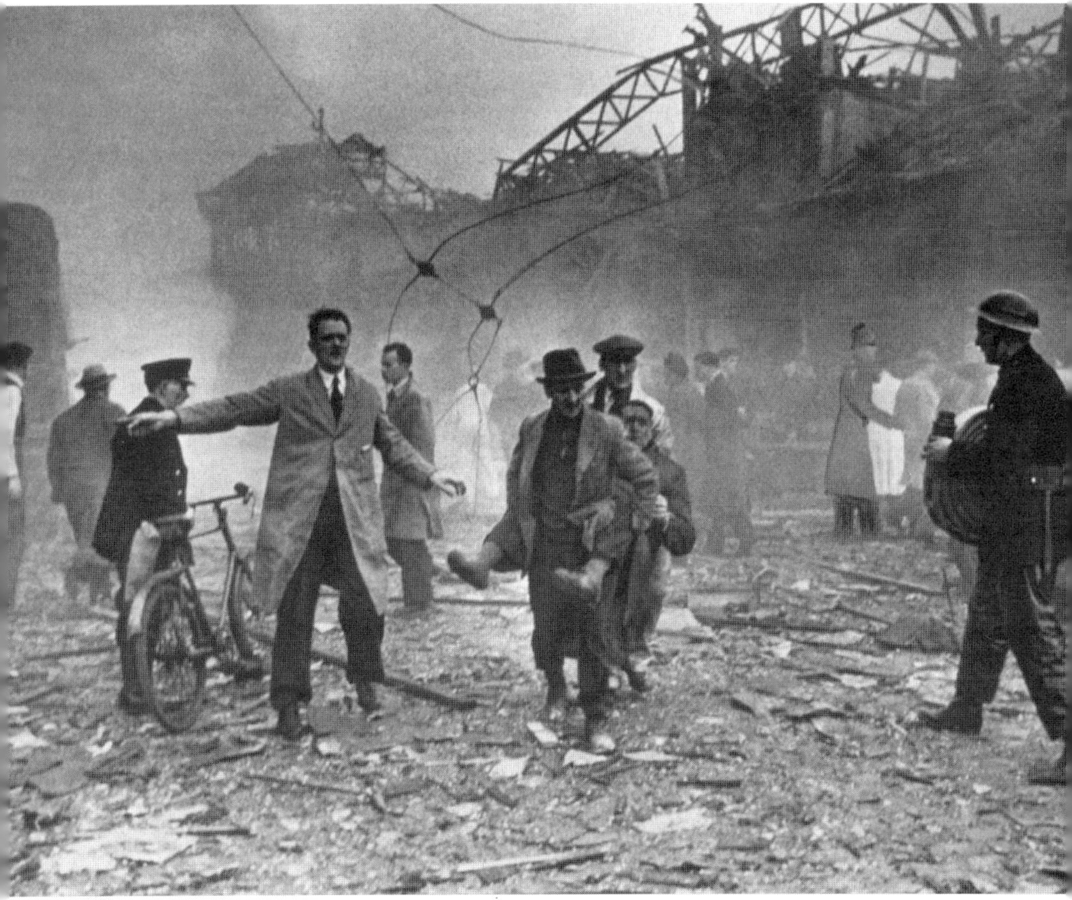

**Farringdon London March 1944** Aftermath of V2 missile attack. The photos the *Picture Post* did not print, thinking the images would demoralise war-weary Londoners. They were finally published in 1948
*Credit: Hulton Getty Picture Library*

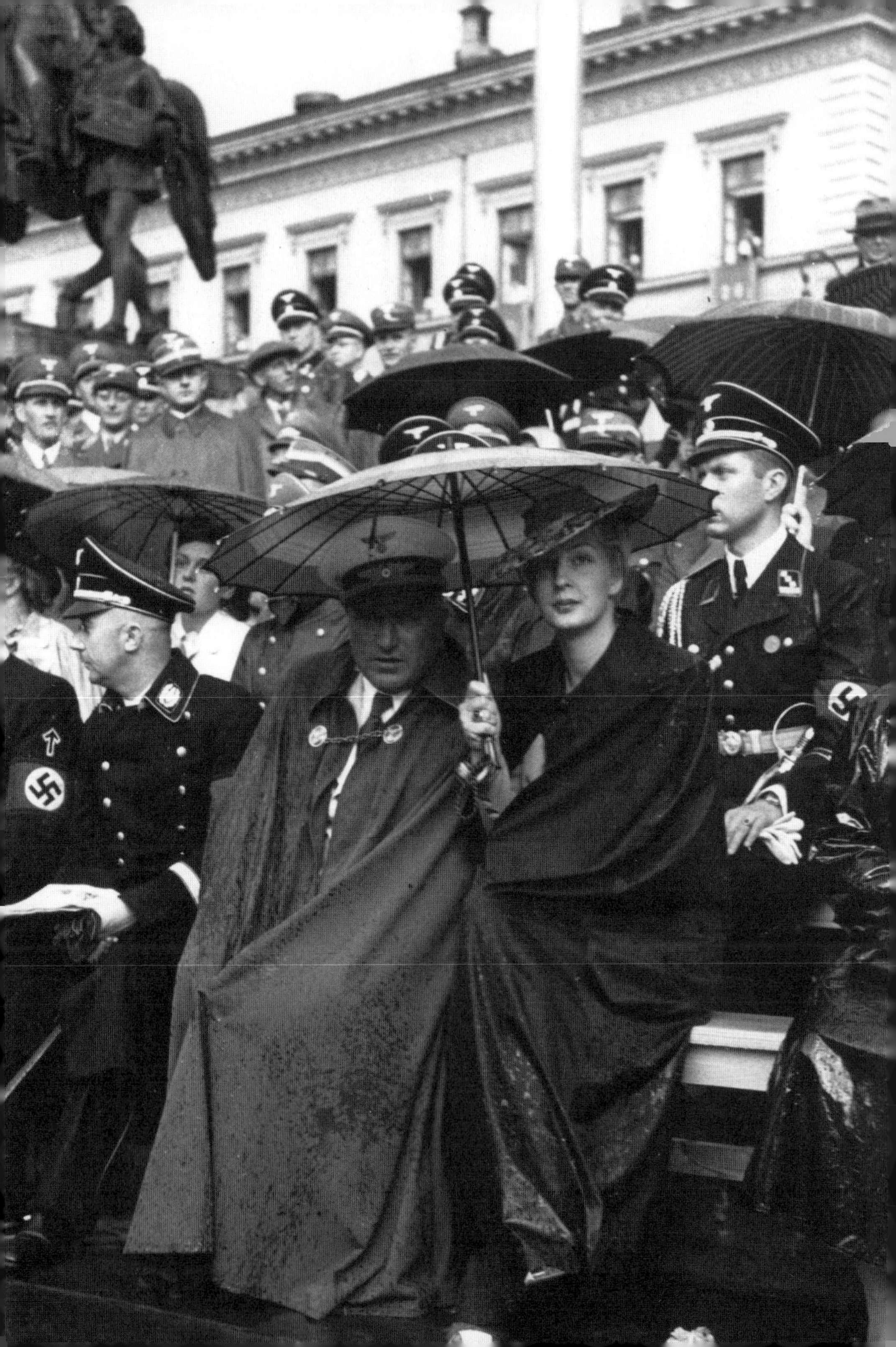

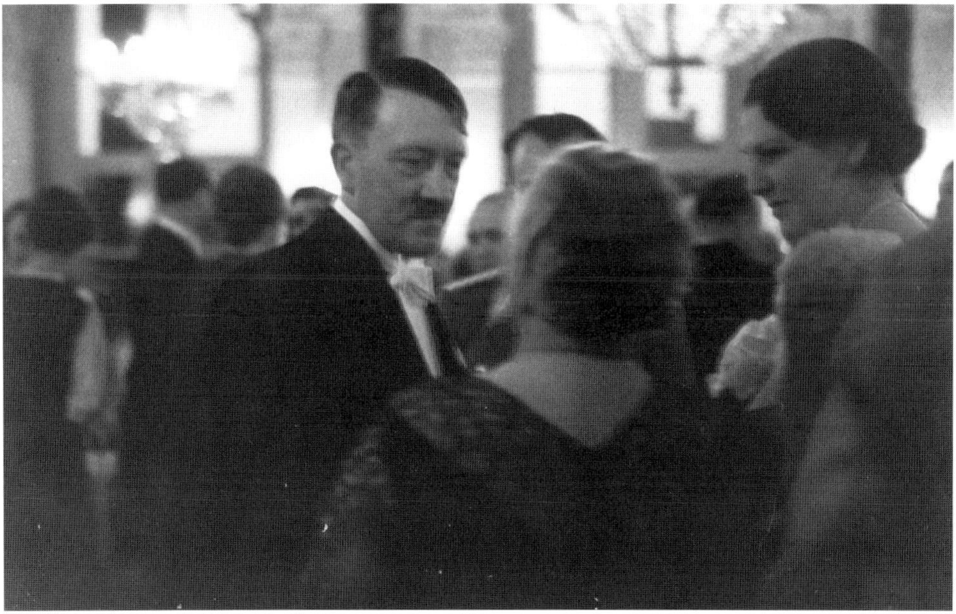

**Munich Germany 1937** Hitler at the opera.

**Munich Germany 1939** Dr Robert Ley and Lore at the Day of German Culture. Both pictures on these pages are held in the *Spiegel* archive where they remain unused as they are thought to glamorise the Nazi years unduly
*Credit: Max Ehlert/Speigel, Hamburg*

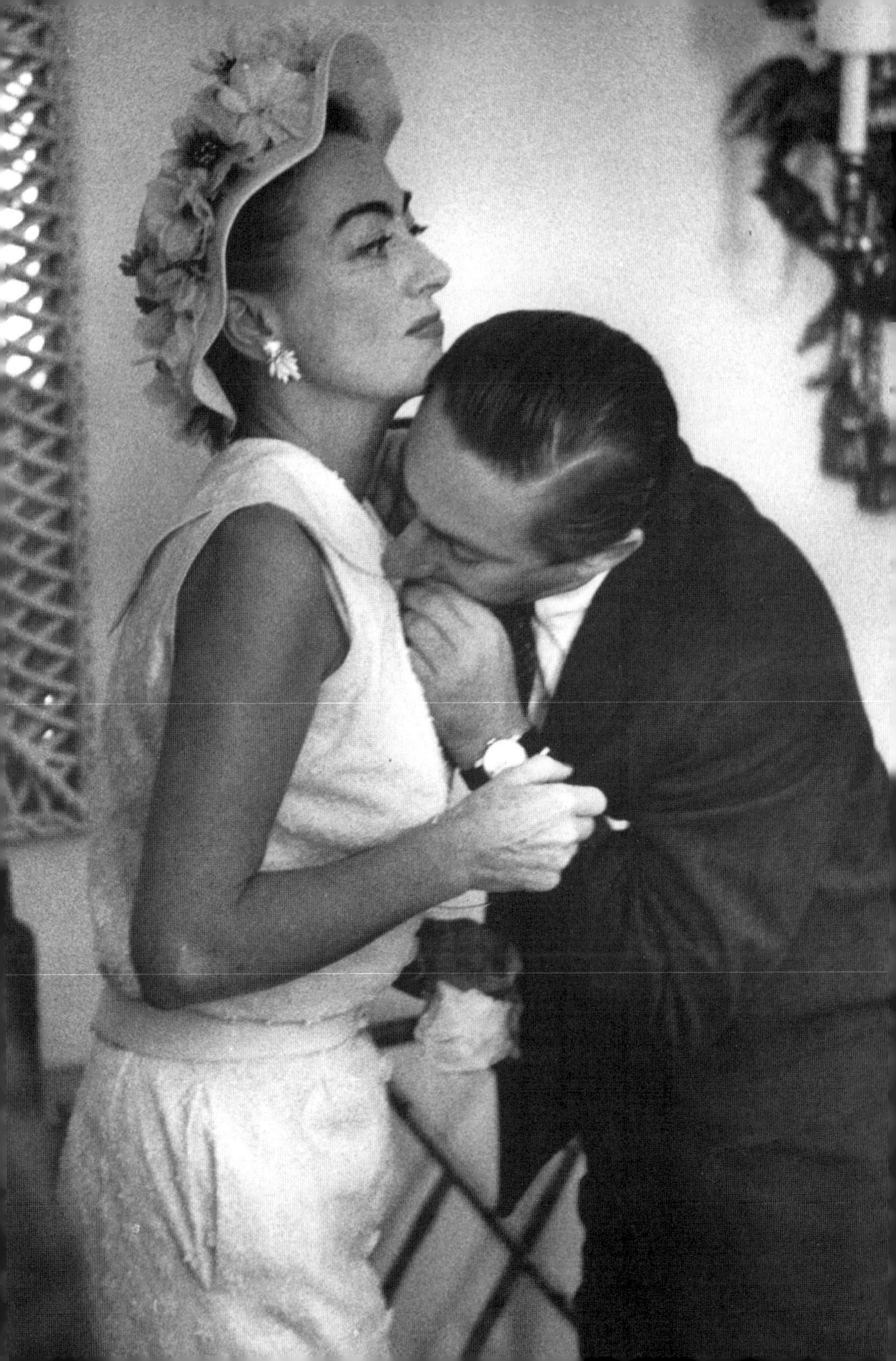

**London 1956** Joan Crawford and admirer at the Dorchester Hotel. Neither the photograph nor the article in which it was to have featured were published
*Credit: Hulton Getty Picture Collection*

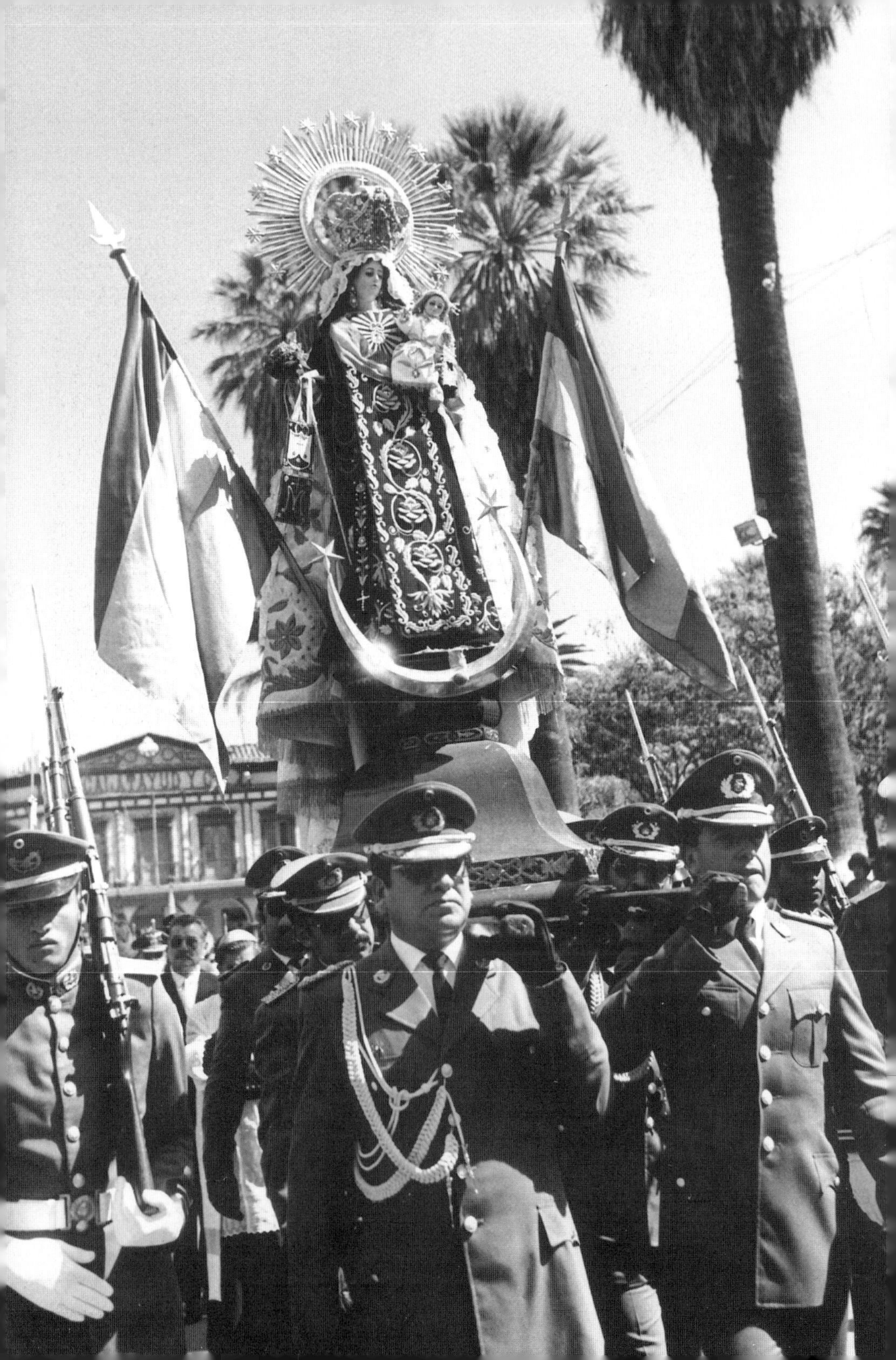

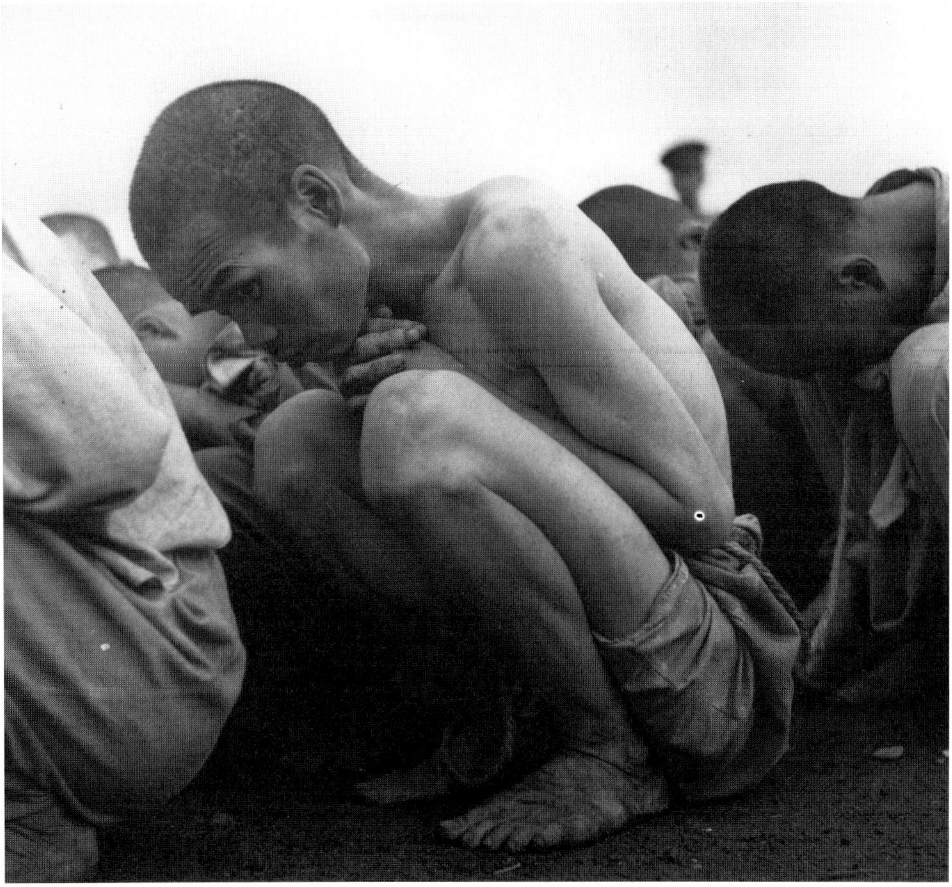

**Chile 1991** Our Lady of Peace parades with the Chilean army. The picture was banned from an exhibition of the photographer's work in Chile in 1992
*Credit: Carlos Reyes/Andes Press Agency*

**South Korea 1950** North Korean prisoners await their fate. Both sides in the war treated prisoners brutally, but a reluctance by its western allies to report South Korean atrocities ensured that publications like *Picture Post* shied away from the more disturbing images
*Credit: Hulton Getty Picture Collection*

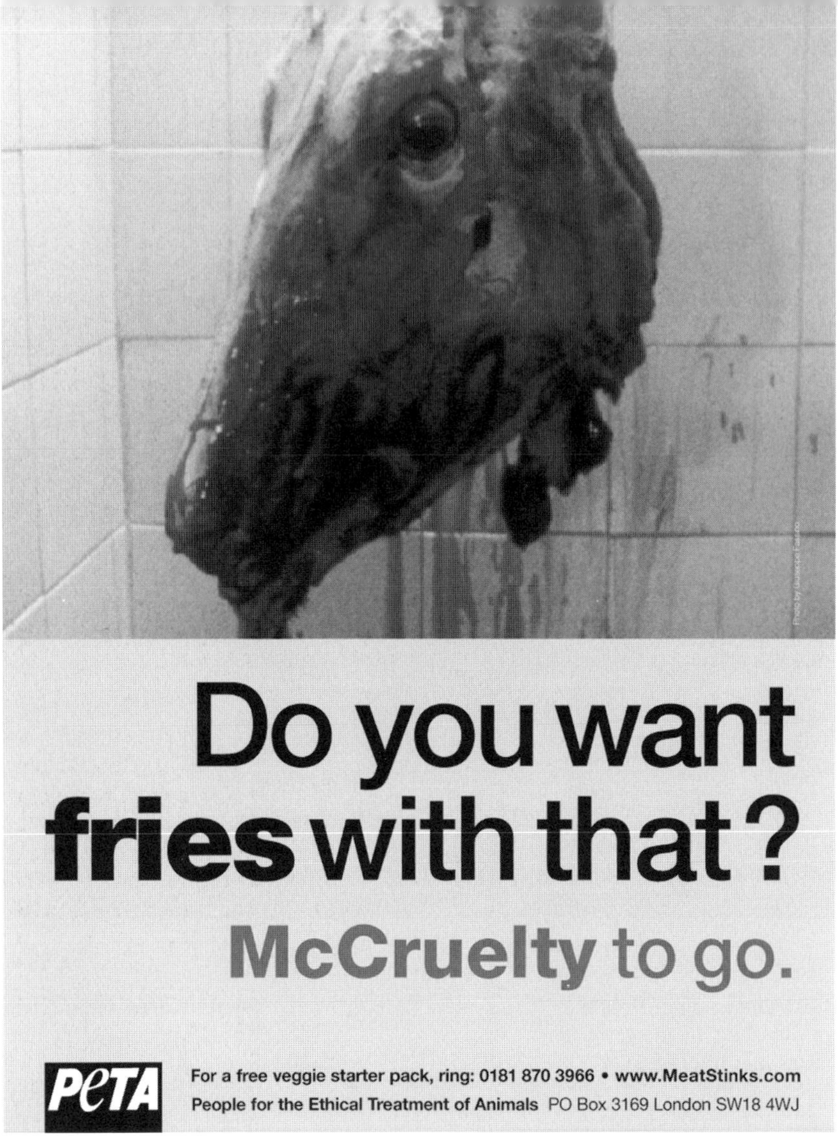


▲
**UK 1999** Taking their cue from the McLibel trial judgement, People for the Ethical Treatment of Animals produced a series of posters echoing the allegations against McDonalds which had been found proven. These included McDonalds' complicity in cruelty to animals during meat production, which the above ad refers to. However, PETA found that no poster operator in the UK would provide space for their advertisments, neither would any national publication accept advertising. Additionally, PETA is currently being refused advertising space in Belfast for their current campaign: 'Jesus was a vegetarian'.

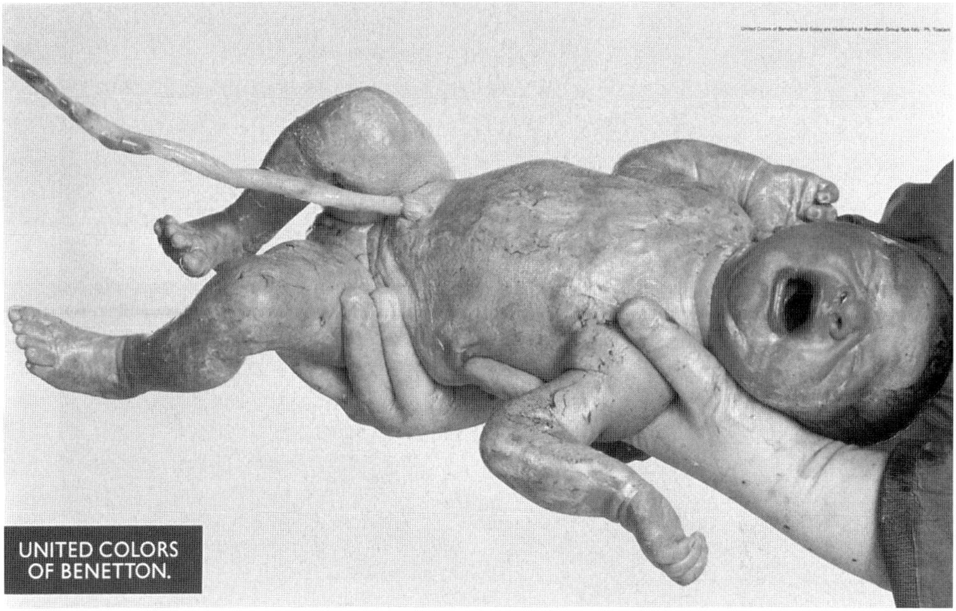


**Italy 1990s** 'Giusy at the moment of birth' appeared on Benetton ads throughout the world. This proved as controversial as other images produced for the Benetton campaigns and was banned in the UK by the Advertising Standards Authority after complaints from 'eminent journalists, sociologists, educationalists, paediatricians and even a few repentant feminists' says the photographer
*Credit: Oliviero Toscani/Benetton*

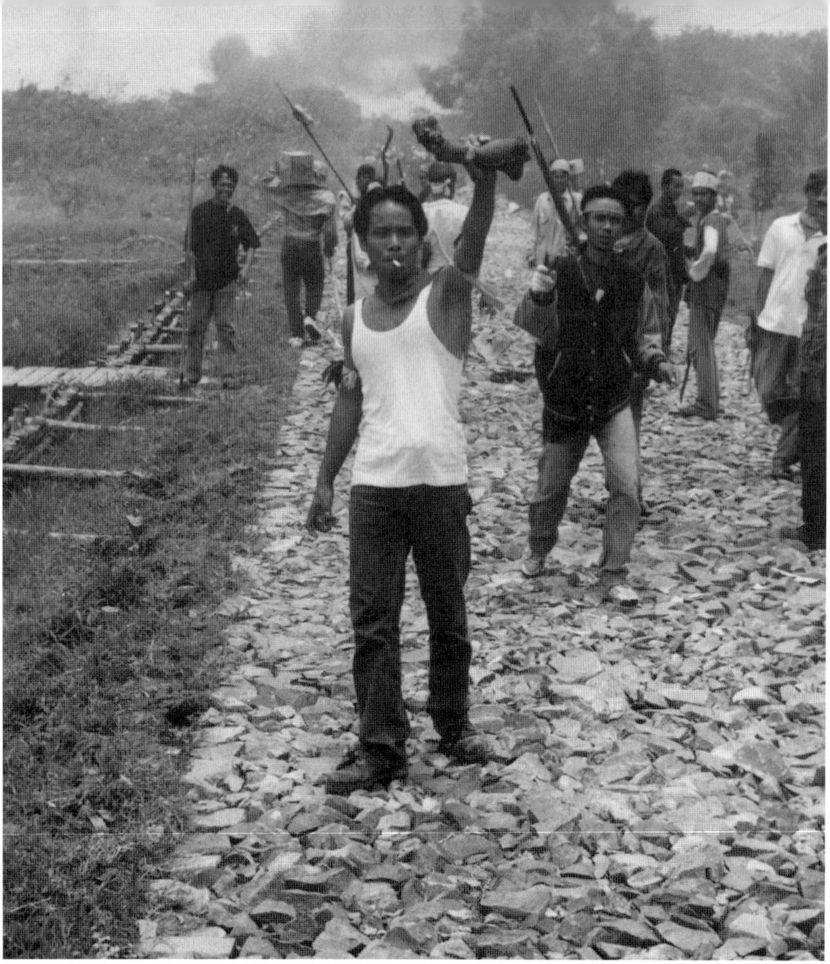

**Sambas West Kalimantan Eastern Borneo Indonesia 1999** Malays and Dayaks take revenge on Madurese settlers. In the wake of President Suharto's departure, sectarian conflict broke out in many parts of Indonesia. In Borneo, old enmities flared, old scores were settled, ancient rituals re-emerged. Thousands were killed and many more driven out. The manner of killing included beheading, mutilation and the ingestion of the victim's organs. Such photos were not published in the Indonesian media at the time
*Credit: Richard Lloyd Parry*

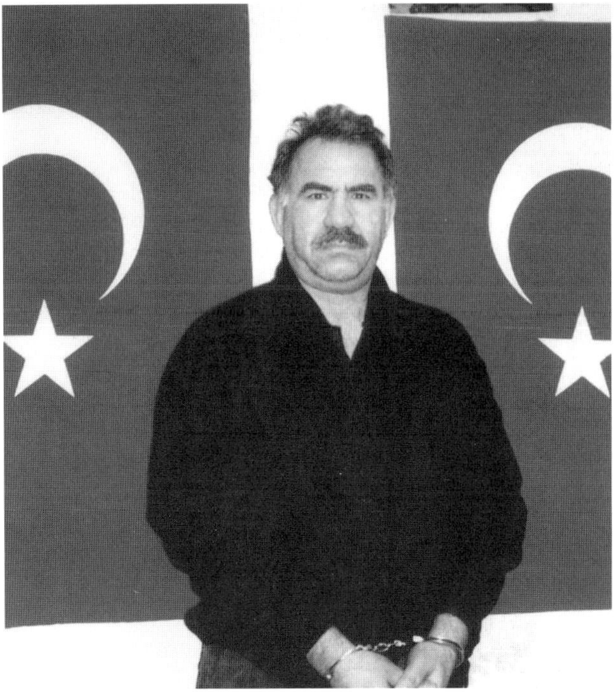

**Turkey 1999** Kurdish leader Abdullah Ocalan at Imrali Prison, Istanbul
*Credit: Sipa*

**Paris 1995** Bomb attack in the Metro

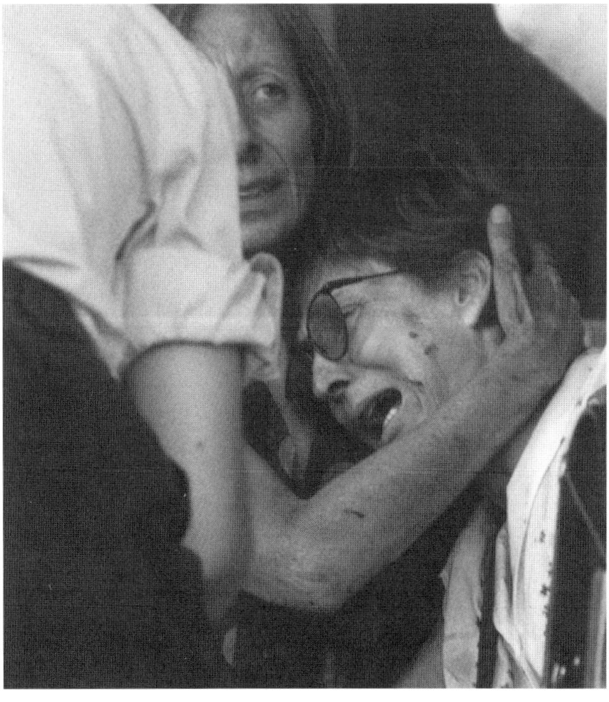

Under the proposed new French law governing the publication of images, neither of the photographs on this page could be used. The law bans the depiction of victims and of prisoners in handcuffs before conviction
*Credit: Sipa & AA/SIPA*

# Propaganda

*Only with effort can the camera be forced to lie: basically it is an honest medium. And contemporary vision, the new life, is based on an honest approach to all problems, be they morals or art. False fronts to buildings, false standards in morals, subterfuges and mummery of all kinds, must be, will be scrapped.*

Edward Weston

**London 1926** Member of the Achille Serre dry-cleaning company Ladies Fire Brigade
*Credit: Hulton Getty Picture Collection*

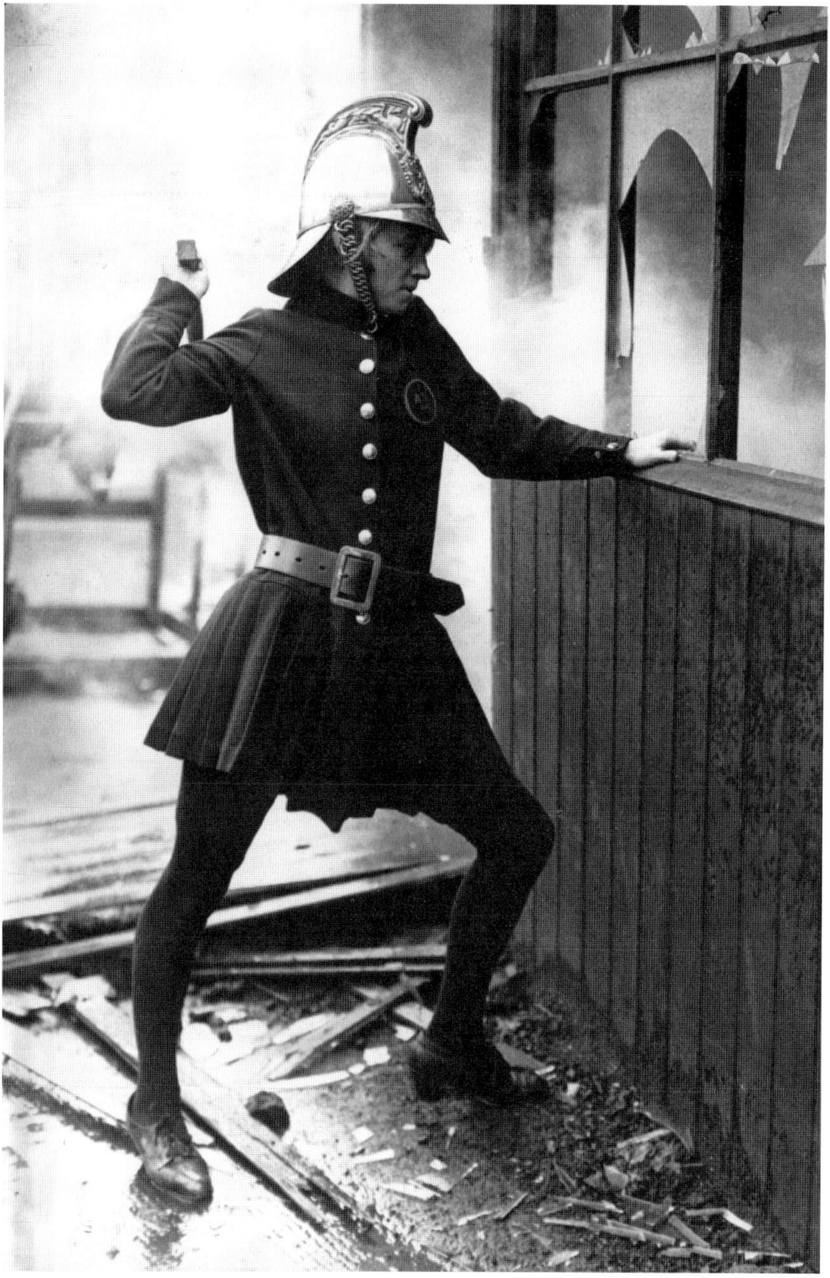

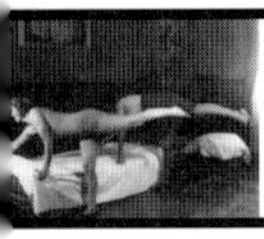

# Propaganda

## *Danny Schechter*

Photojournalism has always had an edge in shaping how we understand world events: impactful images become the private movie we screen in our minds to help us extract meaning from what we see.

Clearly, images can be, and often are, not what they seem to be. In an age of airbrushing and digital enhancement, when colours and backgrounds can be punched in electronically and undetectably, how trustworthy are images? Advertisers and governments alike are shameless manipulators: from the first heroic socialist realist posters celebrating the 'New Soviet Man' that defined one form of propaganda, to the far more carefully constructed advertising campaigns that base their images on psychological probing and focus group research.

Look around. You cannot escape the visual assault – on the streets, in the tubes and subways, in books and magazines and, yes, in the news too. What's true? Ask the editor of the US news magazine who darkened the face of OJ Simpson on the cover because he wanted it clear he was a black man. Ask the many official ministers of information and PR experts who daily sanitise their clients with photos chronicling deceptive stories and heroic accomplishments. It's all here for you to see, and to marvel at the techniques utilised throughout this century to twist the truth and bend the facts.

There are acts of deliberate commission, the fudged, the faked, the phony caption and the old atrocity posing as the new. They can be hard to detect and dissect and we need to be vigilant. Somehow, with the passage of time, that task becomes simpler. We now know what really happened, or so we think, and so can pass judgment on the distortions and manipulations of an earlier era. When we see Hitler goose-step into history on those grainy archival films from 70 years ago, we ask ourselves why wasn't it obvious to all, including the German people, that he was a fraud. Charlie Chaplin realised that early on, but millions were captivated by the carefully pumped-up portrait that he created to promote the mystique of fascism. Perhaps it's just that brainwashed eyes never see.

But the Führer was then. What's now? Goebbels had nothing on the modern practitioners of public relations and political consulting who specialise in the stealth-packaging of politicians and the sale of what passes for their original ideas. The manipulators' trick book has expanded with state-of-the-art refinements tethered to the power of the most powerful media machine in history. Our global TV system is truly a weapon of mass distraction. The commissars used images to mobilise classes and spread ideology. Today so-called 'free market'-driven propaganda has been commercialised and corporatised. Its goal is to depoliticise society and privatise all experience. Its organising slogan is even more seductive: shut up and shop. Its images are used for branding, products and consumers alike. How else to explain the logos plastered on our clothing that have turned us into human billboards? These images bury political culture in a swamp of consumer choice.

The media sin of omission diminishes our world. The media today is like the frog in the well looking up to see a tiny circle of sky above him, and he thinks that's all there is. We know what we see. In the US, we've had a 50% cut in foreign news – the canvas of coverage is shrinking even as globalisation makes world news vital. Deep in our well, we sing 'we are the world' and believe it.

Soundbites substitute for substance and 'bang bang' footage is all we're given of complicated conflicts that are presented with little context or background. CBS News and the *New York Times* asked Americans about Bosnia after four years of nightly coverage. 'Who lives in Sarajevo?' was the question. Fifty-nine per cent answered: 'The Serbs.' Twenty-five per cent said they didn't know. Thus the overwhelming majority of viewers who were exposed only to the daily dose of horror had little clue of what the war was all about, who was fighting whom, or who even lived there.

Another contemporary example. Lori Berenson, a young American woman, was jailed by a military tribunal in Peru, convicted, falsely in my view, of being a terrorist. But the hooded judge who presided over the mockery of her trial overrode the prosecutor's demand for 30 years, giving her a life sentence instead. Why? Because he saw her speak at what was supposed to be a televised press conference and concluded that she *looked* guilty. Sleep-deprived after 11 days in a dank dungeon, she was told to shout because there were no microphones on the stage. She was paraded in chains, spoke for two minutes, and was escorted out. In that moment, Lori looked like a militant, a fanatic even, when she was hauled by armed guards into a room packed with TV cameras, photographers and government plants shouting: 'Treason to the fatherland.' This pseudo 'press conference' allowed no questions or answers. She has still, four years later, not been allowed to offer her side of the story. But her fabricated negative image was broadcast worldwide and carried in all major newspapers, effectively condemning her. In the end, she was convicted by a constructed image in a world where perception often trumps reality.

Pictures can lie – and liars use pictures. Images have become their own imageology. We need to hold the visual media to the same standards of accuracy and credibility as the print media. ❑

***Danny Schechter**, author of* News Dissector *(www.electronpress.com) and* The More You Watch, The Less You Know *(Seven Stories Press, USA) created Globalvision's new Internet supersite, 'The Media Channel' (www.mediachannel.org)*

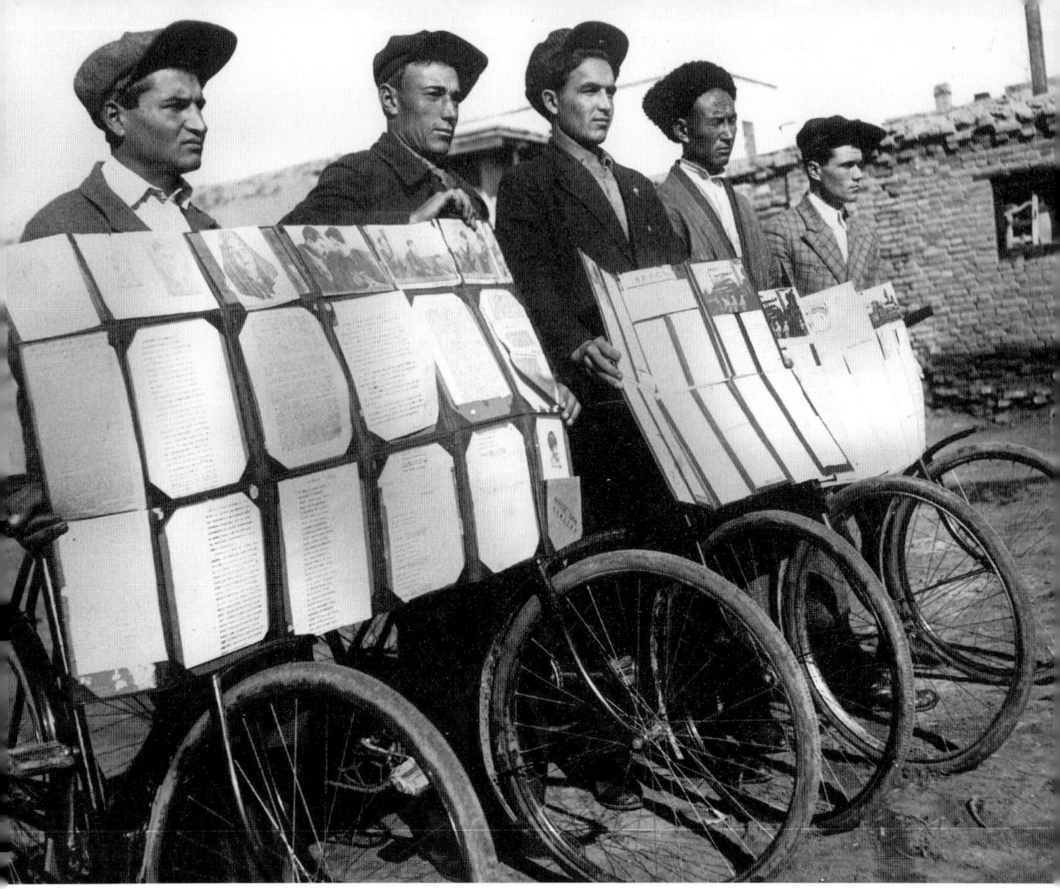

**USSR 1933** Tractors of the Lenin *Kolkhoz* arranged for a propaganda shot extolling the success of collectivisation. In fact, millions died, above all in Ukraine, and famine was widespread in the early years of a disastrous experiment *Credit. G Petrusov/Slava Katamidze Collection/Hulton Getty Picture Collection*

**Turkmenistan USSR 1936**
Wherever, whenever and by whatever means the Party's line was spread across the Soviet Union, as these peddlers of propaganda in a Turkmen village demonstrate
*Credit: Russian State Archive of Film and Photographic Documents, Krasnogorsk/Endeavour Group UK*

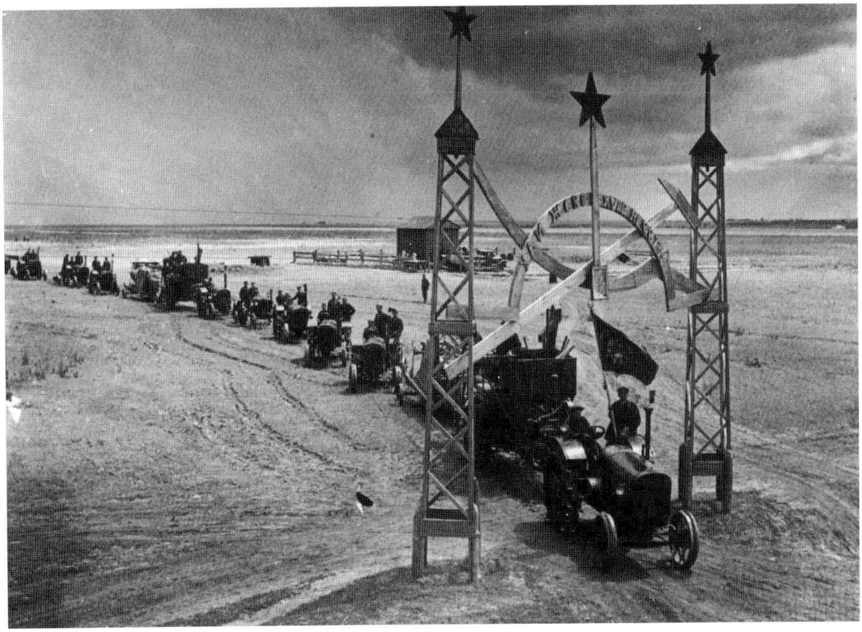

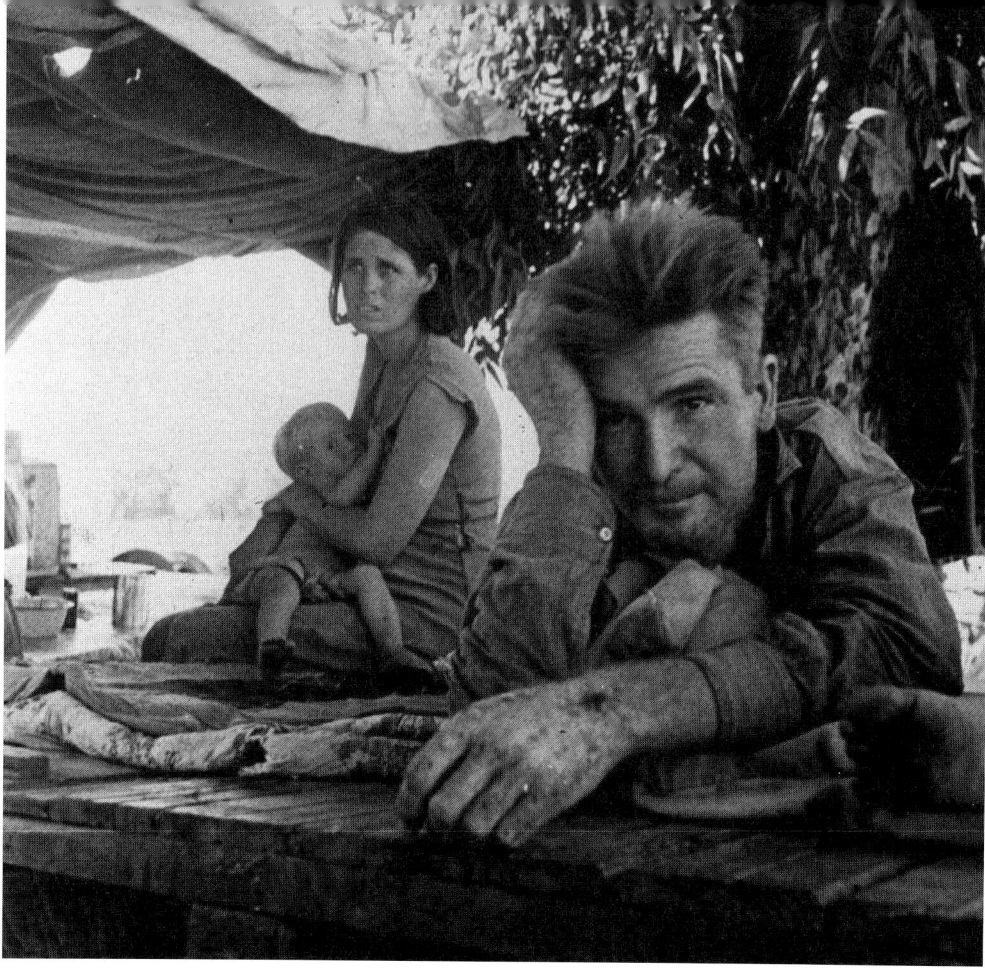

**California USA 1936** Family of migrant workers flee from the Oklahoma Dust Bowl. In 1935, the Farm Security Adminstration, under the direction of Roy Emerson Stryker, set out to compile 'a pictorial documentation of our rural areas and rural problems.' It focused specifically on 'low income groups' and was unashamedly propagandistic. In 1942, with the USA now in WWII, the poor were too downbeat a subject and Stryker changed his instructions accordingly: 'We must have at once men, women and children who appear as if they really believed in the US. Get people with a little spirit.'
*Credit: Hulton Getty Picture Collection*

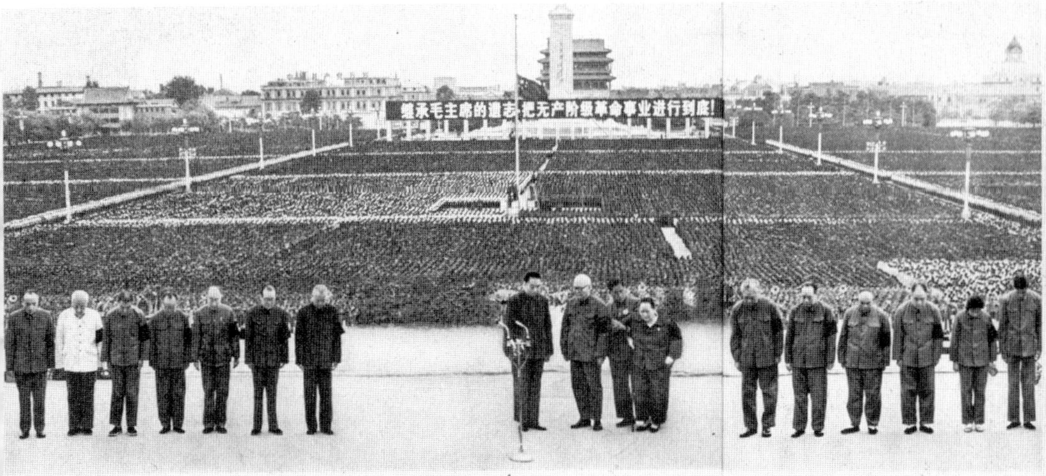


党和国家领导人华国锋、×××、叶剑英、×××、宋庆龄、××、×××、李先念、陈锡联、纪登奎、汪东兴、吴德、许世友、韦国清、李德生、陈永贵、吴桂贤、苏振华、倪志福、赛福鼎在追悼大会上。

"团结起来，到明天，英特纳雄耐尔就一定要实现。"雄壮的歌声激励和鼓舞人们去战斗。

中共中央第一副主席、国务院总理华国锋同志致悼词。

华国锋同志致悼词以后，参加追悼大会的百万群众和全国八亿人民向伟大领袖毛主席遗像三鞠躬。

接着，天安门广场上响起了气势磅礴的《东方红》乐曲。"东方红，太阳升，中国出了个毛泽东，他为人民谋幸福，他是人民大救星……"这高昂激越的伟大颂歌，激动着亿万人民的心，激发了人们对伟大领袖毛主席的无限思念。毛主席永远同我们在一起，毛主席永远活在我们的心中。颂歌在北京上空回响，在我们伟大祖国辽阔土地的上空回响。我国亿万人民将世世代代永远高唱这支颂歌，永远心向毛主席。全党全军全国各族人民决心继承毛主席的遗志，认真学习马列著作和毛主席著作，坚持以阶级斗争为纲，坚持党的基本路线，坚持无产阶级专政下的继续革命，抓革命，促生产，促工作，促战备，巩固和发展无产阶级文化大革命的胜利成果，进一步加强无产阶级专政，永远沿着毛主席的无产阶级革命路线奋勇前进。

参加追悼大会的还有：治丧委员会委员，在北京的人大常委会委员，在北京的政协全国委员会常务委员，工人、农民、人民解放军指战员、赤脚医生、上山下乡知识青年、红卫兵、红小兵的代表，以及科技、文化艺术、教育、卫生、体育、新闻、出版界和服务行业的代表，治丧委员会办公室负责人，在毛主席身边的工作人员和医护人员等。

追悼大会在下午三时半宣布结束。

十八日下午，全国各机关、部队、厂矿、企业、商店、人民公社、学校、街道等一切基层单位的群众都收听或收看了首

**Tiananmen Square China 1976** Mao's wife Jiang Qing with her cronies – the Gang of Four – at Mao's state funeral. Within weeks of his death, all were arrested and charged with conspiracy to seize control. They were also blamed for the untold sufferings of the Chinese people throughout the destructive decades of revolution. The process of 'disappearing' them began: photos were re-touched – in this case with derisory crudity – and the conspirators air-brushed out of existence to be replaced with potted palms and statues
*Credit: David King Collection*

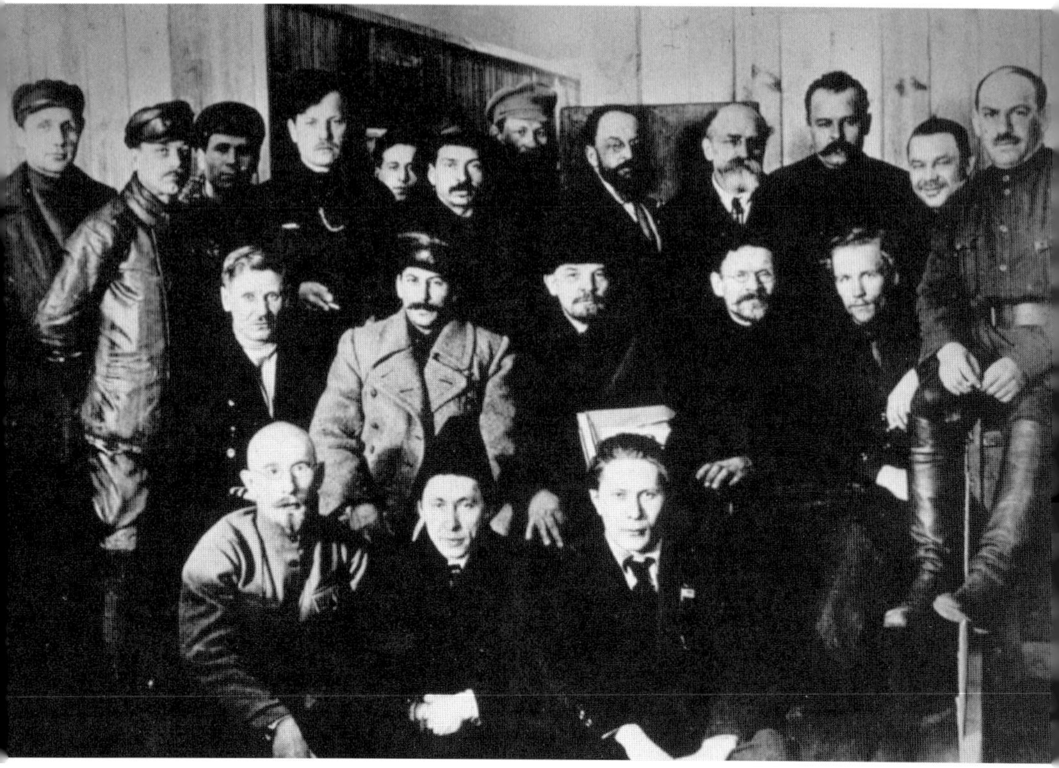

**Moscow 1919** Delegates to the Eighth Congress of the Bolshevik Party in a formerly unpublished portrait. In the years of Stalin's reign, 11 of these delegates were executed on Stalin's orders and three more killed themselves in protest at his policies. The official version of the portrait left only the Stalin, Lenin, Kalinin triumvirate visible. On occasion, Kalinin too was obliterated from reproductions; in 1938, Lenin, too, had been removed from the frame in Alexander Rodchenko's book *First Cavalry*
*Credit: David King Collection*

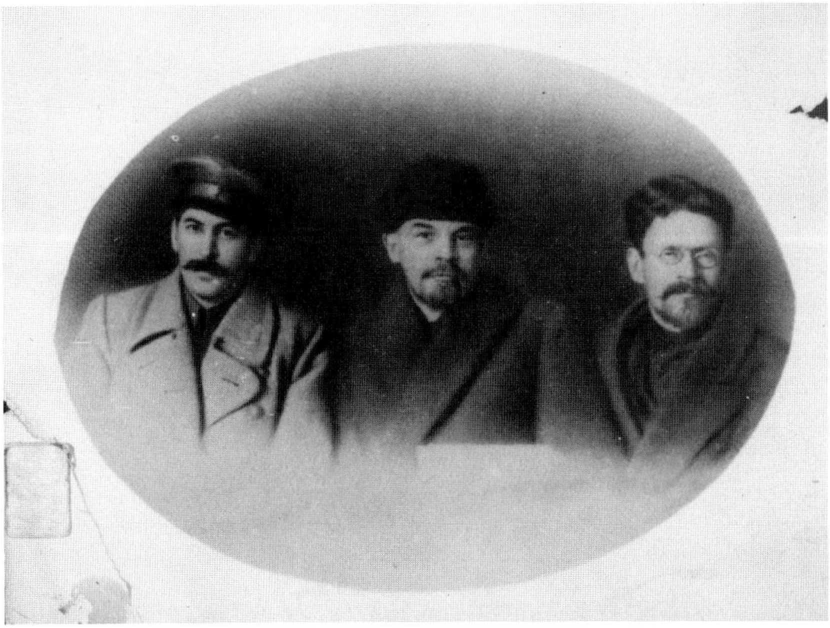

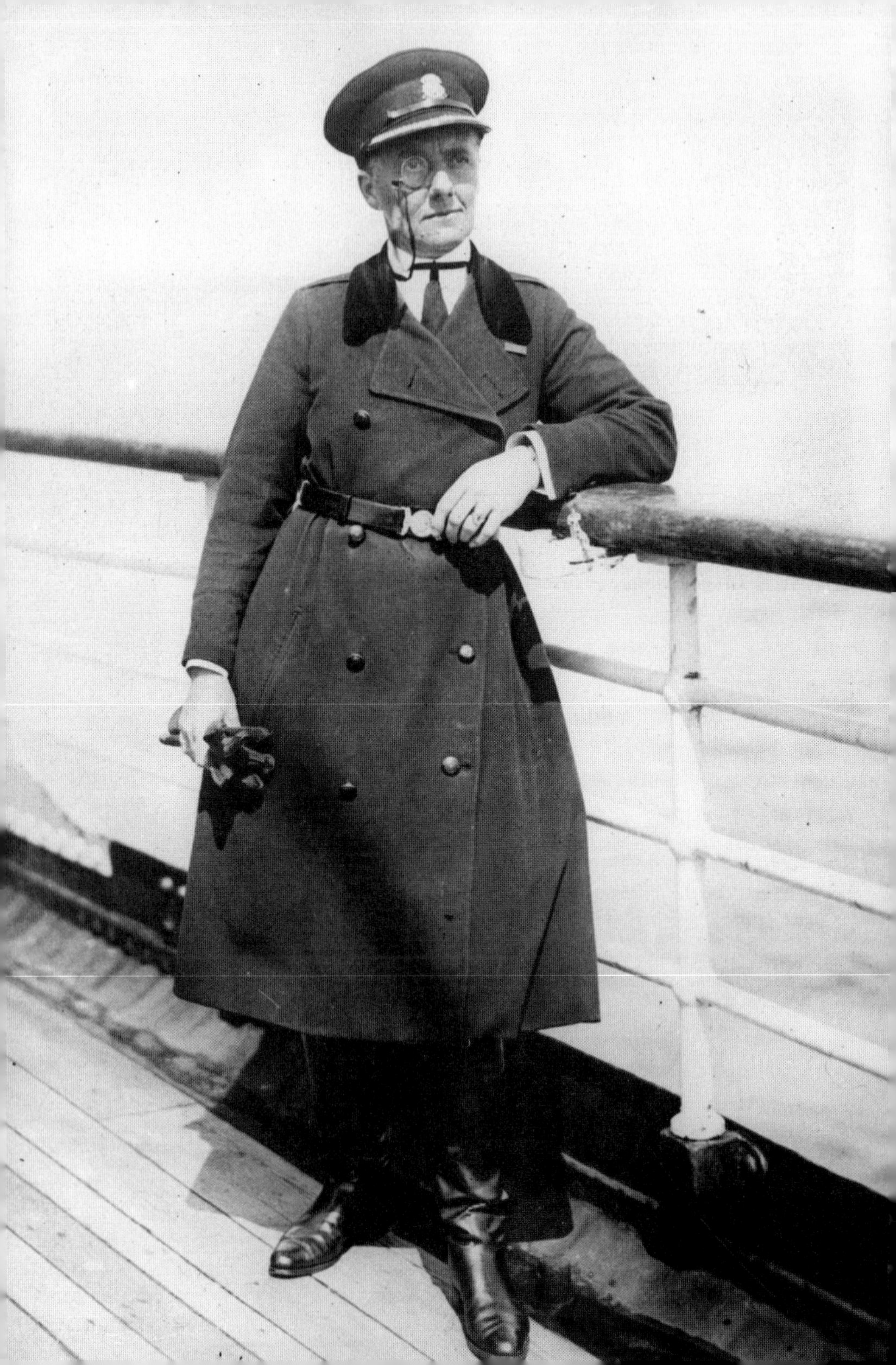

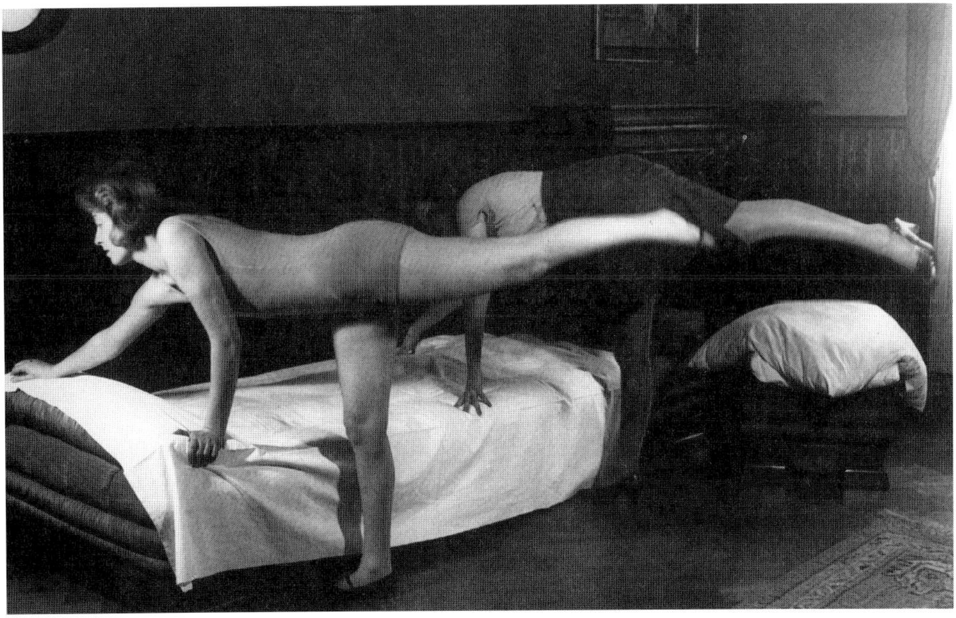

**Health through housework 1935** The original text with the photograph claims that the hapless housewife can tone her muscles as she turns down the sheets
*Credit: Hulton Getty Picture Collection*

**New York 1924** Commandant Mary P Allen, of the Women's Auxiliary Police Force arrives in New York from London to study US police methods
*Credit: Hulton Getty Picture Collection*

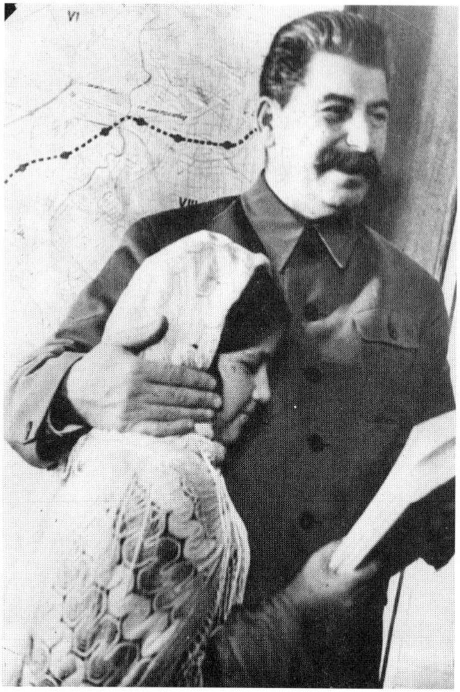

**USSR 1935** Stalin receives a copy of Stalin on Lenin, written in Tajik, from Mamlakat Nakhengova, a schoolgirl from Tajikistan. Even the children of the subjugated Central Asian republics loved him
*Credit: Hulton Getty Picture Collection*

**Germany 1935** Hitler with model Aryan child
*Credit: Hulton Getty Picture Collection*

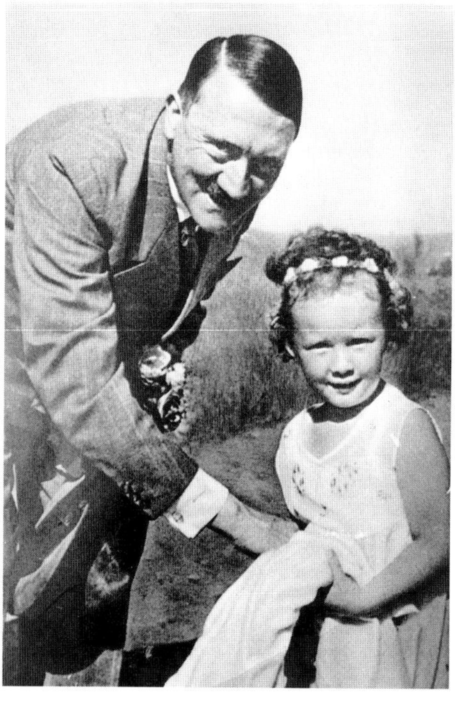

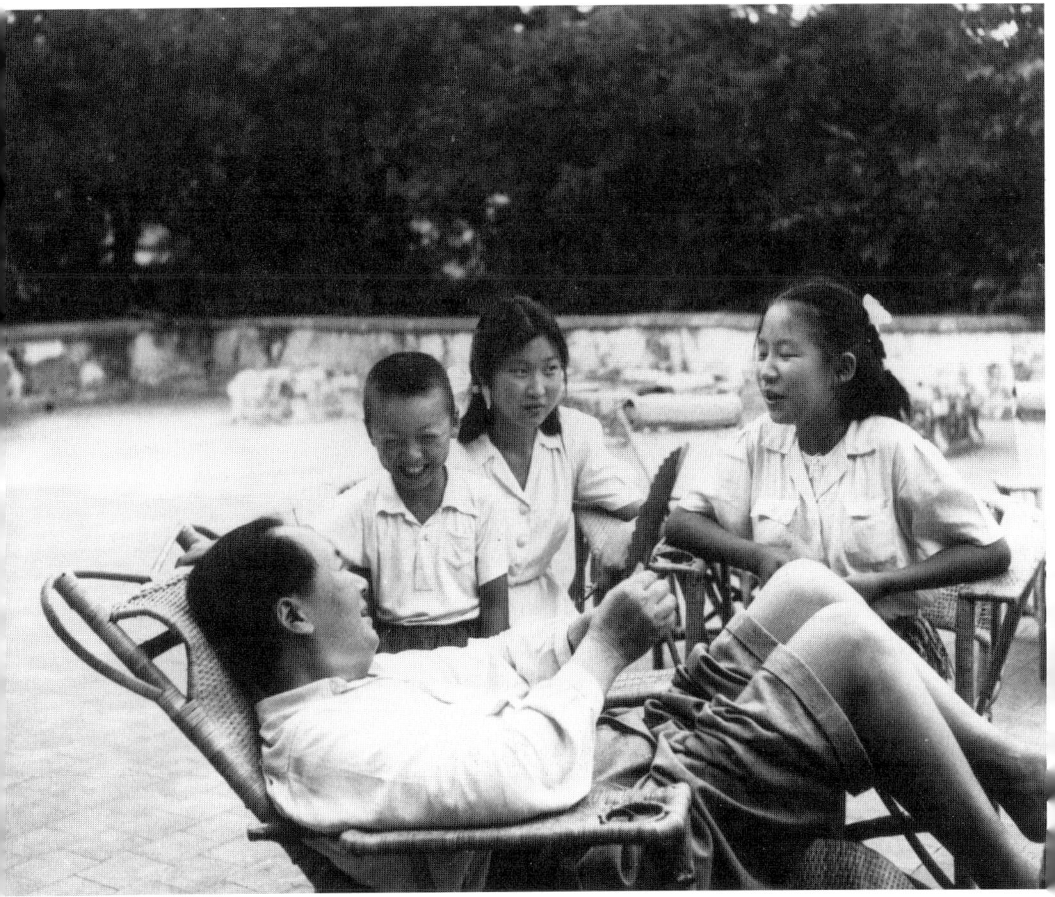

**China 1951** Mao's personal life was a mix of tragedy and farce – but the camera could show the public a semblance of a 'normal' family life. Here in his Zhongnanhai compound in Beijing, Mao with his eldest daugher Li Min (centre) born on the Long March to his second wife – his first was killed during the civil war – and his daughter Li Na, born to his third wife, the ambitious but luckless Jiang Qing. Mao's personal physicain Dr Li said of Li Na that she was 'caustic, mean … downright rude'. Li Min, on the other hand, was 'honest, simple … polite but not very bright'. The little boy is Mao Yuanxin, son of Mao's younger brother, killed along with the Chairman's only other brother in the civil war
*Credit: Xinhua News Agency/Endeavour Group UK*

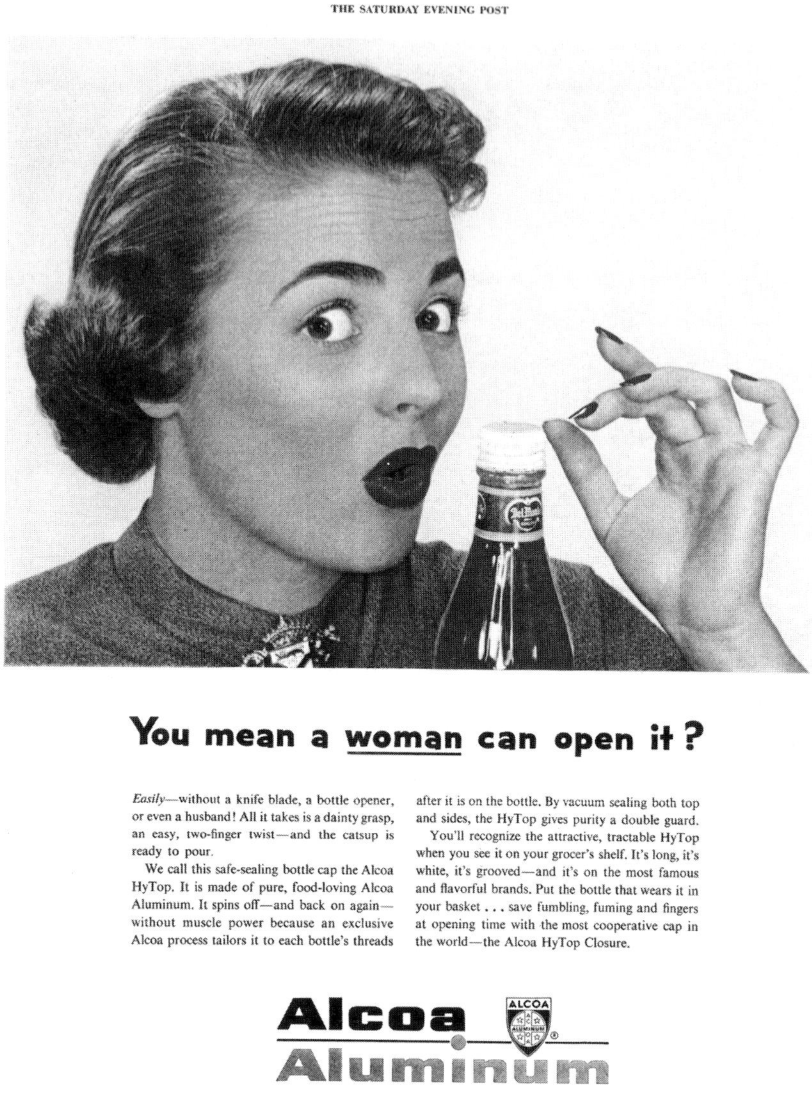


**USA 1950s** Alco Aluminium, not exactly sexual innuendo – but definitely a gender stereotype
*Credit: The Advertising Archive*

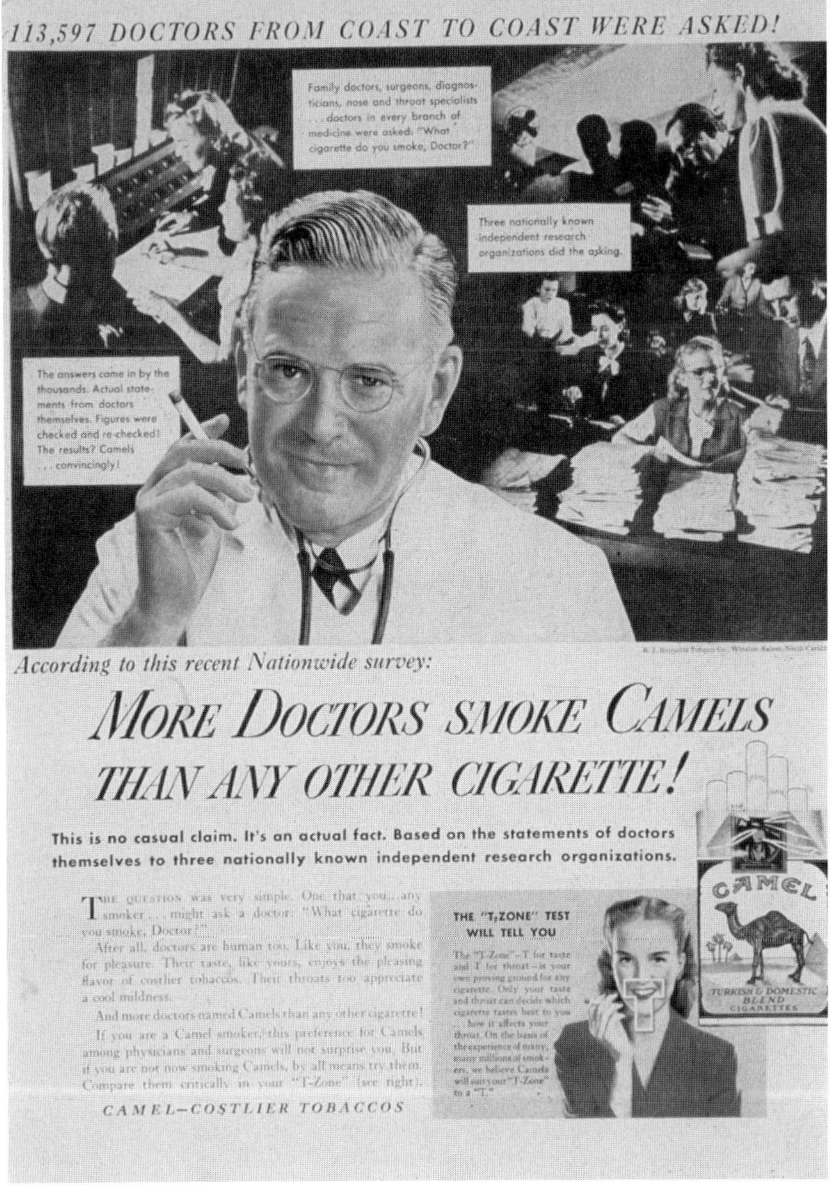


**USA 1960s** Doctors and their false claims for cigarettes after research results showed the damage to public health
*The Advertising Archive*

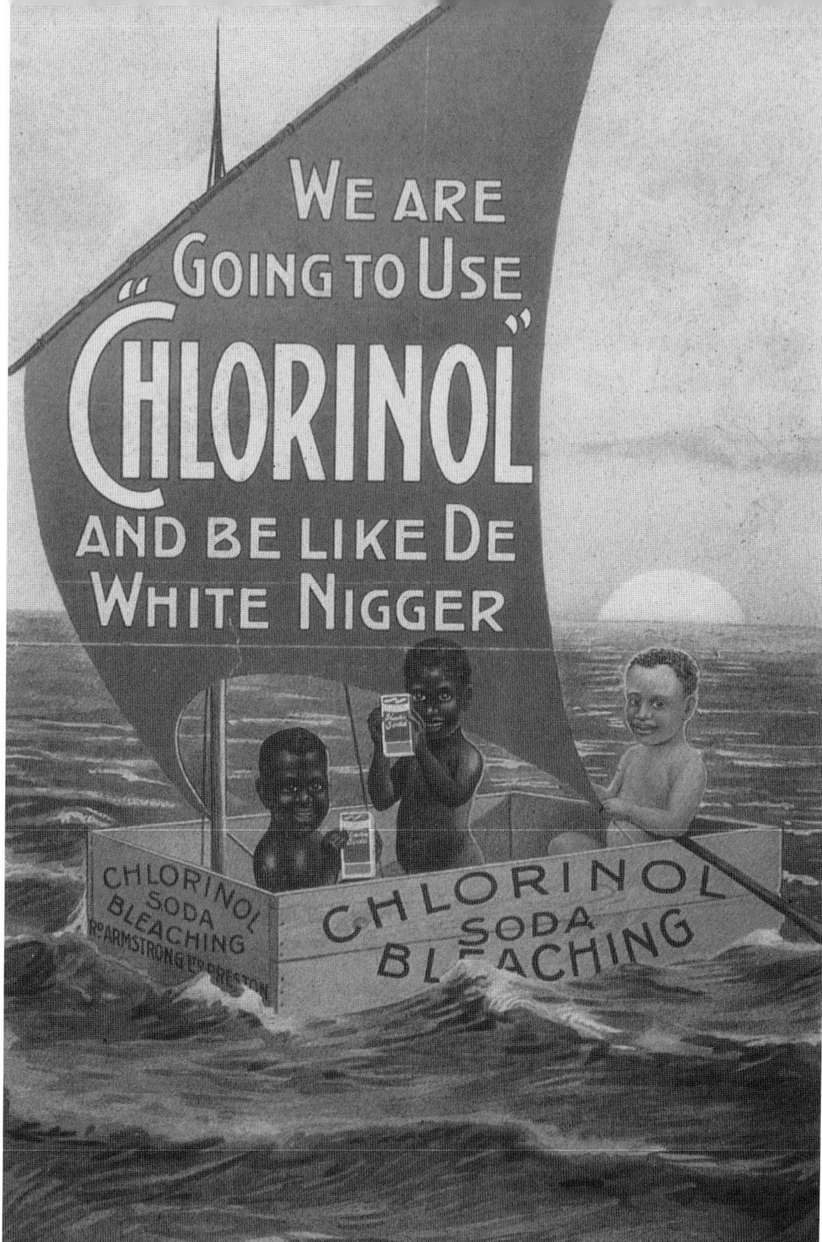


**UK 1907** Chlorinol uses the traditional – and then wholly unexceptionable – stereotypes of race
*Credit: The Advertising Archive*

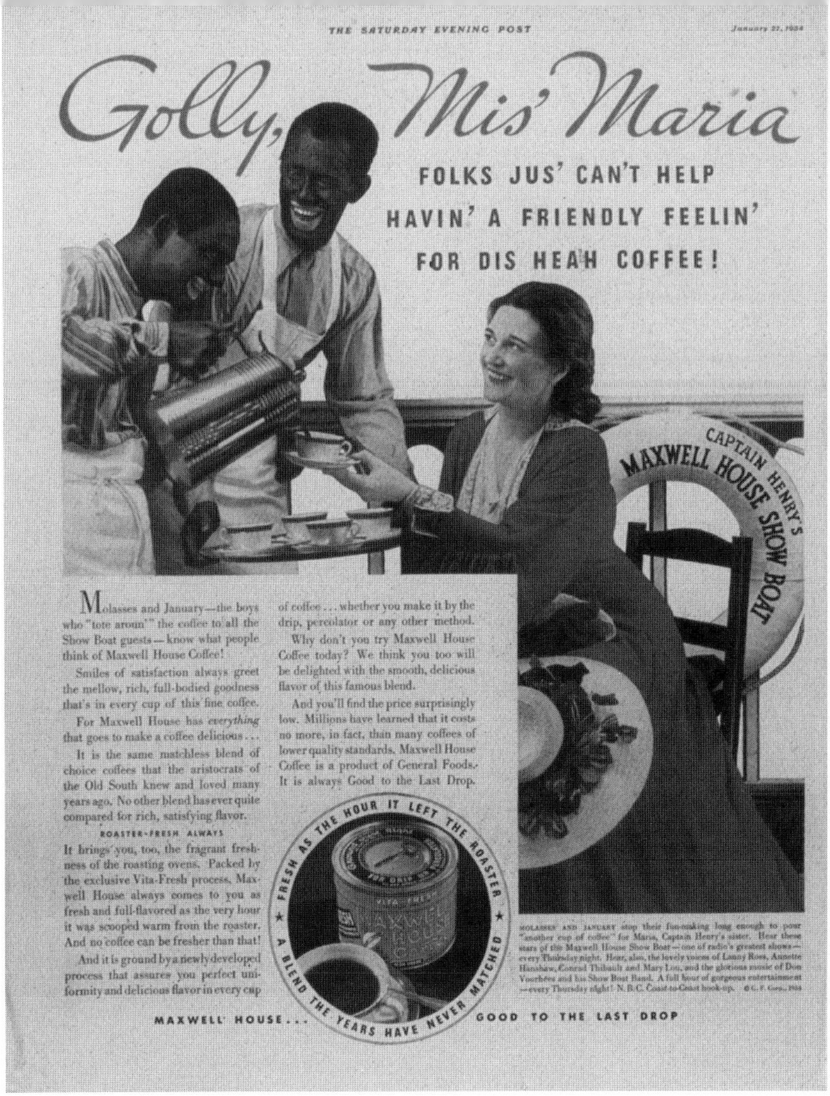


**USA 1934** Maxwell House Coffee shows nothing had changed a quarter of century later
*Credit: The Advertising Archive*

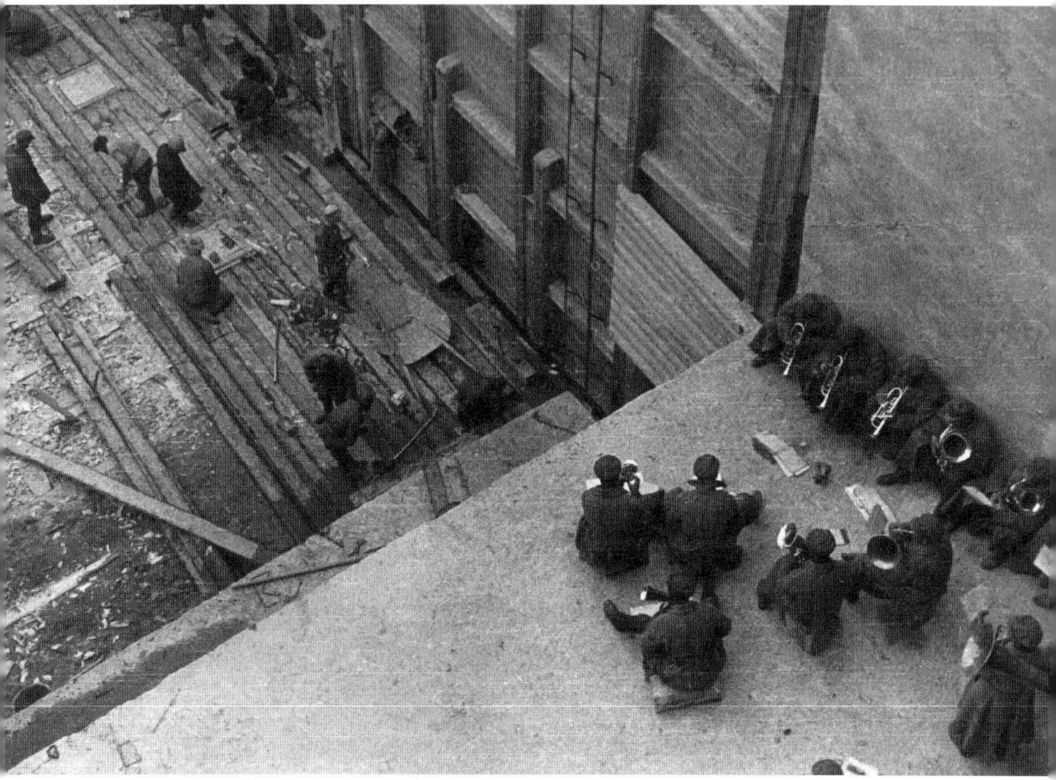

**Prison camp No 7 Vorkuta-Pechora Gulag Siberia USSR 1940s** The camp steam bath from an album compiled by the interior ministry to demonstrate the 'humane' conditions in its gulags
*Credit: Endeavour Group UK*

**USSR 1933** *Zeks* (prisoners) work on the White Sea Canal to the strains of a prison orchestra. Maxim Gorky wrote a book and the leading photographer of the time, Alexander Rodchenko, produced a series of propaganda photographs to lull foreign suspicions about the working conditions of the zeks. As many as 100,000 prisoners, many of them dispossessed *kulaks* from Ukraine, may have died on this project alone
*Credit: Rodchenko Lavrentyev Archive/Endeavour Group UK*

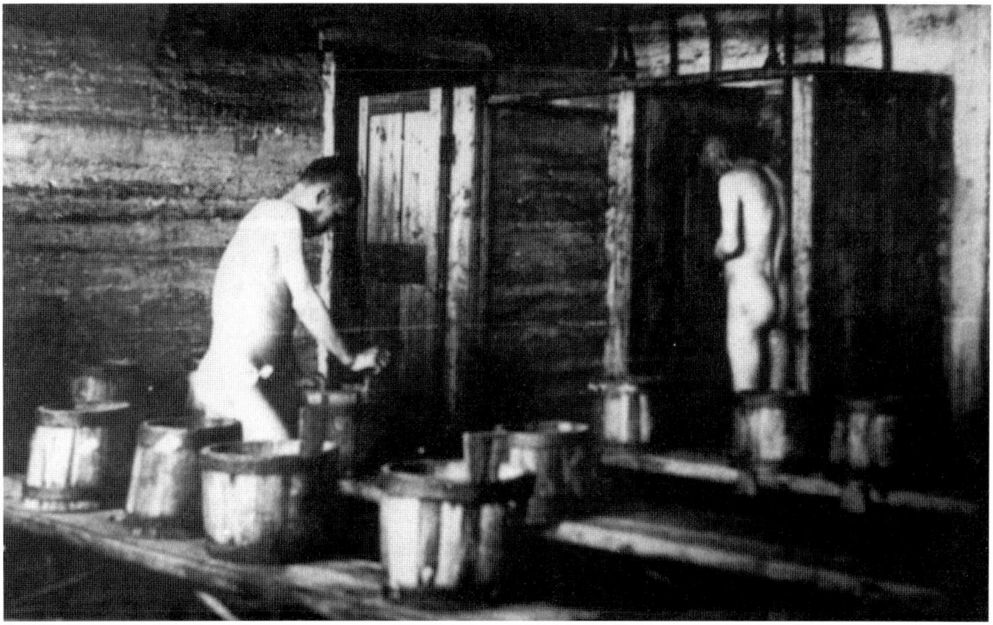

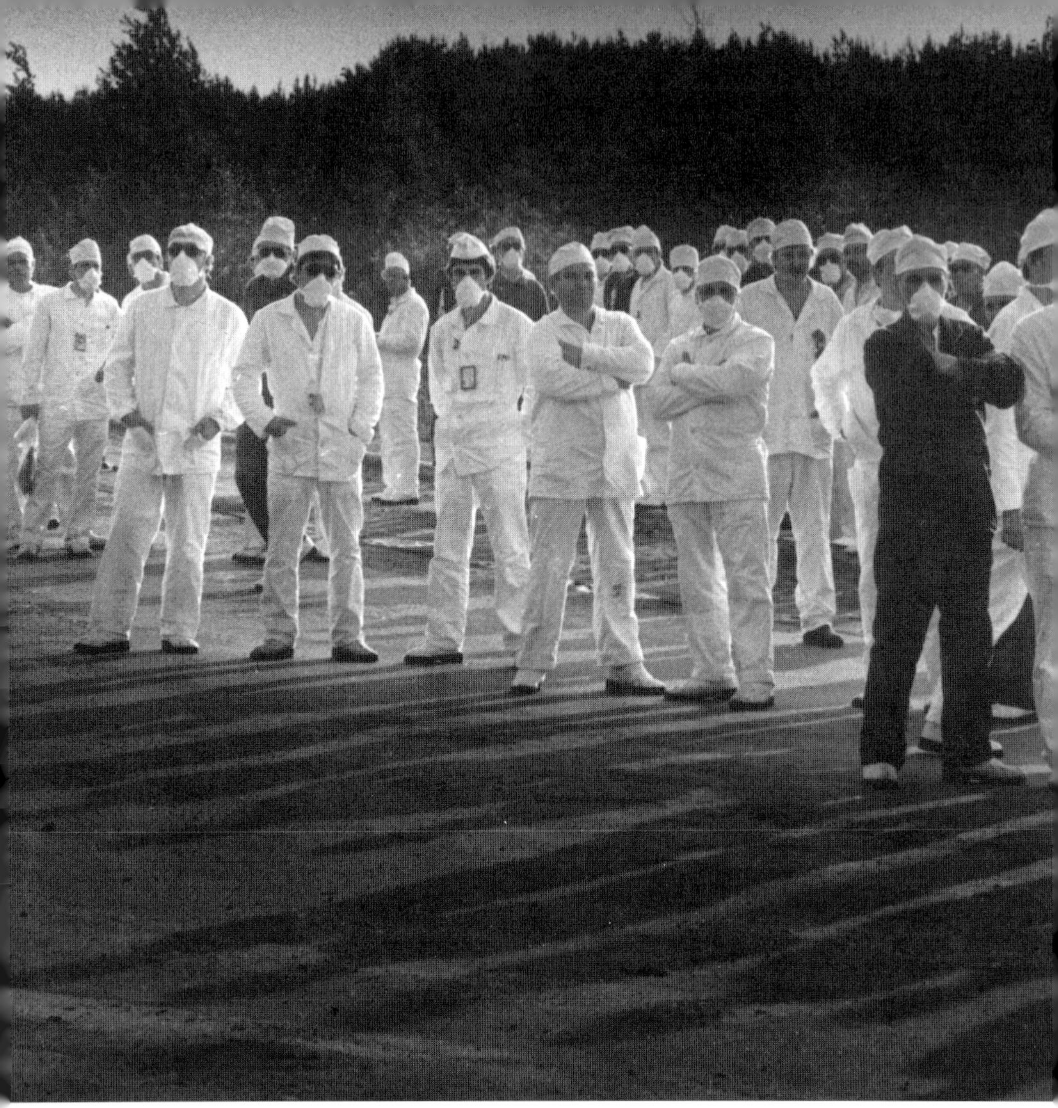

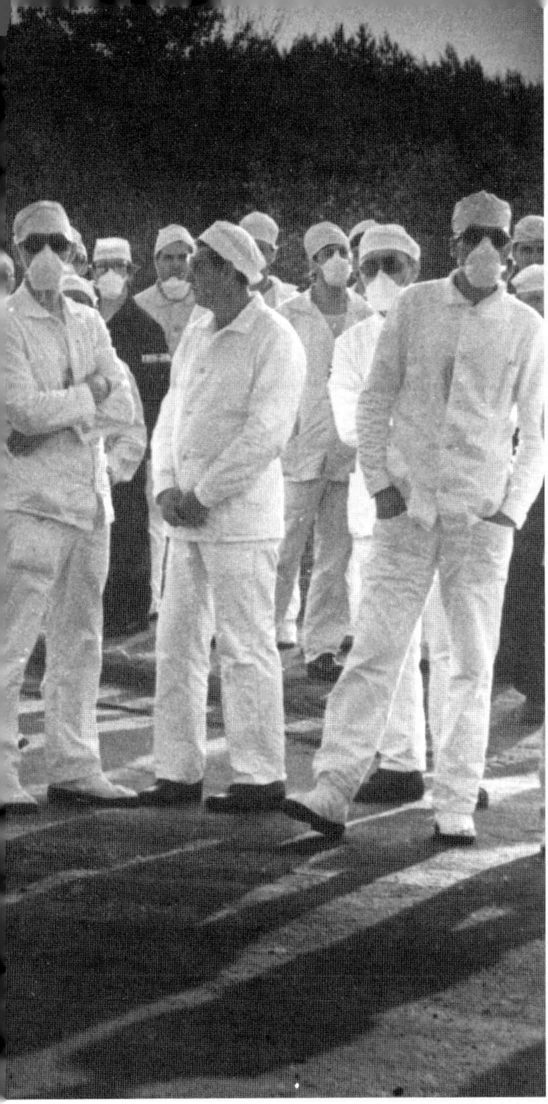

**Chernobyl Ukraine 1986**
Clean-up workers wait for buses to take them home only a week after the explosion of the reactor spread nuclear fuel throughout the surrounding area in April 1986. High levels of incompetence, plus the intense secrecy surrounding the event and the refusal of Mikhail Gorbachev – despite the recent introduction of *glasnost* – to go public, compounded the tragedy. Clean-up teams and assessors, sent into high levels of radiation with only the flimsiest of protection and ignorant of the consequences, were dead from radiation sickness within months. This group have waited for three hours; with radiation levels so high busdrivers refused to go near the site
**Credit: Igor Gavrilov/Endeavour Group UK**

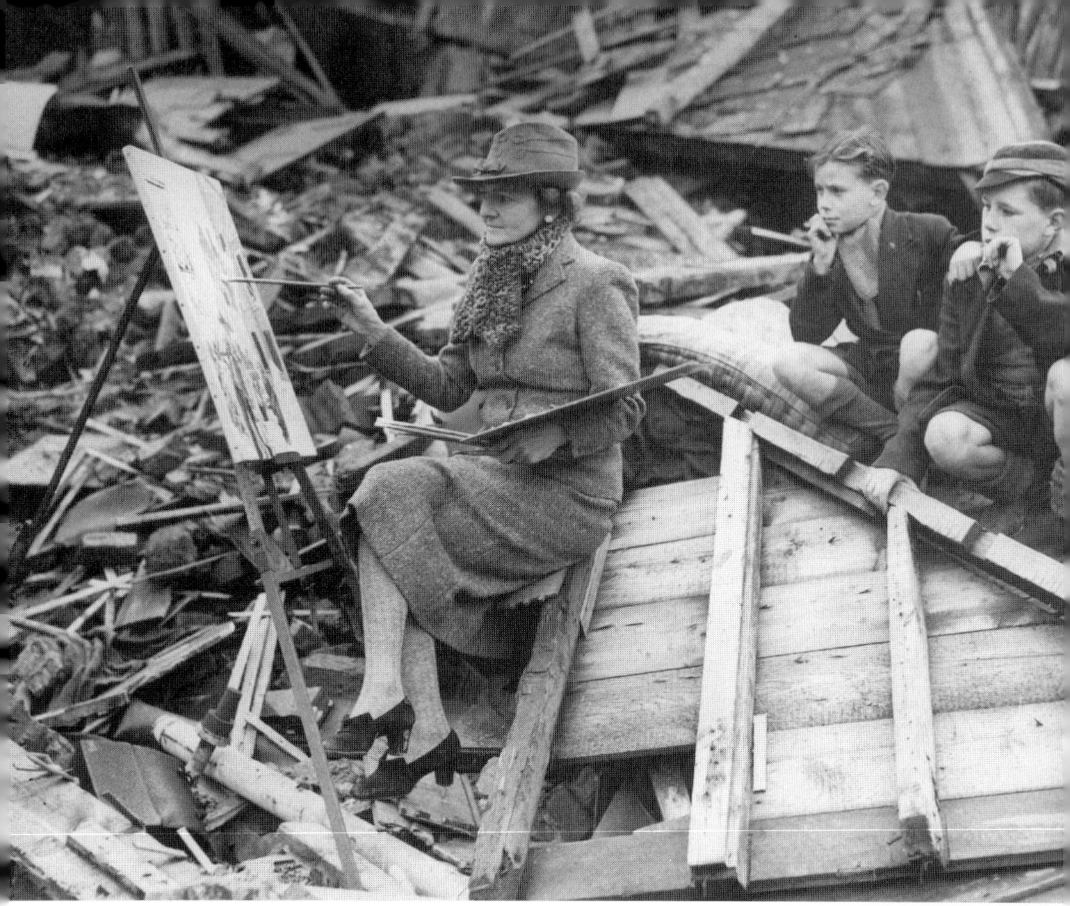

**Germany 1935** Public humiliation of both parties was the price of being caught in a Jewish-Aryan relationship in Nazi Germany. The woman's placard reads, 'I am the greatest swine and only get myself mixed up with Jews.' That of the man, 'I am a Jew, I only take German girls to my room.'
*Credit: Hulton Getty Picture Library*

**London 1940** Ethel Gabain painting air-raid damage for the Ministry of Information. The government believed paintings often made better propaganda than photographs. In this case, the carefully posed artist and onlookers provide the photographer with a second shot for the propaganda machine
*Credit: Hulton Getty Picture Collection*

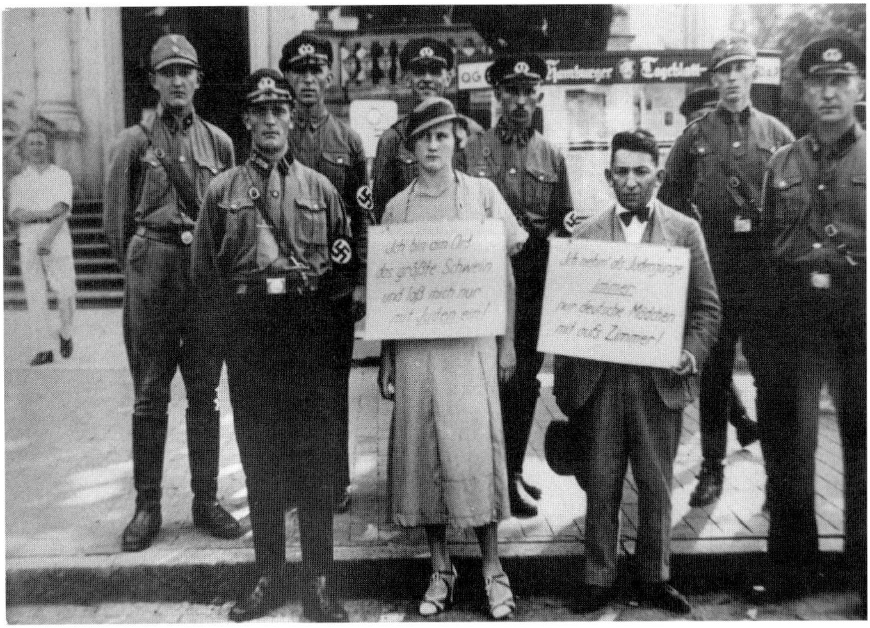

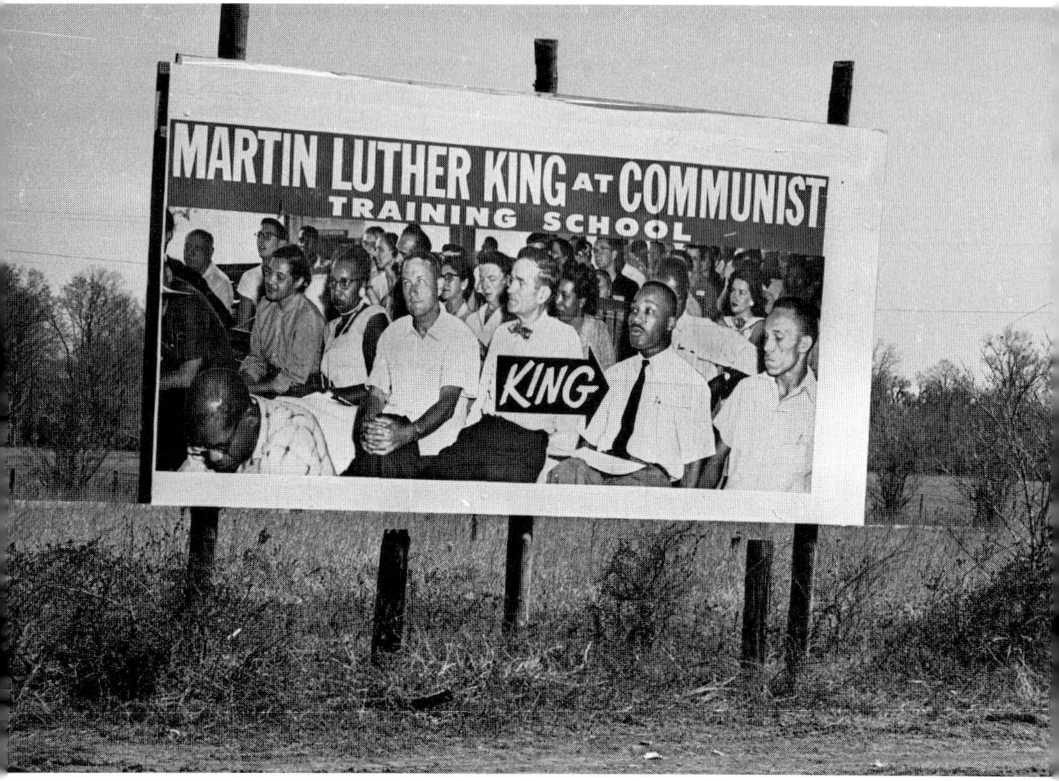


**Hill Timothy Hue Vietnam April 1968** US soldiers huddle for cover while attempting to capture a North Vietnamese stronghold, taken in the Tet offensive two months earlier. Despite President Johnson's assurances that the offensive had been a complete failure, the photo tells a different story: the offensive proved to be the turning point of the war *Credit: Hulton Getty Picture Library*

**Oklahoma USA 1965**
Opposition to Martin Luther King's Civil Rights movement in the 1960s took many forms, including attempts to portray the movement as a threat to national security. The poster supposedly shows King in the front row at a Communist school
*Credit: Hulton Getty Picture Collection*

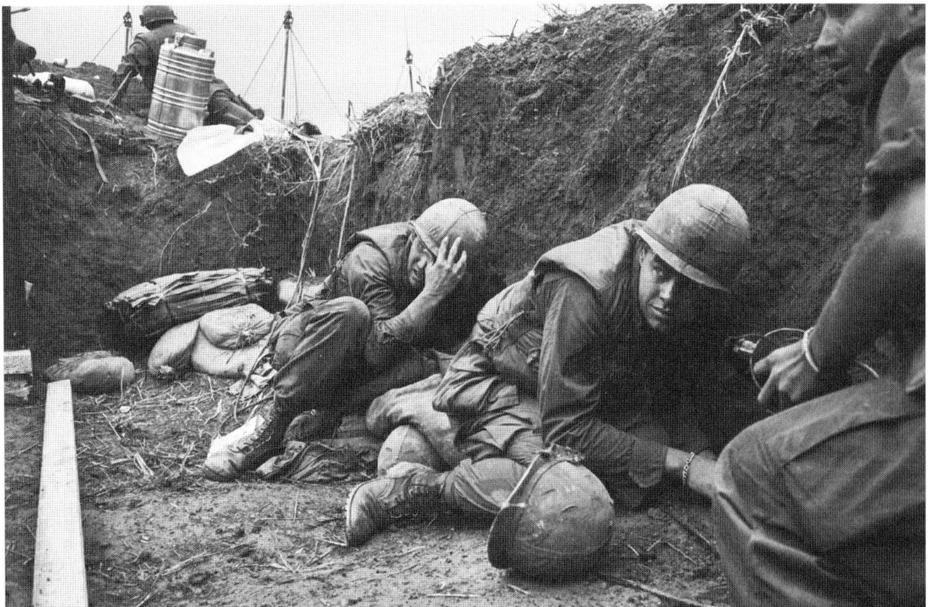

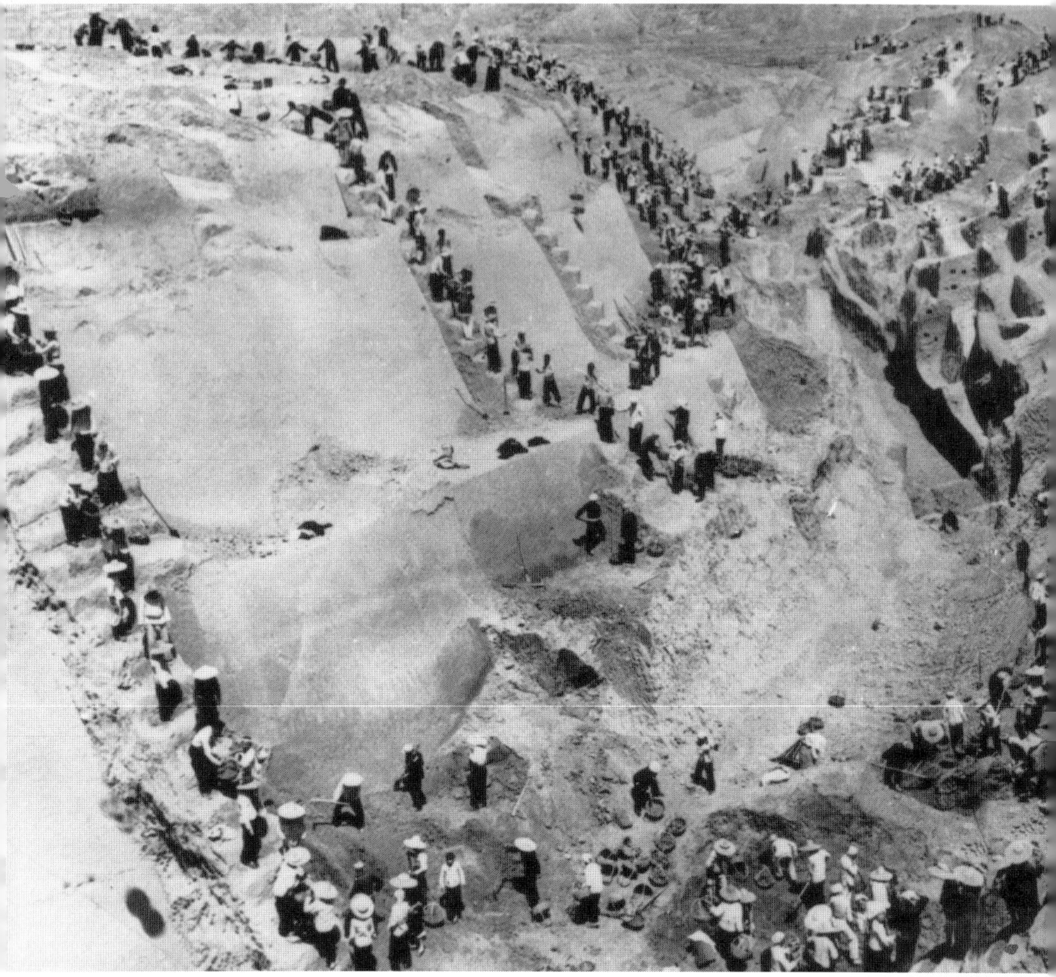

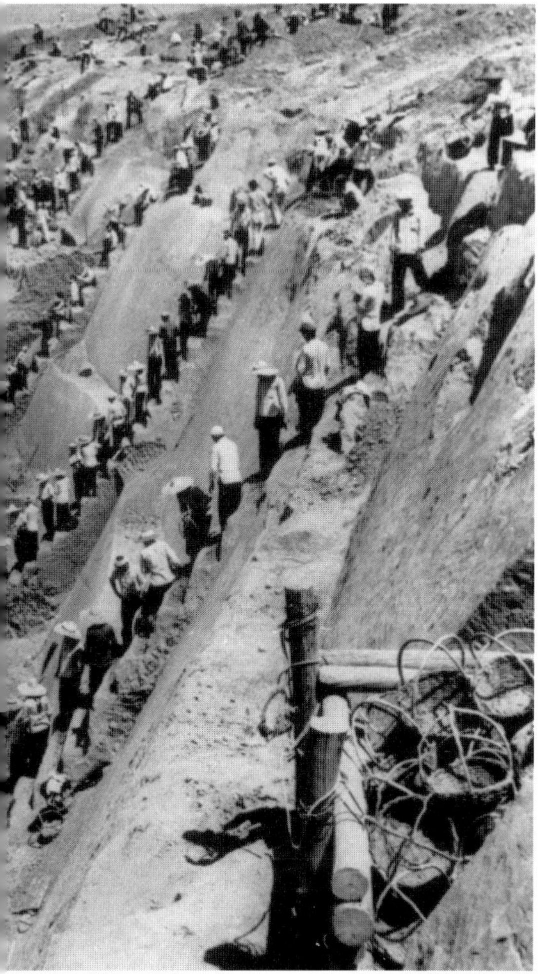

**Jiangxi Province China 1957**
Mao's Great Leap Forward to industrialise China and bring freedom and prosperity to all involved intolerable human costs glossed over by the state propaganda machine. But whatever the public face, a year after the Jiangxi project started, Mao said in a speech to Party leaders, 'Half of China's population will die, and if it's not half, it'll be one third or 10 per cent. If you don't lose your jobs, I at least should lose mine.'
*Credit: Xinhua News Agency Beijing/Endeavour Group UK*

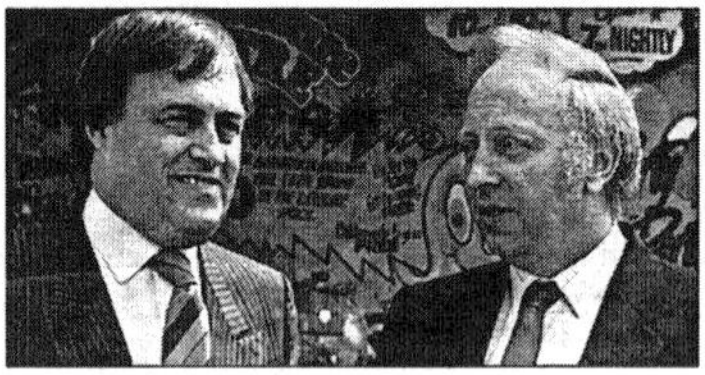


Working class hero: In former days with Arthur Scargill

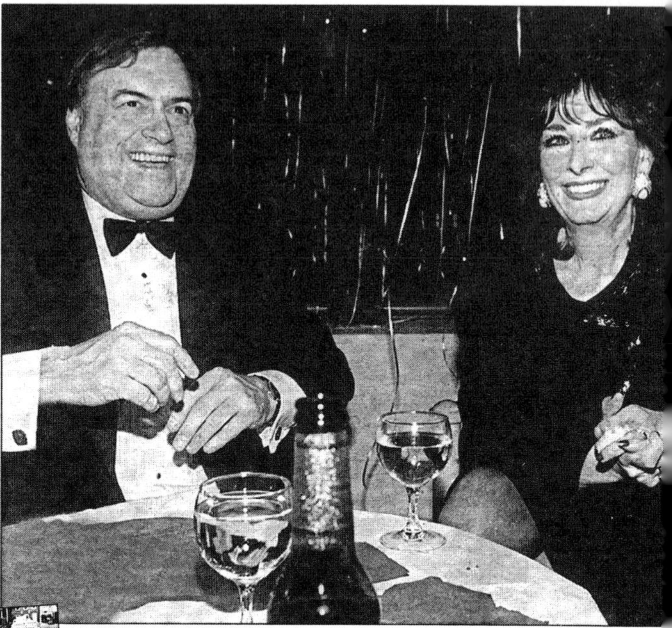

# Aye lad, I'm right middle class, me

## Prescott admits his social rise

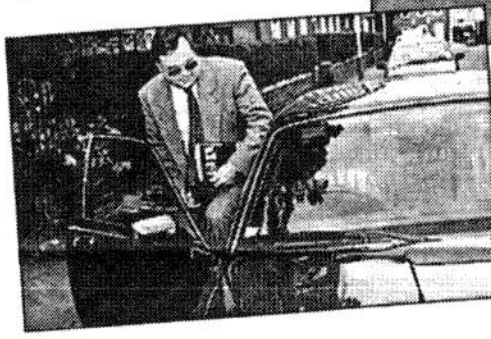

Champagne socialist: Prescott in dinner jacket with wife Pauline and, left, his Jaguar

by PATRICK HENNESSY
Political Correspondent

JOHN PRESCOTT handed Tony Blair's New Labour the ultimate endorsement today by admitting: "I'm middle-class."

The railwayman's son, a former Cunard drinks waiter and union official, stunned fellow Labour MPs with his disclosure.

Labour's blunt deputy leader, whom party activists see as keeper of the working-class flame in Mr Blair's London coterie of mod-

middle-class, I'm middle-class. We welcome votes from wherever they come."

Mr Humprhys said: "I thought you were working-class, but there we are."

Mr Prescott revealed: "Well, I was once

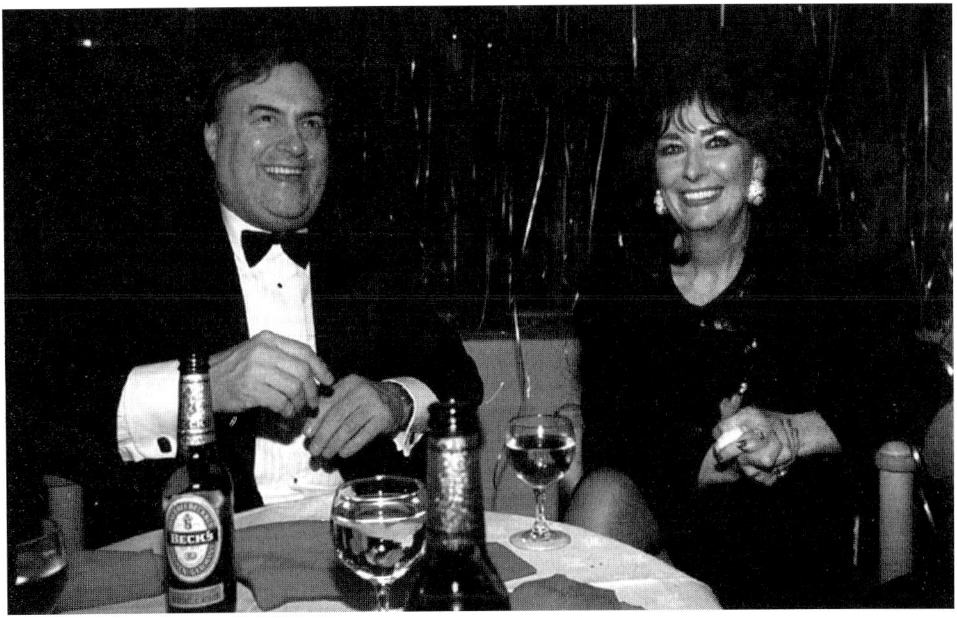


**UK 1996** The London *Evening Standard* set out to prove Labour's John Prescott, then in opposition, a 'champagne socialist'. To do that they digitally manipulated the above photo, taken by freelance Alan Davidson at a social function, to remove the left hand beer bottle and give the impression (*left*) that Prescott was drinking wine. At the time Davidson commented: 'The *Daily Mail* had a picture of mine, of Selwyn Gummer with his daughter eating beef canapes. They removed an arm to make the image tidier. I don't think there's a problem with that. But changing the content of a picture to suit a line is wrong.' The *Standard* later apologised.
*Credit: Alan Davidson*

**Glasgow 1999** Queen Elizabeth II takes tea with Susan McCarron in her housing-association house in Castlemilk, Glasgow. After the death of Princess Diana, the royal family strove to shed its aloof image.
*Credit: David Cheskin Jam/Associated Press*

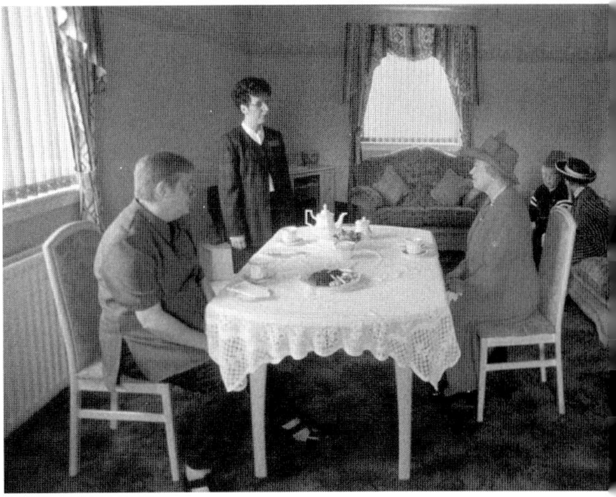

# Forbidden culture

*Good taste at this time in a technological democracy ends up to be nothing more than taste prejudice. If all that art does is create good or bad taste, then it has failed completely... Camera Art must be completely devoid of logic so that the viewer applies his own logic and the work, in fact, makes itself before the viewer's eyes.*

*Les Levine*

**UK 1942** Jacob Epstein unveils his latest work, Jacob and the Angel, at the Leicester Gallery,
*Credit: Hulton Getty Picture Collection*

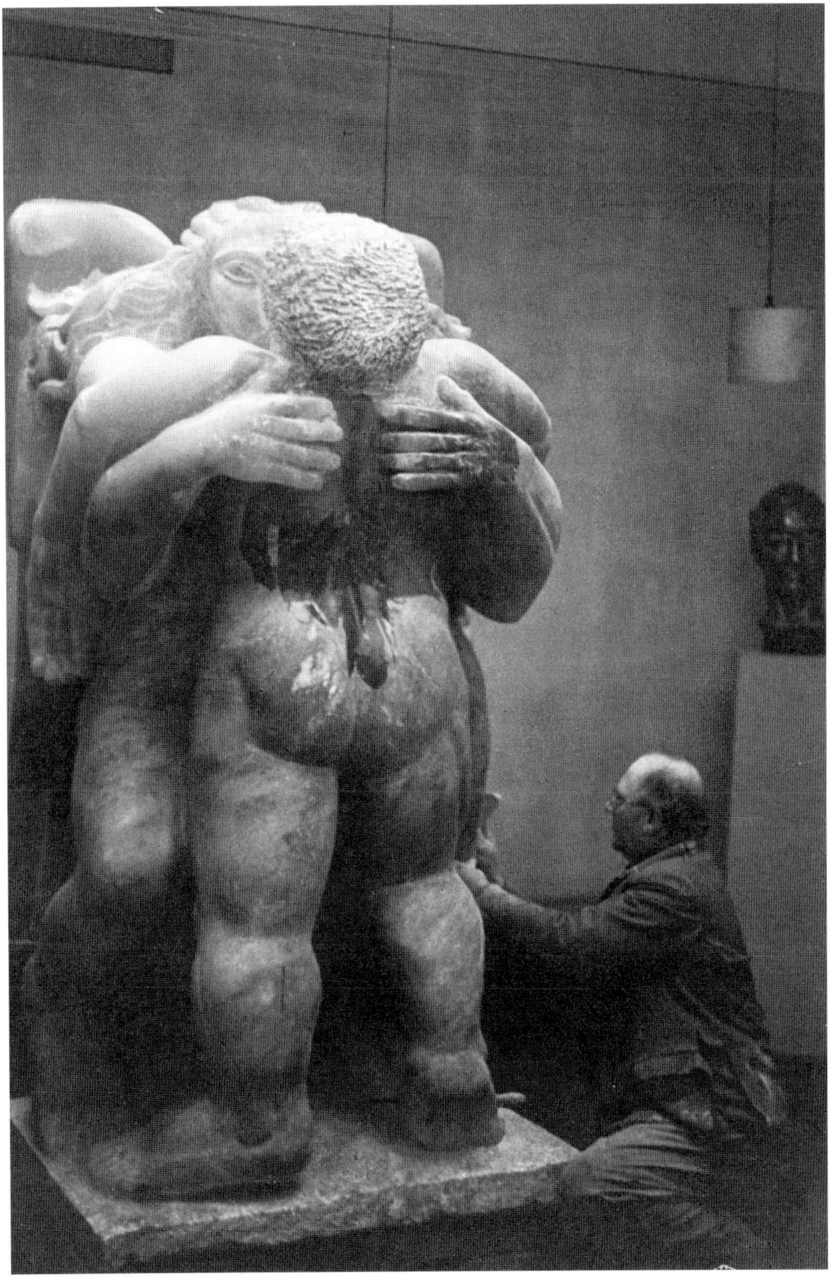

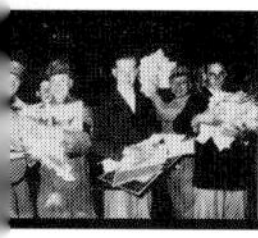

# Forbidden culture

*Edward Lucie-Smith*

On 20 October 1999, *The Times* of London published an editorial defending the entries to the Tate Gallery's annual Turner Prize, which celebrates the activities of so-called 'cutting edge' artists – in other words, the extreme avant-garde. For the anonymous leader writer, the merit of the Prize seemed to be the amount of controversy it aroused: the Turner Prize show has always played to the gallery. For many, its main point is precisely the ruckus that it annually creates. If people are arguing about art, does not that mean, in a way, that even those who loathe them find enjoyment in these pieces?

Perhaps without entirely intending to do so, these sentences sum up the symbiotic relationship that now exists between avant-gardism in the visual arts and the impulse to censor. If no-one wants to ban a contemporary art work, then it cannot be really avant-garde.

There is, however, another element as well – the fact that avant-garde manifestations are now very often, like the Turner Prize itself, supported by the most official kind of patronage. Opposition to this kind of art currently tends to be populist. It is sometimes deliberately whipped up by the popular press. Agitation of this sort may, and sometimes does, result in acts of vandalism – damage to or complete destruction of artworks by enraged individuals or small groups. Destructive acts of this kind cannot accurately be described as 'censorship', which involves the use or misuse of official power.

The images in this section are, among other things, designed to show how this situation has come about, in addition to demonstrating the typical circumstances when censorship is most likely to occur.

The story begins with Epstein's memorial to Oscar Wilde in Père Lachaise cemetery in Paris. Commissioned in 1908 from an already controversial young sculptor, this was installed in Paris in 1912, and was promptly shrouded in a tarpaulin by the administrators of the cemetery, who objected to the size and prominence of the figure's genitals. When the tomb was at long last officially unveiled in August 1914, it wore a small bronze *cache-sexe* in the shape of a butterfly. This object disappeared within a few weeks – the magician Aleister Crowley appeared in the Café Royal in London wearing it as a codpiece. The sculpture then remained undisturbed until it was vandalised in 1961, when the angel's testicles were hacked off. The culprits are said to have been 'two English ladies', offended by the fact that Wilde's tomb was an object of pilgrimage for homosexuals.

The next two episodes also involved celebrated modernist pioneers, and were concerned with sexuality. One centres on Marcel Duchamp's *Fountain*. This is the best known of all his 'readymades'. A male urinal, laid flat and signed with the pseudonym 'R Mutt', was submitted to the supposedly non-juried Independents exhibition held in New York in 1917, with Duchamp as one of the organisers. It caused a predictable uproar. One of its chief opponents was the US realist painter George Bellows, who denounced it as indecent. In the end – as Duchamp had no doubt intended – its removal was voted by a small margin.

Another victim of censorship, the Romanian sculptor Constantin Brancusi, was less content with the situation that confronted him. His polished metal sculpture *Princesse X* was removed from the Salon des Indépendants in 1920 because of its supposed resemblance to a phallus. Picasso is said to have been the first to make the comparison. Ironically enough, the very same sculpture had been shown without trouble in the New York Independents of 1917.

The true age of censorship in 20th-century art coincides with the rise of Soviet communism in Russia and of the Nazi Party in Germany. Though the majority of the pre-Revolutionary avant-garde in Russia became ardent supporters of the Bolsheviks, their enthusiasm was not reciprocated by Lenin and those who surrounded him. Lenin told Clara Zetkin, one of the founders of the German Communist Party, that he disapproved of 'iconoclasts in painting'. The late 1920s saw a violent controversy about 'formalism', a term associated with the Constructivists which soon became a catch-all word of abuse for any artistic style that attracted the disapproval of the authorities. The foundation of the Union of Soviet Artists in 1932 created a mechanism of control which lasted, in one form or another, till the time of Gorbachev. Moments of relaxation were followed by storms, such as Nikita Khrushchev's outburst in 1954 when confronted with some mildly avant-garde work in a large exhibition held at the Manège in Moscow.

In Germany, Hitler, himself a failed painter, detested modern art. Taking up the idea of *Entartung* [Degeneration] proposed by Max Nordau in the 1890s – a concept in step with the mechanical approach to biological science prevalent at that period but already out of date by the 1930s – he denounced the modernists for their internationalism, their slavery to fashion and their supposed connection with Jewish culture. The great exhibition of Degenerate Art held in Munich in 1937 was designed to propagate this doctrine. The exhibition attracted more than two million visitors – until very recent times by far the largest number to have attended any exhibition of contemporary art.

It was Nazi persecution that conferred official status on the Modern Movement in art, as this was now perceived as representative of democratic, anti totalitarian values. Episodes of censorship, since 1945, have usually been linked, first to sexual representation (the most effective but also sometimes the most dangerous weapon in the modernist armoury of shock) and second to social tensions within a particular society.

In Britain, for example, there were two celebrated cases in 1966 – the prosecution of the Robert Fraser Gallery for a show of erotic drawings by the US pop artist Jim Dine, and that of Gustav Metzger, organiser of the Destruction in Art Symposium, for staging an *Aktion* by the Austrian artist Hermann Nitsch in which images of male genitalia were projected on to the carcass of a lamb. These seem to reflect the phobias of a nation then in the throes of radical social transformation.

In the United States, there was a string of art-connected censorship cases in the late 1980s and early 1990s. The series began with the closure of the Robert Mapplethorpe exhibition at the Corcoran Gallery in Washington in 1989. The same show was the subject of an unsuccessful prosecution in Cincinnati the following year. In the same year, the University of the District of Columbia was threatened with loss of official funding if it provided a permanent home for Judy Chicago's feminist installation *The Dinner Party*, and the donation of the work had to be withdrawn. In 1990, another feminist artist, Karen Finley, was denied an NEA grant in reaction to her otherwise solo performance *We Keep Our Victims Ready*, which had attracted the attention of conservative newspaper columnists. She initiated a lawsuit against the NEA, settled in her favour in 1993. In that year she also received a Guggenheim Fellowship.

Once again, sexual representations and references were an issue in all these cases, which seem to reflect the current struggle in the USA between the neo-puritan revival and constitutional guarantees of freedom of expression. This struggle, however, cannot be accurately represented as one between unestablished artists and official forces. It has more the character of a civil war within the establishment itself. ❑

***Edward Lucie-Smith** is an art critic and historian. His latest book is* Women and Art, *jointly written with Judy Chicago (Weidenfeld Illustrated, October 1999)*

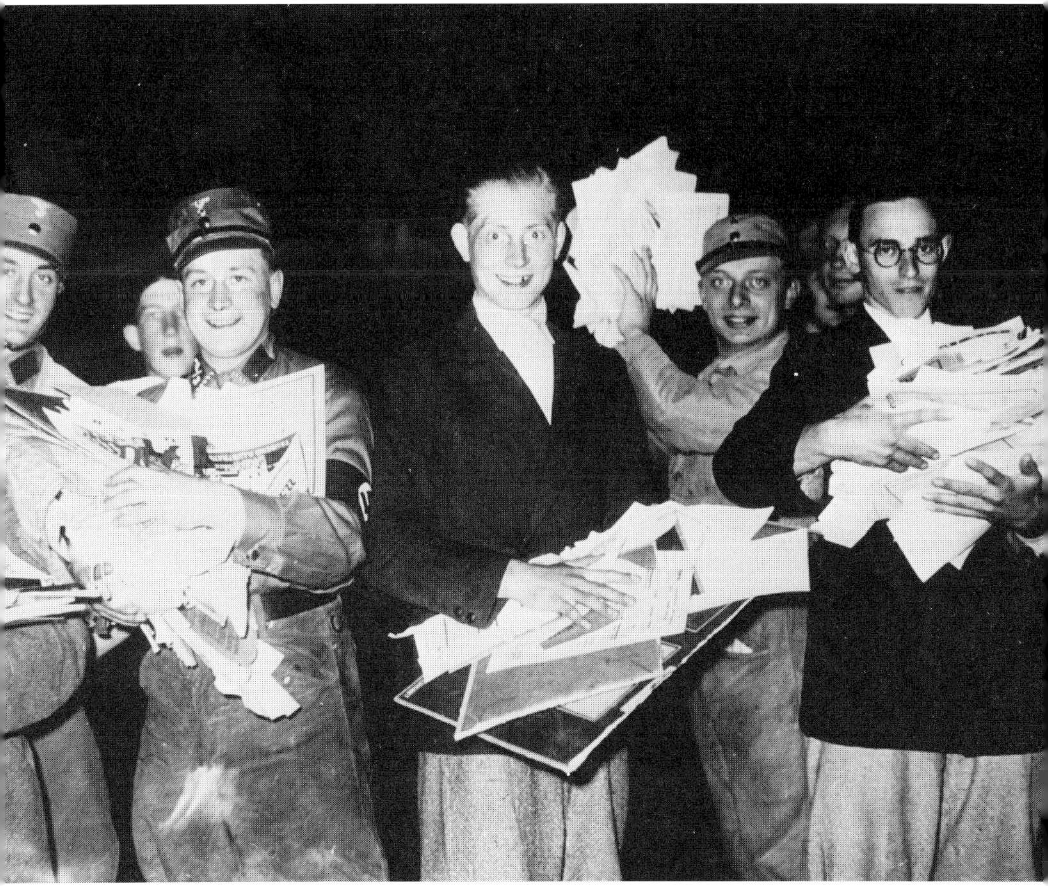

**Berlin 1933** 'Burn this!' In 1933 the Nazis ordered all 'offensive' books to be gathered and burned. The Hitler youth joined in with a will
*Credit: Hulton Getty Picture Collection*

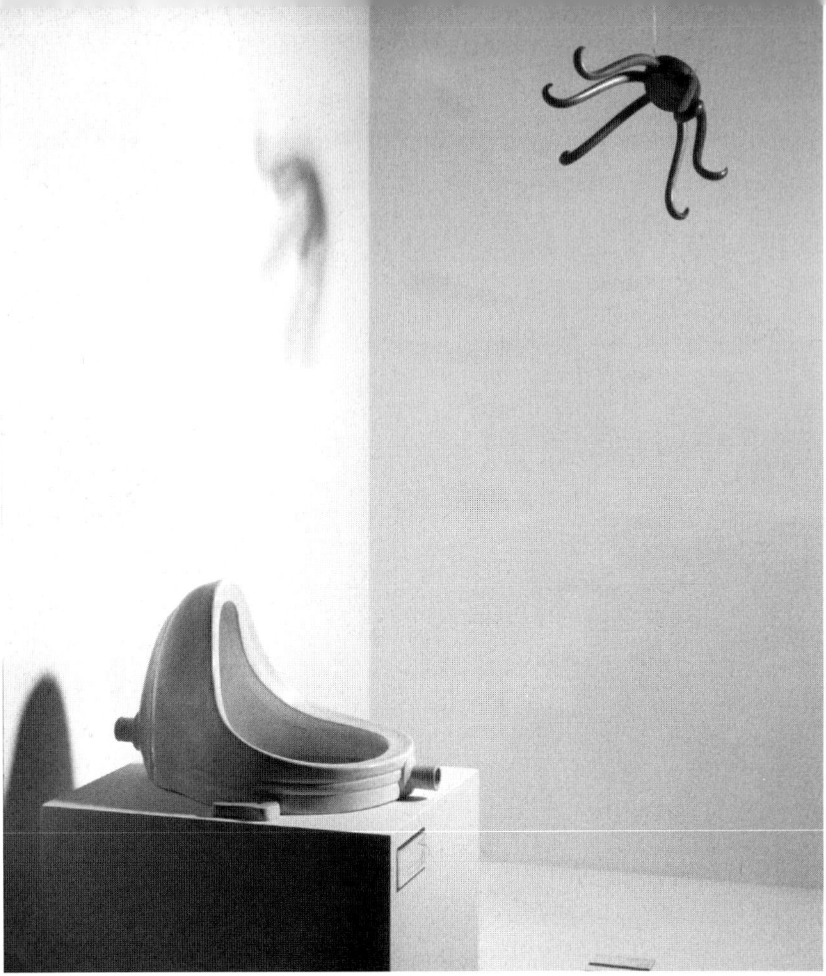

**New York, 1917** Marcel Duchamp's *Fountain*, one of the artist's 'readymades', removed from a supposedly unjuried exhibition in New York
*Credit: AKG London/Cameraphoto*

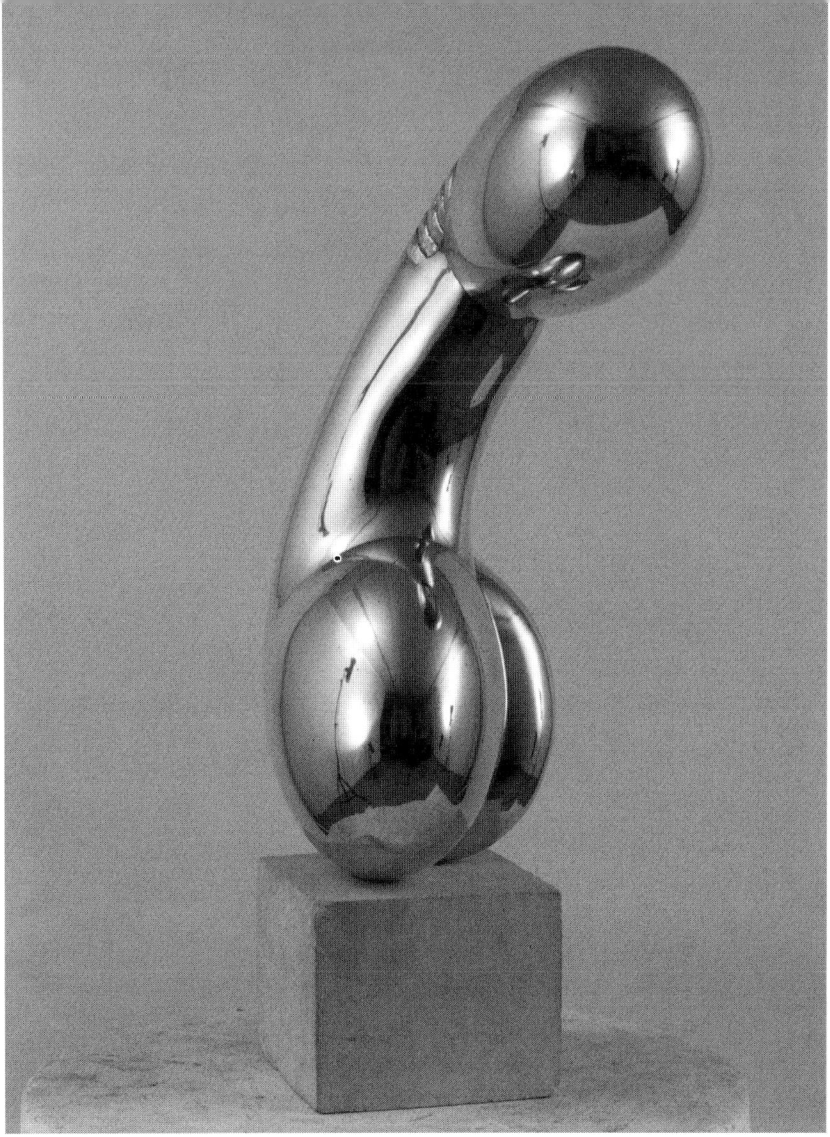

**France 1920** Constantin Brancusi's *Princesse X* removed from the Salon des Indépendants because of its alleged resemblance to a phallus
*Credit: Centre Georges Pompidou*

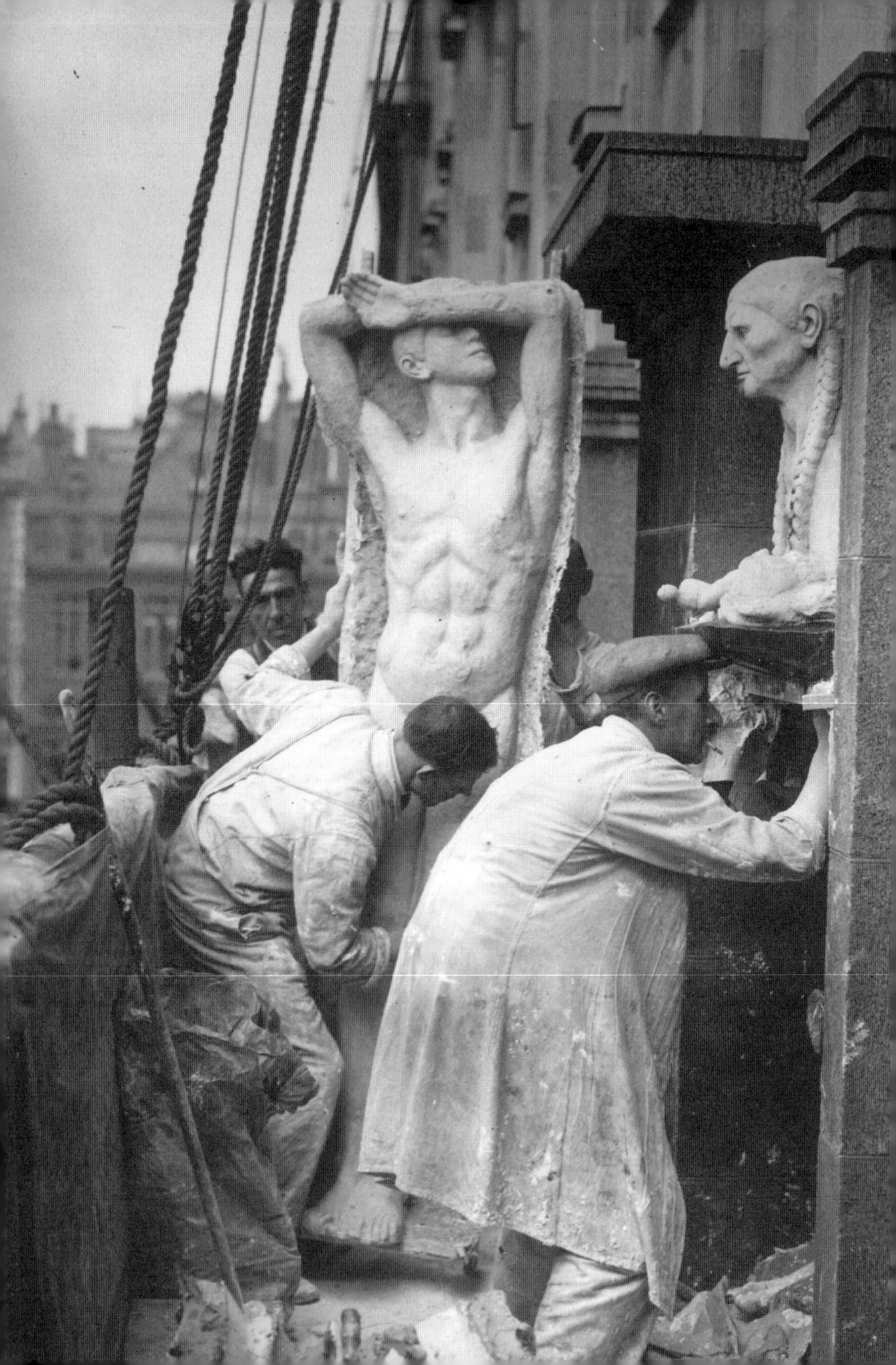

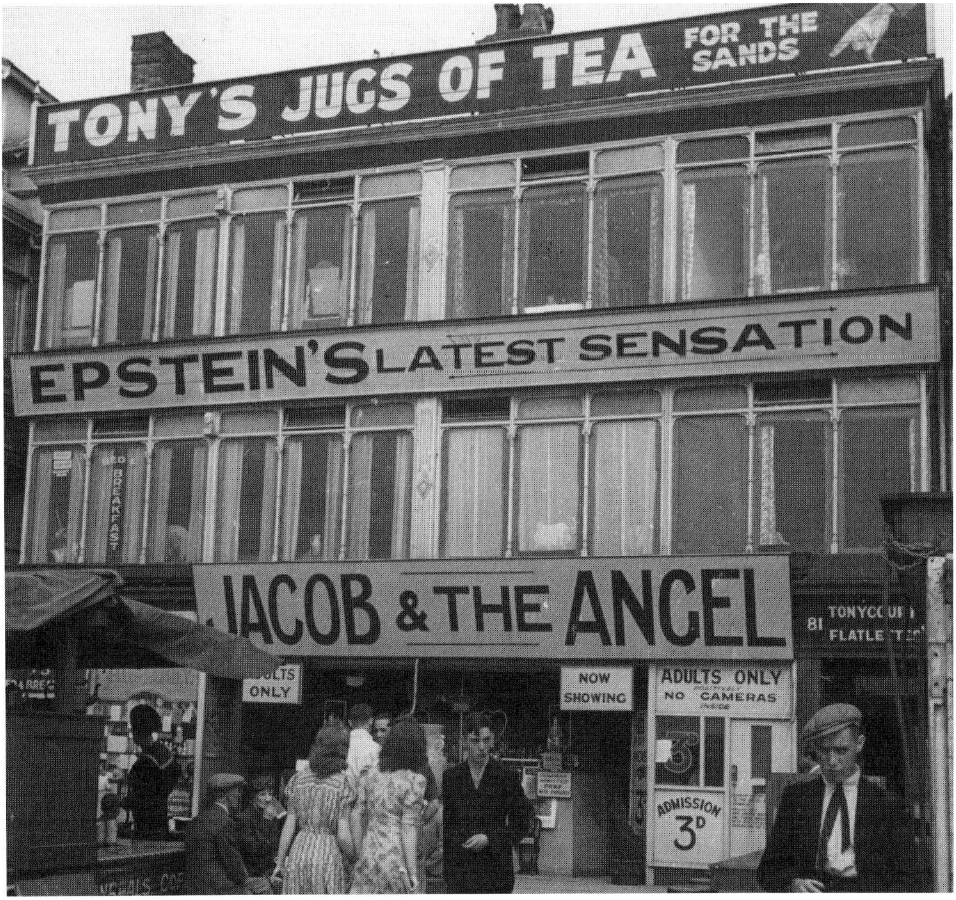


**Rhodesia House, London 1937** After years of controversy and abuse, Epstein's 1908 statues decorating the façade of Rhodesia House were removed and destroyed, without the artist's knowledge or consent, on the pretext that they had become unstable and were a danger to passersby
*Credit: Hulton Getty Picture Collection*

**Blackpool 1942** Like others of Epstein's more controversial works, Jacob and the Angel was exiled to a seaside pier where it provided 'adults only' entertainment out of sight of its critics
*Credit: Hulton Getty Picture Collection*

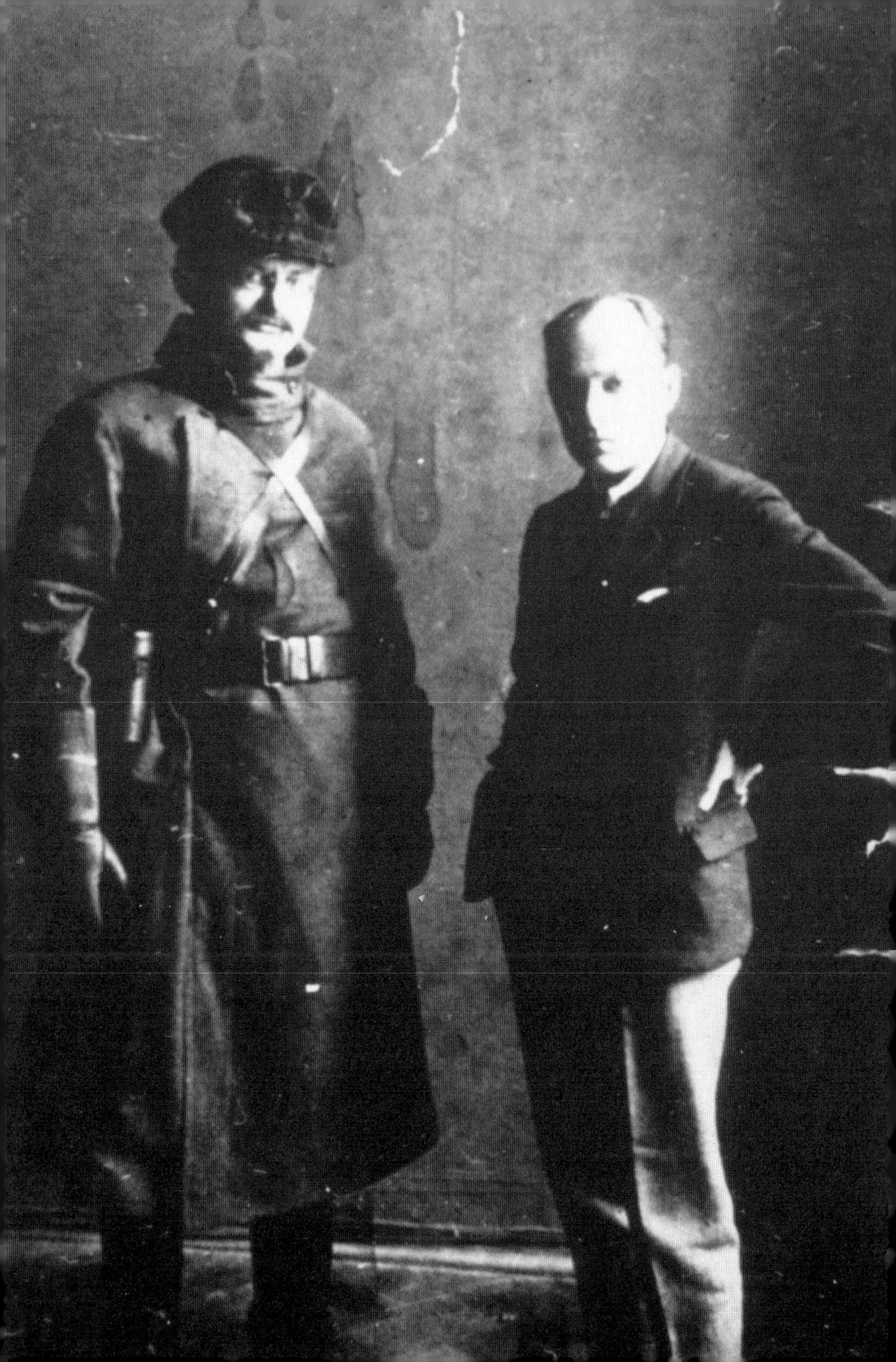

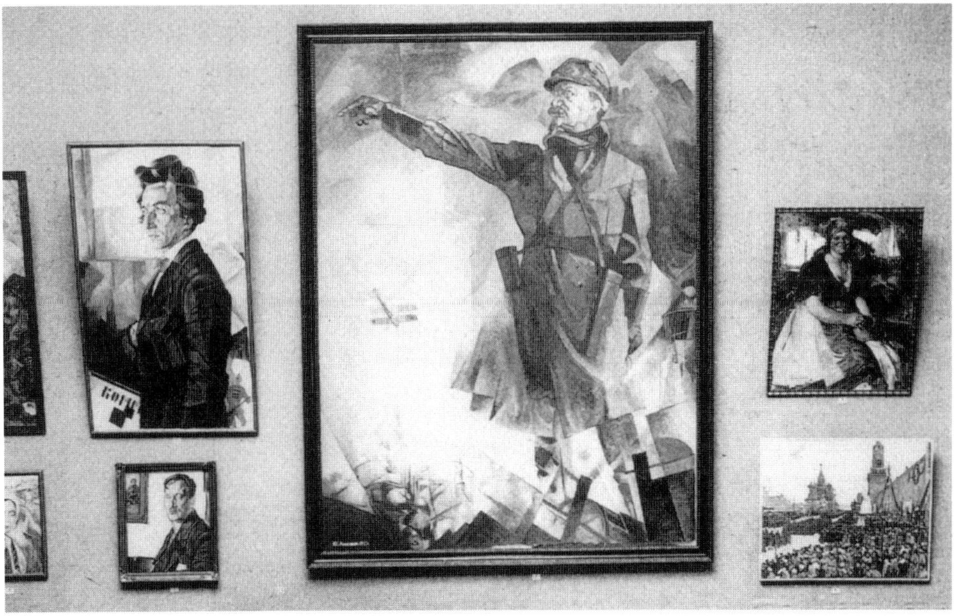

**Venice 1924** In 1923, the cubo-futurist artist Yuri Annenkov's portrait of Trotsky was so well received that it became the centrepiece of the Russian exhibit at the 1924 Venice Biennale. Following Trotsky's fall from favour, the picture disappeared. Seventy years later, no record of it exists and its fate remains unknown
*Credit: David King Collection*

**Russia 1923** Trotsky and Annenkov in the artist's studio
*Credit: David King Collection*

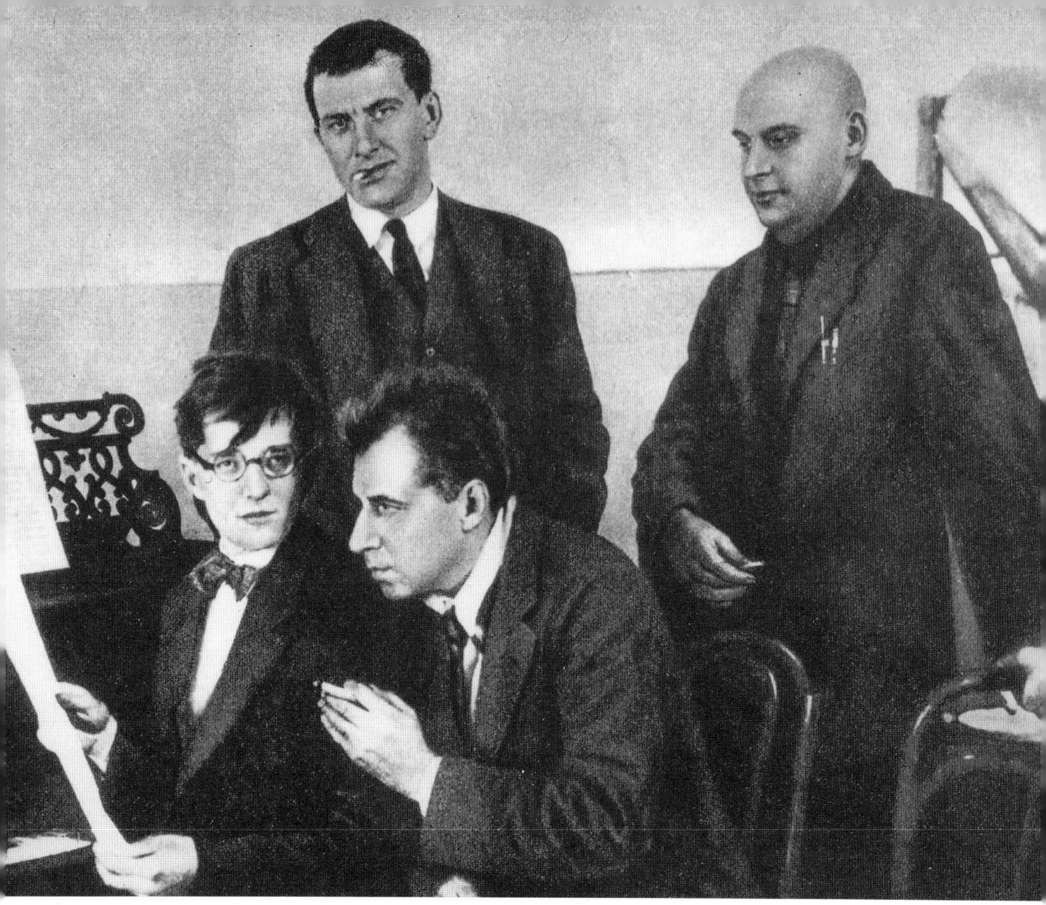

**Moscow 1929** Vladimir Mayakovsky's *The Bedbug* at the Meyerhold Theatre. Until the imposition of the officially-approved Socialist Realism in the 1930s, Vsevolod Meyerhold's theatre was at the centre of the Soviet avant-garde. However, *The Bedbug*, a satire on Bolshevik bureaucracy, was suppressed and, in 1938, the theatre was closed and Meyerhold disappeared into the *gulag* whence he never returned
*Credit: Literature Museum Moscow/Endeavour Group UK*

**Moscow 1929** Vsevolod Meyerhold (director), Alexander Rodchenko (designer), Dmitri Shostakovich (music) with Vladimir Mayakovsky discussing Shostakovich's score for *The Bedbug*
*Credit: Lebrecht Collection*

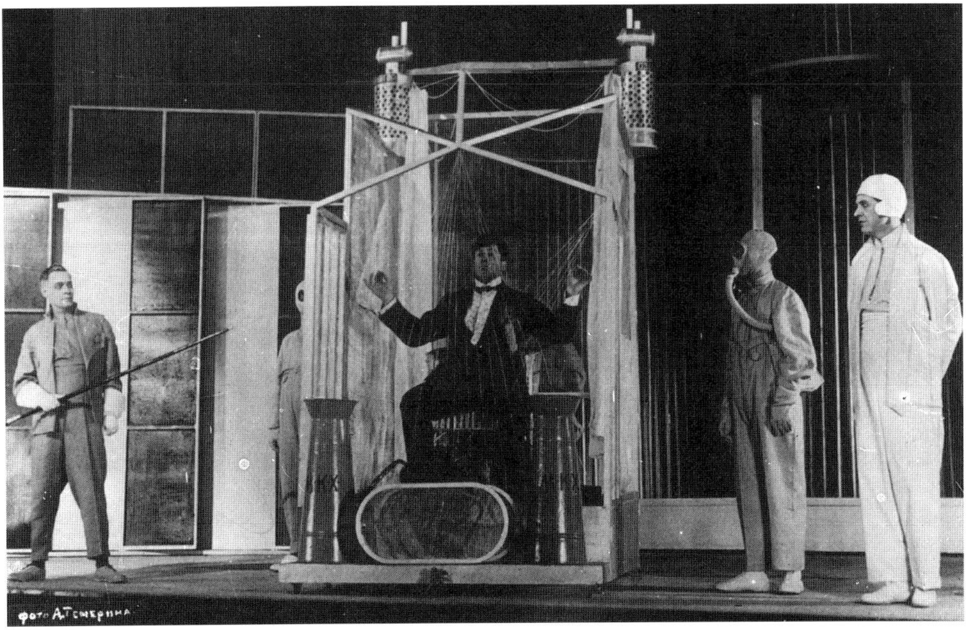

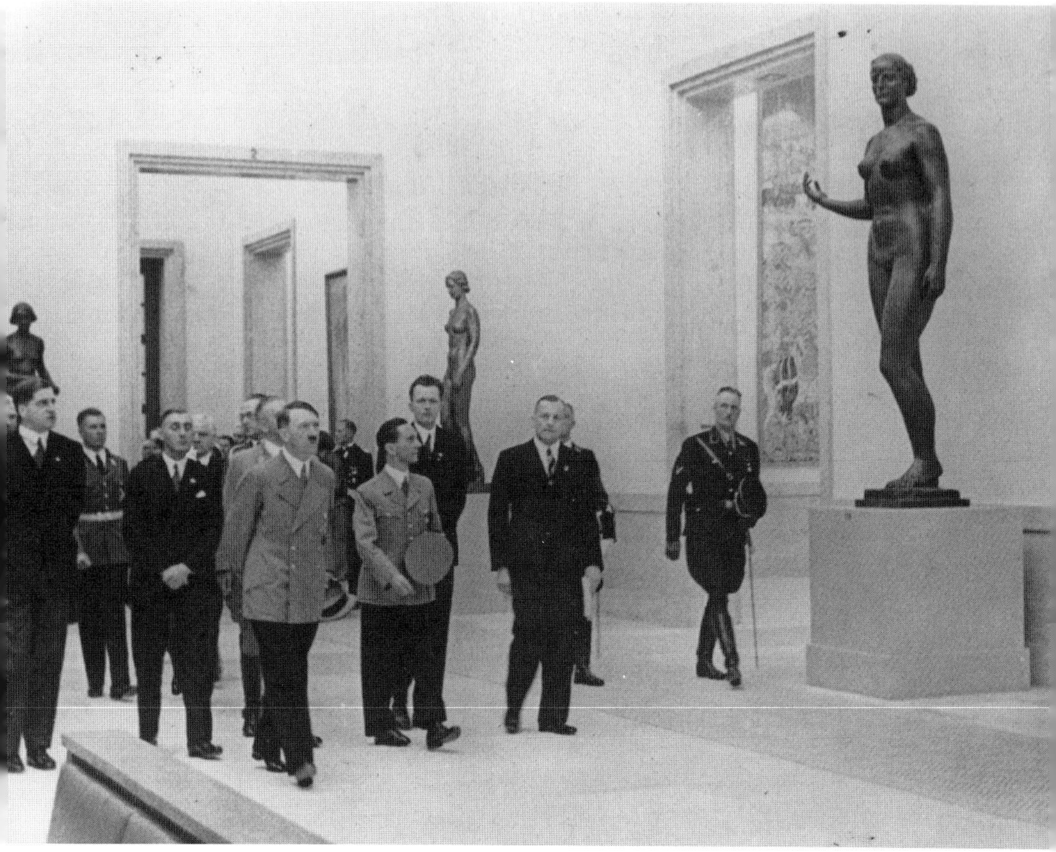

**Munich 1938** Adolf Hitler accompanied by Josef Goebbels at the Nazi Art Exhibition. This showcased 'good' German art and included a five-mile parade extolling 2,000 years of German culture
*Credit: Hulton Getty Picture Collection*

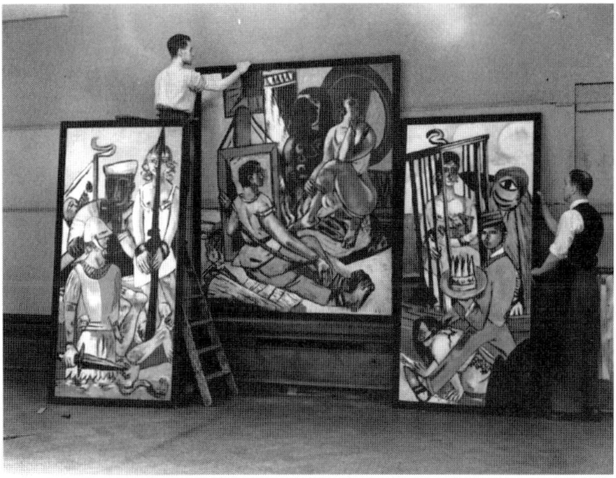

**London 1938** Hanging the German expressionist Max Beckmann's triptych *Temptation* at the Twentieth Century German Art exhibition at the New Burlington Galleries. The show included work by all the artists pilloried by Hitler in the Entartete Kunst exhibition a year earlier *Credit: Hulton Getty Picture Collection*

**Munich 1937** Hitler's *Entartete Kunst* (Degenerate Art) exhibition 'denounced the modernists for their internationalism, their slavery to fashion and their supposed connection with Jewish culture' *Credit: A Grimm/Bildarchiv Preussischer Kulturbesitz Berlin*

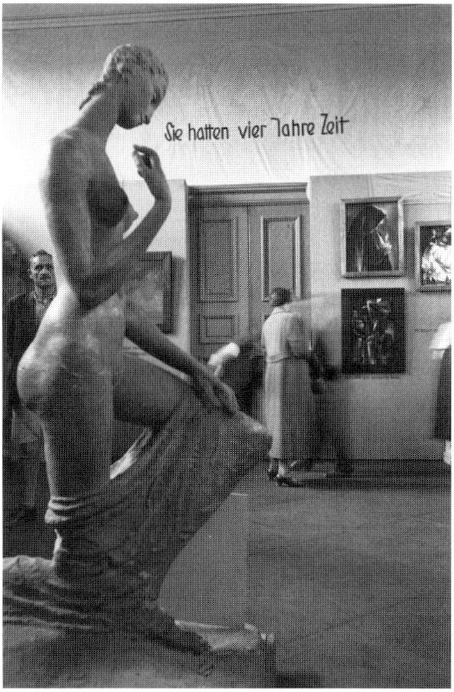

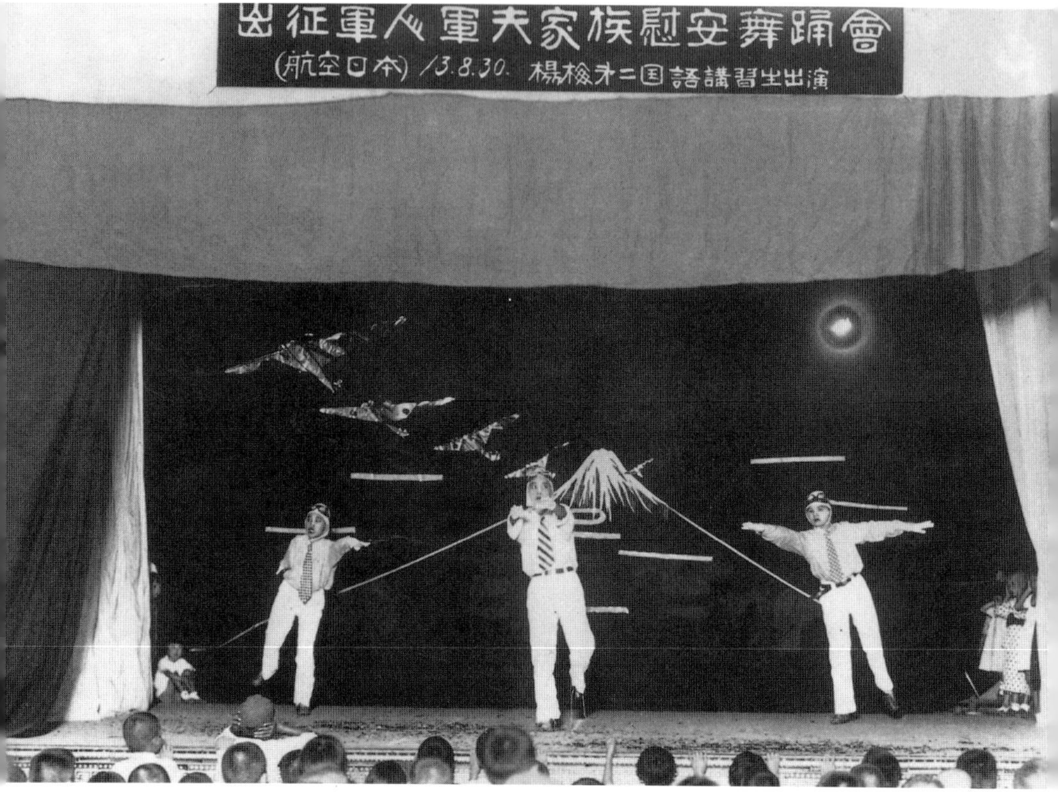


**Taiwan 1935** As part of the build-up to their occupation of China, Japanese authorities closed down the traditional Taiwan opera, *Gezai*. Chinese actors were ordered to wear only western- or military-style dress and perform only scripts that glorified Japan. Here, *Gezai* actors mime bombing raids on China beneath paper models of Japanese war planes
*Credit: Endeavour Group UK*

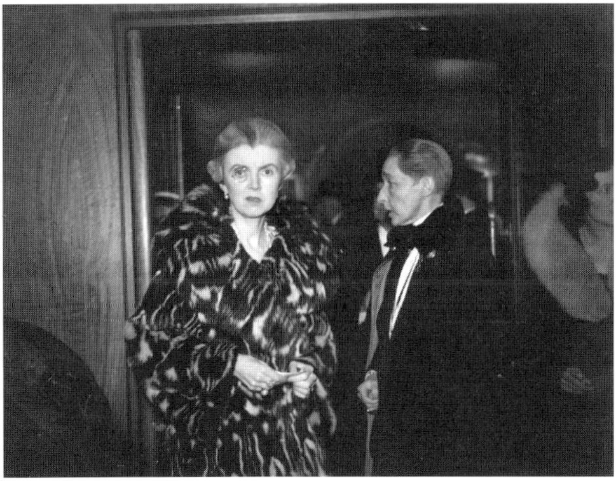

**London 1933** Radclyffe Hall (right), author of the lesbian novel *Well of Loneliness*, with her lover Una, Lady Trowbridge, at the Lyric Theatre. Hall was tried for obscenity in 1928 and the UK ban on the book was not lifted until 1949
*Credit: Hulton Getty Picture Collection*

**Shakespeare and Company Paris 1922** The French publisher of James Joyce's *Ulysses*, Sylvia Beach, with the author. *Ulysses* first appeared in a heavily bowdlerised serial form in the USA in 1918 to storms of abuse. The trials of *Ulysses* lasted until 1934 in the USA and the book was refused entry to the UK until 1936
*Credit: Poetry/Rare Books Collection University Libraries State University of New York at Buffalo*

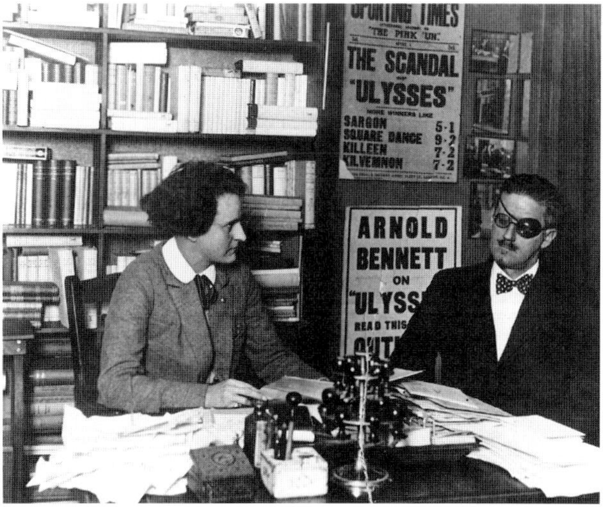

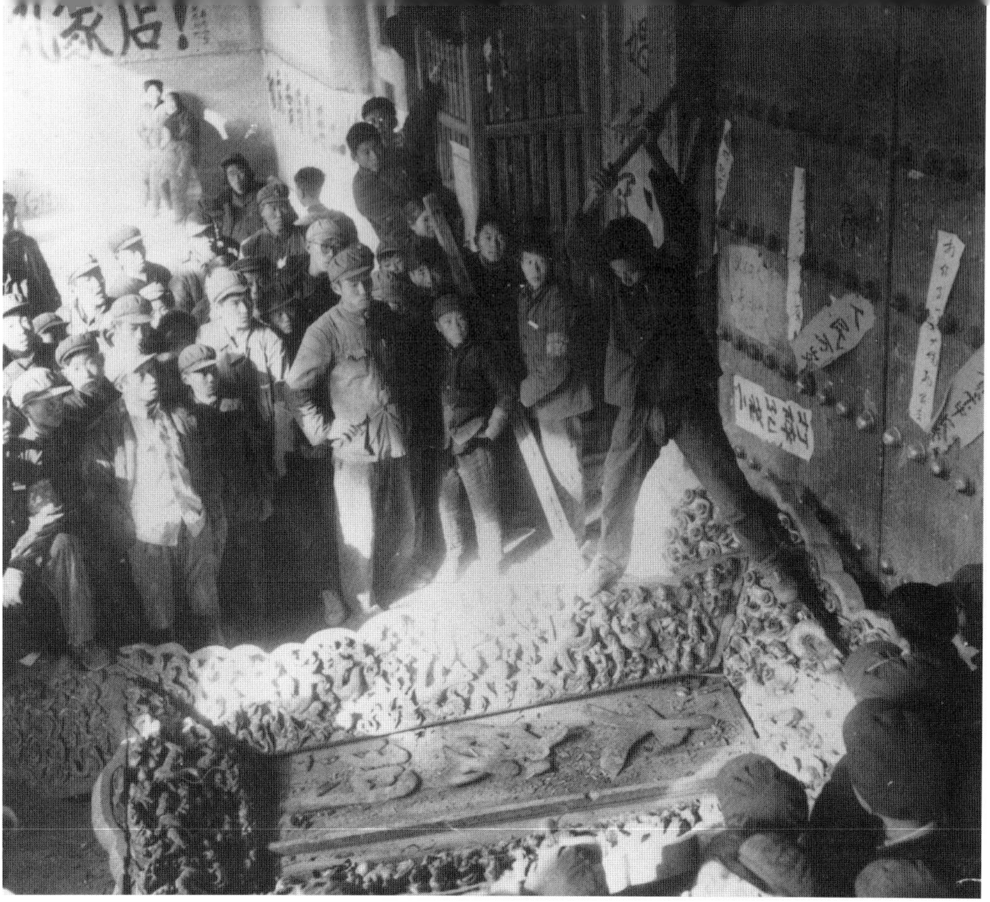

**USSR 1935** Demolition gang with the ruins of the Giorgievsky Church near Nizhny Novgorod. Over 50,000 churches were destroyed under Stalin and Khrushchev in an orgy of cultural destruction
*Credit: Nizhny Novgorod City Museum (M Dmitriev Photo Archive/Endeavour Group UK*

**China 1966** Red Guards destroy the 2,000-year-old shrines of Confucius. Destruction of shrines and temples in China and Tibet was widespread during the Cultural Revolution
*Credit: Xinhua News Agency Beijing/Endeavour Group UK*

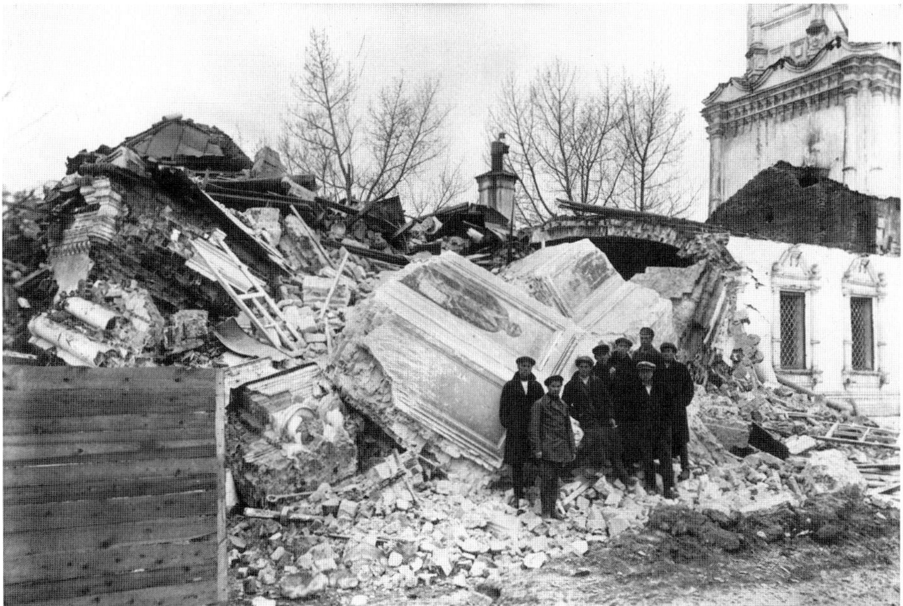

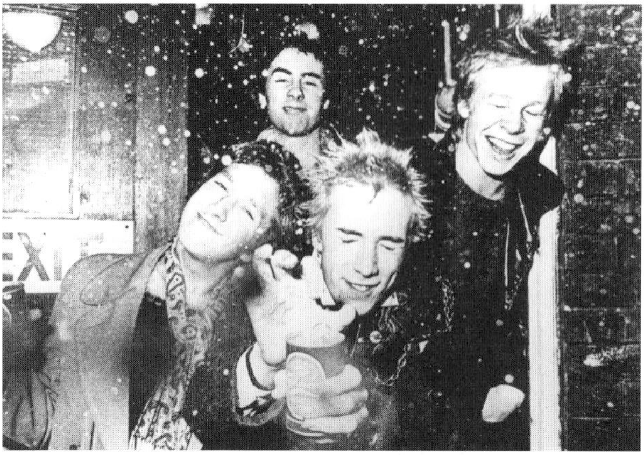

**London 1976** After resorting to a string of obscenities in a TV interview, the Sex Pistols had the majority of their gigs cancelled
*Credit: Hulton Getty Picture Collection*

**London 1977** Malcolm McLaren and Vivienne Westwood, the leading creators of punk clothing, leave Bow Street Magistrates' Court after being charged with a breach of the peace incited by Westwood's use of bondage gear in her designs
*Credit: Hulton Getty Picture Collection*

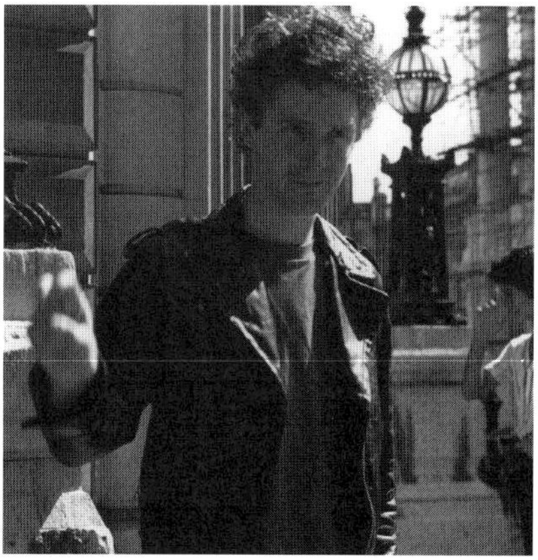

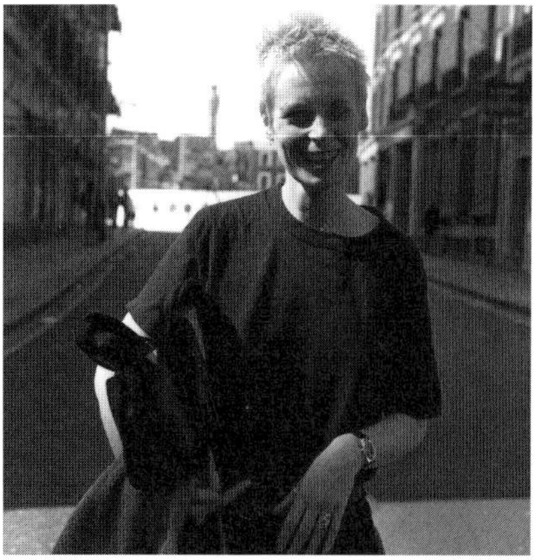

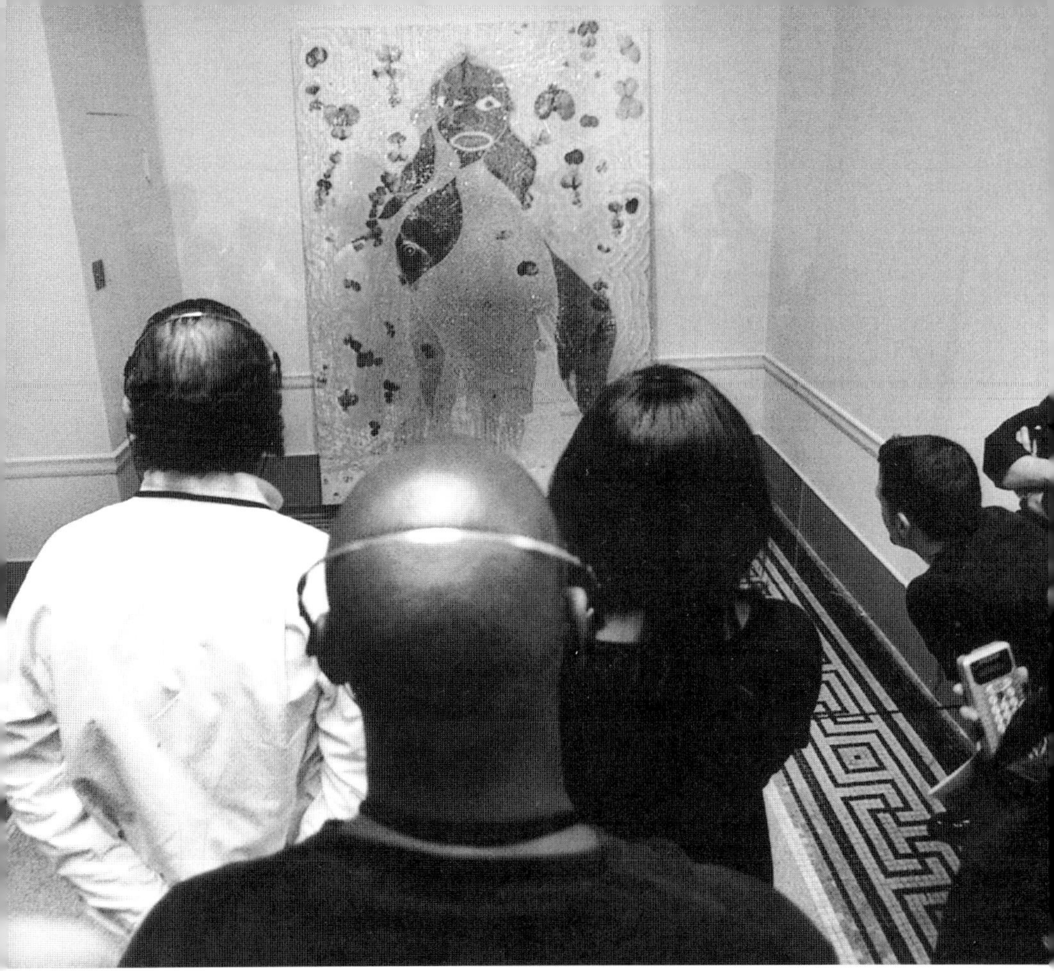

▲
**New York 1999** New York mayor Rudolph Giuliani attempted to run the exhibition Sensation: Young British Artists from the Saatchi Collection out of town by withdrawing Brooklyn Museum of Art funding – US$7.2 million. His main objection was to Turner Prize winner Chris Ofili's *Virgin Mary*, which he described as 'desecrating people's most deeply held views'. The museum won the first round of what promises to be a protracted case by securing an injunction against Giuliani.
*Credit: Lynsey Addario/Associated Press*

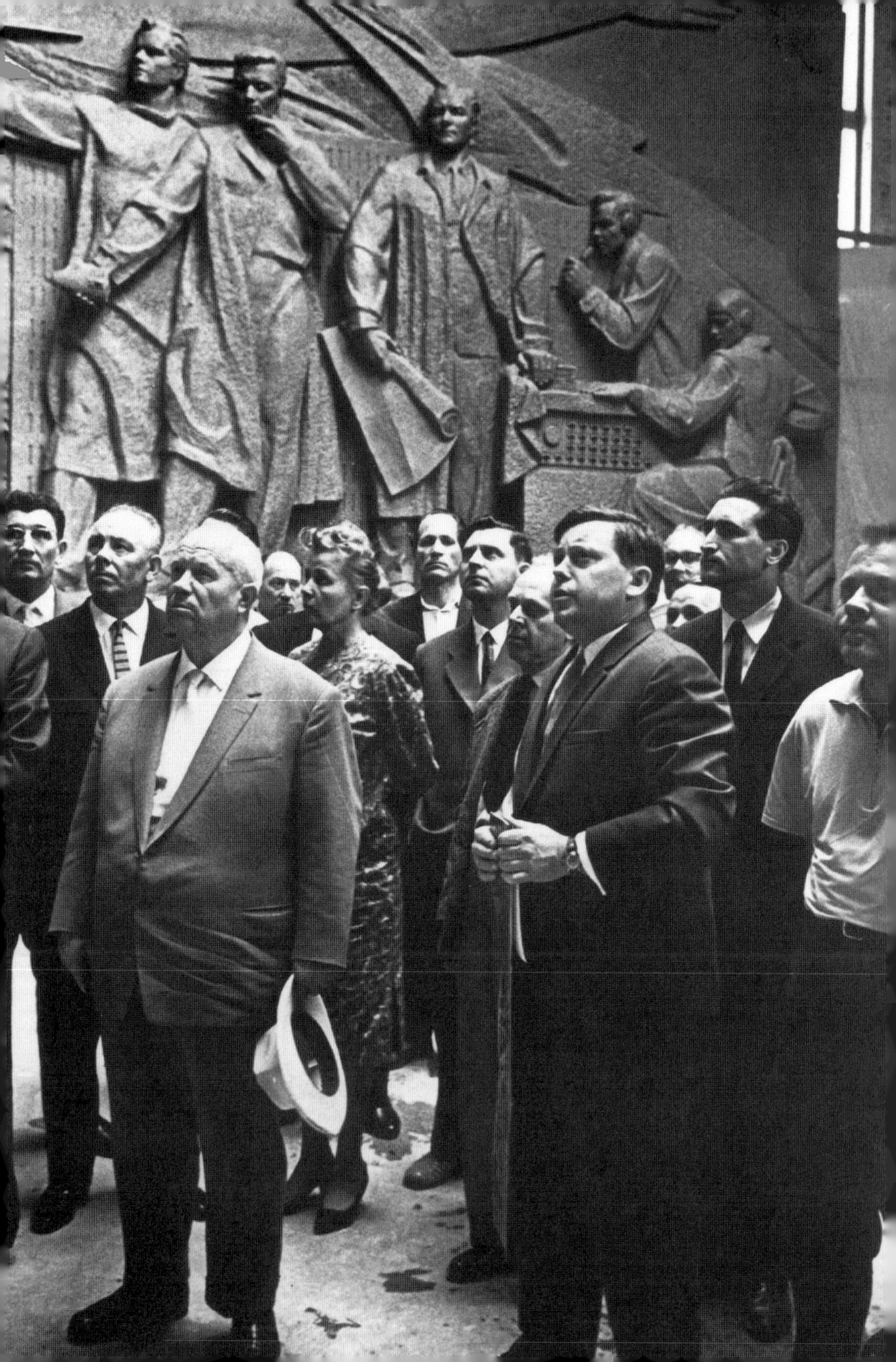

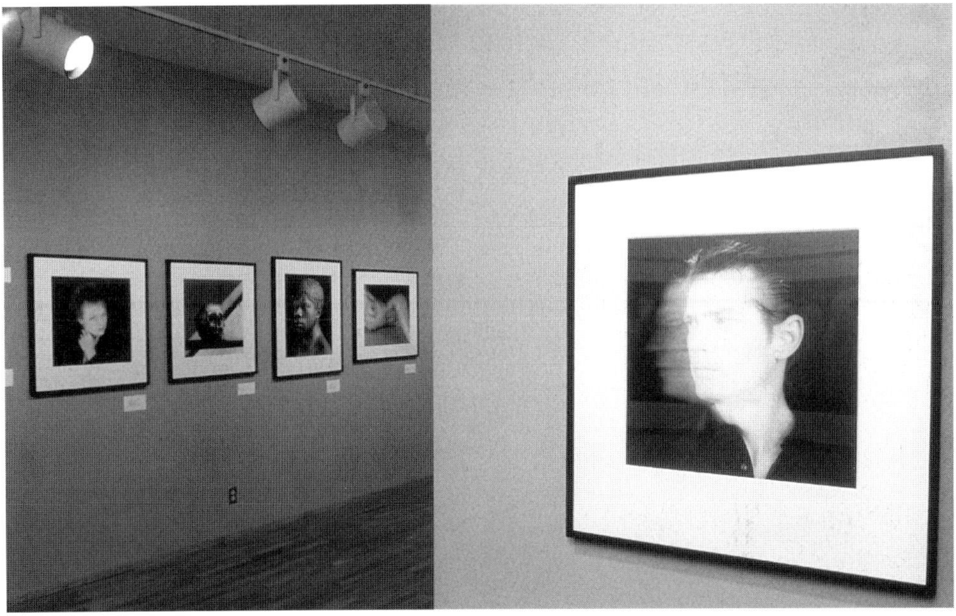

**Washington DC 1989** The exhibition of Robert Mapplethorpe's work at the Corcoran Gallery in Washington DC was closed down
*Credit: WPA/Corcoran*

**Moscow 1954** Khrushchev about to storm out of a modern art exhibition at the Manège. 'Any donkey could have done better,' he raged – and closed the exhibition
*Credit: A Ustinov/Endeavour Group UK*

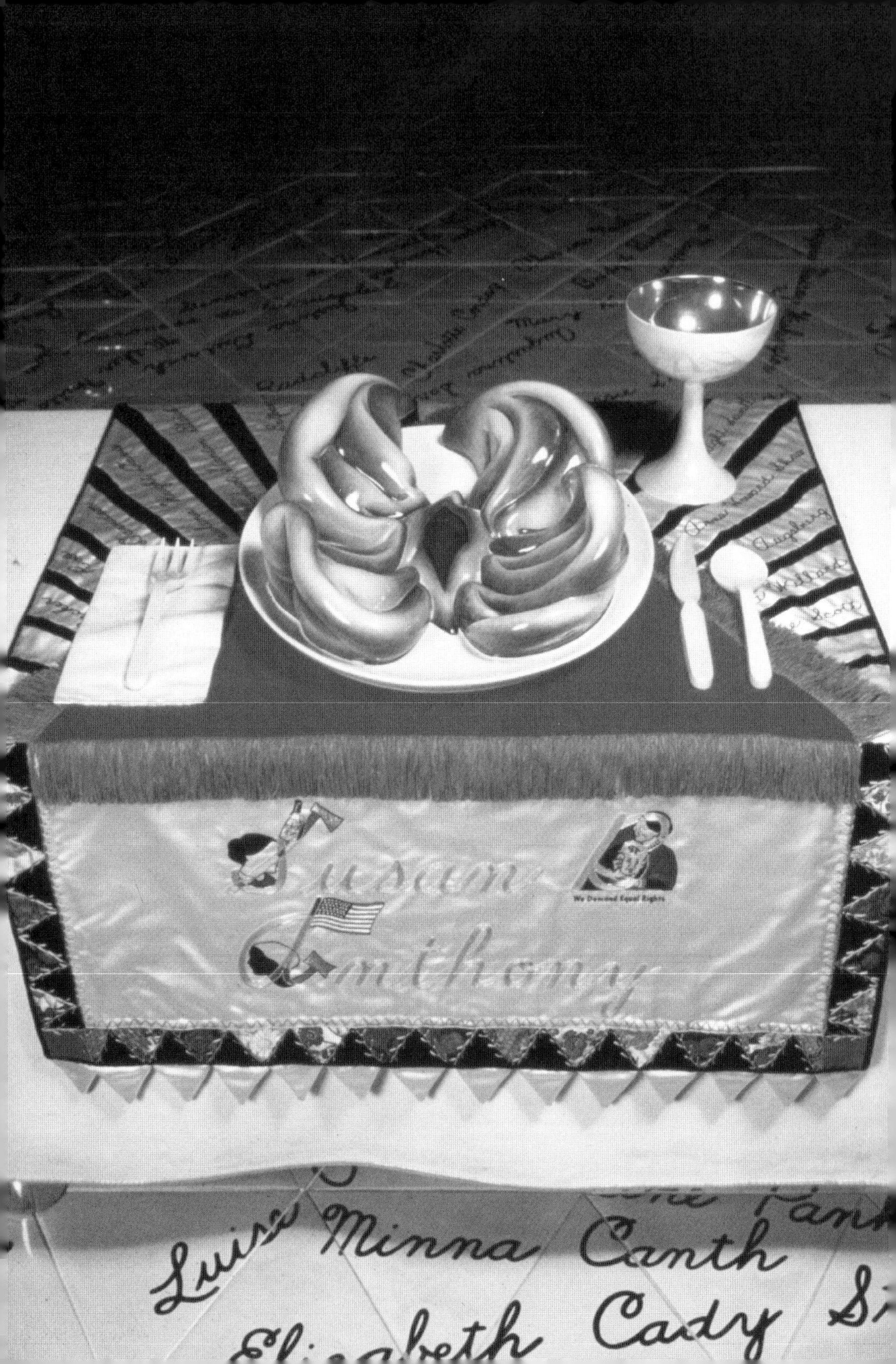
Minna Canth
Cady

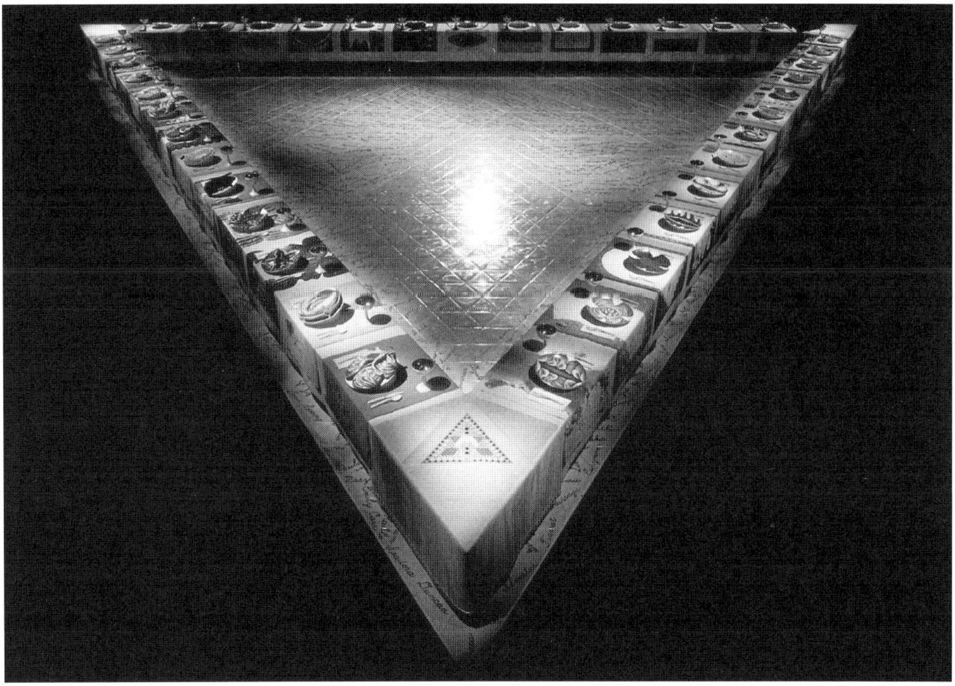

**USA 1979** Ever since its appearance Judy Chicago's *The Dinner Party* has provoked controversy, failing for many years to find a permanent home. When the University of the District of Columbia finally promised the installation a resting place, it was threatened with loss of funding by Congress and the offer was withdrawn
*Credit: Judy Chicago*

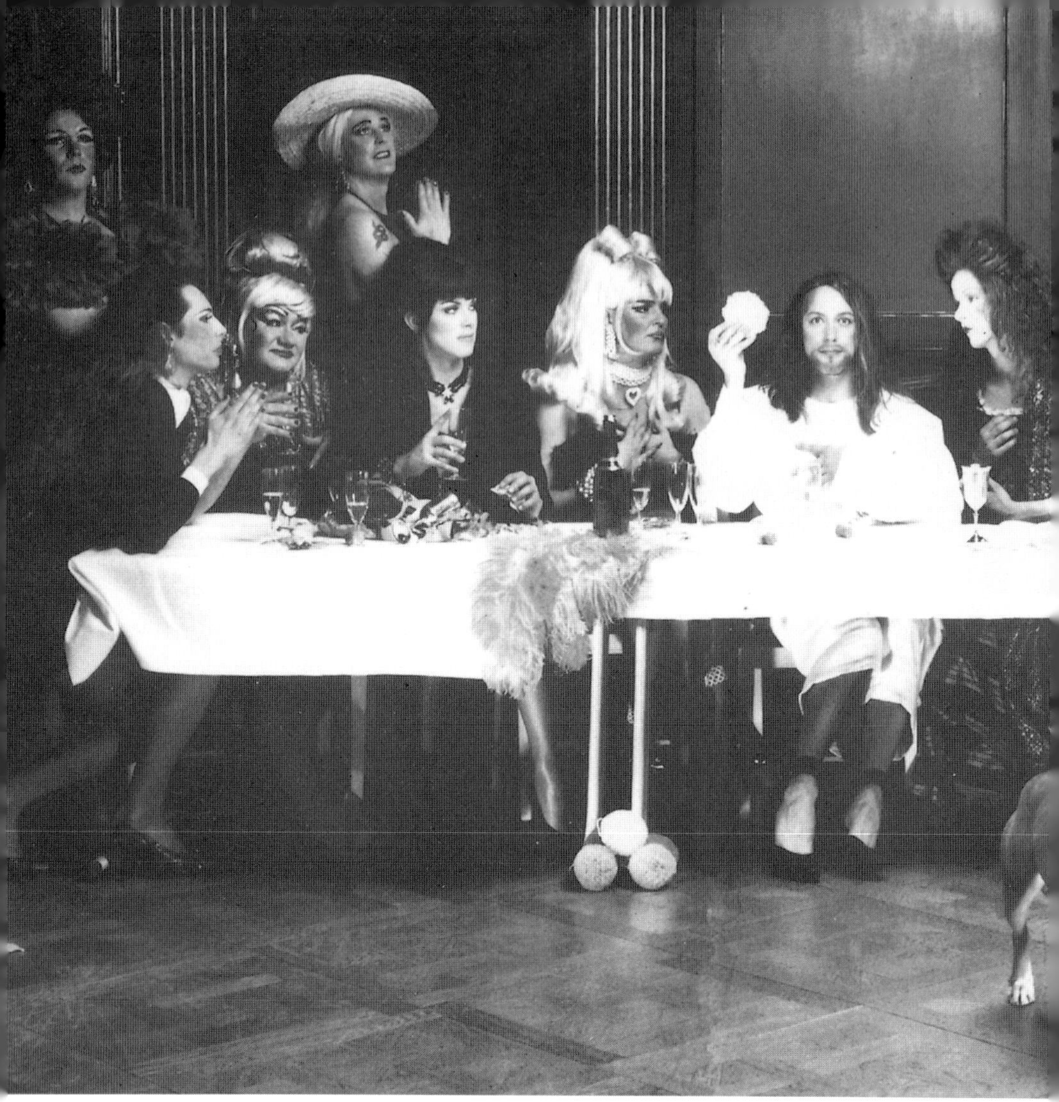

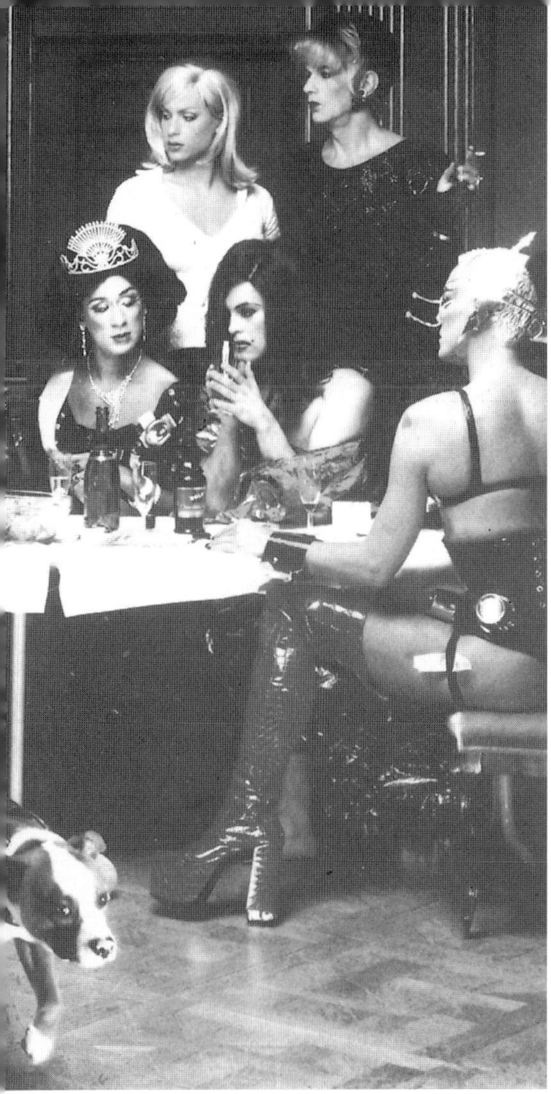

**Sweden 1998** *The Last Supper*. When Elisabeth Ohlson's *Ecce Homo* – a photographic Stations of the Cross – was hung in Uppsala Cathedral in 1998, it created an uproar throughout Sweden and there were calls for its removal. The series portrays the lives of gays and lesbians in *tableaux vivants* based on traditional Christian iconography
*Credit: Elisabeth Ohlson*

# Recovered memory

*Suddenly a small boy dropped to the ground next to me. I realised then that the police were not firing warning shots. They were shooting into the crowd. More children fell… I began taking pictures of the little boy who was dying next to me. Blood poured from his mouth… It was like a dream. A dream I will never forget.*

Alf Khumalo, writing on the outbreak of riots in Soweto, South Africa

**El Salvador 1979** A mother holds a picture of the son who 'disappeared' in the 1979 military coup. Between 1979 and 1982, 750,000 fled the country as refugees, 9,000 disappeared and 20,000 to 30,000 were killed
*Credit: Etienne Montes/Liaison Agency*

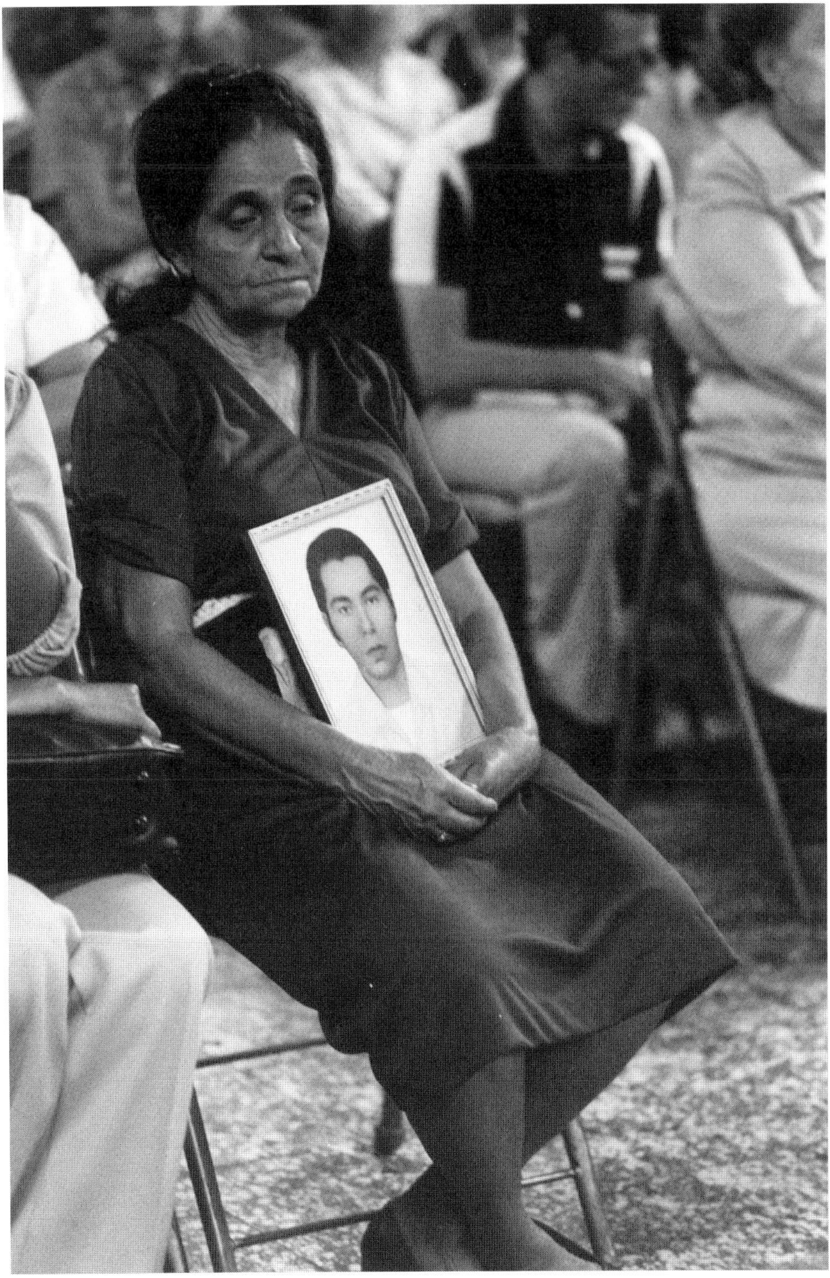

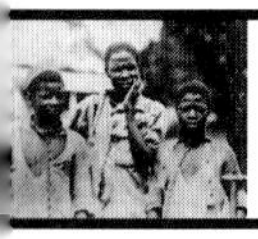

# Recovered memory

*Adam Phillips*

Remembering everything is a form of madness. It would also be a form of madness – perhaps a particularly modern form – to believe that such a thing was possible. A form of madness made plausible only by our increasingly sophisticated technologies for recording and retrieving the past. And yet when this striking remark is made in Brian Friel's play *Translations* it also serves to remind us that we tend to think of memory as redemptive. As though remembering, in and of itself, were salutary, and that we suffer above all from forgetting. But whenever we privilege memory we are always, more or less covertly, promoting specific kinds of remembering. It is not, for example, Germans 'remembering' their glorious Teutonic past in the 1930s that we even call remembering. But even if we call it mythologising the past to manufacture the future, we are unavoidably confronted with the selective nature of memory. We are not simply doomed to repeat what we forget, we are also enabled to repeat what we can remember. Our images of the past are our eye on the future. Remembering, that guarantees nothing, is unpredictable in its consequences. It only proves what we make it prove.

So in looking at these photographs – both the ones that we have chosen to forget, and the ones we may never have noticed – we may wonder what we are looking for, what use they are. If they are instuctive, they force us to connect things we prefer to keep separate – the Ku Klux Klan and our idea of Britain; the brutality of those on the 'right side', on the side of freedom and democracy, abusing collaborators. If they are evocative we might find ourselves stirred, against our better judgment as it were, as though the images were a kind of pornography. We might find ourselves taking awkward pleasure in the insidious violence we are being shown. The photograph, that is to say, can teach us – can serve as a reminder that is also a warning – but it can also undermine us. It challenges our ways of seeing if we refuse to be too easily recruited; if we take sides before we take thought. The photography is propaganda if we immediately know where we are with it. It is the complicity in voyeurism that tells us it's better to look, and yet without looking such complicities can never be undone.

In the dream, Freud suggested, the dreamer is all the characters. In the stilled life of the photograph, which has become so quickly an essential part of our cultural dream-work, we are at once invited and implicated. So it may be more revealing to think of these photographs – the ones that fascinate us and the ones we disown – along these lines. More revealing and more usefully disturbing. To see ourselves everywhere in the photographs – while unerringly acknowledging that these are real, other people living their predicaments – may be our best refuge from the worst refuge of all, which is righteous indignation. It's never enough now to be shocked by a photograph; and perhaps these daunting photographs are best seen as part of an attempt to get beyond shock, to think more promisingly about the uses of memory, and the trickiness of images.

If trauma is that which, by definition, we cannot bear, it is not surprising that we work so hard to make it seem unreal; to make it appear as spectacle, rather than lived experience. The question becomes how can one reproduce, or record, or elaborate an experience – in these photographs, the horrors of what is still contemporary history – but keep it imaginably real. The unbearable has to be made bearable in order to be remembered. If the image is too terrible we can only look away; we can only go on looking if we can in some way use the image to punish and/or excite ourselves with. It is what we need to do with memories, with the images, to make them acceptable and therefore available for consideration – to aestheticise them, to censor them, to eroticise them, to idealise them – that makes the act of memory so fraught. So if these photographs remind us of what we would rather forget – or are a bit too keen to remember – they also confront us with a question: with what desire, with what kind of project in mind are we going to take a look at them?

Pieties about the perils of forgetting have made it increasingly difficult to think differently about the purposes of memory; and indeed, about the virtues of forgetting. When we say (or assume) that memory is selective, that forgetting is motivated, we imply that we are purposive beyond our knowledge of ourselves. That we only turn a blind eye with a view to our future. The photos we choose to recirculate, now at the end of the century, encode our wishes for the future. The pictures of the past we choose – and there is, as always, more past than ever before – are conjectural politics. But they predict nothing, they only tell us, more obscurely than we might wish, what it is we want. ❑

***Adam Phillips** is an author and psychotherapist. His latest book is* Darwin's Worms *(Faber and Faber, 1999)*

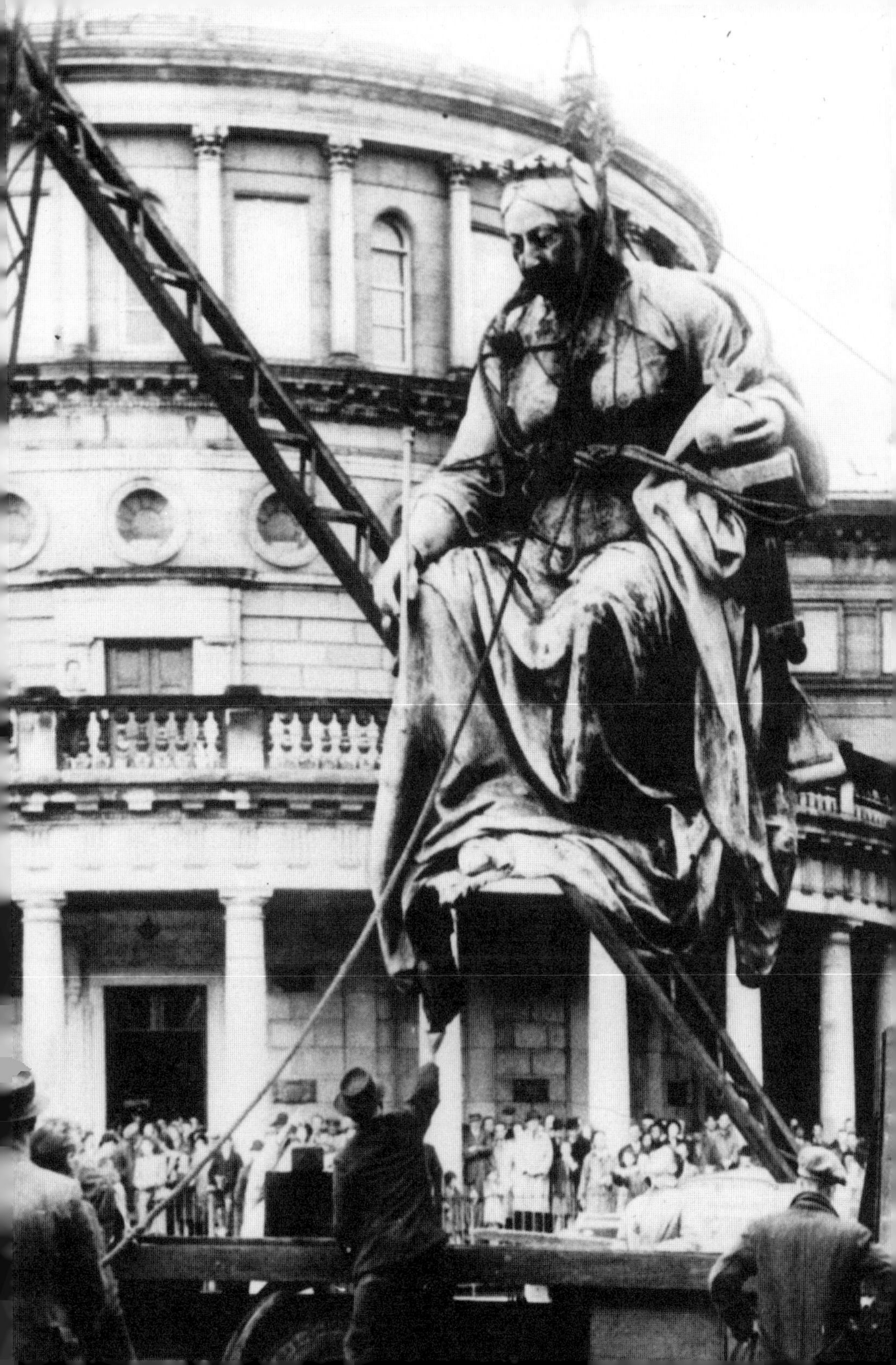

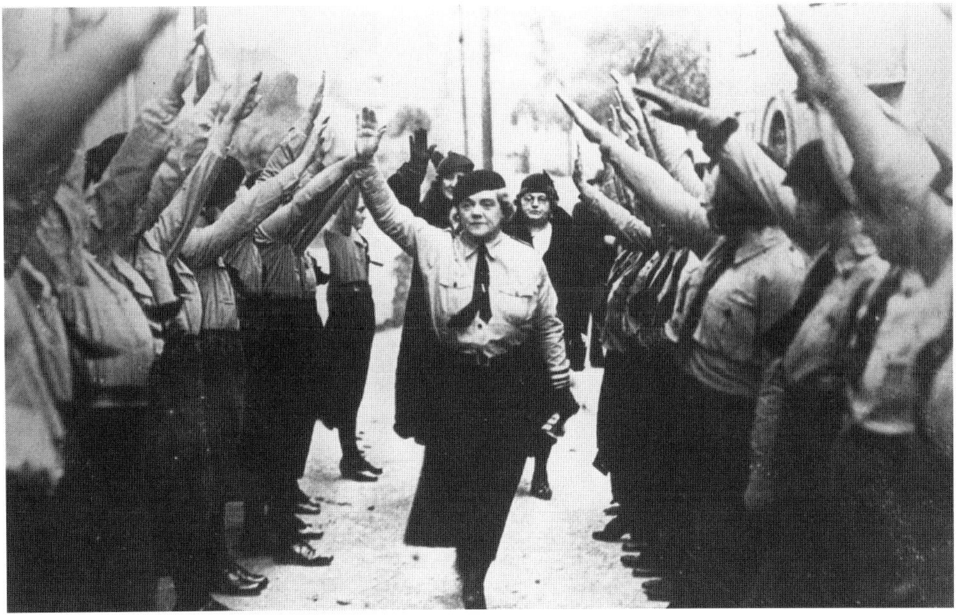

**County Cork Ireland 1933** Mrs 'General' O'Neill takes the fascist salute in Kinsale. Irish attitudes to Britain's war in Europe remained ambivalent: 50,000 men volunteered for the British Army – a well-kept secret within Ireland – others, with the memory of British colonialism still strong, favoured the German cause. In the interests of preserving its neutrality, strict military censorship was applied to the Irish press throughout WWII
*Credit: Michael McInerney/RTE*

**Dublin Ireland 1948** One of the last vestiges of a troubled past is removed: Queen Victoria comes down from her pedestal – only to rise again in Australia in 1986
*Credit: Mrs G A Duncan*

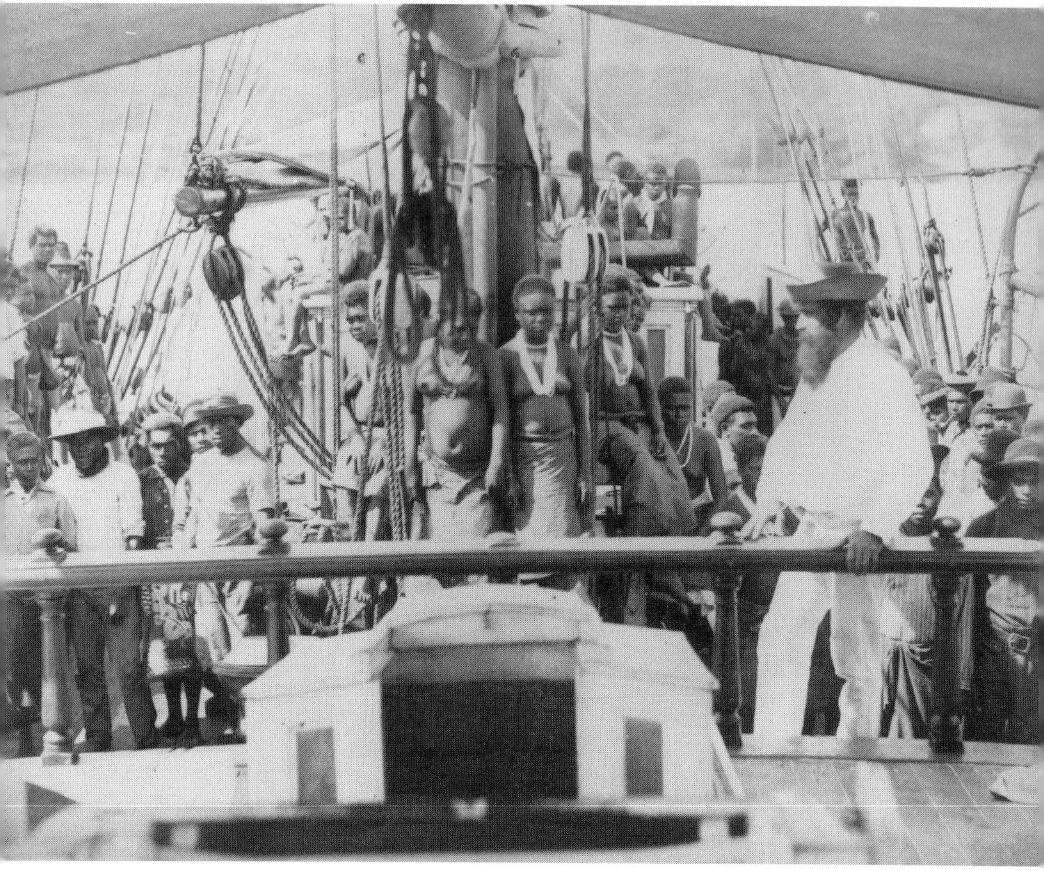

**Abyssinia 1930** Slaves in their shackles. Despite the abolition of slavery in the UK a century earlier and its gradual erosion throughout the West, the trade persisted in much of Africa and the Arab world
*Credit: Hulton Getty Picture Collection*

**Bound for Australia turn of the century** A 'blackbirder' and his human cargo, kidnapped from the Solomon Isles, the New Hebrides and Fiji as indentured labour for the plantations of Australia. In 1904, the practice was outlawed because of the serious depopulation it caused in parts of Melanesia
*Credit: Royal Commonwealth Society Collections/Cambridge University Library*

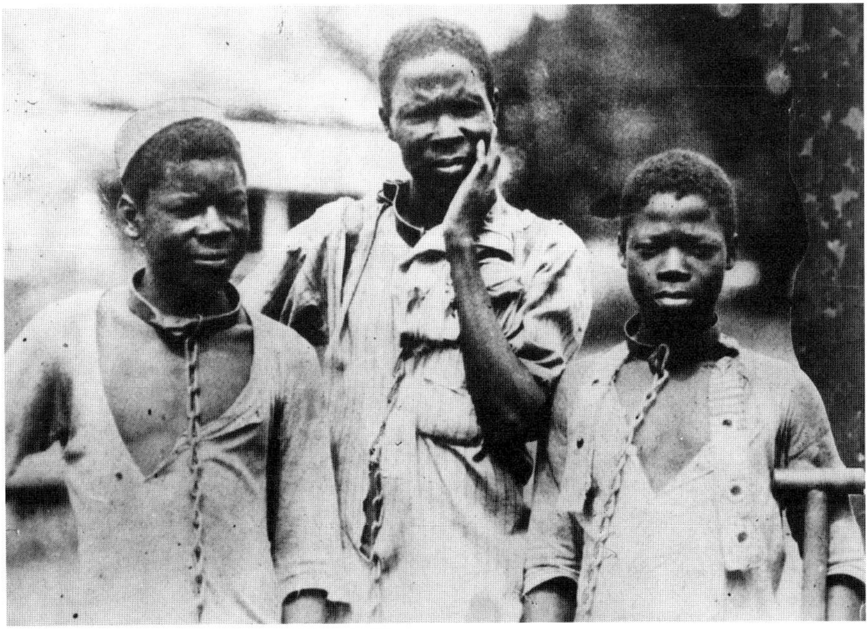

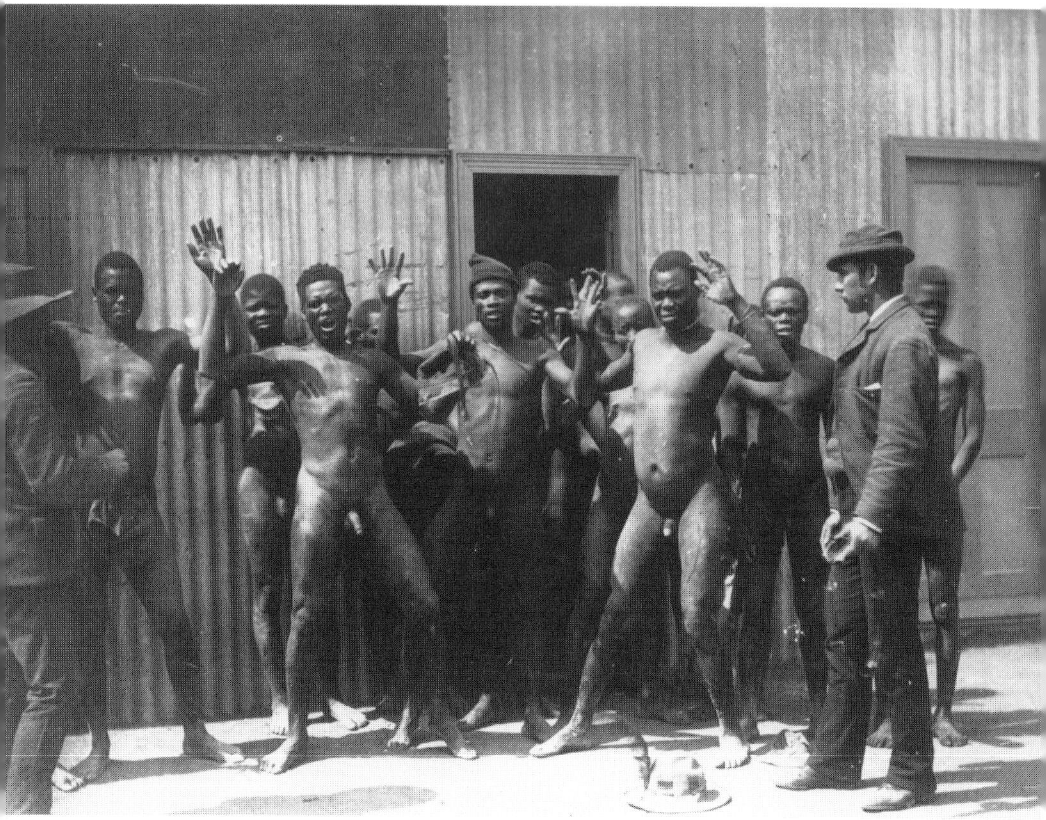

**Burma, early-20th century**
Captured Burmese rebels 'chastised', it was, many of the British colonialists said, the only way of keeping the Empire under control
*Credit: British Library, London*

**Colonial Africa 1900s** Miners at the Kimberley mines stripped at the end of their shift and searched in every orifice for smuggled rocks. By the turn of the century, Sir Cecil Rhodes's British South Africa Company controlled 90 per cent of the world diamond business
*Credit: Royal Photographic Society Collection Bath*

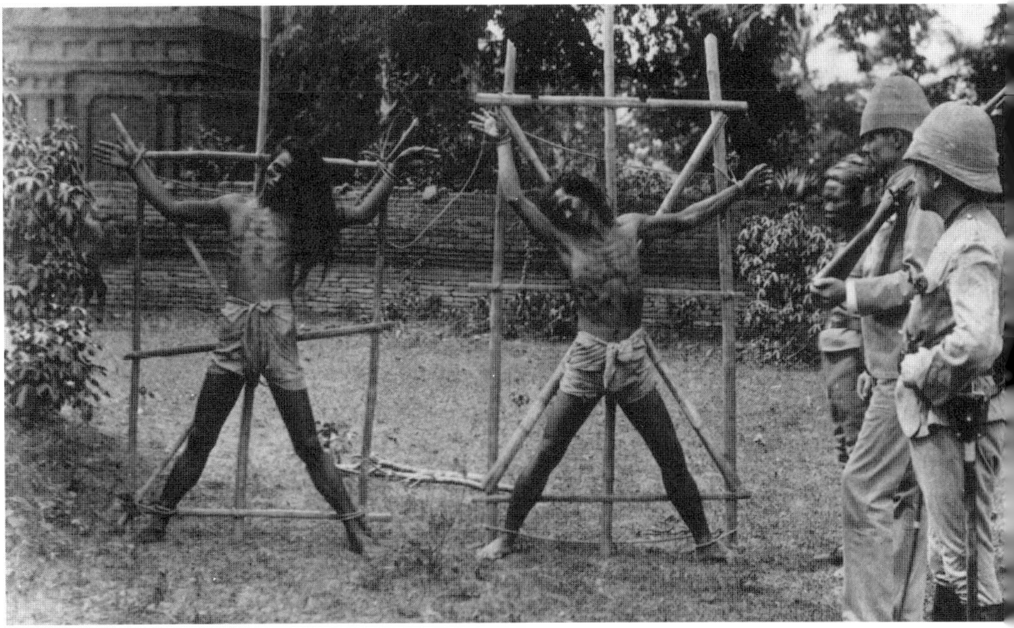

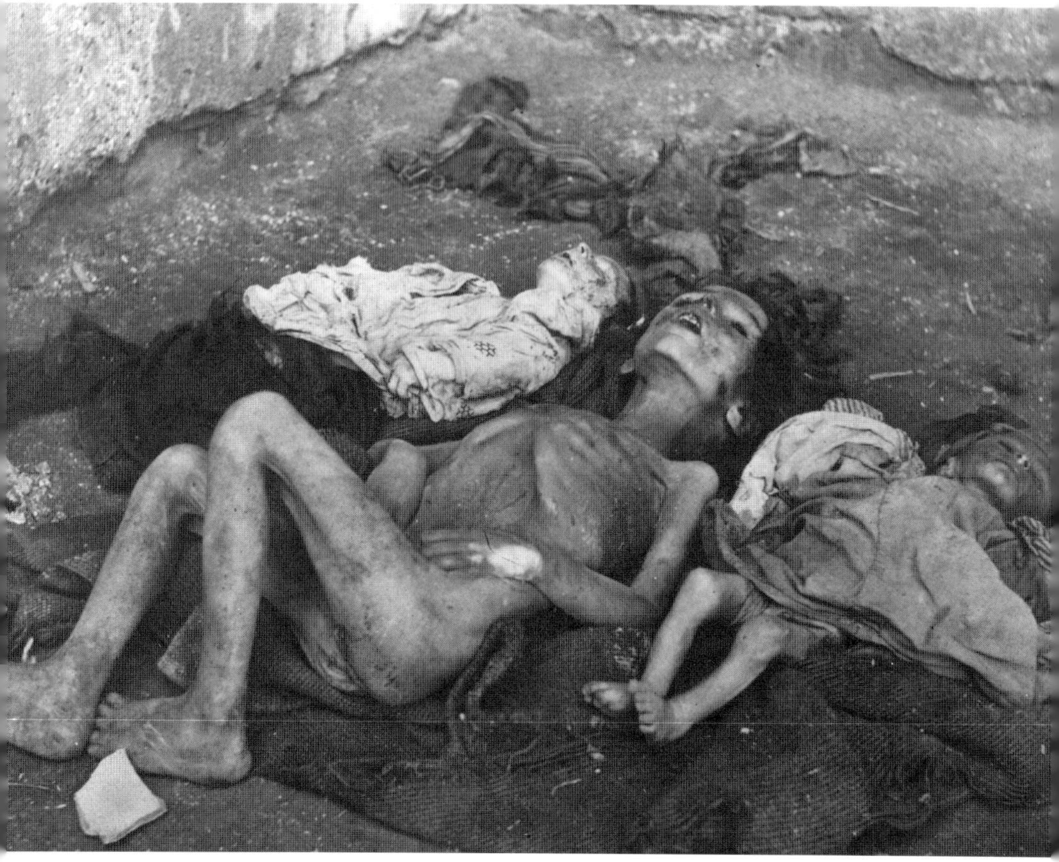

**Ottoman Empire 1915** Armenians massacred by Turks. The Turks deny any massacre or genocide of the Armenians in the early years of WW1; the latter claim up to 1.5 million were killed or driven from the country
*Credit: Hulton Getty Picture Collection*

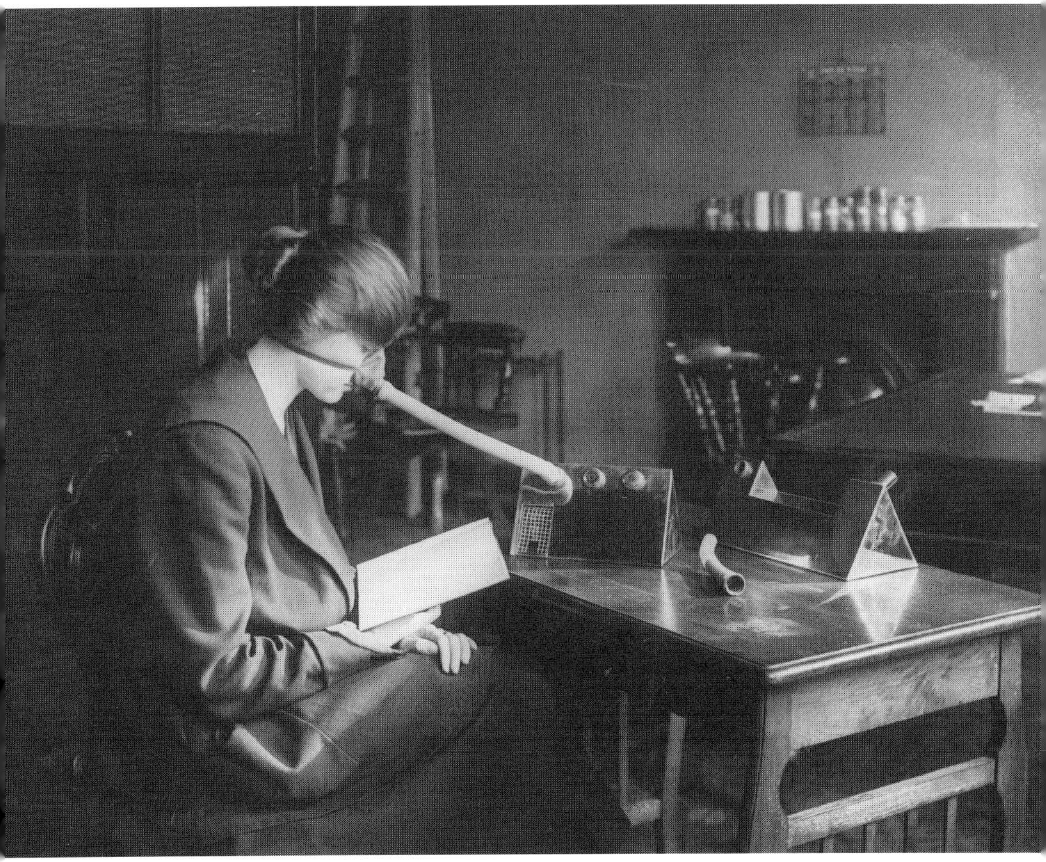

**Post-war world 1918** An ingenious – and completely ineffectual – device for warding off the dreaded influenza. Though the figures were not revealed at the time, more people died of flu after WWI than were killed in the war
*Credit: Hulton Getty Picture Collection*

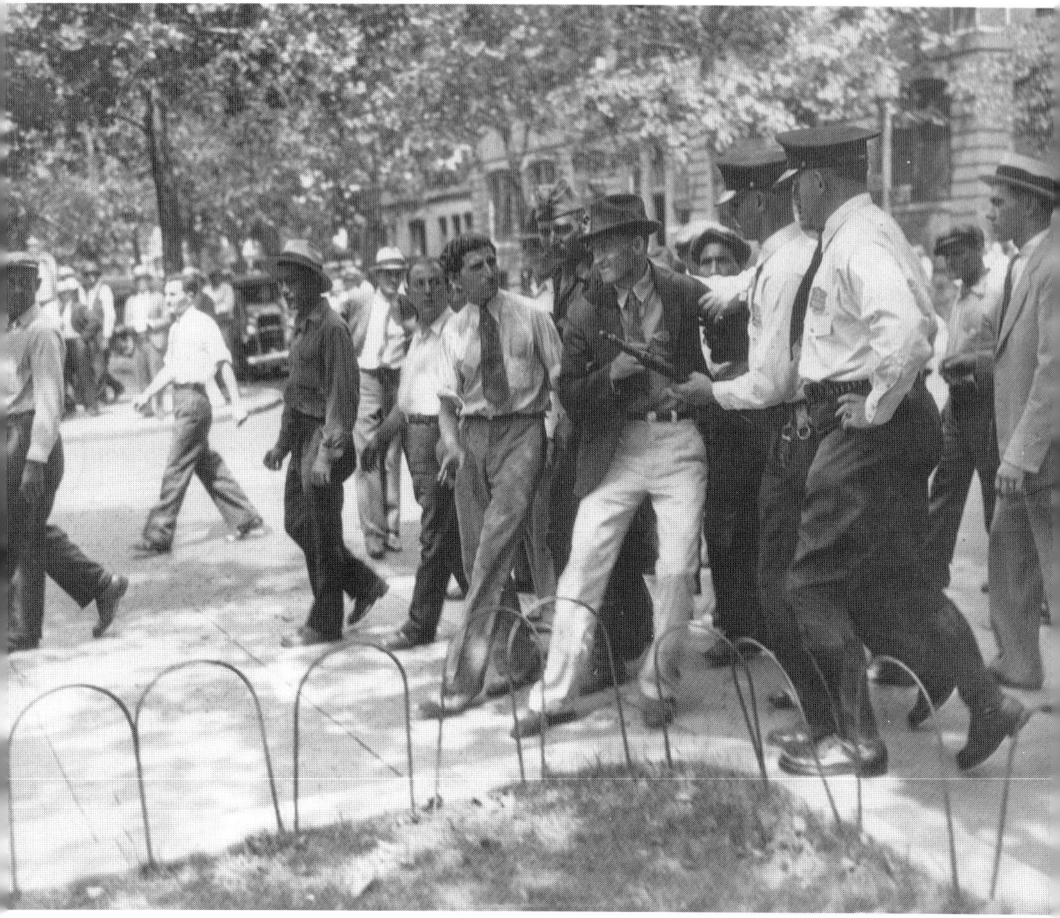

**Washington USA 1932** The arrest of John Page, a leader of the Bonus Army, during a picket of the White House. Fourteen years after the end of WWI, and at a time of rampant unemployment, veterans of the US army were still attempting to claim their unpaid war bonus from Congress
*Credit: Hulton Getty Picture Collection*

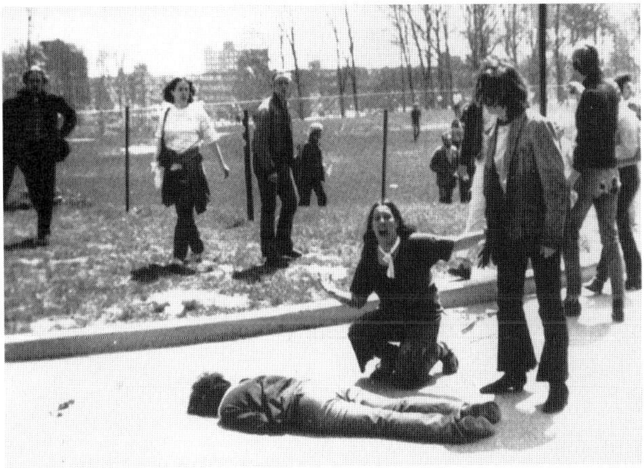

**Kent State University Ohio 1970** Anti-war victim. Four students were killed and nine wounded when troops opened fire on 4 May on 2,000 students protesting against the entry of US troops into Cambodia
*Credit: John Filo/Associated Press*

**Chicago USA 1938** City police fire tear gas canisters into a crowd of strikers from the Chicago Hardware Foundry Company
*Credit: Hulton Getty Picture Collection*

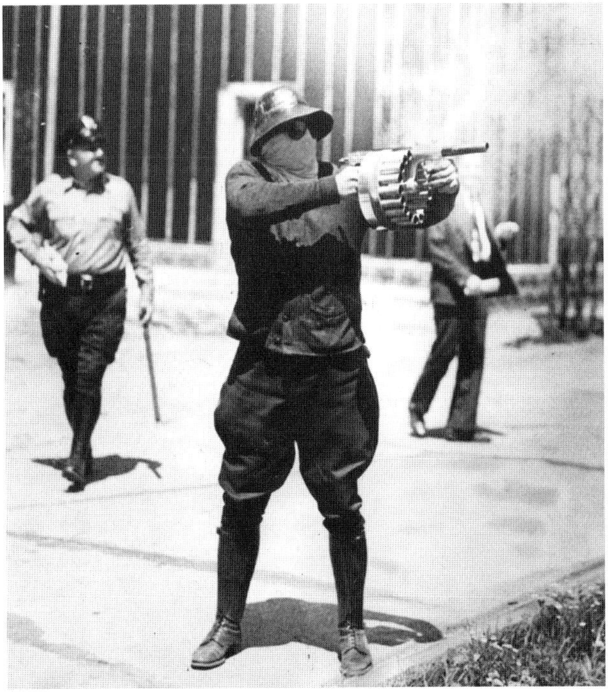

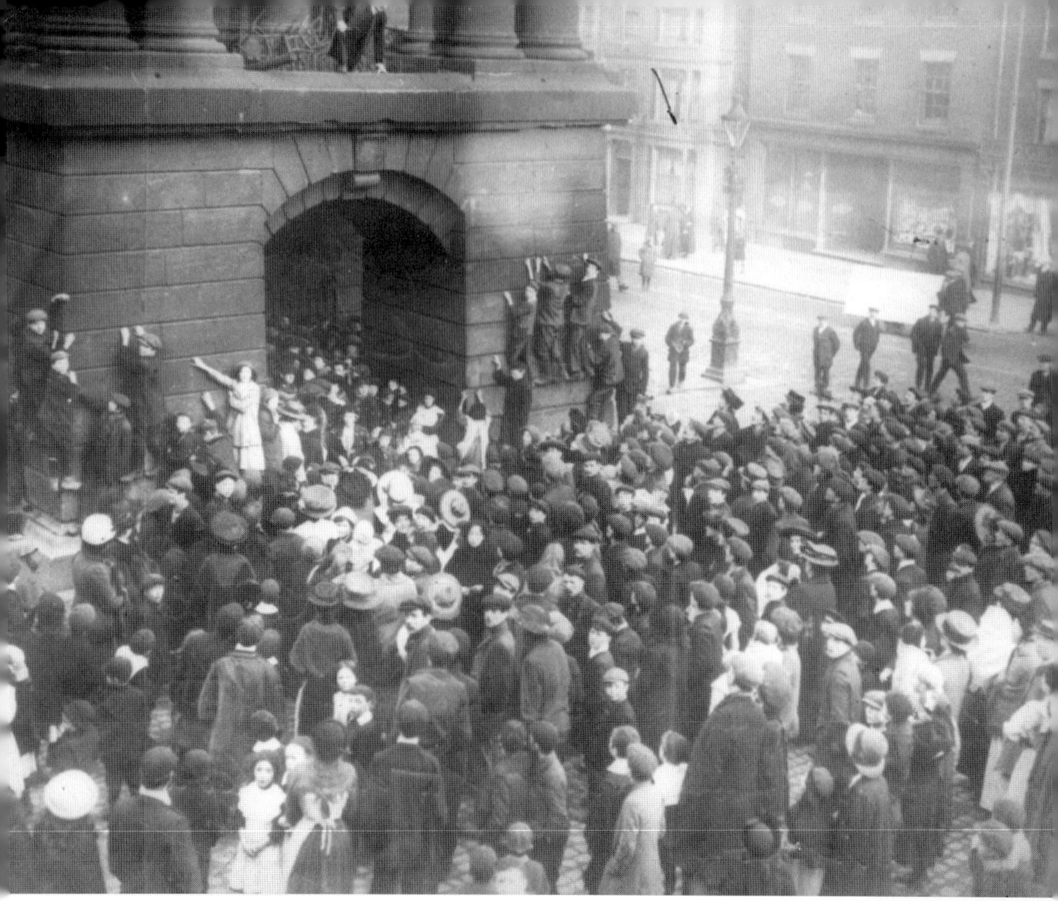

**London 1920/1921** A government propaganda poster attempts to alienate public sympathy for striking miners ... while hungry crowds converge on a government office during the strike only to be told there is no more food
*Credit: Hulton Getty Picture Collection*

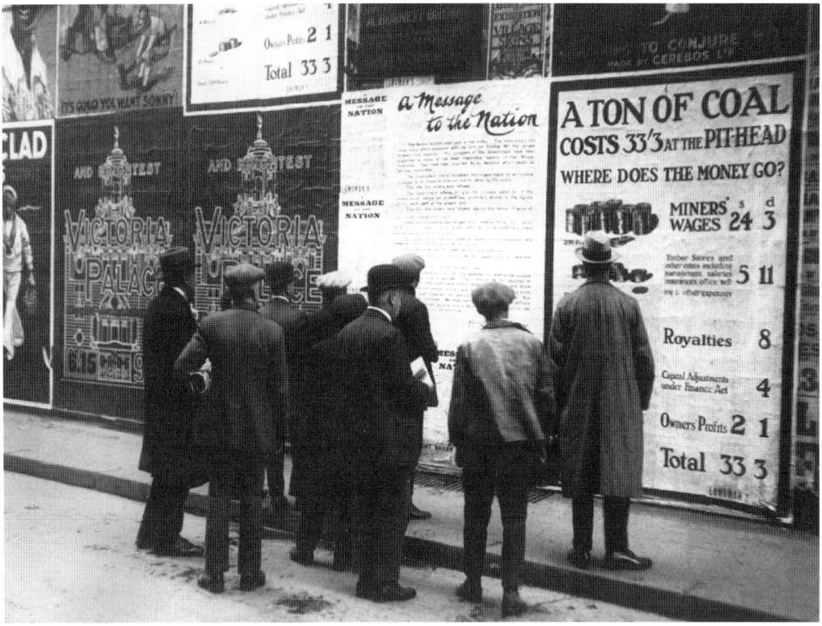

A TON OF COAL
COSTS 33/3 AT THE PIT-HEAD
WHERE DOES THE MONEY GO?
s d
MINERS' WAGES 24 3
5 11
Royalties 8
Capital Adjustments under Finance Act 4
Owners Profits 2 1
Total 33 3
a Message to the Nation
MESSAGE
NATION
VICTORIA PALACE
CLAD
TO CONJURE

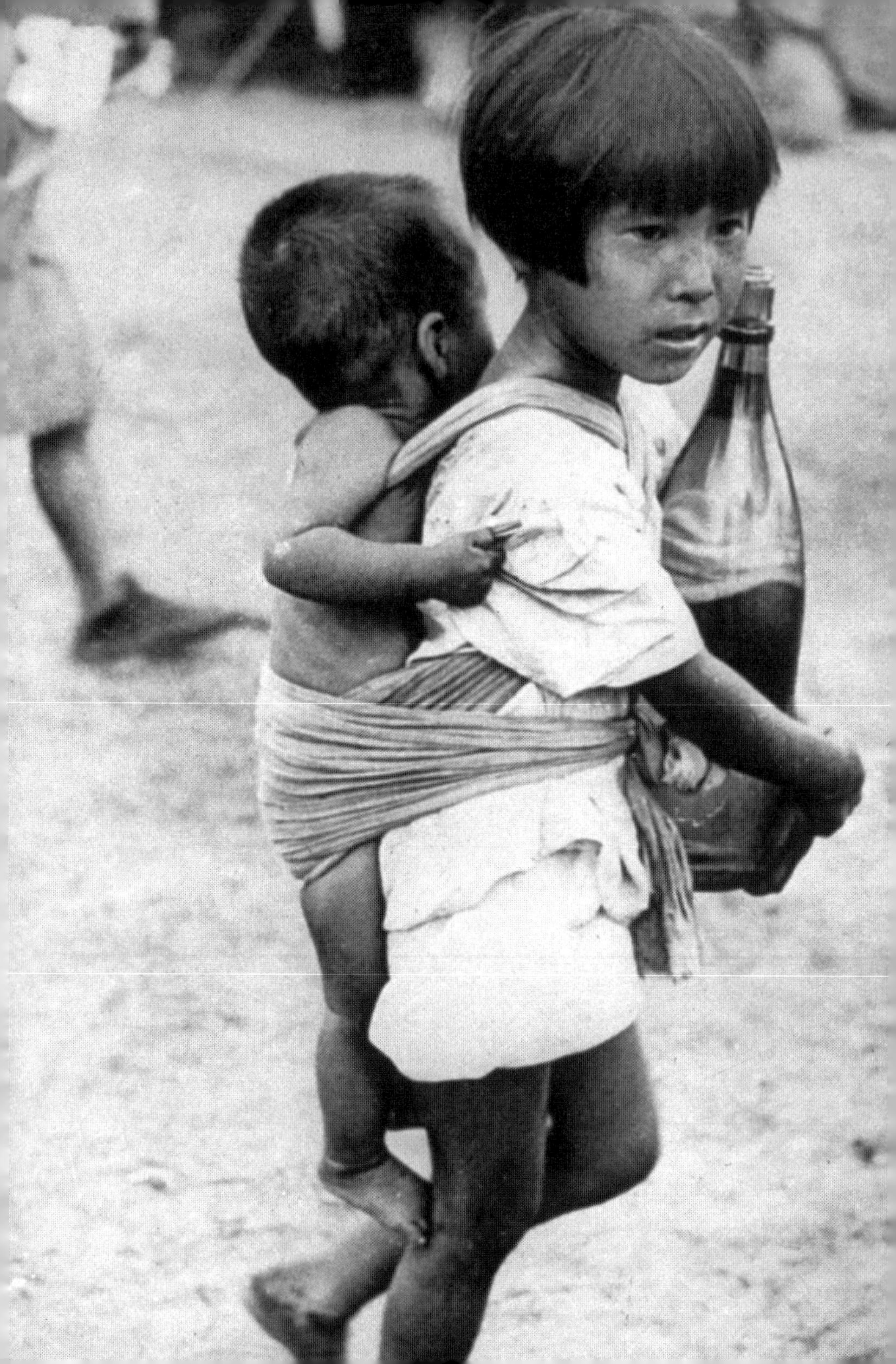

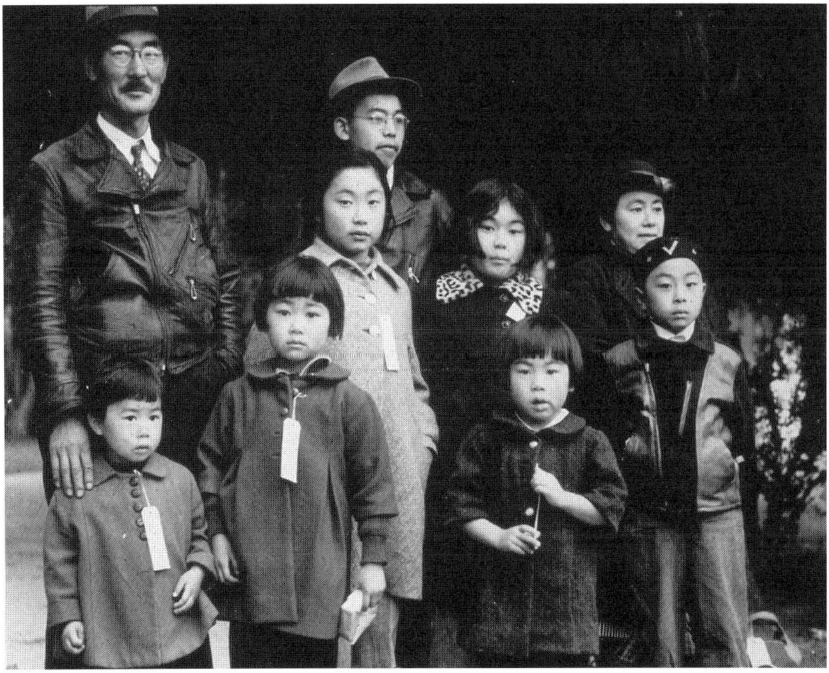

**USA 1942** Once the USA entered WWII in the wake of the Japanese destruction of their fleet at Pearl Harbour, all Japanese-Americans, no matter how long they had been in the country or their US citizenship, were interned in War Relocation Centres for the duration of the war. The measure smacked more of vengeance than concern for national security. In 1988, the US Civil Liberties Act apologised to Japanese-Americans 'on behalf of the people of the United States' for their internment
*Credit: Hulton Getty Picture Collection*

**Internment camp USA** 1945
Sister and brother struggle to survive the often appalling conditions in the internment camps for American-Japanese citizens
*Credit: Hulton Getty Picture Collection*

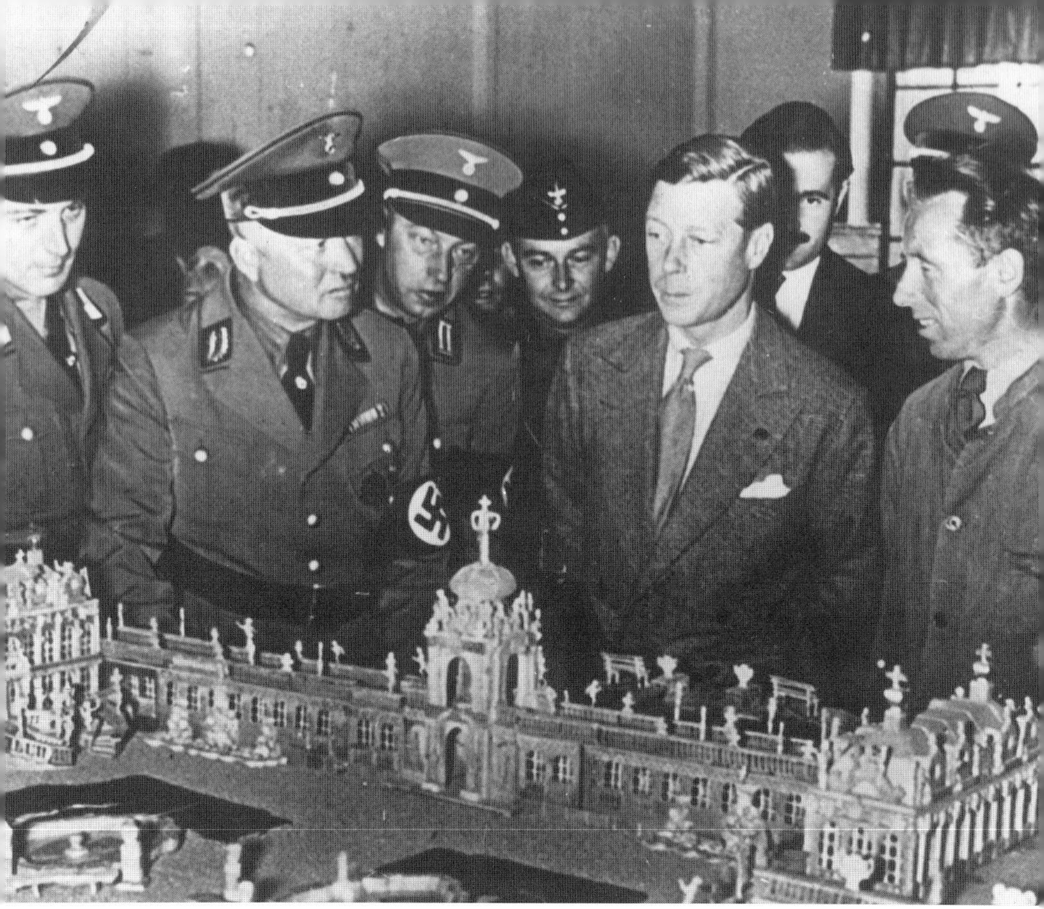

**Dresden Germany 1937 and 1946**
The fantasy and the reality The deposed and disgraced Edward VIII, now Duke of Windsor, flirted with fascism to the end. On one of his numerous pre-war visits to Nazi Germany, he discusses Hitler's schemes for Dresden, the flower of Germany's baroque cities ... but the Allies had different ideas. With the end of the war in sight, in March 1945 the RAF and USAF reduced the city to a smouldering ruin. Over 125,000 people died in the fires. A year later, Gustav and Alma Piltz pick through the rubble. It took over 50 years for the Allies to offer an apology for their wanton and unnecessary attack
*Credit: Hulton Getty Picture Collection*

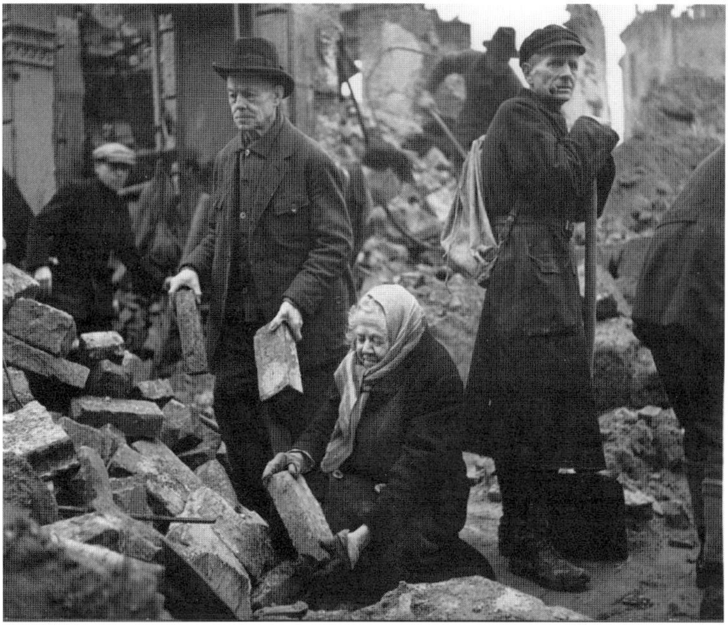

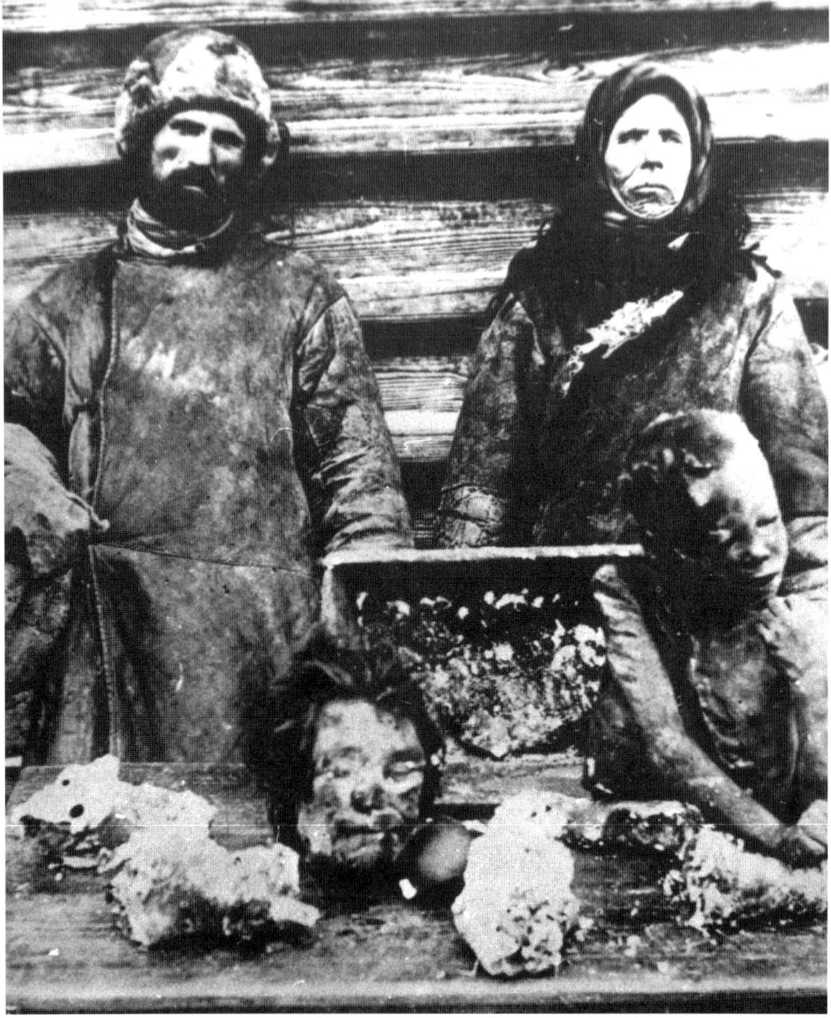

**Volga 1921** Caught red-handed with their cuts of human flesh, cannibals with their victims in one of the repeated famines that devastated the fledgling USSR. The disruption of civil war and widespread requisitioning of grain from the countryside to feed the towns and the armies led to widespread famine. By 1921, food output had fallen to half that of 1913; famine swept the Volga – as it was later to do in the Ukraine where 25% of the population died during collectivisation in the 1930s
*Credit: Slava Katamidze Collection/Hulton Getty Picture Collection*

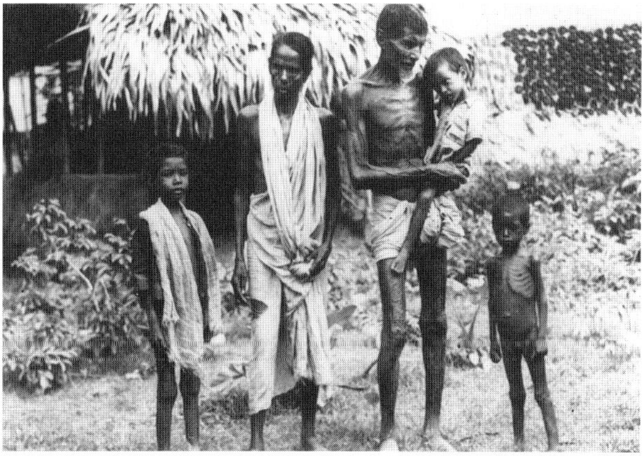

**Calcutta British India 1943** The Bengal famine, completely hidden by the British during WWII for fear of alienating this crucial region on the border of Japanese-occupied Burma, was one of the worst on record, compounded by the diversion of food supplies to British troops
*Credit: Hulton Getty Picture Collection*

**North Korea 1998** One of North Korea's best kept secrets. Despite international warnings of impending famine as early as 1995, the authorities refused food aid. By 1999, estimates from South Korea put the death toll at around one million
*Credit: Buddhist Sharing Movement*

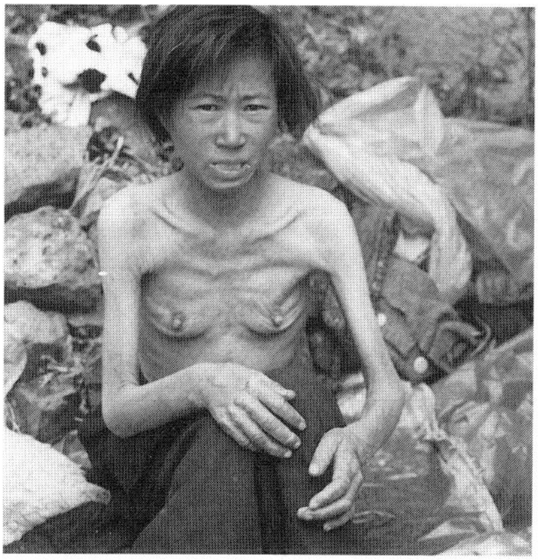

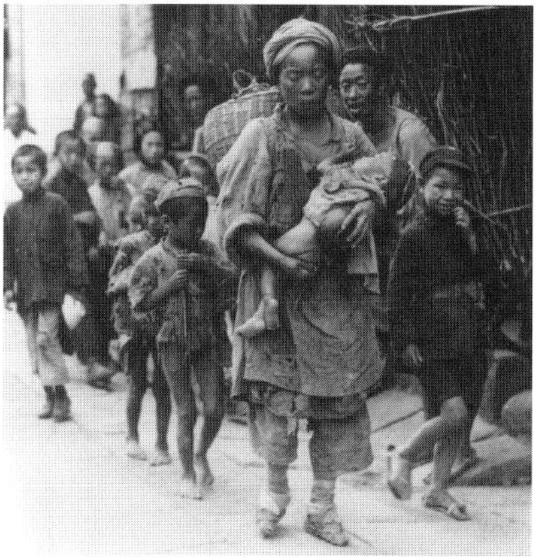

**Shanghai China 1920s** Refugees from the countryside. The city of Shanghai sheltered extremes of wealth and poverty: while the profits from prostitution and narcotics were vast, as many as 400 corpses a day were swept up from the city streets
*Credit: Shanghai Historical Museum/Endeavour Group UK*

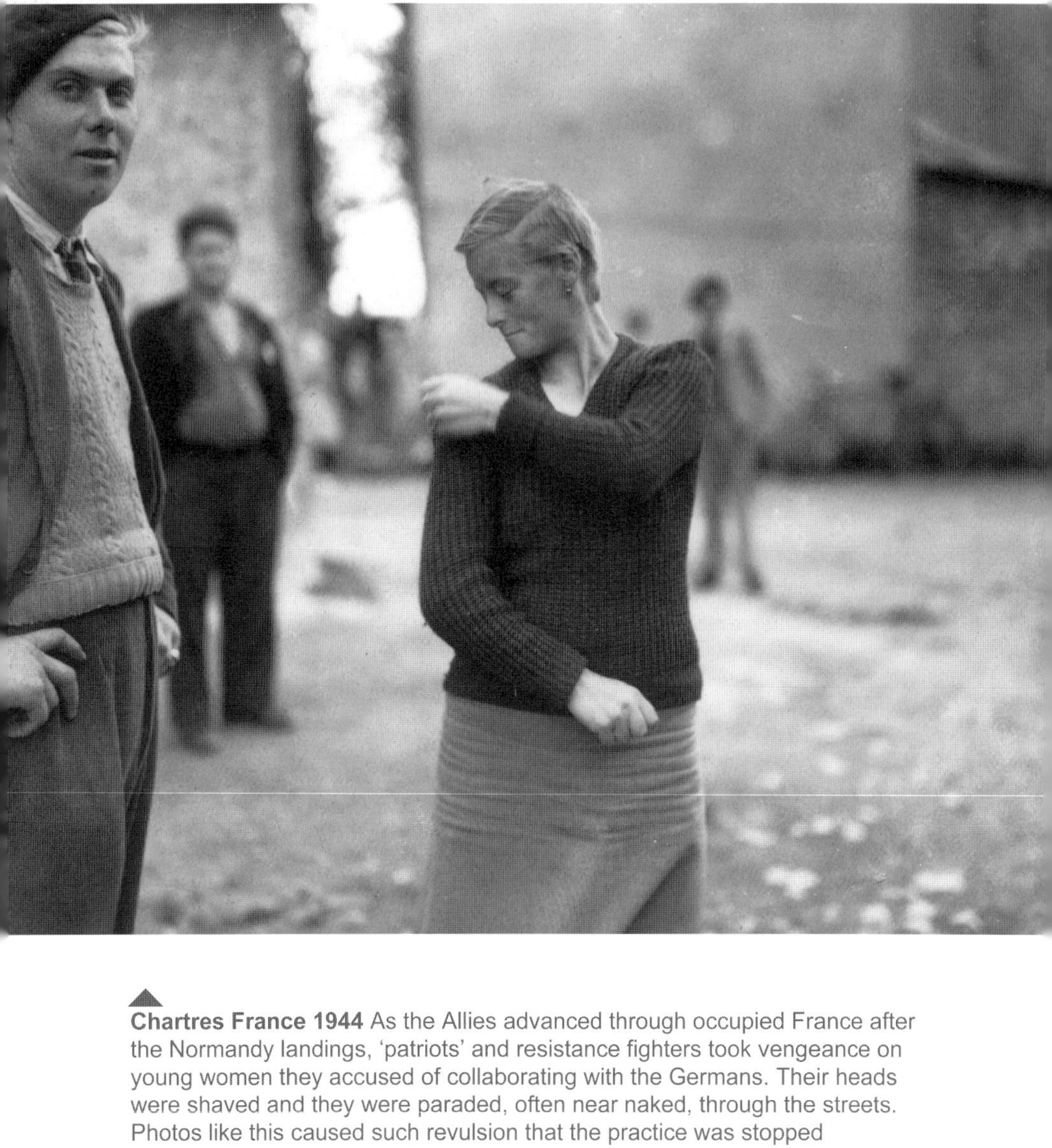

**Chartres France 1944** As the Allies advanced through occupied France after the Normandy landings, 'patriots' and resistance fighters took vengeance on young women they accused of collaborating with the Germans. Their heads were shaved and they were paraded, often near naked, through the streets. Photos like this caused such revulsion that the practice was stopped
*Credit: Hulton Getty Picture Collection*

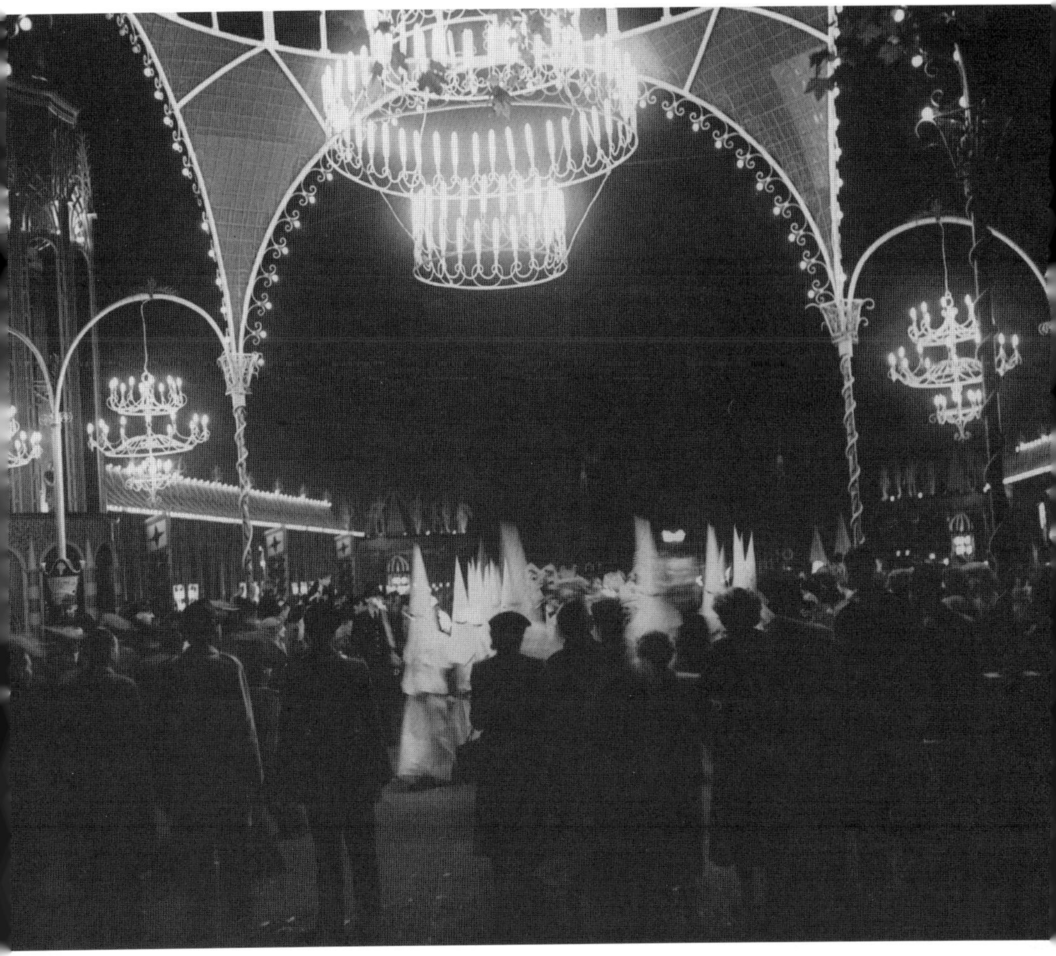

**London 1951** Torchlit procession of Ku Klux Klan members at the Festival of Britain, the UK's first major post-war celebration
*Credit: Hulton Getty Picture Collection*

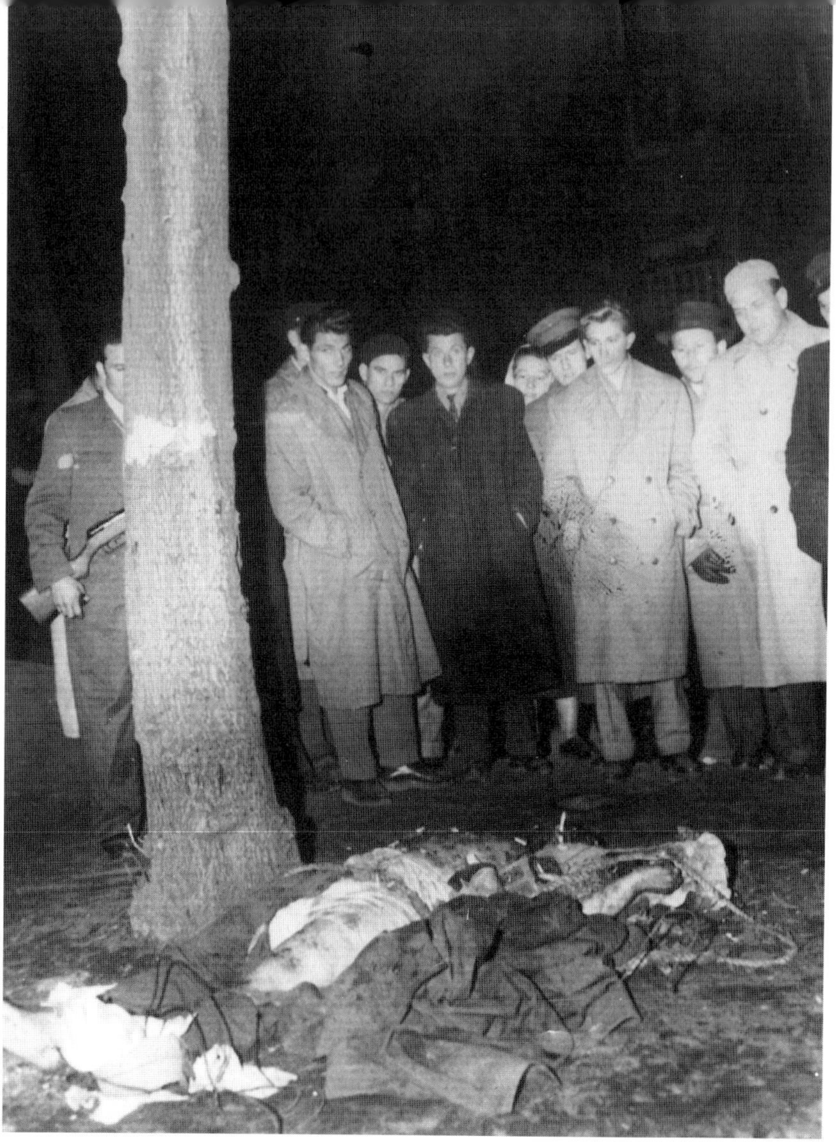

**Hungary 1956** Summary execution of a member of the much hated AVH (secret police). In the weeks before Soviet tanks moved in to crush their uprising, Hungarians exacted a savage revenge on the AVH, who had sparked the popular rising by firing on a student demonstration against the Communist rulers of the country
*Credit: Associated Press*

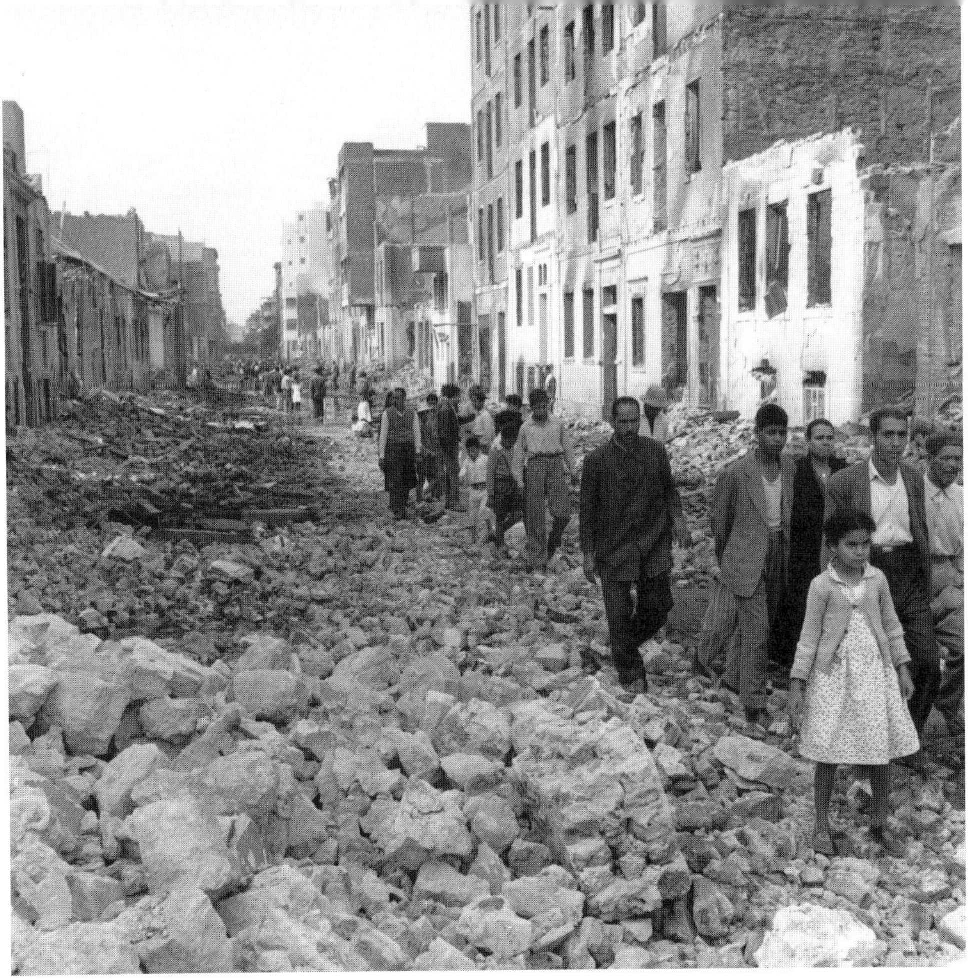

▲
**Egypt 1956** A street near Suez during the Suez 'crisis'. The level of damage inflicted by UK bombing was far from clear at the time
*Credit: Hulton Getty Picture Collection*

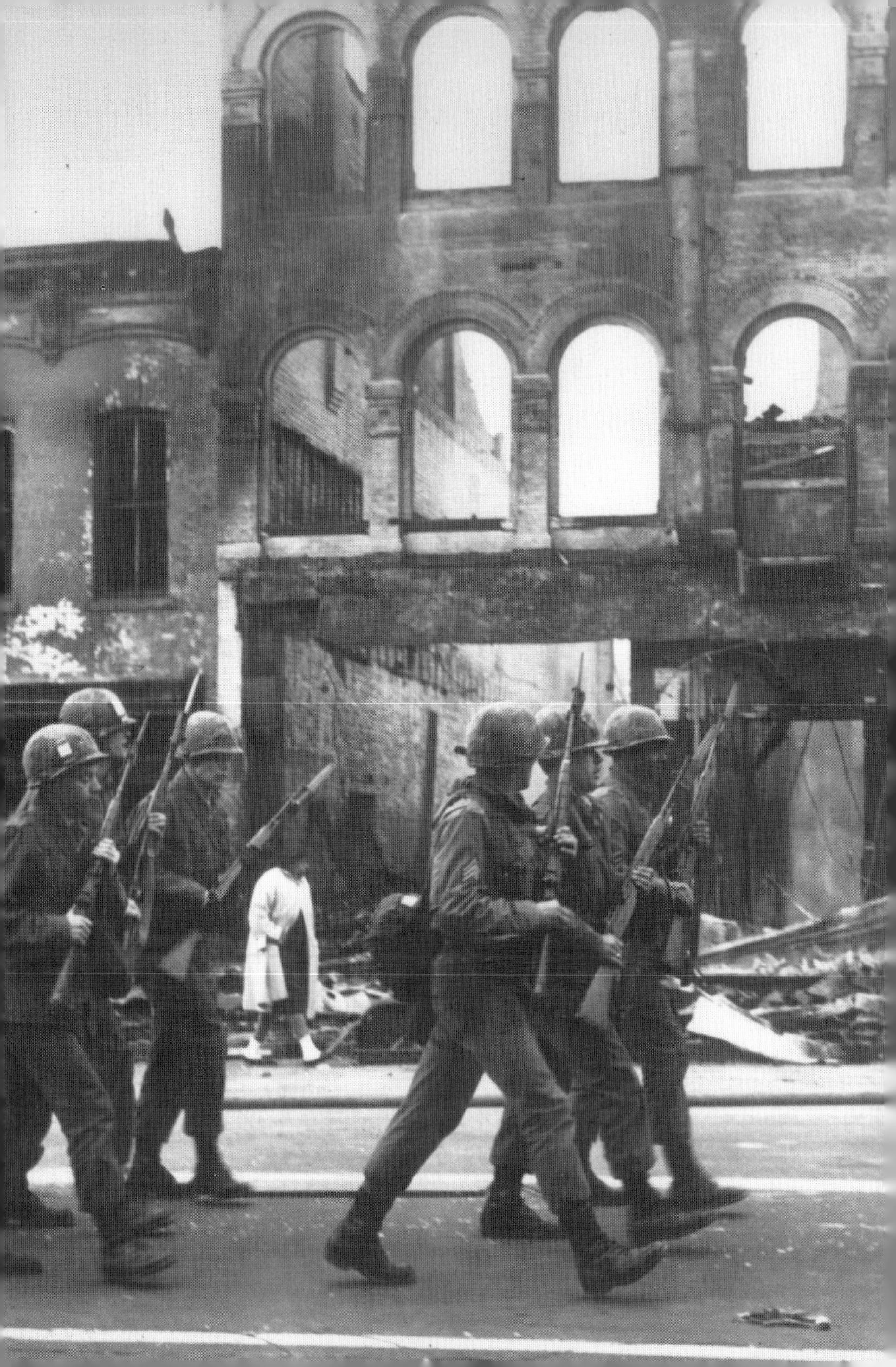

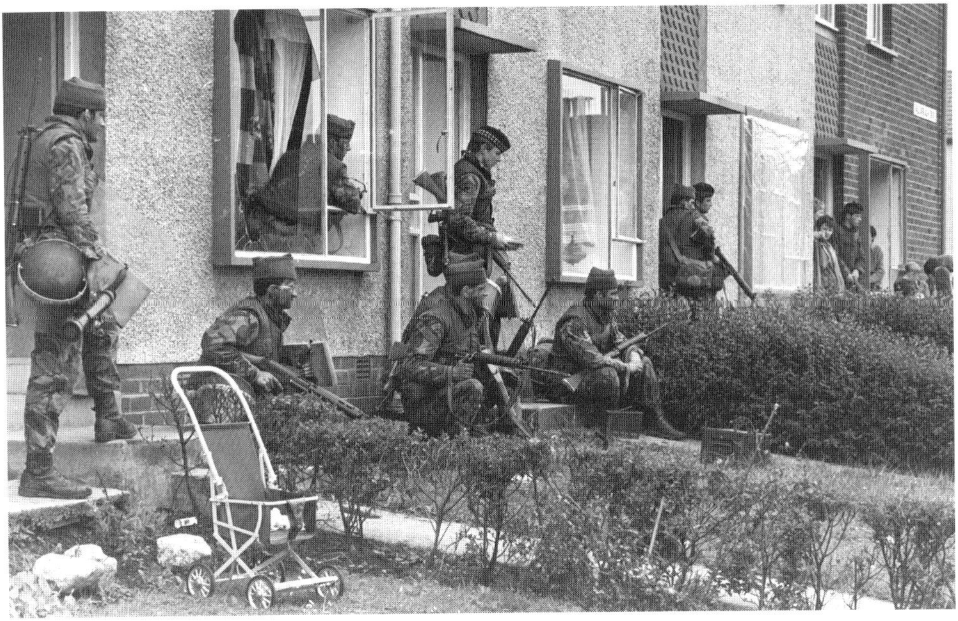

**Northern Ireland 1972** In what looks all too like overkill, British troops take over the streets – and houses – in the troubled province
*Credit: Mirror Syndication International*

**Paris 1968** The CRS charge demonstrators during the student/worker *évenements* that threatened the government that summer
*Credit: Hulton Getty Picture Collection*

**Washington DC USA 1968** National guardsmen patrol the streets after the riots following the assassination of Martin Luther King. Eight people were killed and large residential areas went up in flames
*Credit: Hulton Getty Picture Collection*

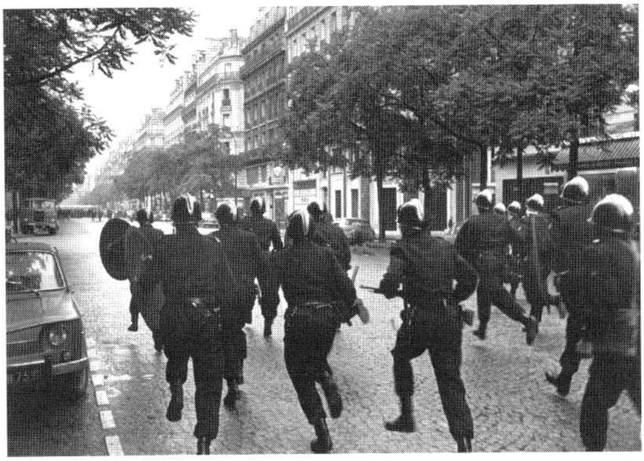

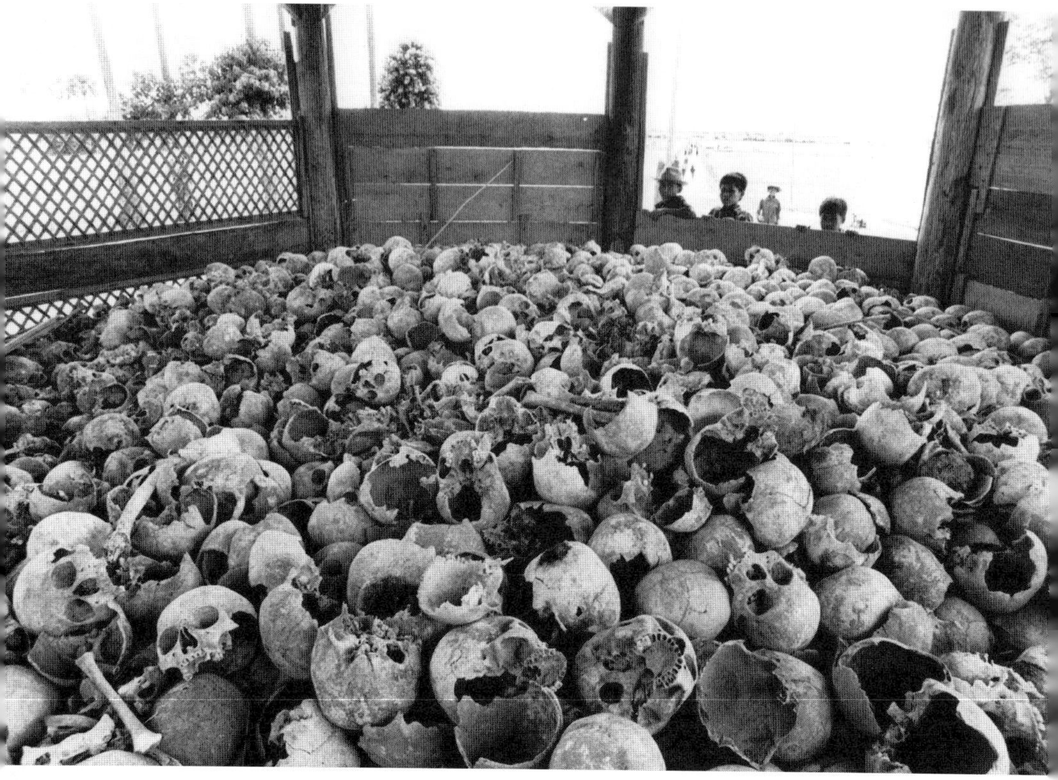

**Ukraine 1990s** Victims of Stalin's purges lifted from their secret resting place in a mass grave. With the coming of *glasnost* and the end of the USSR, Russian organisations like Memorial – responsible for uncovering many such graves – were able to provide testimony to Stalin's excesses *Credit: D Grafov/Endeavour Group UK*

**Tuoi Sleng camp Cambodia post-1979** Evidence of Cambodia's return to 'Year Zero'. One million – maybe two million – Khmers were killed by the Pol Pot regime between 1975 and 1979 by a combination of war, starvation and arbitrary execution
*Credit: Brian Eades/Observer/Hulton Getty Picture Collection*

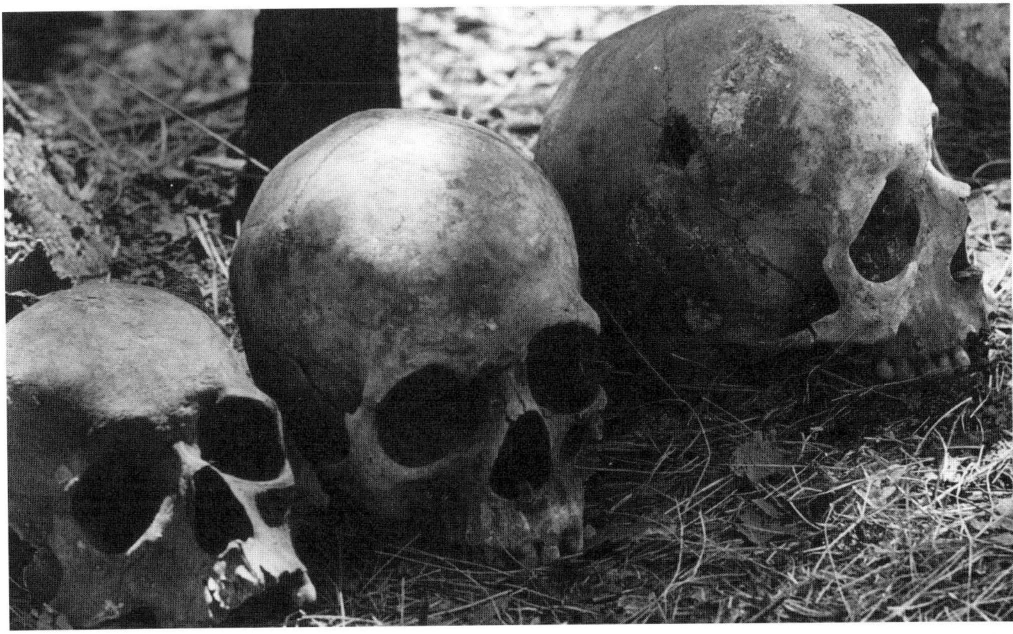

# Covert

*I went to Marseille... I prowled the streets all day, feeling very strung up and ready to pounce, determined to 'trap' life – to preserve life in the act of living. Above all, I craved to seize the whole essence, in the confines of one single photograph, of some situation that was in the process of unrolling itself before my eyes.*

Henri Cartier Bresson

**Germany 1935** Keeping track of the population. German police with the latest in communications technology
*Credit: Hulton Getty Picture Collection*

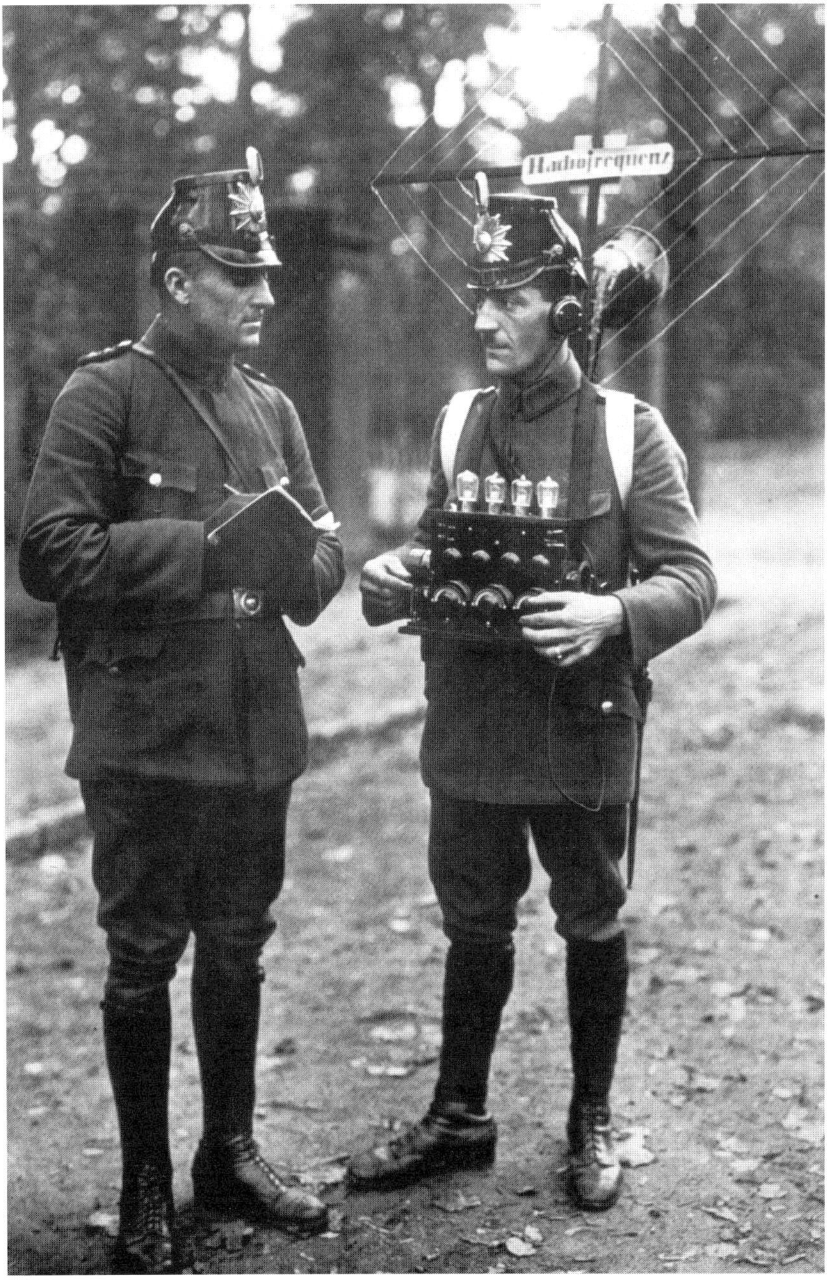

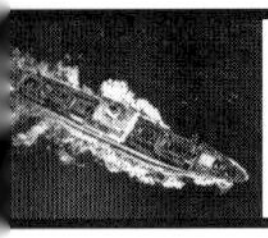

# Covert

*John le Carré*

We said goodbye to him not long ago, but I may not tell you when. I may not tell you whether we burned him or buried him, whether we did it in the town or in the country, or whether his name was Tom, Dick or Harry, or whether the funeral was Christian or of another sort. I will call him Harry. It is even possible that what I am telling you is fiction, and never happened at all. Or perhaps it happened to a former colleague from the secret world who is scared of losing his pension, and I am standing in for him.

Harry's wife was there, the same wife he had had for 50 years, and she had been spat on in the fish queue for him, jeered at by neighbours for him, and had her house burgled by the local police force who thought they were doing their patriotic duty by shaking out the local Communist Party firebrand.

There was a child, now grown up, who had suffered similar humiliations, at school and later. But I may not tell you whether this was a boy or a girl, or whether he or she has found a safe corner in the world Harry believed he was protecting. The wife, now a widow, was as steady as she had always been under pressure, but the grown-up child was crumpled with grief, to the mother's evident contempt. A life of hardship had taught her to value bearing, and she expected it of her offspring.

I went because, for a short time, 40 years ago or so, I had the management of Harry, which was a sacred trust as well as a delicate one, since all his energies from late childhood onward had been directed at frustrating his country's enemies by becoming one of them. Harry had absorbed the Party's dogma until it was second nature to him. He had bent his mind until he scarcely knew its old shape any more. With our help he had schooled himself to think and react from the hip as one of its faithful. Yet he always managed to come up smiling for his furtive weekly debriefings with his case officer:

'All right then, Harry?' I would ask, or someone would.

'Hunkydory, thank you, John. How's your good self and the missus?'

Harry had taken on all the dirty jobs, in the evenings and at weekends, that other comrades were only too glad to be relieved of. He had sold or failed to sell the *Daily Worker* at street corners. He had acted as runner and talent-spotter for visiting Soviet 'cultural attachés' and 'third secretaries', and accepted their dreary assignments to collect tittle-tattle about technical industries in the area where he lived. And if none came his way, then of course we provided him with it, having first made sure it was harmless or inaccurate. But nothing really dramatic ever happened to him. Gradually, through diligence and devotion to the cause – you might say both causes – he rose to become an influential and valued comrade, entrusted with semi-conspiritorial errands which – though he played them for all they were worth, and so did we – seldom amounted to anything of substance in the intelligence marketplace.

But this lack of visible success didn't matter, we assured Harry, because he was the right man in the right place, the essential listening post: 'If you didn't hear anything, Harry,' ran our argument, 'that means we can sleep a little easier in our beds at night.' And Harry would remark cheerfully that, well John, *somebody* has to clean out the drains and mop up the vomit, don't they? And we'd say, somebody has to, Harry, and thank you for being the one.

From time to time, perhaps to bolster his morale, we'd enter the dark world of *staybehind*:

'If those Reds ever *do* come, Harry,' we'd remind him – and there were times when we almost thought they might – 'and you happen to wake up one morning to find yourself the big Pooh-bah for your district – that's when you'll become the linkman for the Resistance Movement that's going to have to drive those bastards into the sea.'

In earnest of which, we would dig his radio-transmitter out of its hiding-place in his attic, and blow the dust off it, and watch him send dummy messages to an imaginary underground headquarters Somewhere-in-England, and receive dummy orders in return, all by way of practice for the Soviet occupation of Britain that was just around the corner. We all felt a little awkward about doing this, and so did Harry, but it was part of the job, so we got on with it.

Ever since I left the secret world, I pondered the motives of Harry and his wife, and of other Harrys and other wives. Sometimes it was the wives who took the Party ticket while their husbands toiled in the local factory and didn't make foremen because their wives were Red. Shrinks would have had a field day with Harry, but Harry would have had a field day with the shrinks too. 'So what am I supposed to do, then?' he'd have asked them, all combative. 'Sit back and watch the Party steal the bloody country from underneath my nose?'

Harry took no delight in his duplicity. He bore it as a necessary burden of his calling. We paid him a pittance, and if we'd paid him more, he'd have been embarrassed. Besides, he could never have enjoyed his money. So we gave him a tiny private income and a tiny pension, and called it his alimony, and we threw in all the respect and friendship that security allowed. With time, furtively, Harry and his wife became a little bit religious. The minister of the religion they espoused seems never to have asked why two such dyed-in-the-wool atheists came to him to pray.

When the funeral was over, and the bereaved friends and family and Party comrades had dispersed, a pleasant-faced man in a raincoat and black tie walked over to my car and shook my hand. 'I'm from the Office. Harry's my third this month,' he murmured shyly. 'They all seem to be dying off at the same time.'

Harry was one of the poor bloody infantry of honourable men and women who believed that the communists were set on destroying the country they loved, and felt they'd better do something about it. He thought the Reds were a nice enough bunch of boys and girls in their way, idealistic but a bit warped. So he put his life where his convictions were, and died an unknown soldier of the Cold War. ❑

***John le Carré's*** *latest book is* Silent, Silent. *This article first appeared in the* New York Times. *©David Cornwell 1999*

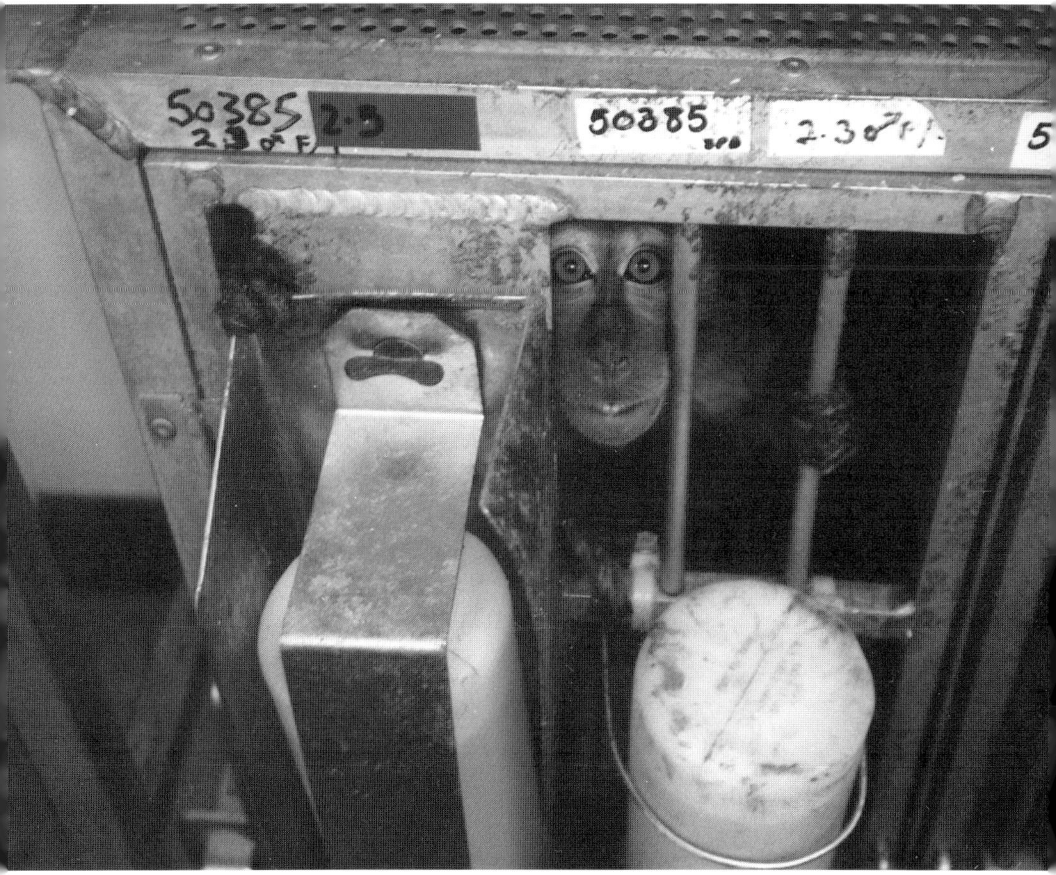


**UK 1991** Monkey awaiting shipment from Shamrock Farm primate breeding facility in Sussex. The photograph was taken as part of an undercover investigation into conditions and treatment at the farm.
*Credit: British Union for the Abolition of Vivisection*

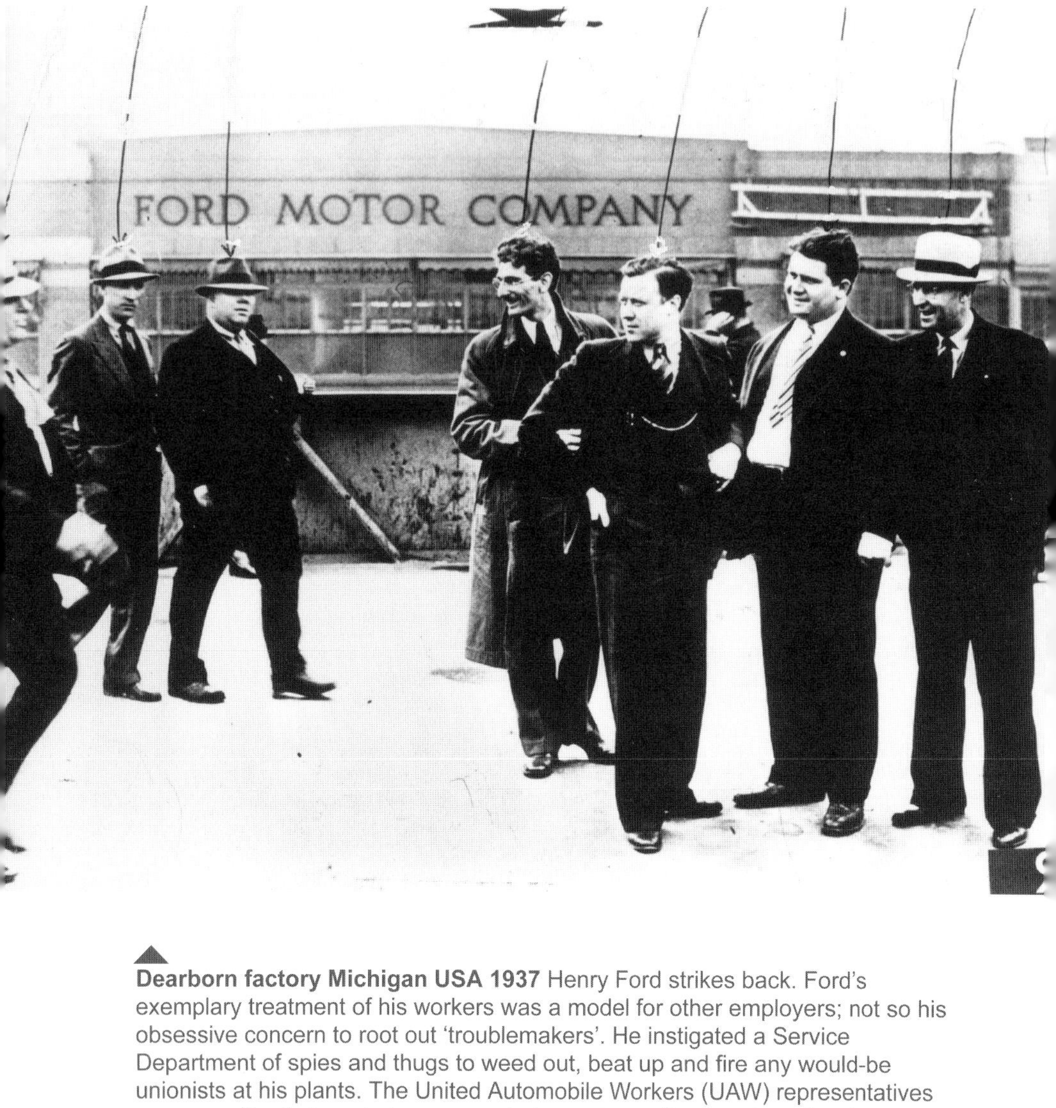


**Dearborn factory Michigan USA 1937** Henry Ford strikes back. Ford's exemplary treatment of his workers was a model for other employers; not so his obsessive concern to root out 'troublemakers'. He instigated a Service Department of spies and thugs to weed out, beat up and fire any would-be unionists at his plants. The United Automobile Workers (UAW) representatives were specifically targeted, as were photographers after the story. Service men (left) about to assault UAW delegates outside the factory
*Credit: Hulton Getty Picture Collection*

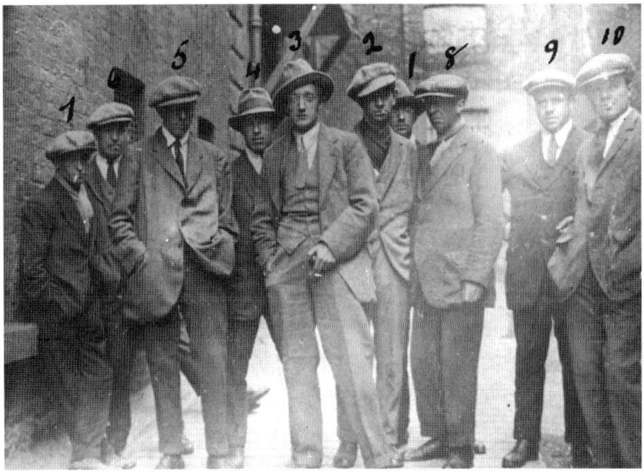

**Ireland 1920** The Cairo Gang, British intelligence agents so-called because of their Middle-Eastern experience, caught and executed by Michael Collins' men *Credit: Hulton Getty Picture Collection*

**Shanghai 1932** A Chinese agent is led to his execution by Japanese secret police. The Japanese were granted concession areas in Shanghai as their control in China extended in the 1930s; Shanghai became a key Japanese naval base *Credit: Goumindang Party Archives Taiwan/Endeavour Group UK*

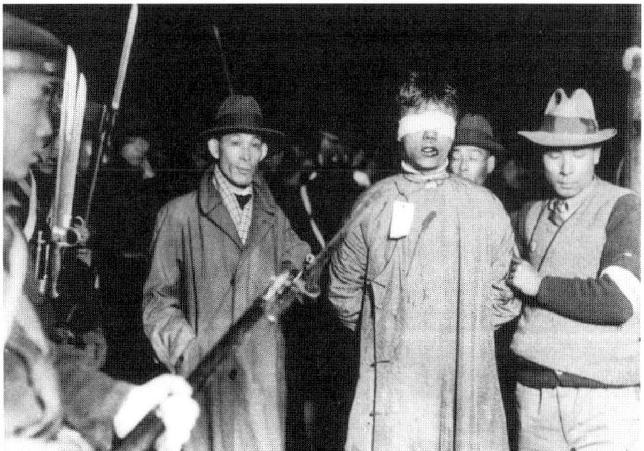

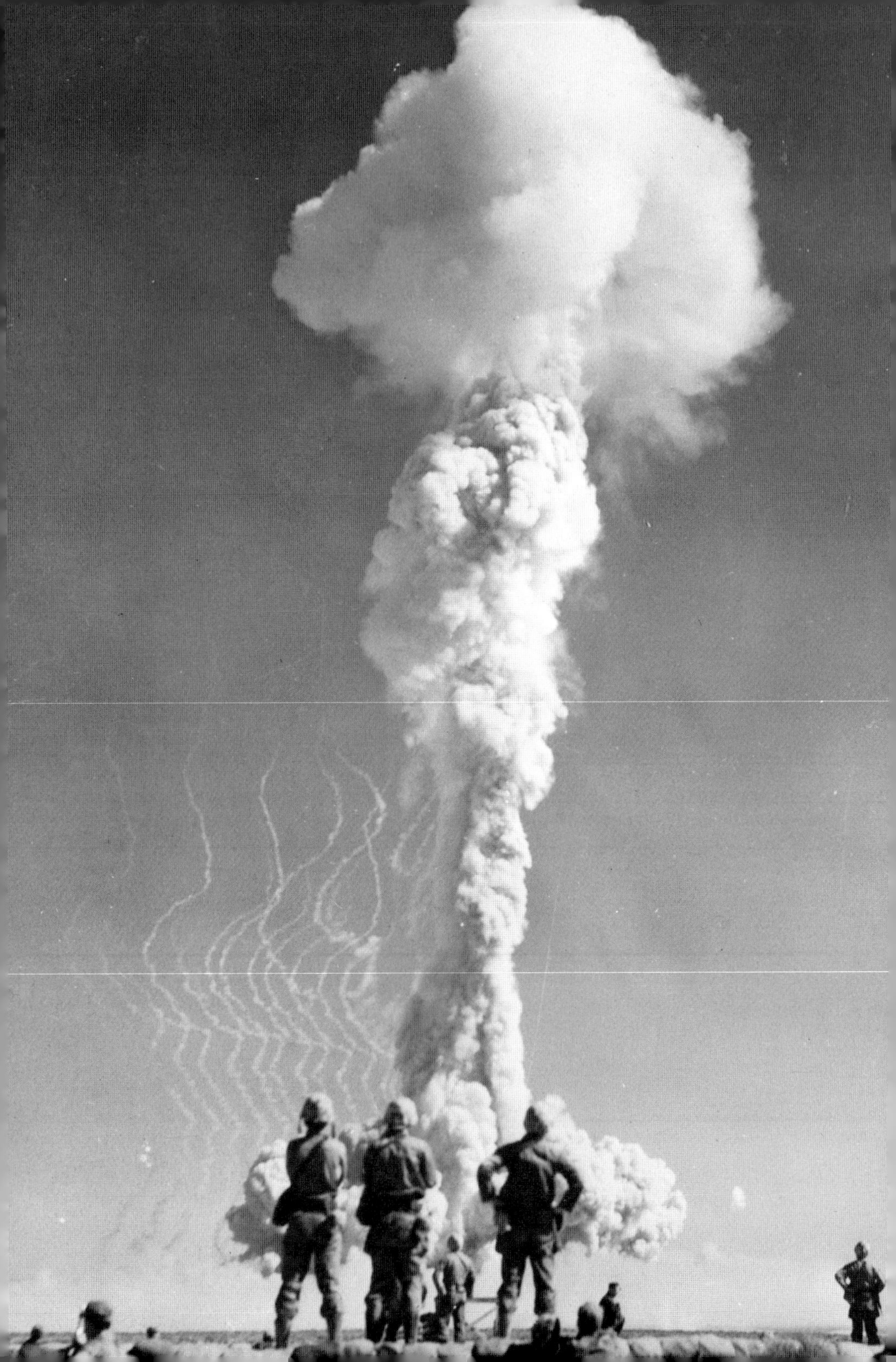

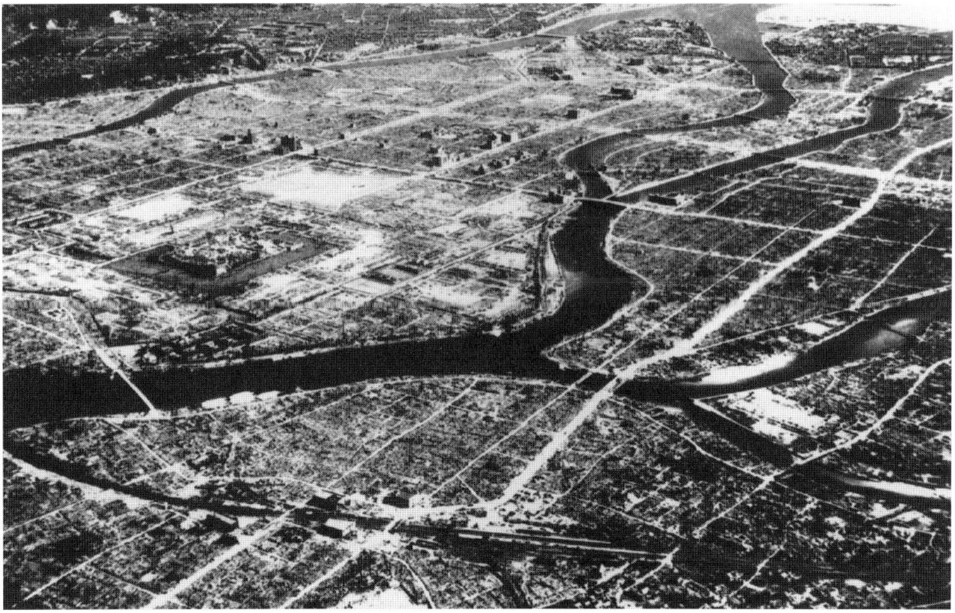

**Japan 1945** Within days of dropping the atom bomb on Hiroshima on 6 August, the US airforce surveyed the damage. The photos of the city were not released until almost 50 years after the event. A 1995 Smithsonian Institute exhibition commemorating the event that displayed some of the photographs taken at this time was censored by Congress
*Credit: Hulton Getty Picture Collection*

**Nevada USA 1952** Nuclear bomb test at Yucca Flats observed by US marines. All nuclear powers used their armed forces as guinea pigs in this way. Only in the last generation has compensation for damage caused become an important public issue
*Credit: Hulton Getty Picture Collection*

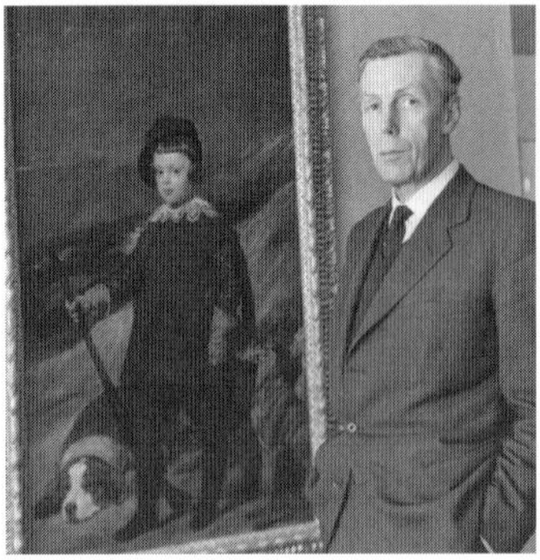

**Anthony Blunt** Art historian and surveyor of the Queen's pictures, later exposed as a Soviet spy
*Credit: Hulton Getty Picture Collection*

**Kim Philby** British intelligence officer and Soviet spy after being cleared of spying charges against Harold Macmillan in 1955.
*Credit: Hulton Getty Picture Collection*

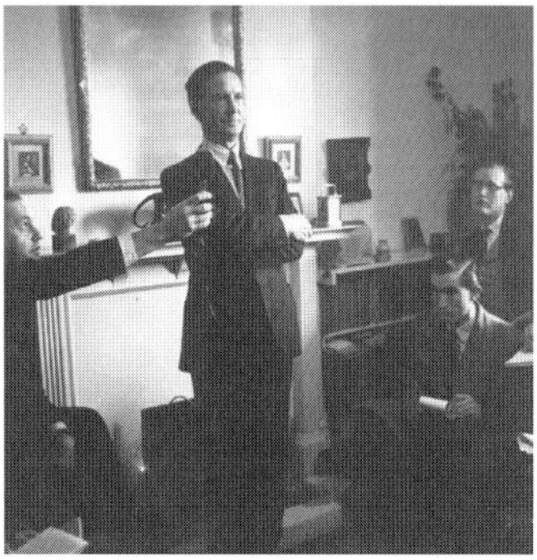

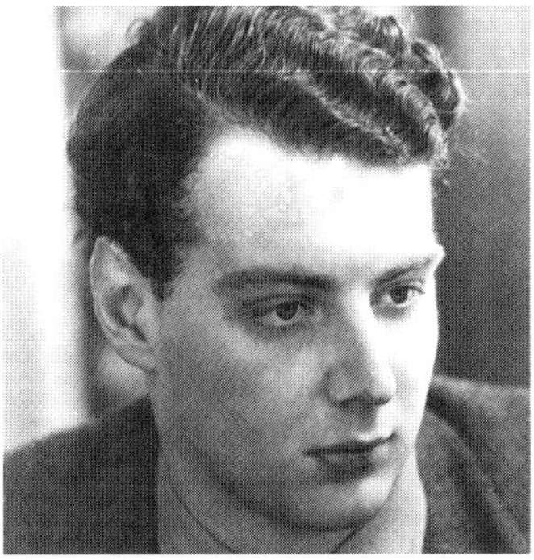

**Guy Burgess** British diplomat and Soviet spy in 1950 before his exposure
*Credit: Hulton Getty Picture Collection*

**Donald Maclean** British double agent and Soviet spy before his exposure and flight
*Credit: Hulton Getty Picture Collection*

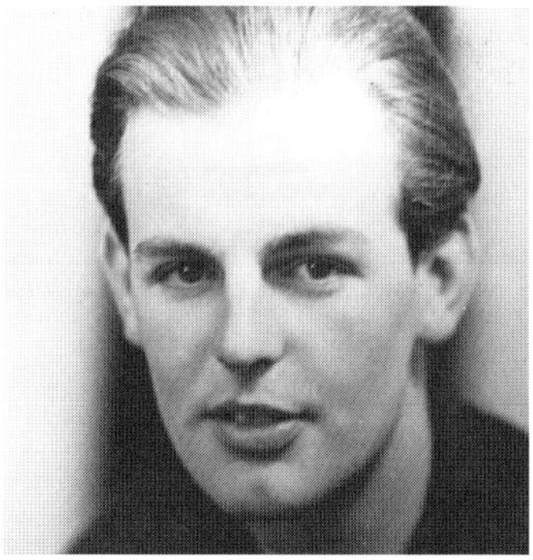

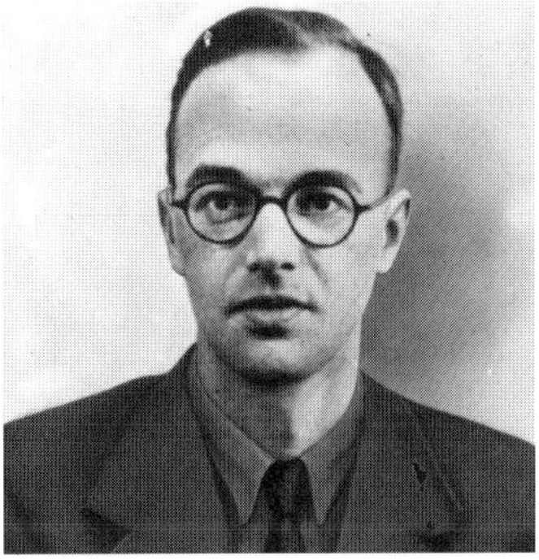

**Klaus Fuchs 1950** German-born British physicist, who was tried at the Old Bailey for handing the Russians atomic secrets *Credit: Hulton Getty Picture Collection*

**Borodin (left) 1927** This Russian agent was a pivotal instigator and adviser to China's communist movement *Credit: Milly Bennett Collection/Hoover Institution Archives (Stanford University)*

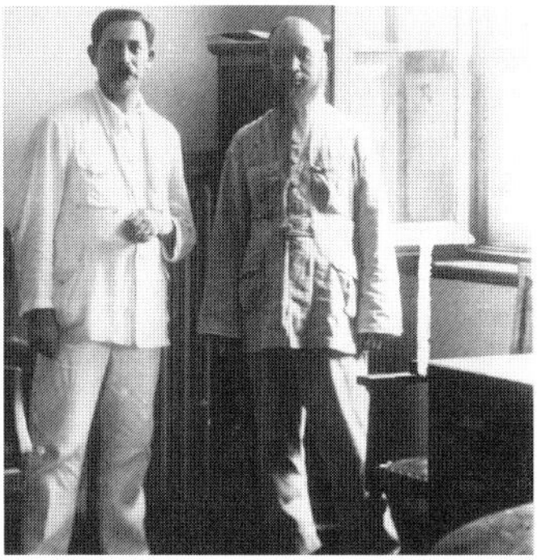

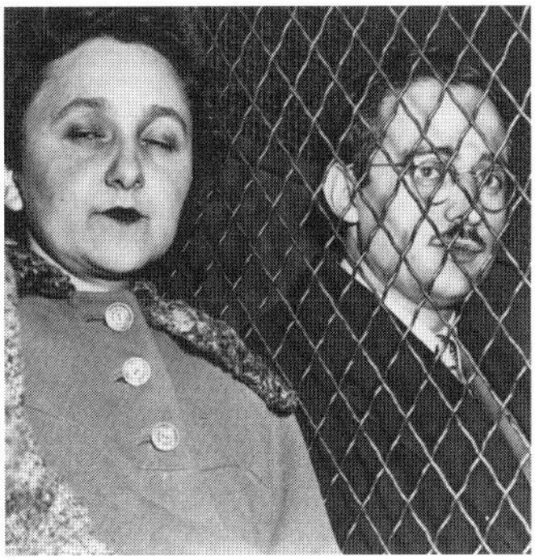

**Julius and Ethel Rosenberg** after being found guilty of nuclear espionage in the USA at the height of Cold War hysteria. They protested their innocence to the end, but were sentenced to death on 5 April 1951 *Credit: Hulton Getty Picture Collection*

**Mata Hari 1907** Femme fatale, darling of the halls and WWI spy performs the 'Dance of the Seven Veils' *Credit: Hulton Getty Picture Collection*

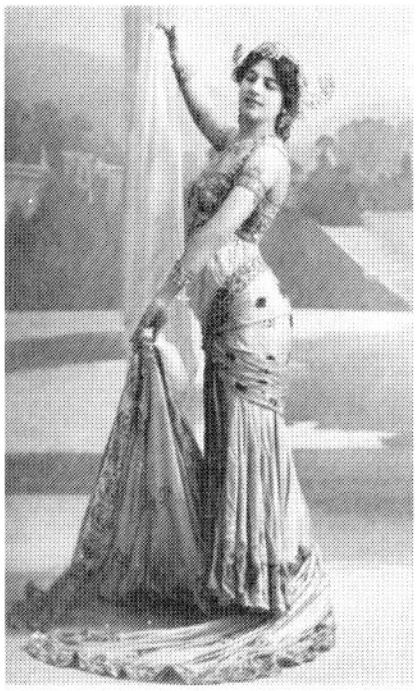

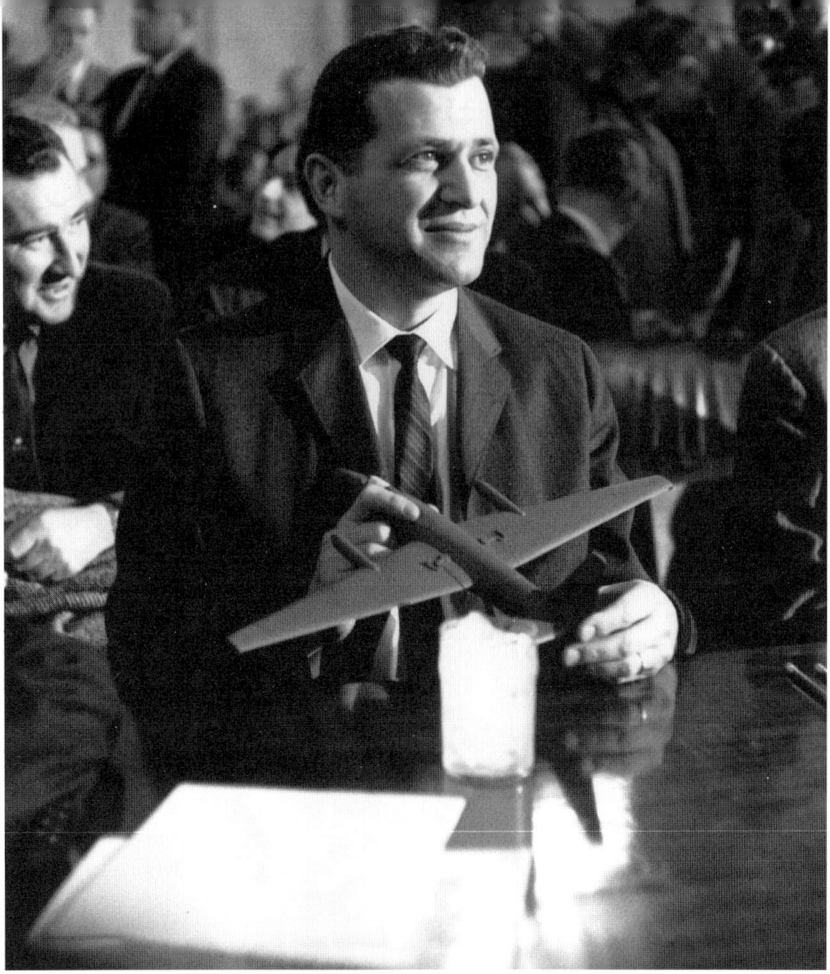

▲
**USA 1962** Francis Gary Powers sits before a US Senate committee shortly after his release from the Soviet Union in exchange for a Russian spy. He holds a model of the U-2 spy-plane, a CIA reconnaissance machine that had remained a secret until Powers was shot down in one over the USSR on the 1 May 1960. U-2s are still in use, most recently over Bosnia
*Credit: Hulton Getty Picture Collection*

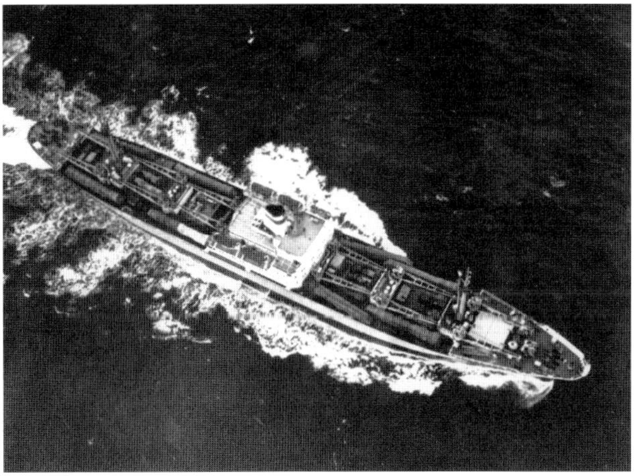

**Homeward-bound from Cuba 1962** Soviet missiles, observed by a US reconnaissance aircraft, only days after their discovery in Cuba took the world to the brink of nuclear war as Presidents Kennedy and Khrushchev faced each other off in public. Khrushchev blinked first and withdrew
*Credit: Hulton Getty Picture Collection*

**USA 1926** Not what they seem. The height of prohibition and US customs officials examine a cache of torpedoes on board a schooner. They will later be towed into port and deliver their cargo - gallons of illicit alcohol - undetected
*Credit: Hulton Getty Picture Collection*

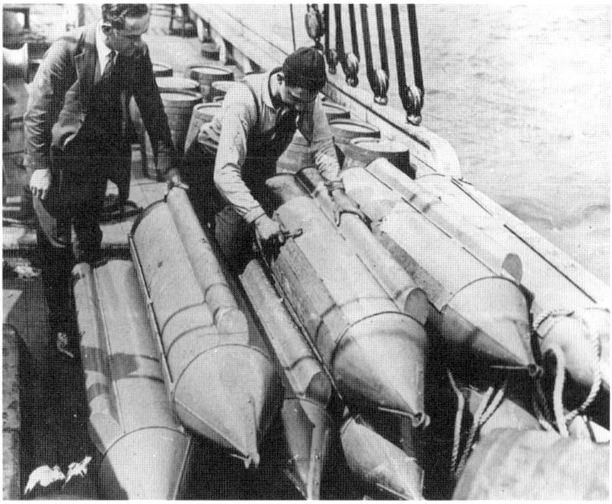

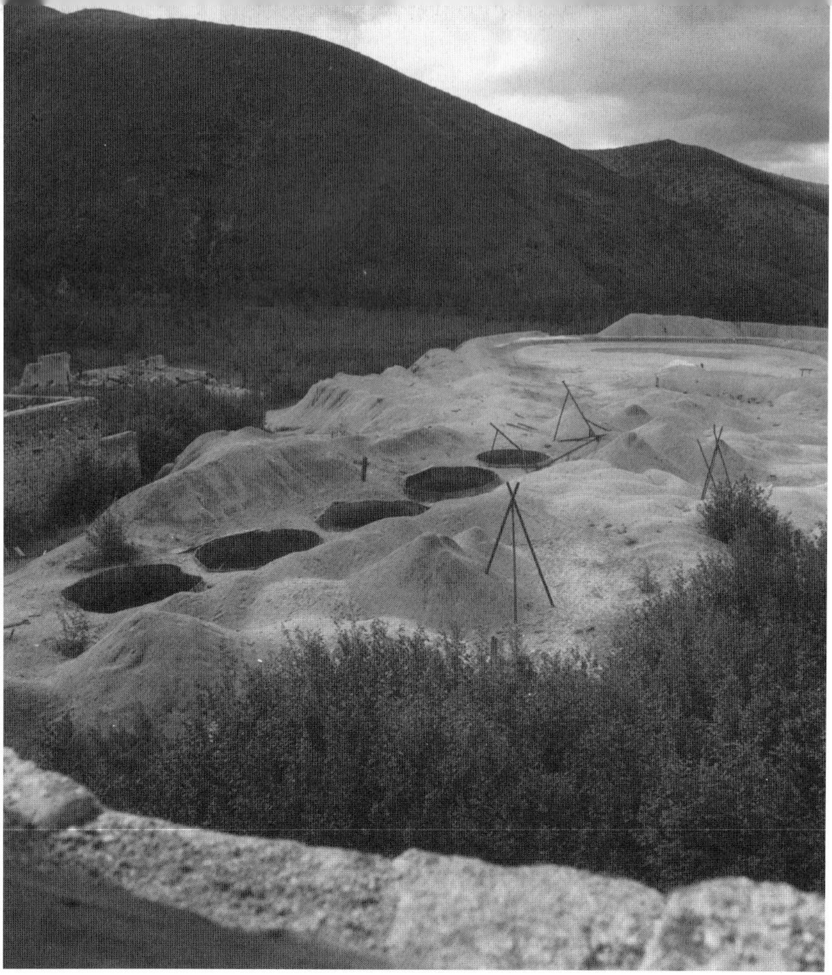

**Russia 1930s** Secret Soviet uranium mines at Butuguchak deep inside Siberia. Uranium ore for the USSR's first atomic bombs, as well as silver and tin, was mined and processed here by prison labour; inmates were usually dead from radiation sickness within three months. Although closed in 1954, the site remains highly radioactive, with lethal quantities of uranium strewn about the surface. Locals still refer to it as 'the place of death' and they and their animals stay well away
*Credit: A Kotlyarov/Endeavour Group UK*

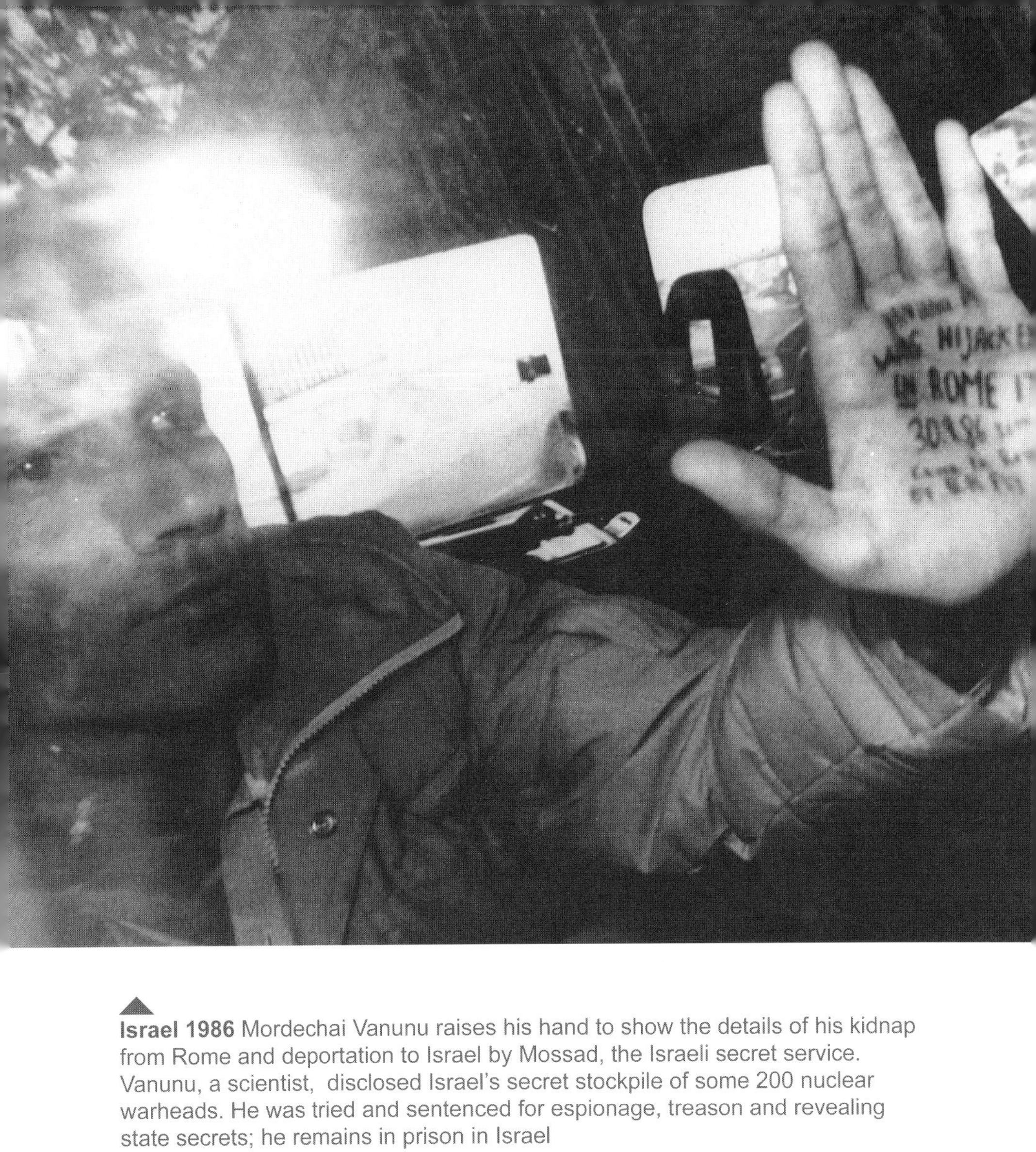


**Israel 1986** Mordechai Vanunu raises his hand to show the details of his kidnap from Rome and deportation to Israel by Mossad, the Israeli secret service. Vanunu, a scientist, disclosed Israel's secret stockpile of some 200 nuclear warheads. He was tried and sentenced for espionage, treason and revealing state secrets; he remains in prison in Israel
*Credit: Associated Press*

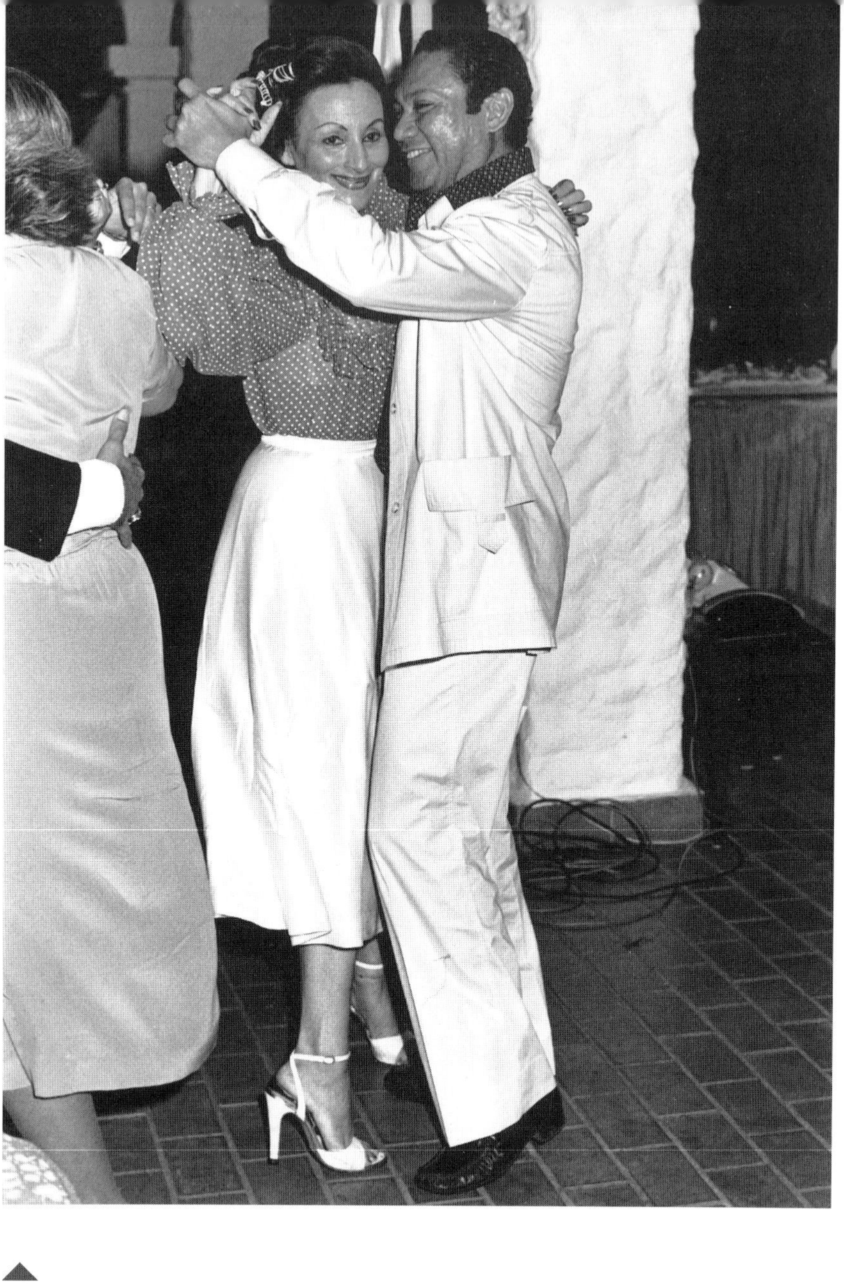

**Panama 1979** Manuel Noriega, right-hand man of President Torrijos, faces the music with the president's sister shortly before the US-backed coup that killed Torrijos and eventually brought Noriega to power. He was a thorn in the US side but turned out to be secretly on the CIA and US Army payroll. The USA put an end to their embarrassment by invading Panama in December 1989 and unseating yet another of their home-grown dictators
*Credit: Carlos Reyes/Andes Press Agency*

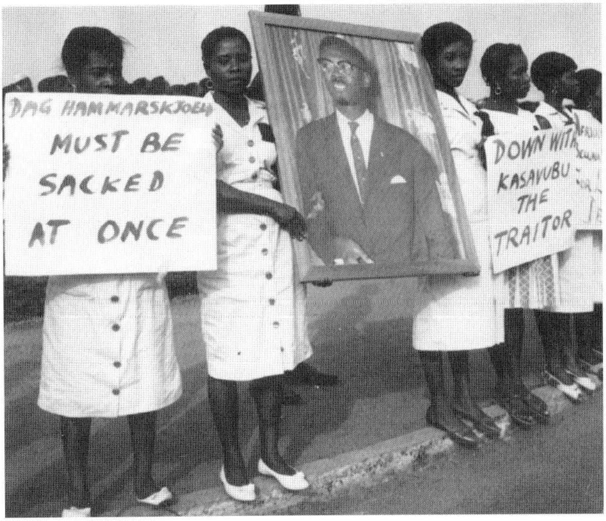


**Congo 1961** Women mourn Patrice Lumumba, Moscow-friendly first premier of newly independent Congo, assassinated in 1960 in a covert CIA coup. The US feared the mineral-rich republic would fall into Soviet hands
*Credit: Hulton Getty Picture Collection*

**Nicaragua 1990** A secret contra camp in the north of the country. CIA support for the opponents of the Sandanista regime was financed by drug-trafficking and continued from the Sandinista takeover to the end of the 1980s
*Credit: Bosio/Liaison Agency*

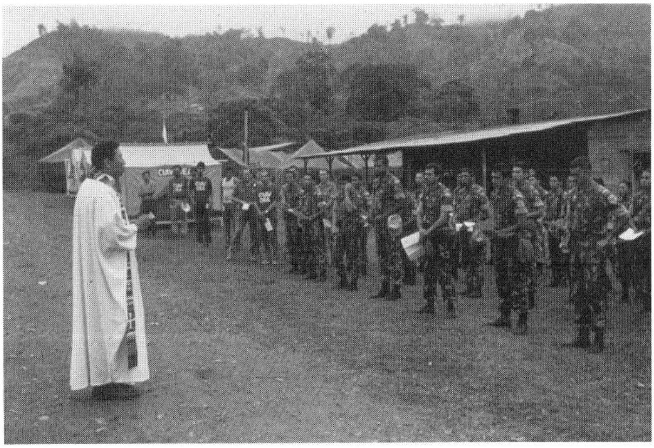

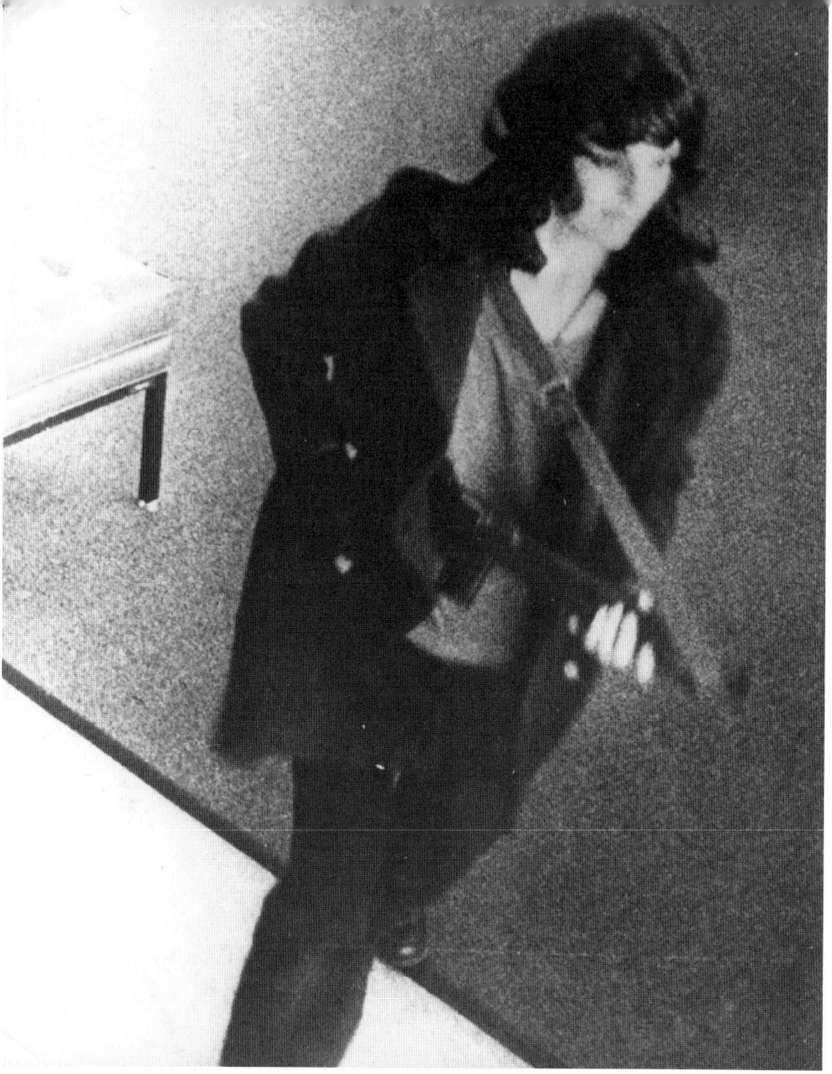

**San Francisco USA 1975** US heiress Patty Hearst caught on a surveillance camera during a raid on a bank by the Symbionese Liberation Army. This was an early instance of CCTV pictures being used as evidence in court and led to her subsequent conviction and imprisonment
*Credit: Hulton Getty Picture Collection*

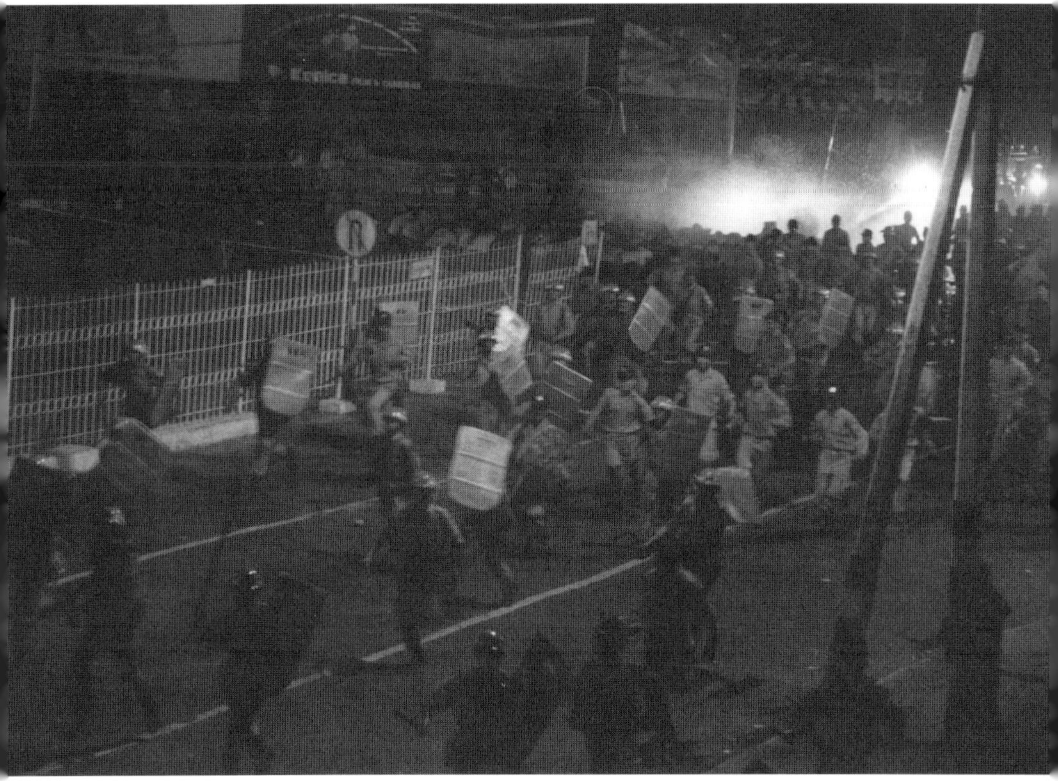

**Burma 1996** Violent dispersal of student protest in the capital, Rangoon. This was the biggest anti-government demonstration since the nationwide democracy uprising of 1988. Covertly photographed with a concealed camera
*Credit: Andres Hernandez/Liaison Agency*

# Body

*I often feel that people come to me to be photographed as they would go to a doctor or a fortune teller – to find out how they are. So they're dependent on me. I have to engage them. Otherwise there's nothing to photograph... And when the sitting is over ... there's nothing left except the photograph and a kind of embarrassment.*

Richard Avedon

**England some time between the wars** Lady Diana Cooper as Charity
*Credit: Hulton Getty Picture Collection*

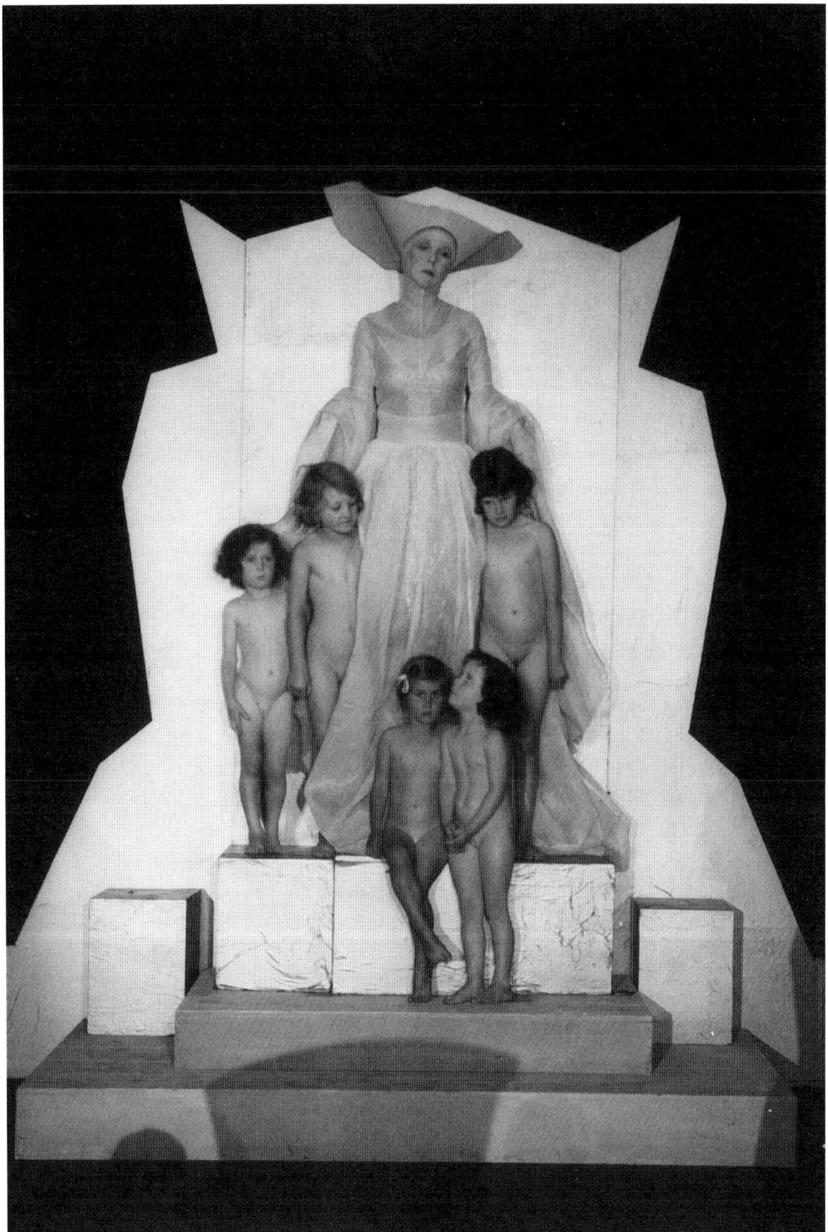

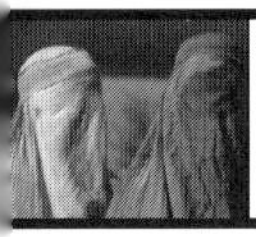

# Body

*Peter Brooks*

The story of the eroticised gaze at the body is, from one perspective, the story of *pudeur*, modesty, of the hiding of those parts known as *pudenda*, shameful, or at least private. The development of civilisation is for Freud, in large measure, a question of instinctual renunciation, learning to repress, sublimate and delay various gratifications – a renunciation that takes a high toll, in that it virtually makes civilisation synonymous with neurosis. Norbert Elias has traced what he calls 'the civilising process' as a lowering of the threshold of disgust, particularly in relation to the body and its products, a progressive hiding of bodily parts and functions. The story told by Elias is in part one of an increasingly socialised body learning to discipline itself, to be more self-contained, controlled, autonomous and private. It is also the story of an increasing psychologising of mankind, where questions that originally pertain to the body – how one eats with others, when one farts or belches – become subsumed in more general psychological and ethical categories such as shame and modesty. While this story is not linear, and progresses differently for different social classes as well as for different cultures, it is in the main characterised by increasing privatisation and hiding. Recent historians of private life have demonstrated that privitisation and hiding affect all aspects of existence: architecture, sleeping and eating arrangements, relations to servants, the raising of children – indeed, the 'invention' of childhood as a separate stage of development needing isolation from adulthood, and especially from adult sexuality. When the body becomes more secret, hidden, covered, it becomes all the more intensely the object of curiosity. As Michel Foucault has argued, modern societies have created a massive discourse of sexuality that produces sexuality as that which is hidden, secret, and therefore most desirable to know. In this sense, discourse of the sexual body has perhaps replaced theological discourses of the arcane and the sacred for a desacralised era.

These generalities apply to both the male and the female body, but there are profound asymmetries in the specific treatments of the two genders. It appears that in patriarchal societies, the male body is ostensibly deproblematised, decathected as an object of curiosity or of representation, and concomitantly more thoroughly hidden. There is an apparent paradox here: if the male body in patriarchy becomes the norm, the standard against which one measures otherness – and thus creates the enigma of woman – one might expect the male body to be more openly displayed and discussed. But a moment's reflection allows us to see that the paradox is merely apparent. Precisely because it is the norm, the male body is veiled from enquiry, taken as the agent and not the object of knowing: the gaze is 'phallic,' its object is not. Barthes suggests that in our culture, narrative itself, as the individual unveiling of truth is a 'staging [*mise en scène*] of the Father (absent, hidden, or suspended) – which would explain the interdependence of narrative forms, familial structures, and prohibitions of nudity, all brought together, for us, in the myth of Noah covered by his sons'. In this view, the nakedness of the drunken patriarch Noah would be the central scandal of our culture, one that must at all costs be veiled since it reveals the very principle of patriarchal authority. Despite – or because of – the attention paid to viewing woman naked, the paternal phallus may be the ultimate taboo object of our culture. As the controversy aroused in 1989 by the exhibit of photographs by Robert Mapplethorpe confirmed, the erect penis is virtually the only object still rated obscene in contemporary American society – the very definition of 'hard core' – and subject to restrictions. ...

The postmodern age is intensely visual, defined by film, video, dance, performance art, blockbuster museum shows. As Jean-Louis Comolli suggests, since the late nineteenth century we have lived in a 'frenzy of the visible', and certainly our own time has seen only an intensification of the frenzy. Even though George Eliot and Freud taught us, in different ways, to listen to the body, our knowing of the body still seems to be obsessed with viewing it, striving to see it in its moments of most intense sensation. Linda Williams has discussed the pornographic film as an example of Michel Foucault's 'knowledge of pleasure': the apparently insatiable need to see the body perform erotically, organised around moments of orgasm – especially male orgasm, which is visually demonstrable, the orgasm that cannot be faked. Although pornography remains a special realm, its demarcations from acceptable artistic expression have been repeatedly questioned, in ways that define some of the issues of the body and knowledge in our time. ❑

***Peter Brooks*** *is Tripp Professor of Humanities at Yale University and is the author of* The Novel of Worldliness, The Melodramatic Imagination *and* Reading for the Plot. *This extract is taken from* Body Work: Objects of Desire in Modern Narrative *(Harvard University Press, 1993). His most recent book is* History, Painting and Narrative: Delacroix's 'Moments', *published in 1999*

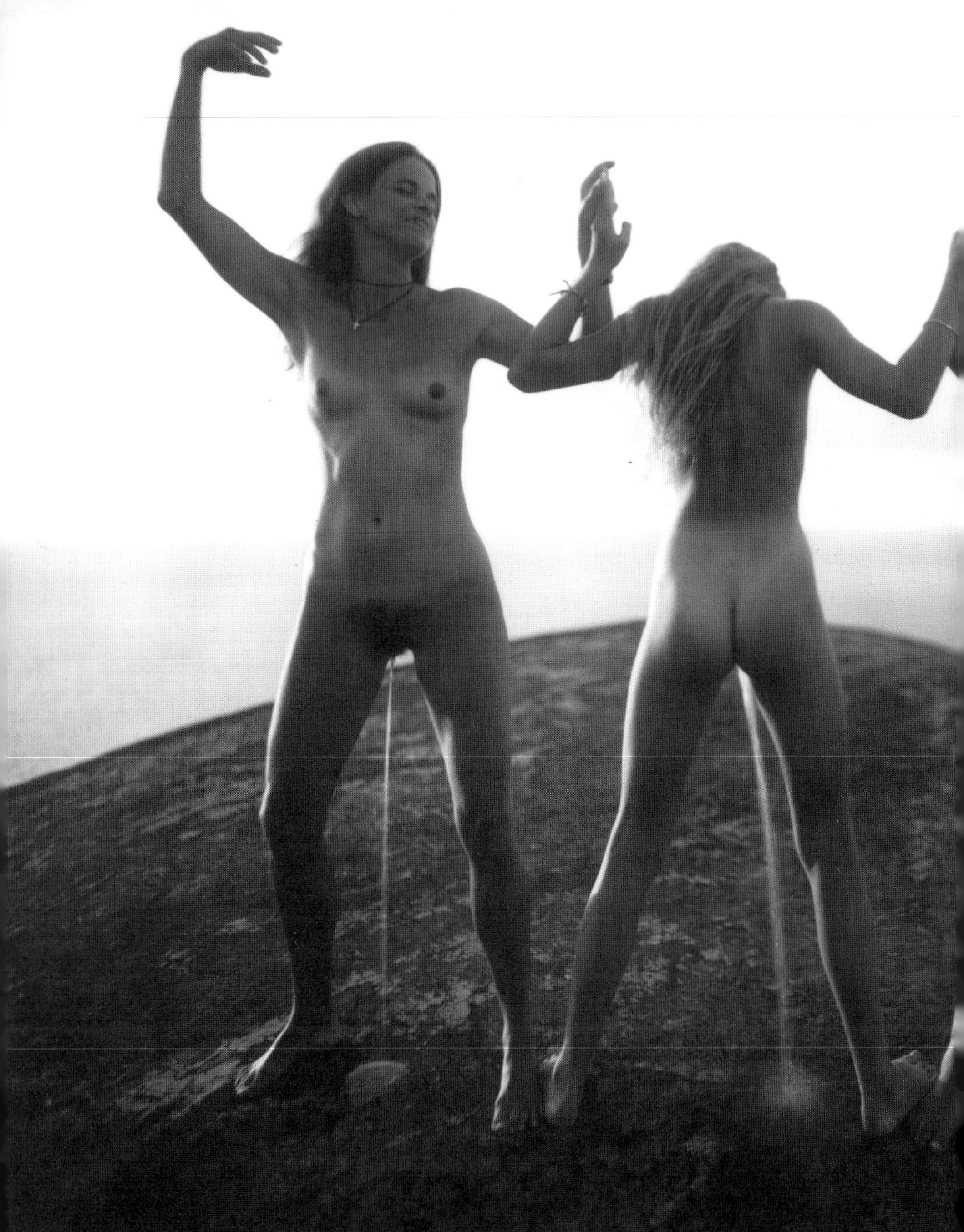

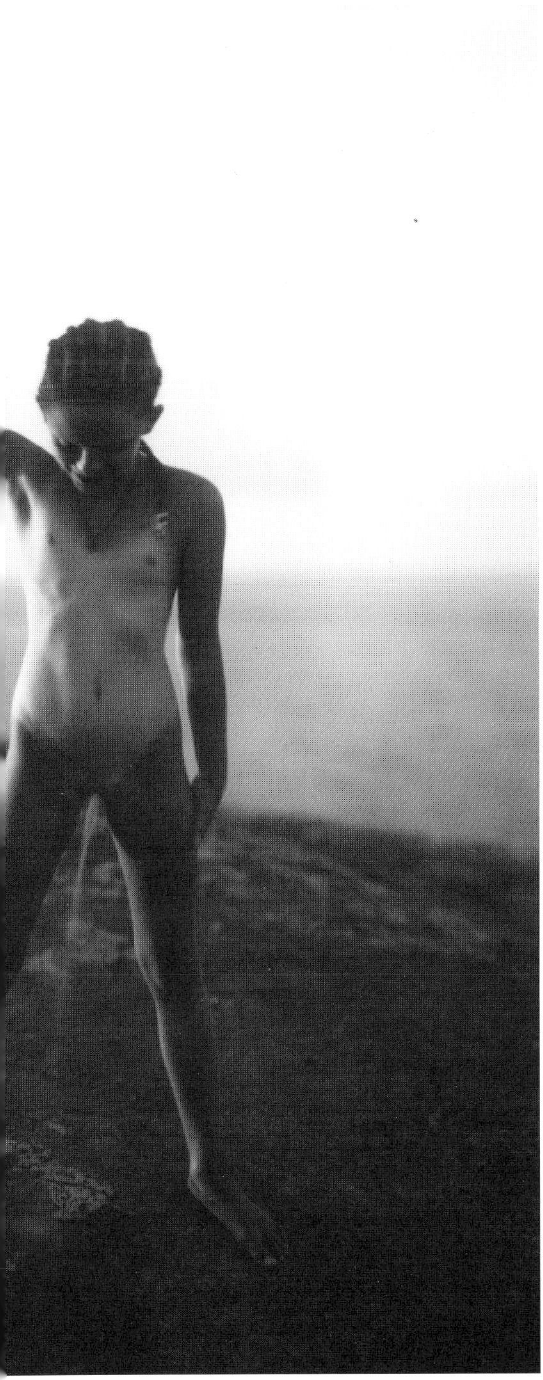

**USA 1994** *The Three Graces*
Photographer Sally Mann and her daughters Jessie and Virginia peeing
*Credit: Sally Mann/Edwyn Houk Gallery New York*

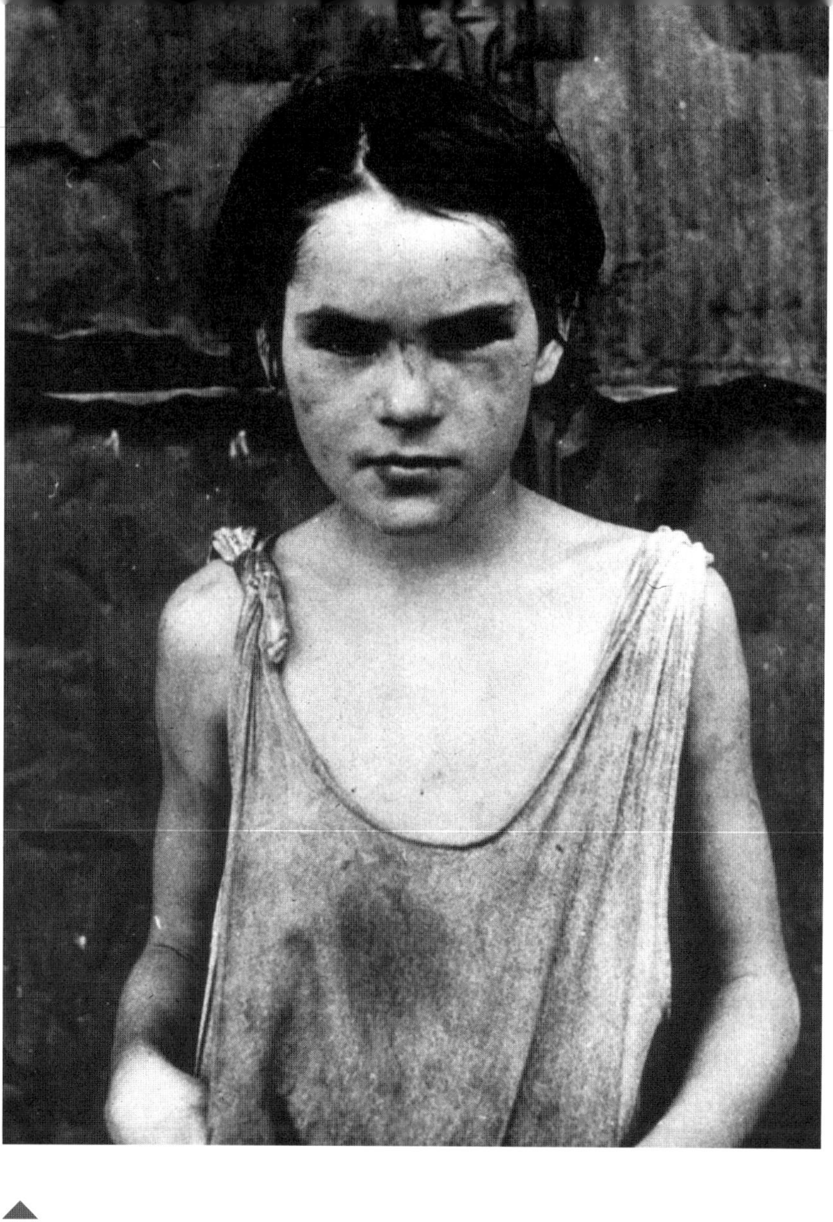

**Shacktown Oklahoma USA 1936** Damaged child, from Dorothea Lange's work for the Farm Security Administration (see p40)
*Credit: Hulton Getty Picture Collection*

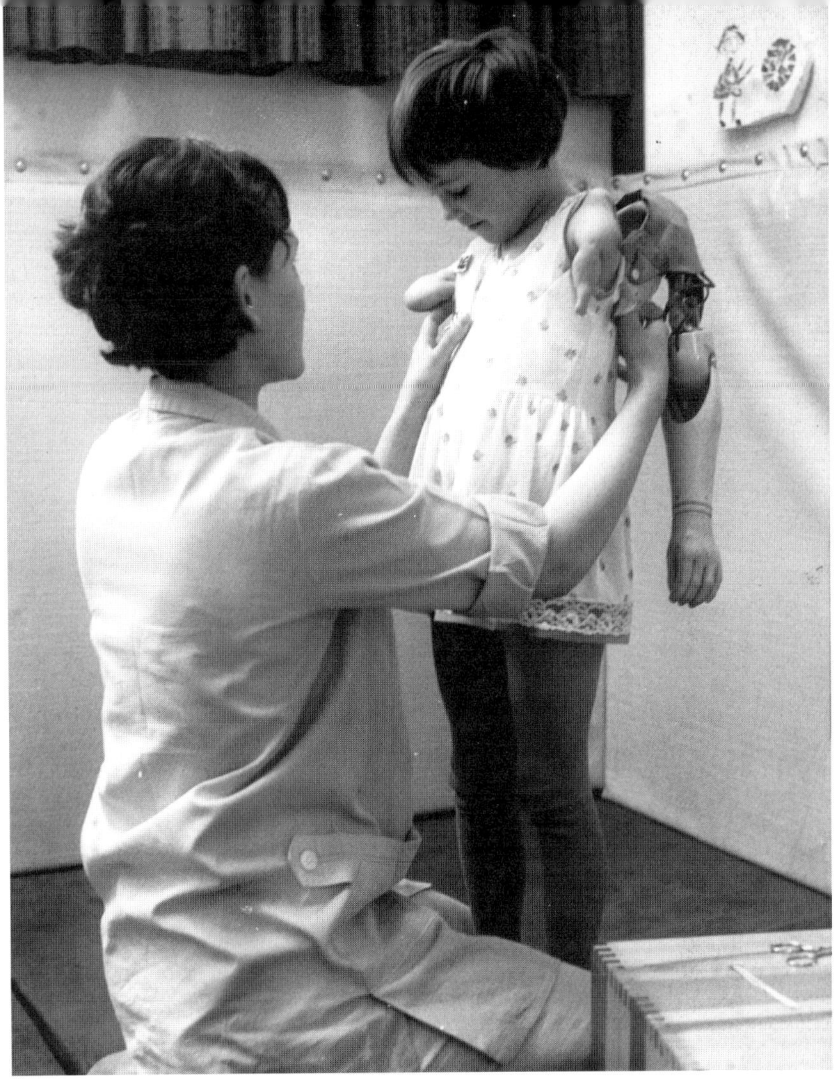

▲
**West Germany 1967** Up to 10,000 children were affected by the drug Thalidomide. Introduced as a sedative in 1956 and most frequently prescribed for pregnant women, it affected the growth of the foetus. It was withdrawn in 1961
*Credit: Hulton Getty Picture Collection*

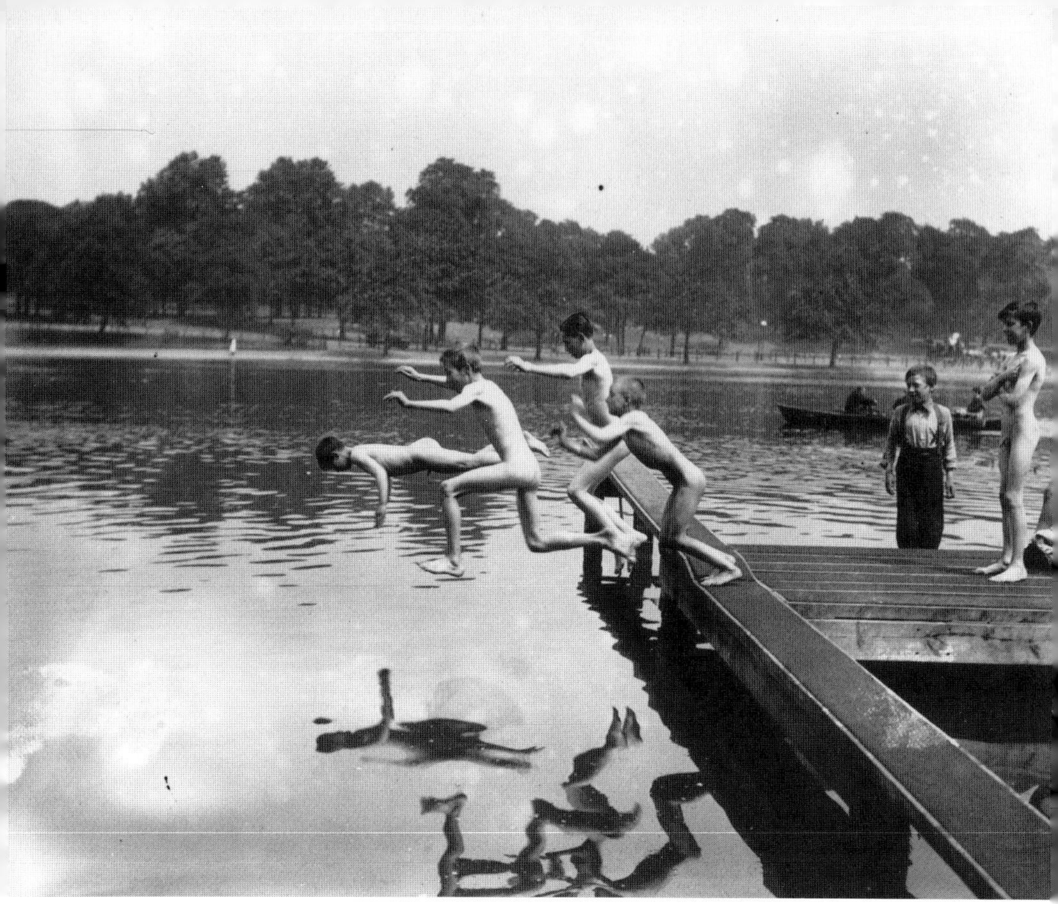

**Germany 1990s** Published in 1973 as a sex education book for use with children, *Zeig Mal! (Show Me!)* became the immediate object of abuse and prosecutions for its frank portrayal of children's sexuality. The US edition was banned; in Germany, there is an active campaign working for its removal from libraries and bookshops and its suppression as an 'abusive' book
*Credit: Will McBride*

**London 1926** During the heat-wave. The joy was short-lived: the next photo in the sequence shows them pursued naked through the streets by a female policeman brandishing her birch *Credit: Hulton Getty Picture Collection*

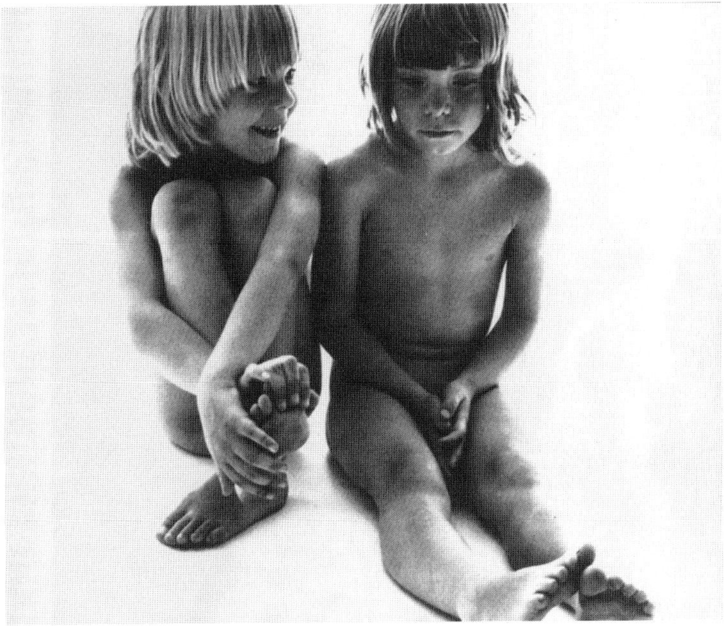

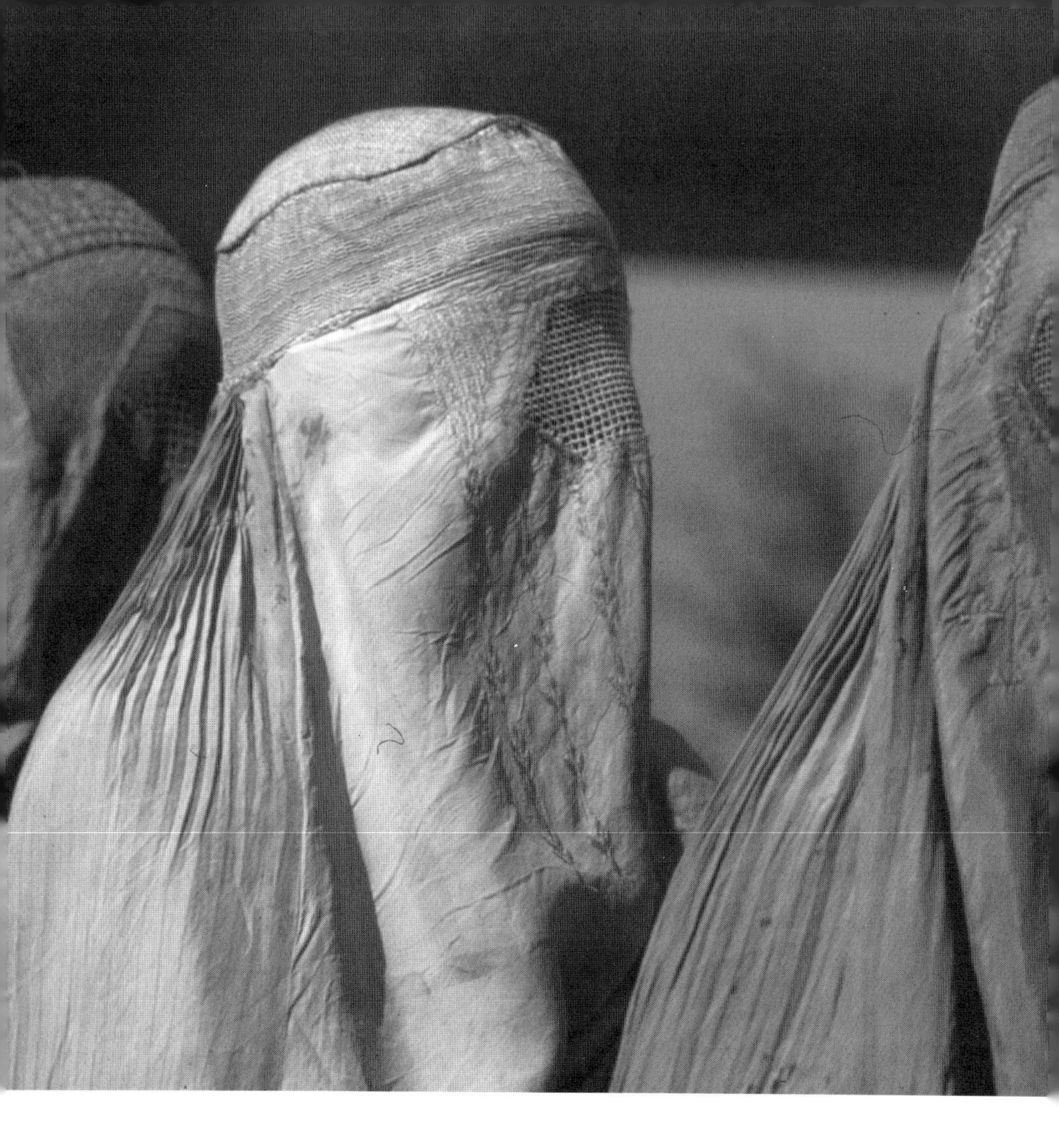

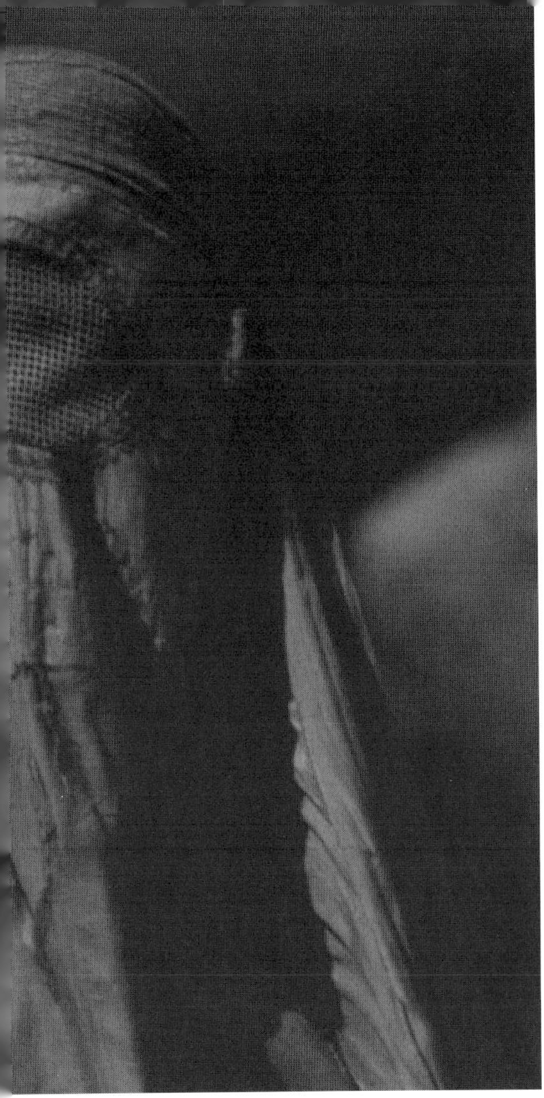

**Afganistan 1999** In Taliban-ruled Afganistan, the bodies of women are rendered invisible by the obligatory wearing of the chador in public. Women may not practise their professions nor work in public institutions *Credit: Lenoyne/Liaison Agency*

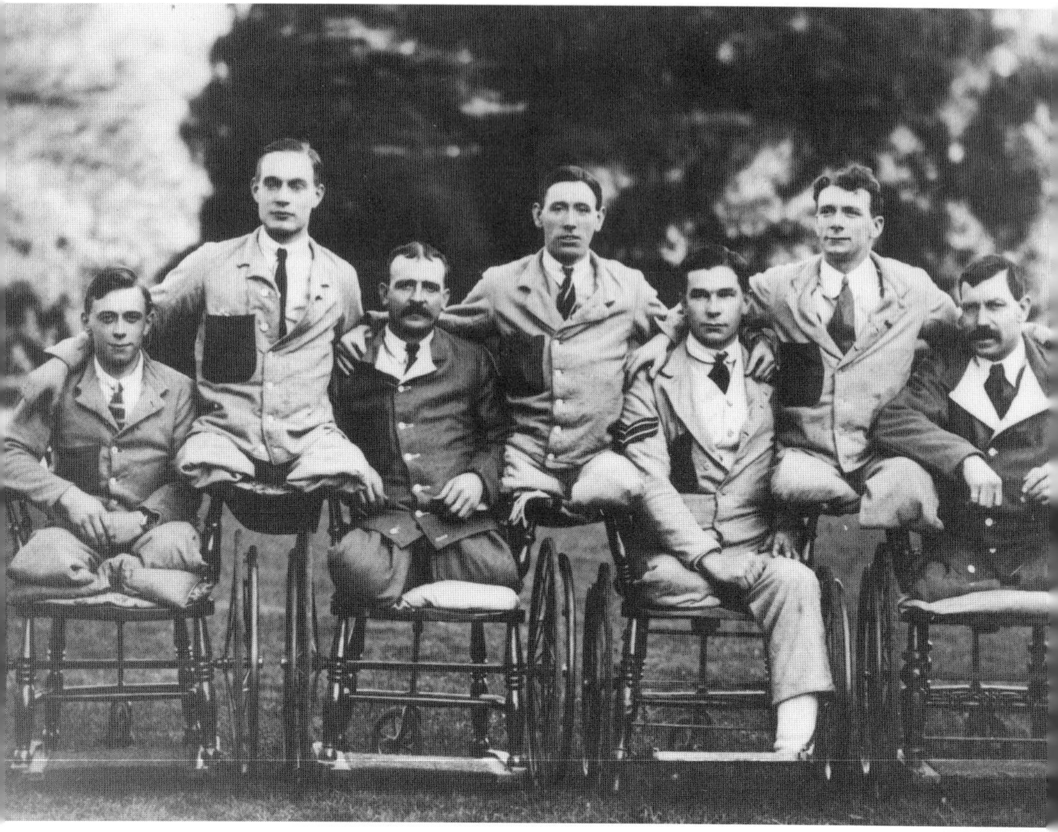

**South Vietnam 1973** Ten-year-old Le Luy (right) and six-year-old Cu Van Anh (left) in Thi Nge orphanage
*Credit: Mirror Syndication International*

**UK 1918** War amputees at Roehampton Military Hospital
*Credit: Imperial War Museum London (Q108161)*

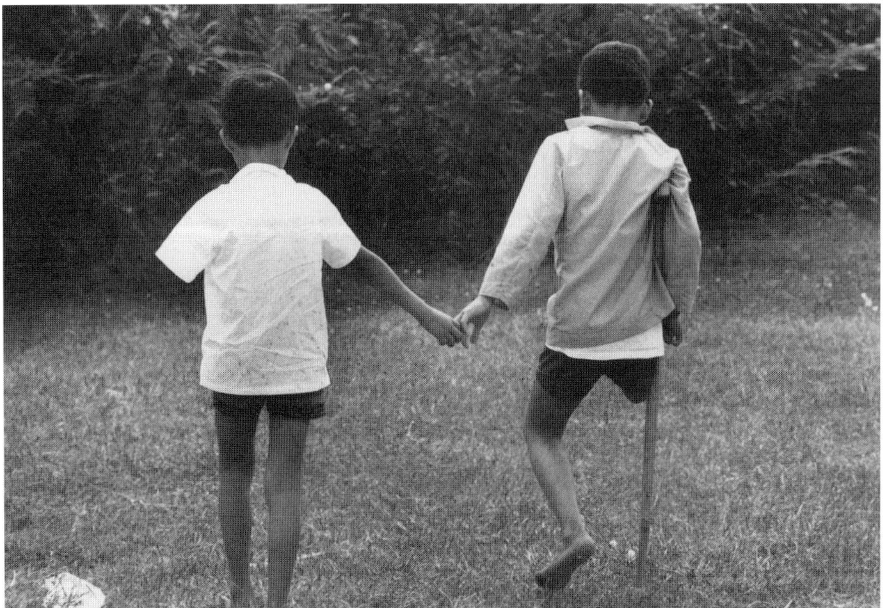

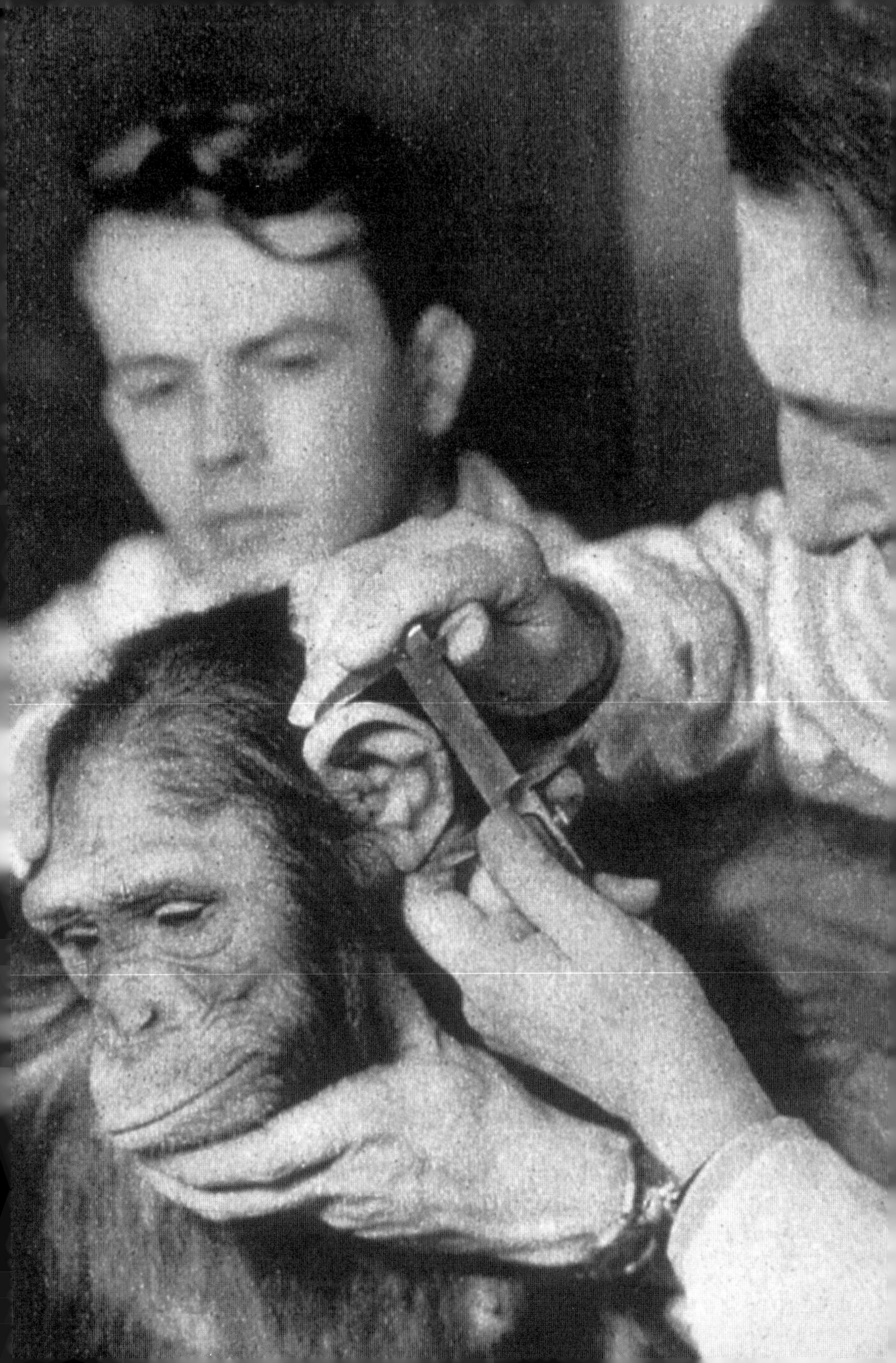

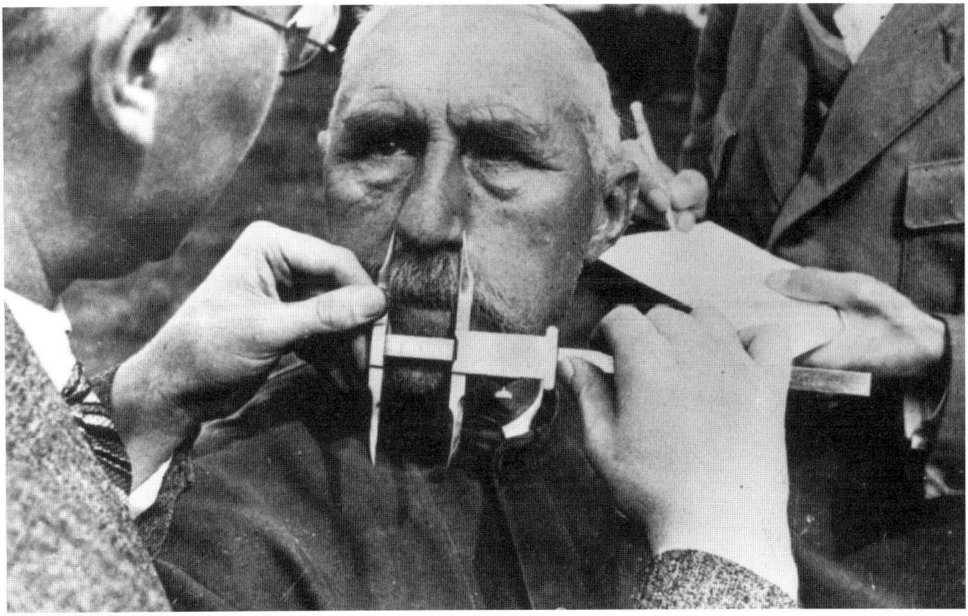

**Germany 1940** Ear and nose job. Nose measurement was among the more bizarre of the Nazi's 'Aryan race determination tests' to detect 'crypto Jews' at the height of anti-Jewish hysteria ... and German scientists chart the progress of evolution with the Aryan ear test
*Credit: Hulton Getty Picture Collection*

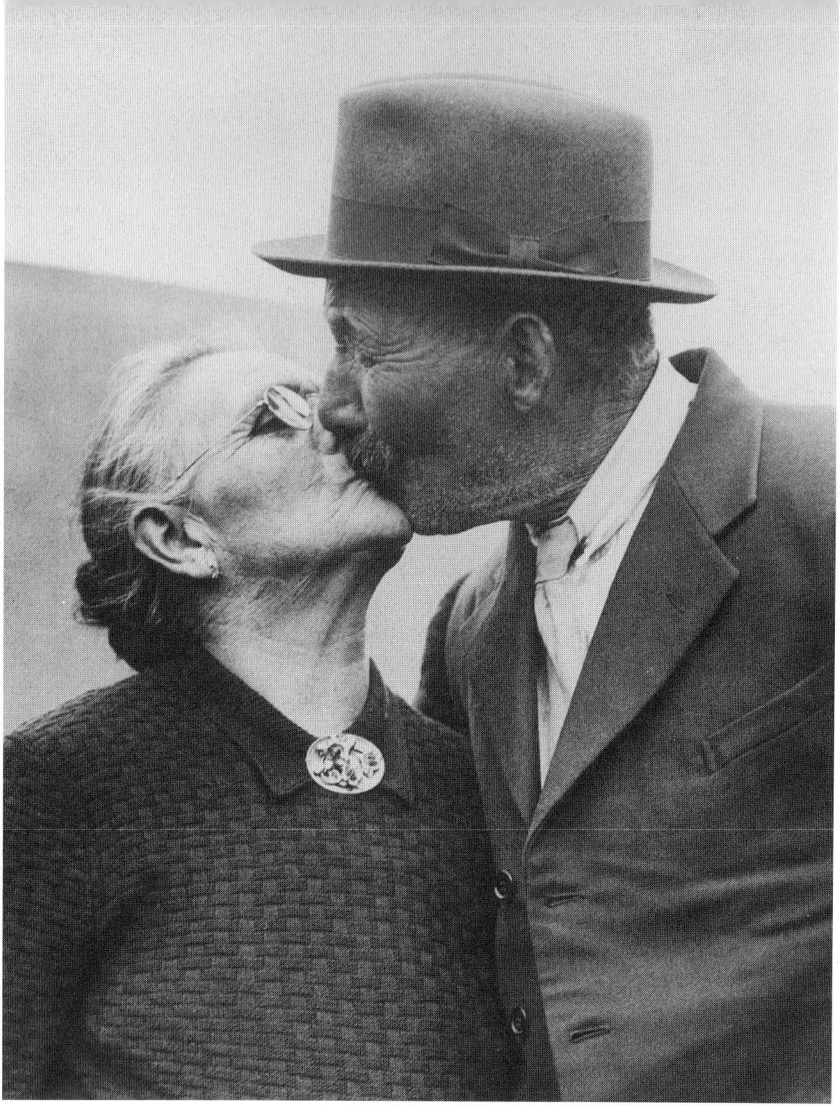

**Stanton Harcourt Oxfordshire UK 1939** Mr and Mrs Townsend celebrate their golden wedding
*Credit: Hulton Getty Picture Collection*

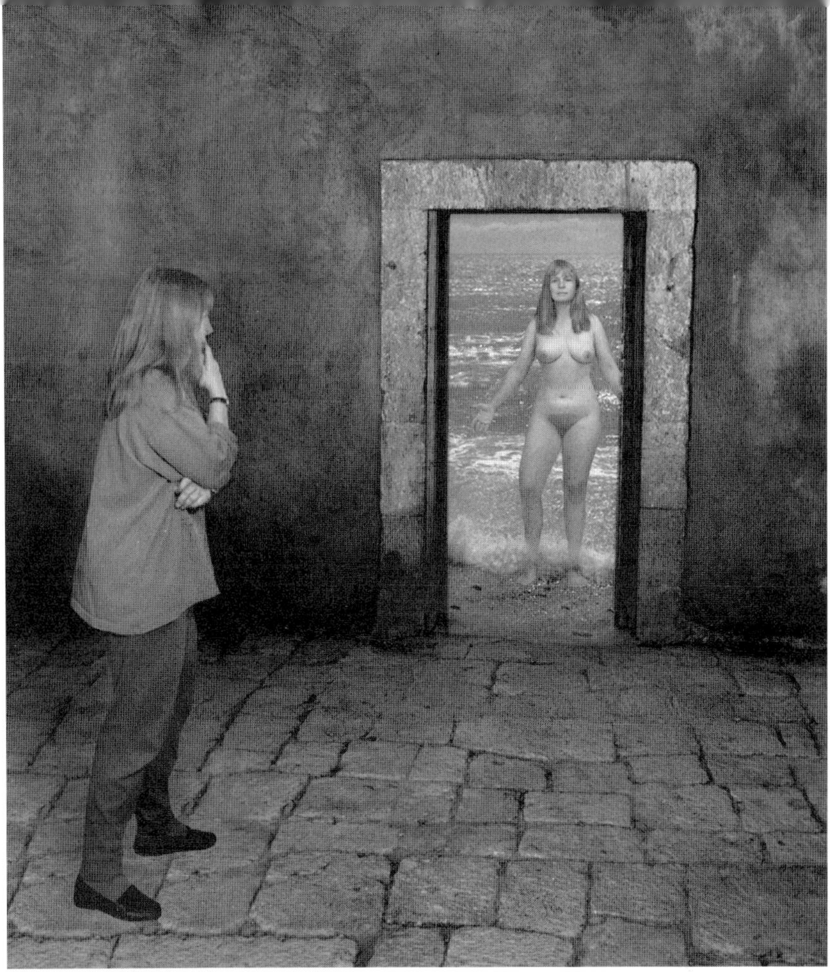

▲
**USA 1994** 'Much of my photography involves nudes, and one issue I often deal with is that of how difficult it can be for people to accept and like their own body. When I made my first foray into digital manipulation of photographs, one of the obvious choices was to use the digital manipulation to give my models the ability to see what they really wished they could see.
The model in Body Image #2 had some common concerns about weight, surgical scars, and asymmetry of her breasts, and articulated a wish to become a Venus-like figure, with some of her power and mystery.' Saelon Renkes
*Credit: Saelon Renkes*

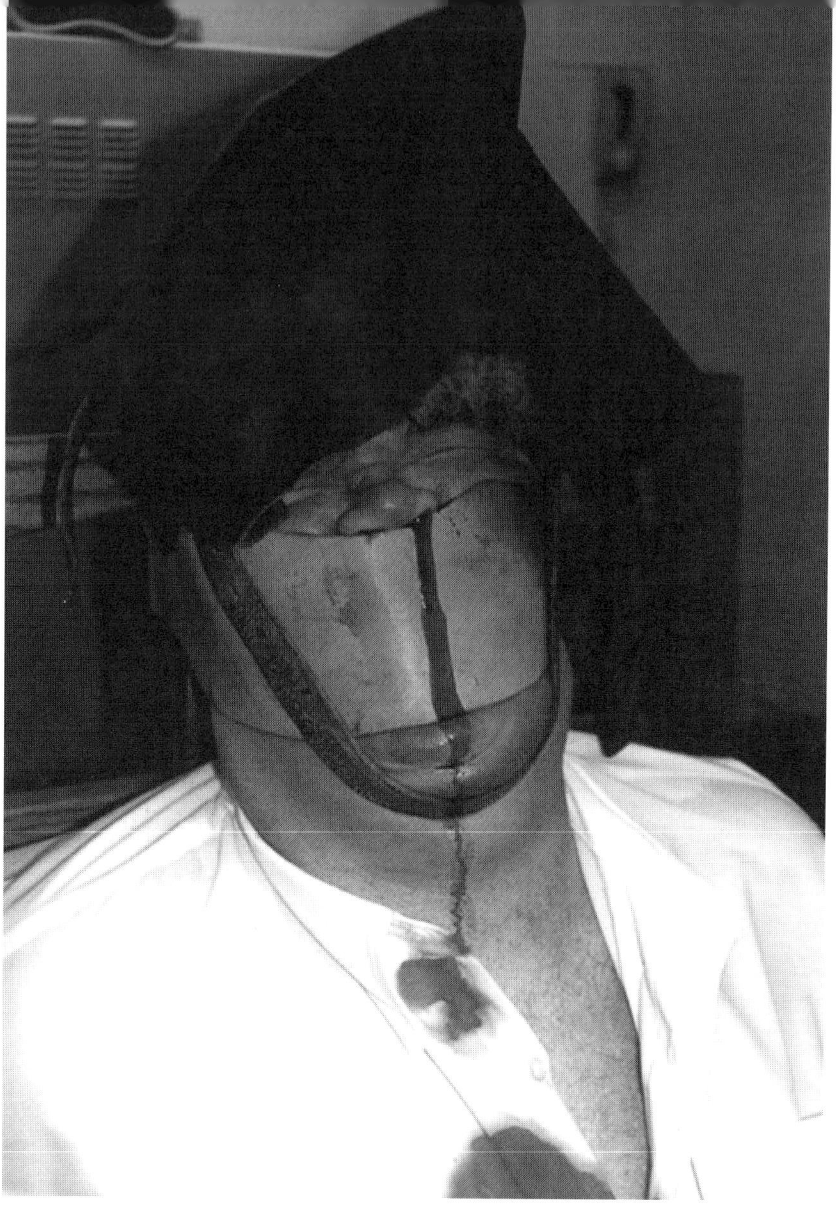

**Florida 1999** Allen Lee Davis, 54, executed for a triple murder committed during a robbery 17 years earlier. He was the first person electrocuted in the replacement for 'Old Sparky,' which was retired by the state of Florida following a 1997 execution in which foot-long flames burst from the dying man's head. Davis's unexpectedly bloody end prompted Governor Jeb Bush to remark that: 'The [new] chair functioned as it was designed to function, and we're comfortable with that'

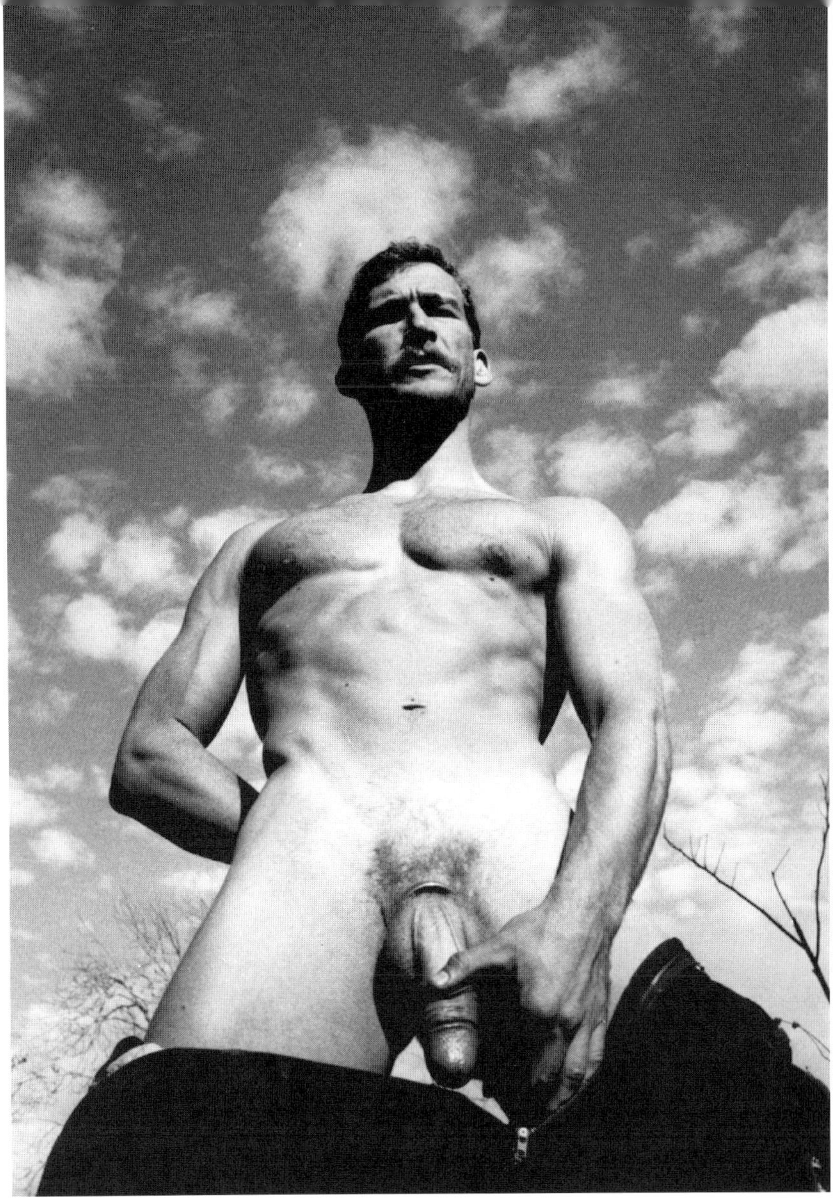

▲
**USA 1997** Mike Welder by Jack Fritscher banned from Edward Lucie-Smith's
*Ars Erotica*
*Credit: www.JackFritscher.com*

# Planet

*I attempt, through much of my work, to animate all things – even so-called 'inanimate' objects – with the spirit of man. I have come, by degrees, to realise that this extremely animistic projection rises, ultimately, from my profound fear and disquiet over the accelarating mechanisation of man's life… The creative photographer imparts humanity to the inhuman world around him*

Clarence John Laughlin

**Cameroon 1999** 'The hunters blasted into the trees until the gorillas and their two babies fell out. I persuaded the hunters to huddle the bodies together for this photograph before they began butchering them. They told me they would get about £30 for the adults' meat, but that the babies would fetch nothing, and would be given to children to play with, cut up and cook' Karl Ammann
*Credit: Karl Ammann/BG Wildlife Photographer of the Year organised by BBC Wildlife magazine and the Natural History Museum, London*

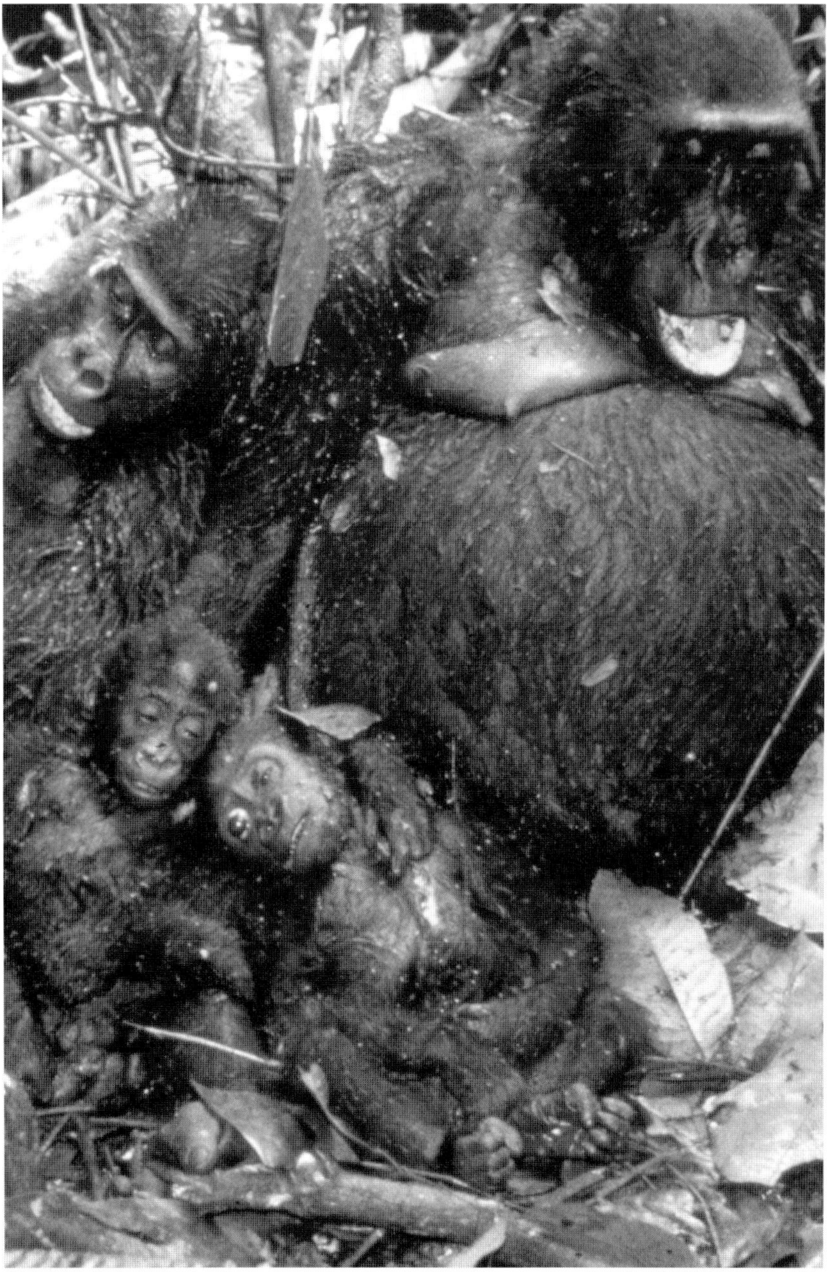

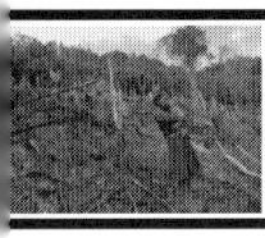

# Planet

*Colin Tudge*

Prophets in every century warned that the end of the world was nigh – but those of the 20th have had more reason than most. Thomas Malthus predicted around 1800 that we would starve before long if numbers continued to rise but the population has grown six-fold since then and, at the present rate of increase, would rise from the present six billion to an almost inconceivable 100 billion by 2150. Malthus's timing may have been out but something has definitely got to give soon. Meanwhile, extinction rates among other creatures are 100 times greater than was usual this past 50 million years – and about half the species now on Earth are endangered, including most big mammals and virtually all cats and primates. Even some deep-ocean fish, like the bluefin tuna, seem all but scuppered.

The greatest threat is loss of habitat. Virtually all the world's fertile valleys are long since farmed, so we already think of 'wilderness' as the places where agriculture is uneconomic: mountain, desert, tropical forest – which carry at least 90% (probably nearer 98%) of all the world's species. This is why loss of tropical forest is so serious. Fragmentation can be as bad as total removal. Thus there are plenty of woods left in India – but very few are large enough to hold viable populations of elephants, whose population has fallen in the 20th century from hundreds of thousands to an estimated 30,000, and surely will fall to around 15,000 before it stabilises, if indeed it does. Asia as a whole once had elephants from Iran to China and the islands beyond, but only India, Sri Lanka, Malaysia and perhaps Nepal now have viable numbers. Pollution is a form of habitat loss – making the habitats uninhabitable – and takes many strange and subtle forms. Orang-utans are threatened not simply by the loss of trees but by the sound of chainsaws, which cause them to abandon their territory.

The second greatest threat, surprisingly, is importation of exotic species: by accident (as with New Zealand's gorse, or rats and groundsel everywhere), for fun (as with Australia's rabbits and foxes, and the American rainbow trout introduced to rivers worldwide), for commerce (India's eucalyptus, and the Nile perch that virtually wiped out hundreds of native fish species in Lake Victoria), or for misguided biological control (as with the cane toad in Australia, brought in to control rats in the sugar cane fields, now wiping out everything).

Hunting is an unexpected third in the league table of dangers but, especially for slow-breeding species, it can be critical. Africa still has plenty of good habitat for black rhinos, but poachers will risk their lives for the horns. Zimbabwe had the biggest population in the 1980s and apparently protected them heroically, but it lost two-thirds of them to poachers in a decade. Great Indian rhinos in Nepal's Chitwan National Park are poached in many ingenious ways: by diverting power cables into their paths, for example. The beautiful hyacinthine macaws in Brazil yield about as much meat as a small chicken leg but the last few are still being shot at. So are many species of monkey. Some creatures are just too easy to pick off.

But there have been signs of hope. The theory of conservation has improved vastly in the present century: ecology, animal behaviour, genetics and in particular the notions of island biogeography, which show why animal populations need to be large (generally several hundred) if they are to survive at all. At least it is now known that fragments of habitat must be linked by 'corridors'. Zoos have had an often ghastly century but some at least now realise their essential role in maintaining numbers. The return of the Arabian oryx to the wild (first Jordan, then Oman) in the late 1970s after last-ditch rescue in California, shows what can be done; while the European bison, Père David's deer, Przewalski's horse and the Hawaiian goose are among other notable 20th-century successes. High-tech plays an increasing part: in radiotelemetry (to track animals in the wild), artificial insemination and DNA studies to establish genetic relationships and maximise diversity. Many more species are bound to be lost but we could yet stop short of disaster.

Most encouragingly, the UN suggests that human numbers could level out in the mid 21st century (at around 12 billion) not through coercion but because more and more people elect to have fewer children. Best of all, the only controls that work are the benign ones: more personal wealth, greater autonomy and freedom for women, better pensions (so people do not rely on their children in their old age). Attitudes may be improving too. Evironmentalism is now a serious force and the Arabian oryx can be a wild animal again mainly because the men of the Middle East decided that Allah no longer wanted them to hunt it.

The next century could be like the present only worse, truly the *coup de grâce*. Or we could turn the corner. ❑

***Colin Tudge's*** *latest book,* The Variety of Life: The Meaning of Biodiversity *will be published by Oxford University Press early in 2000*

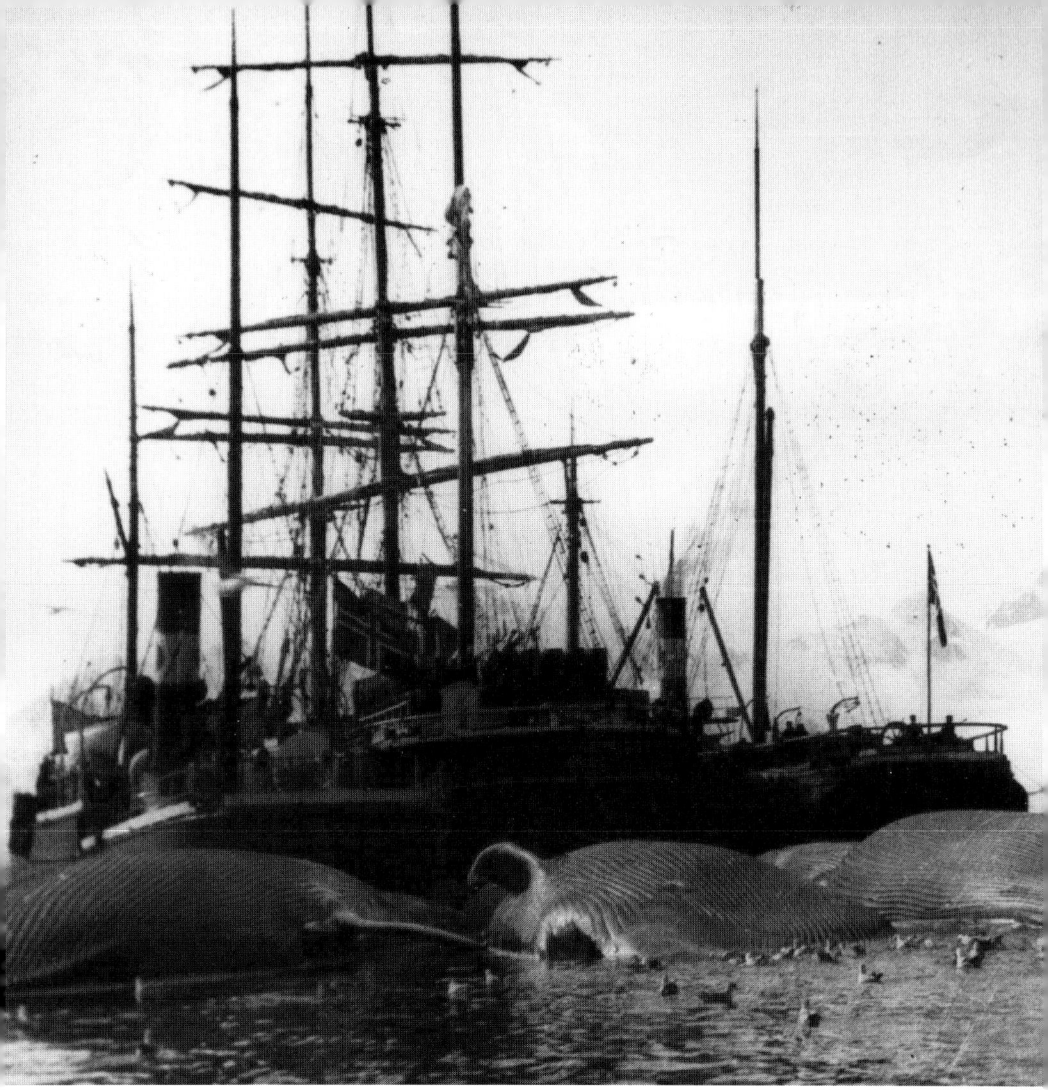

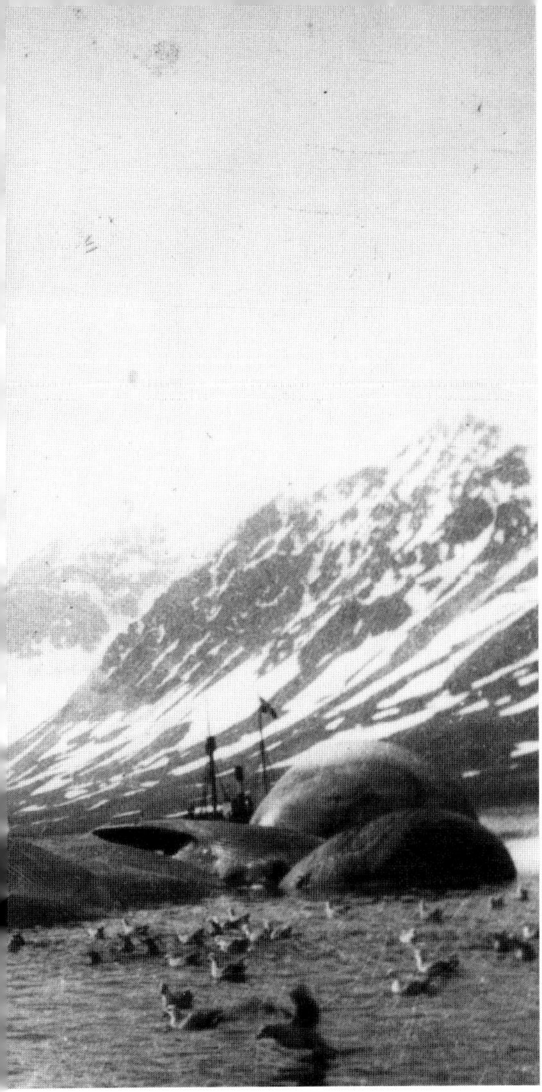

**Spitzbergen 1905** Whaling ship with its catch. The advent of factory whaling at the beginning of the century began the annihilation of many species. The process continues today; Japan and Norway are the main offenders
*Credit: Hulton Getty Picture Collection*

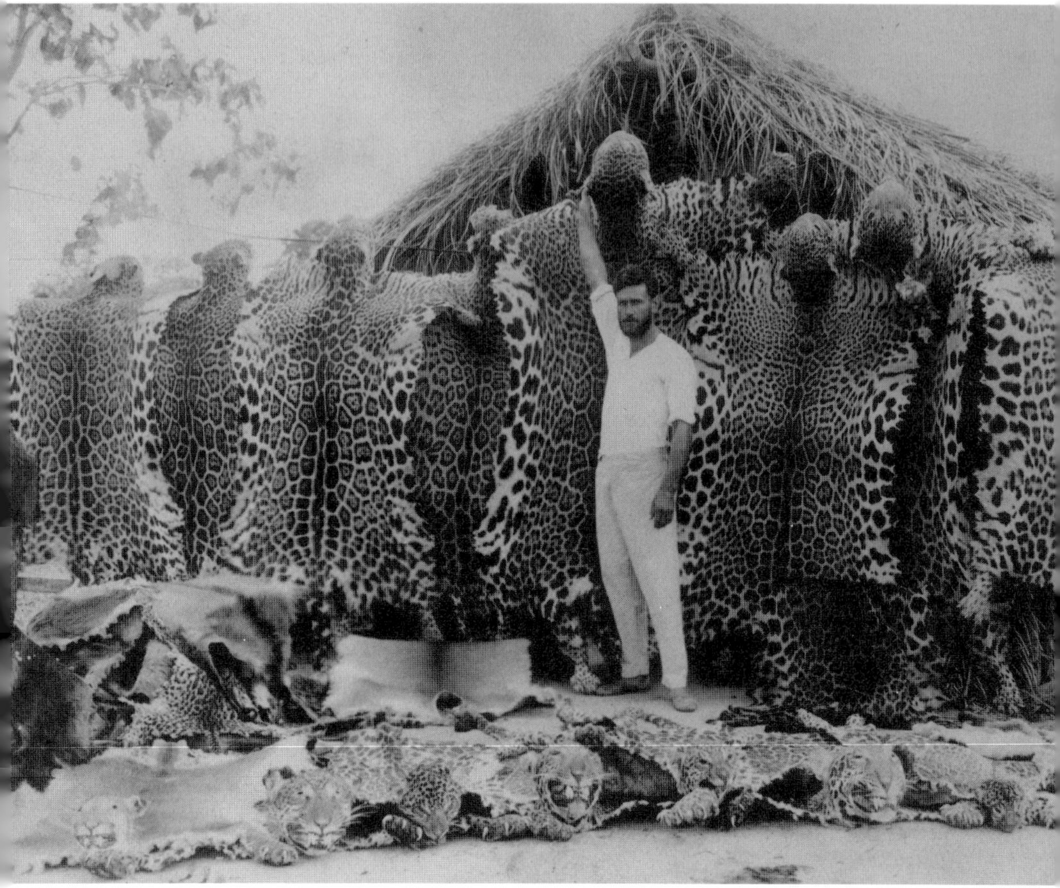

**Bolivia 1932** Jaguar Man and his prey. Before extinction threatened and conservationists stepped in, the 'great white hunters' like Sacha Siemel slaughtered indiscriminately; in the name of sport they began the process of extinction that now threatens so many species
*Credit: Hulton Getty Picture Collection*

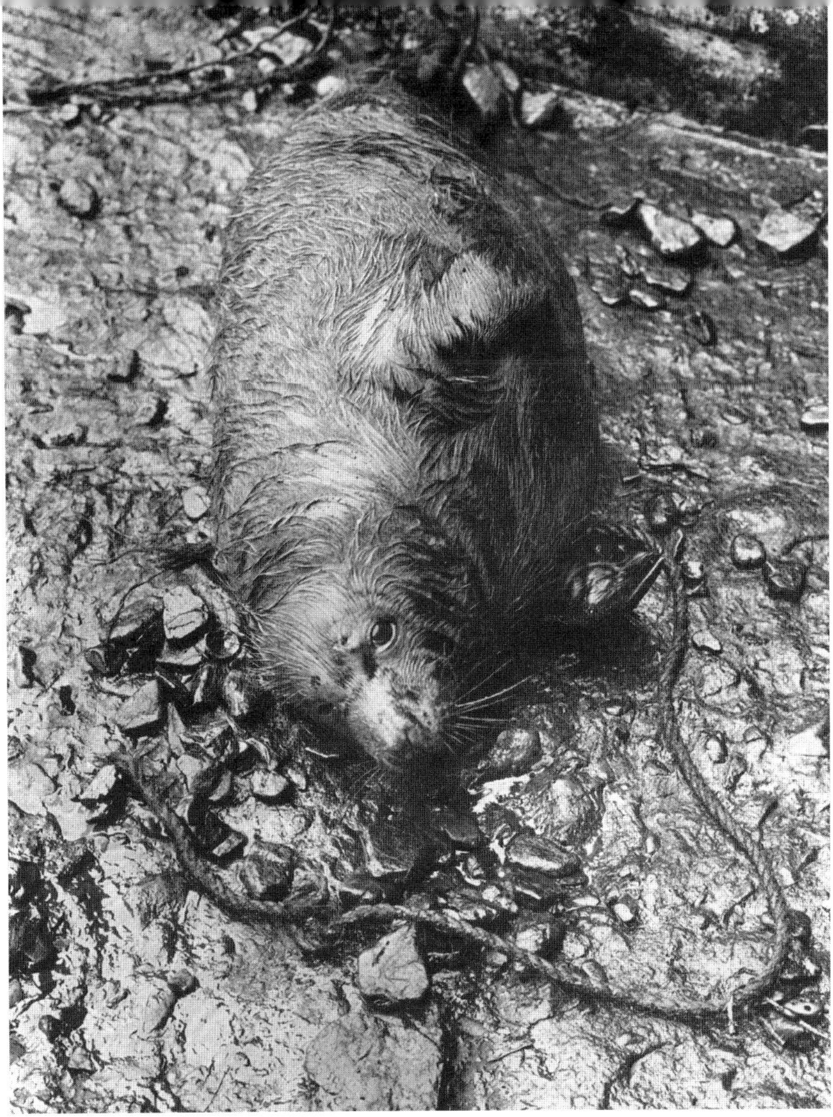

**Welsh coast 1975** An oil-drenched seal beached on the shore
*Credit: Hulton Getty Picture Collection*

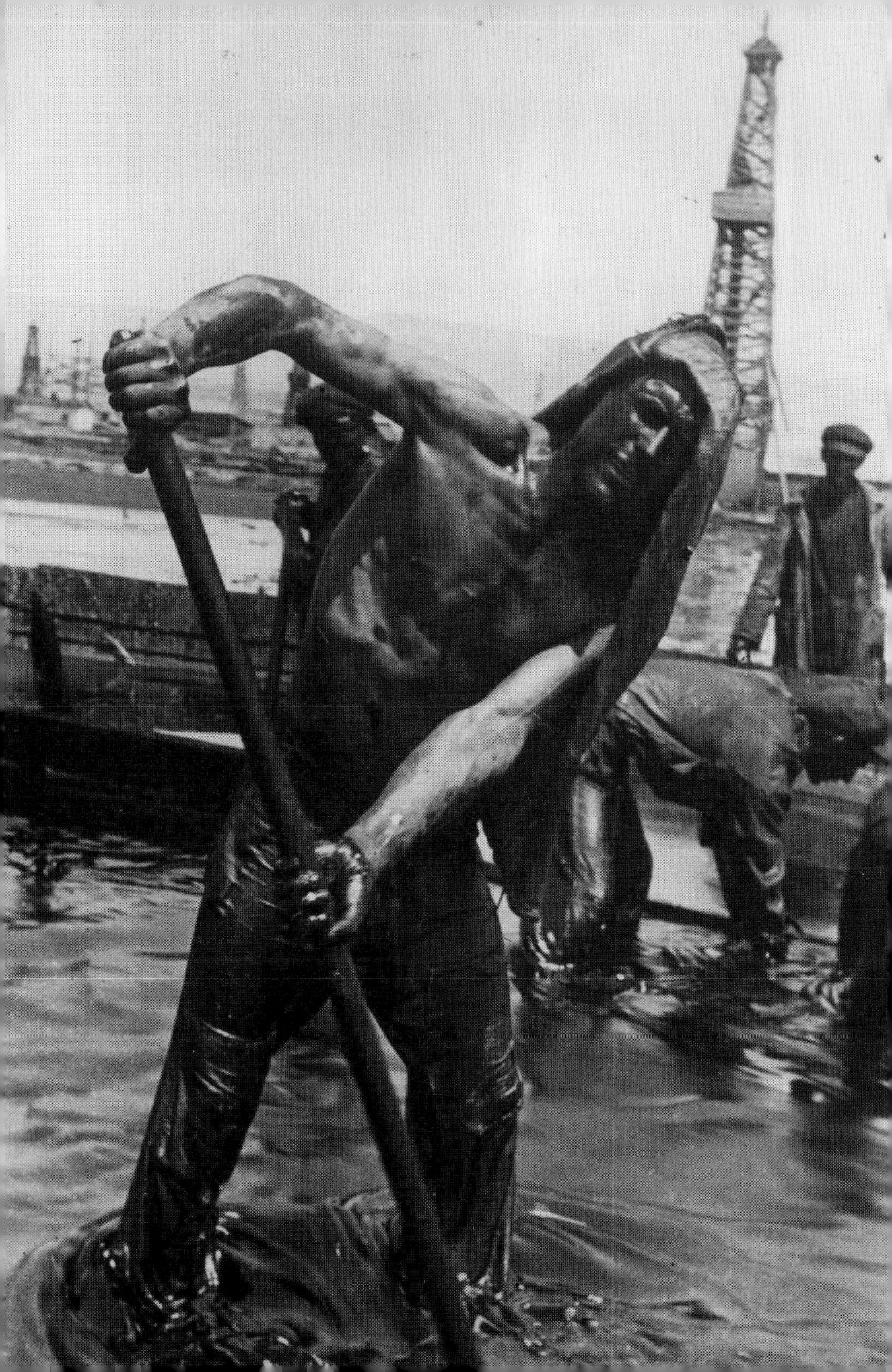

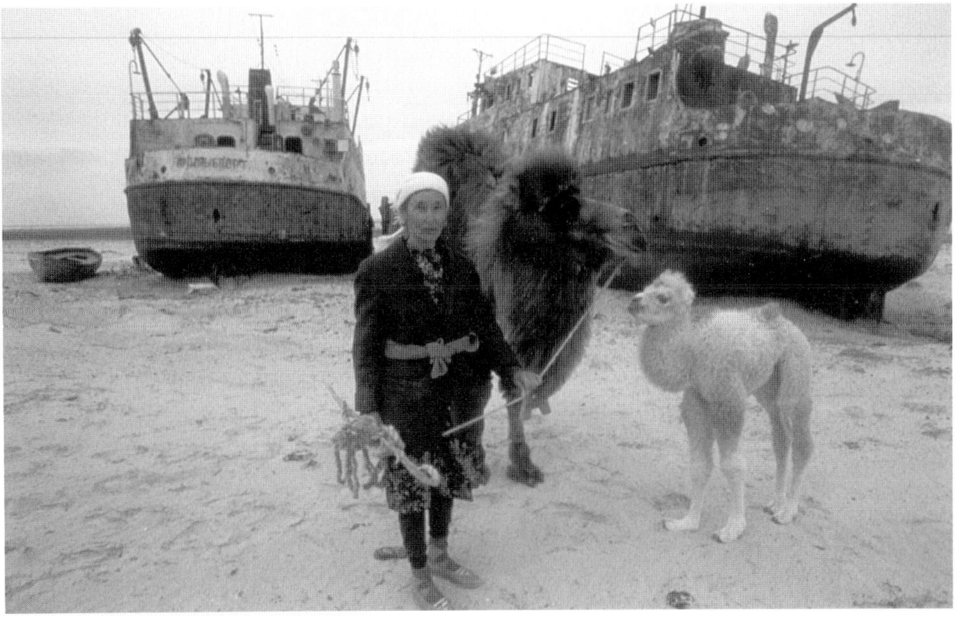

**Aral Sea Central Asia 1990**
The first known death of a sea in the modern era, and the most dramatic man-made environmental disaster this century. Overexploitation for irrigation has shrunk the sea by 50%; fisheries have declined; salts, toxic herbicides and pesticides are blown in dust clouds dust over nearby towns; respiratory disease is endemic, mortality has increased. Experts predict the sea could have disappeared entirely by 2015
*Credit: Gilles Saussier/Liaison Agency*

**Baku Azerbaijan 1933** A model oil worker toils in the vast oil and gas reserves that were crucial to Soviet development and were to become the largest in the world. Baku today promises an oil bonanza to rival that of Kuwait, but now, as then, rampant pollution is ignored and the environment is not a priority
*Credit: Russian State Archive of Film and Photographic Documents Krosnogorsk*

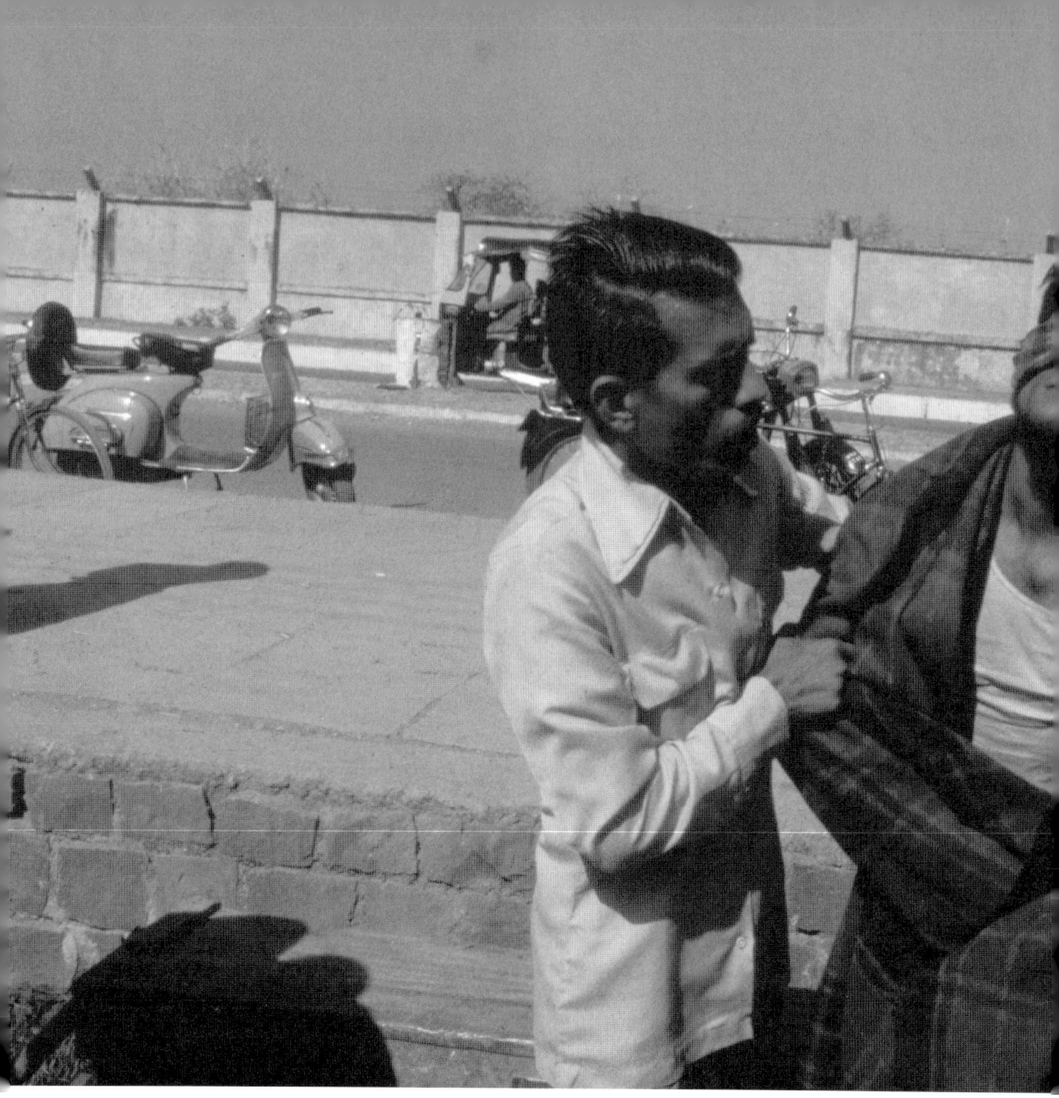

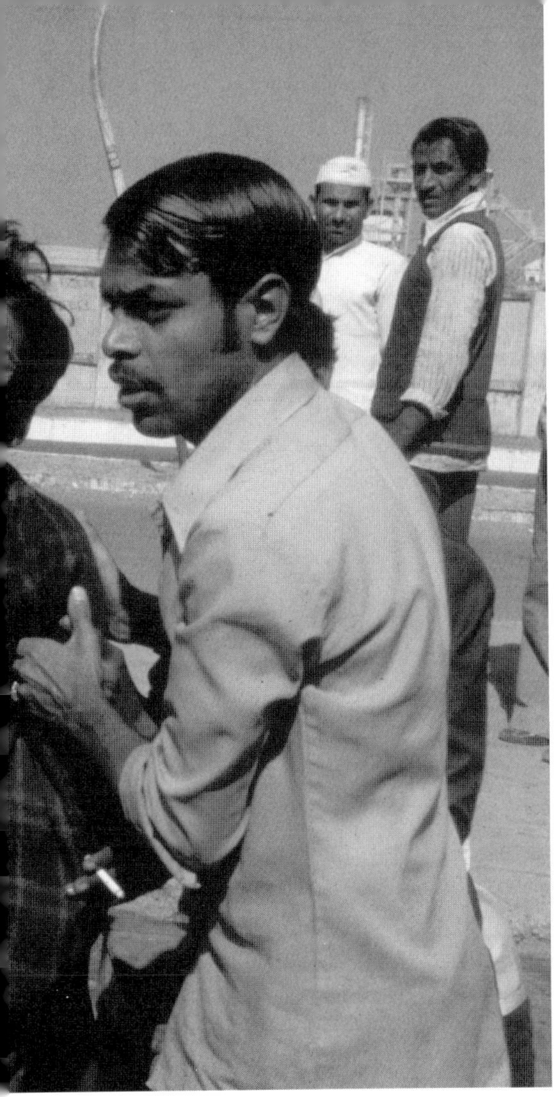

**India 1984** Victims of the Union Carbide disaster in Bhopal. Methyl isocyanate gas seeped into the sprawling slums around the plant. Official estimates say 3,800 died over the next few days; 2,720 were left with permanent damage to eyes and lungs. Unofficial sources place the casualty figure in the hundreds of thousands
*Credit: Pablo Bartholomew/Liaison Agency*

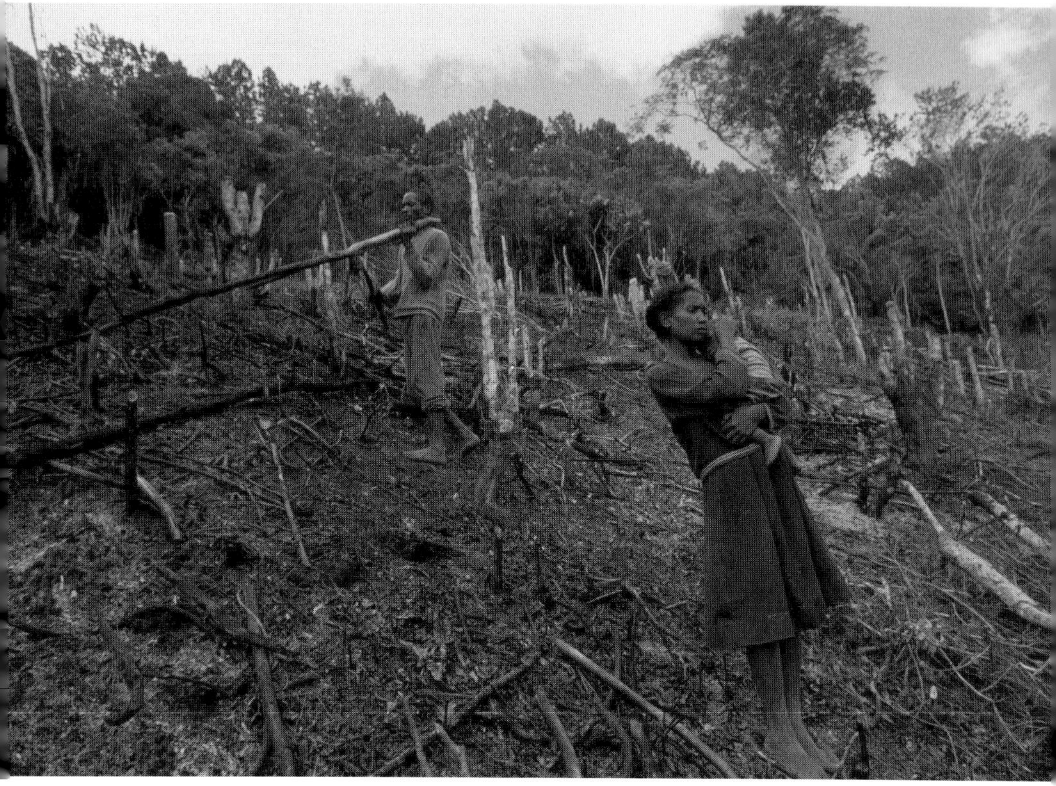

**Carlin Nevada 1993** The devastation wrought by the Newmont Gold Company. Open-cast mining is the cheapest and most destructive form of extraction. But with land at US$2.50 an acre, and no legislation to prevent it, why worrry
*Credit: Karl Gehring/Liaison Agency*

**Madagascar 1992** Madagascar has a unique environment, home to flora and fauna and plants found nowhere else in the world. All is under threat as the forests are brought down through traditional slash-and-burn agriculture. With growing populations, shifting cultivation now accounts for 70% of the deforestation in Africa and 50% in Asia: more than 10 million hectares of tropical forest are lost every year with consequent climate change, soil erosion, watershed degradation and loss of biodiversity
*Credit: Raphael Gaillarde/Liaison Agency*

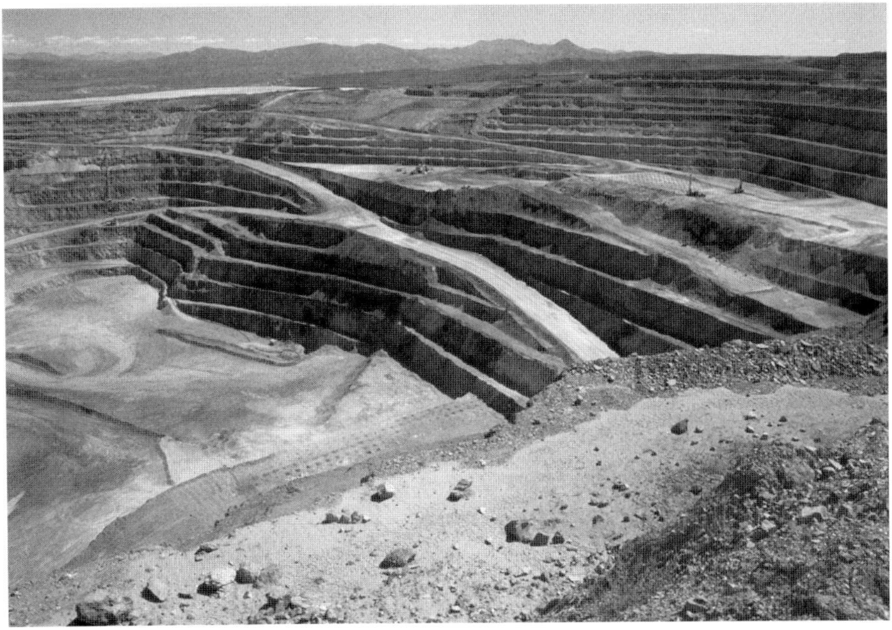

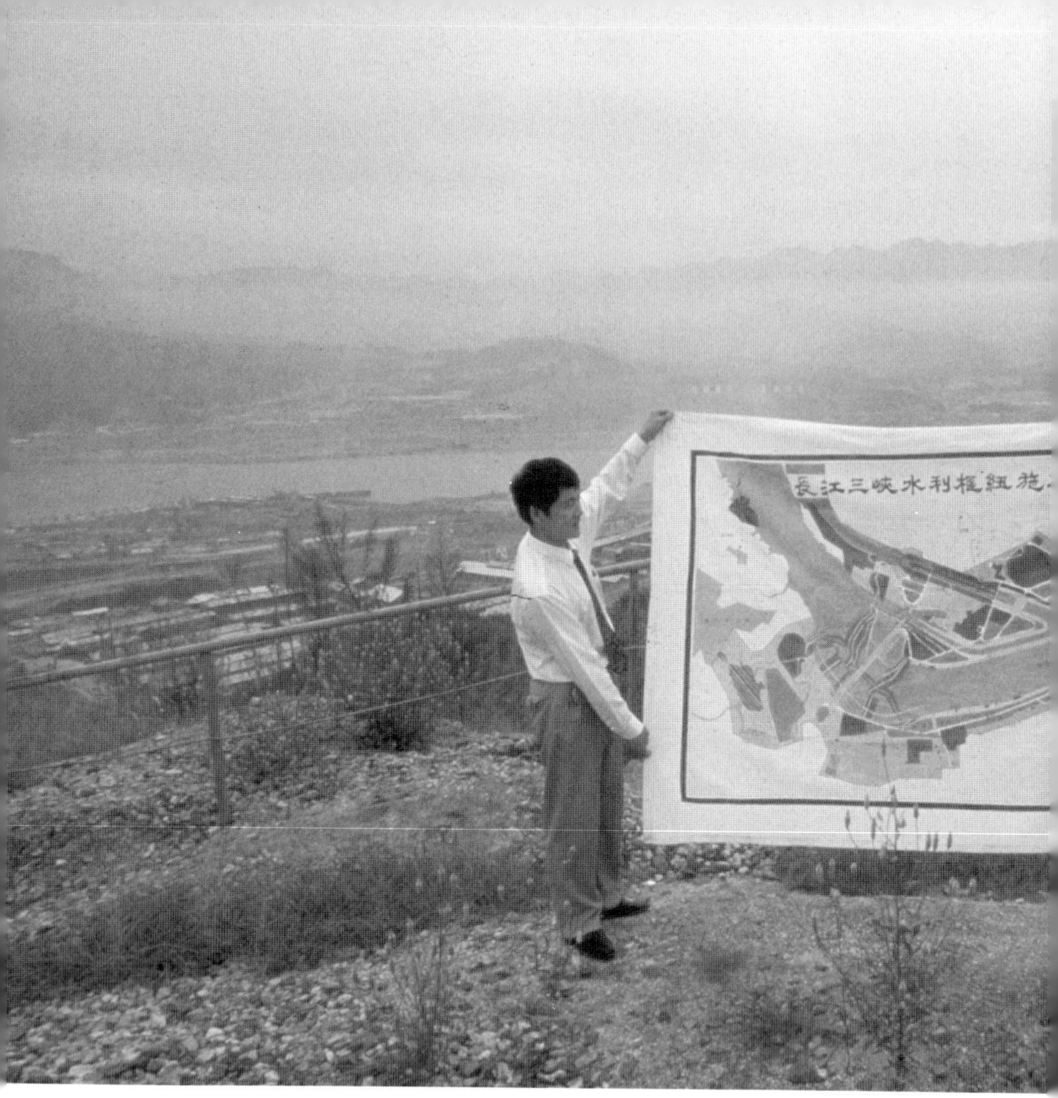
長江三峽水利樞紐施

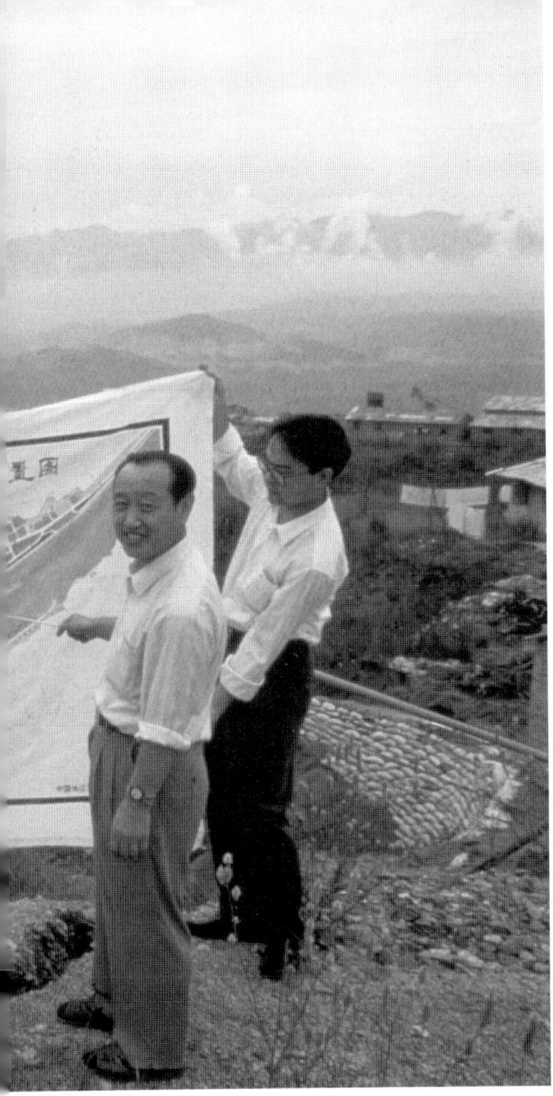

**China 1998** Chinese officials proudly display their map of the Three Gorges Dam on the Yangtze river. When finished, the dam will cover 28,000 hectares of arable land including thousands of square kilometres of unique forest and landscape and will have displaced 1.2 million people. Unusually, the project has harnessed open opposition within China on account of the environmental degradation and corruption and misappropriation of funds for rehousing
*Credit: Chip Hires/Liaiason Agency*

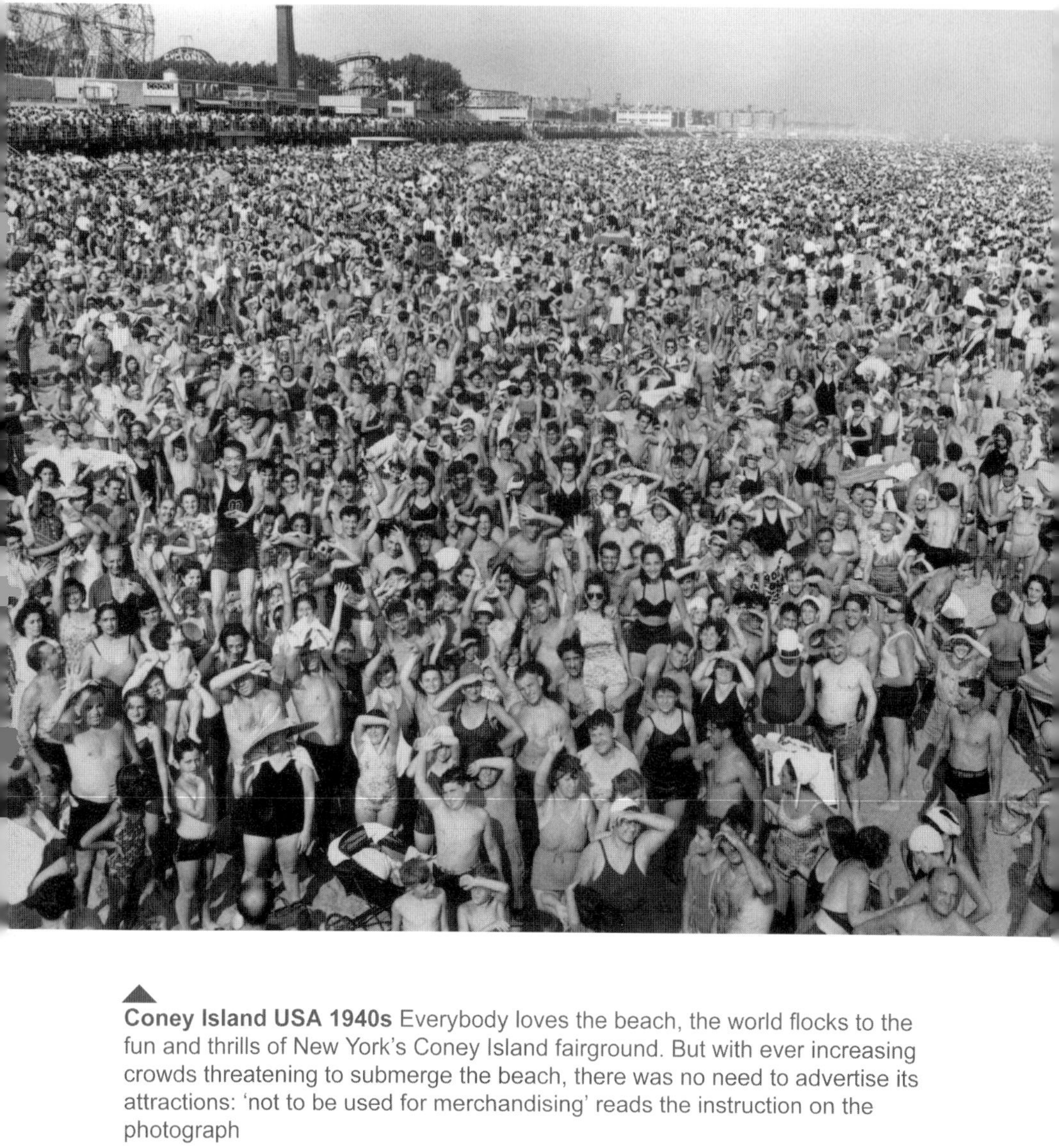

▲

**Coney Island USA 1940s** Everybody loves the beach, the world flocks to the fun and thrills of New York's Coney Island fairground. But with ever increasing crowds threatening to submerge the beach, there was no need to advertise its attractions: 'not to be used for merchandising' reads the instruction on the photograph

*Credit: Weegee (Arthur Fellig)/ICP; Hulton Getty Picture Collection*

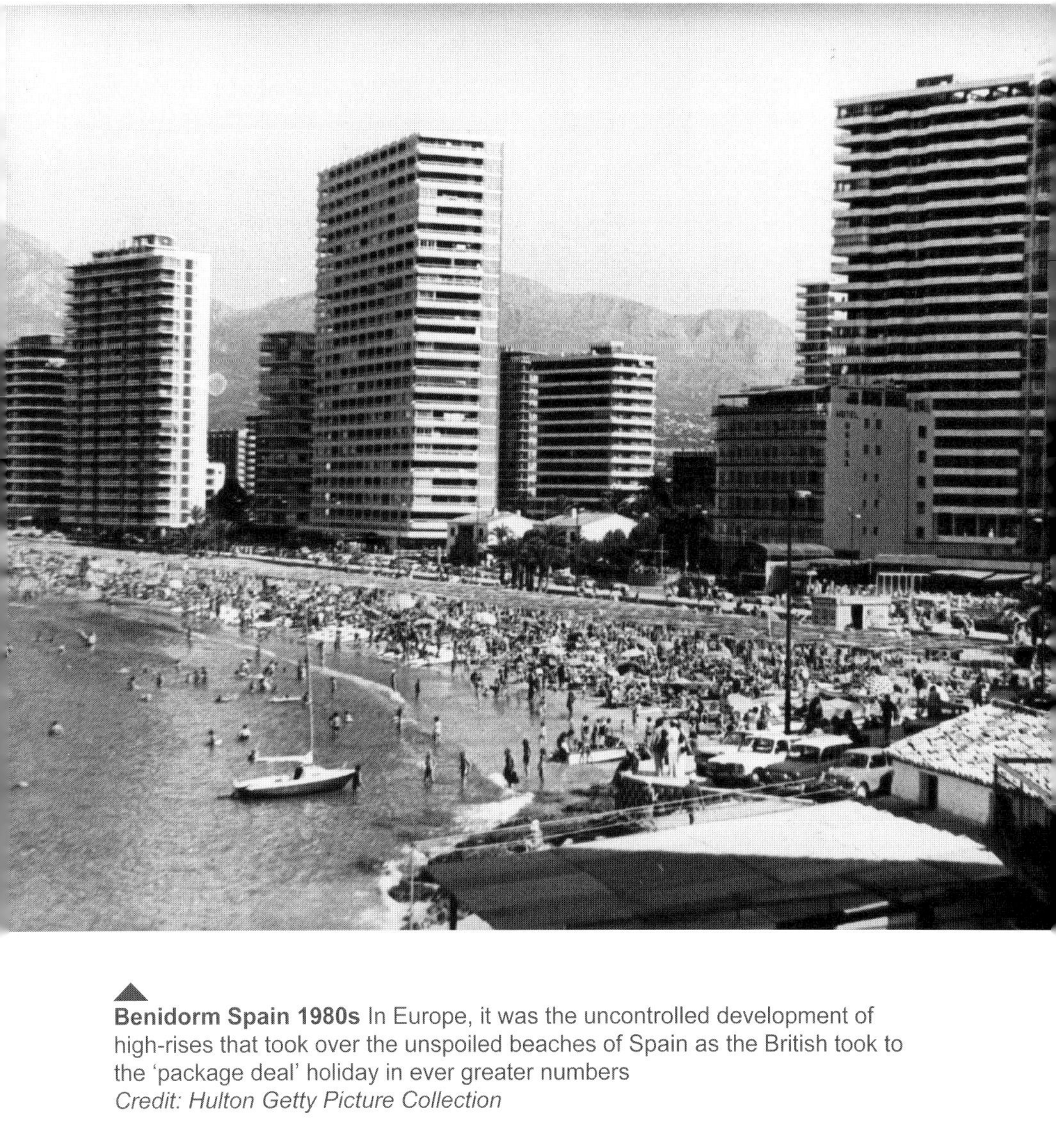

▲
**Benidorm Spain 1980s** In Europe, it was the uncontrolled development of high-rises that took over the unspoiled beaches of Spain as the British took to the 'package deal' holiday in ever greater numbers
*Credit: Hulton Getty Picture Collection*

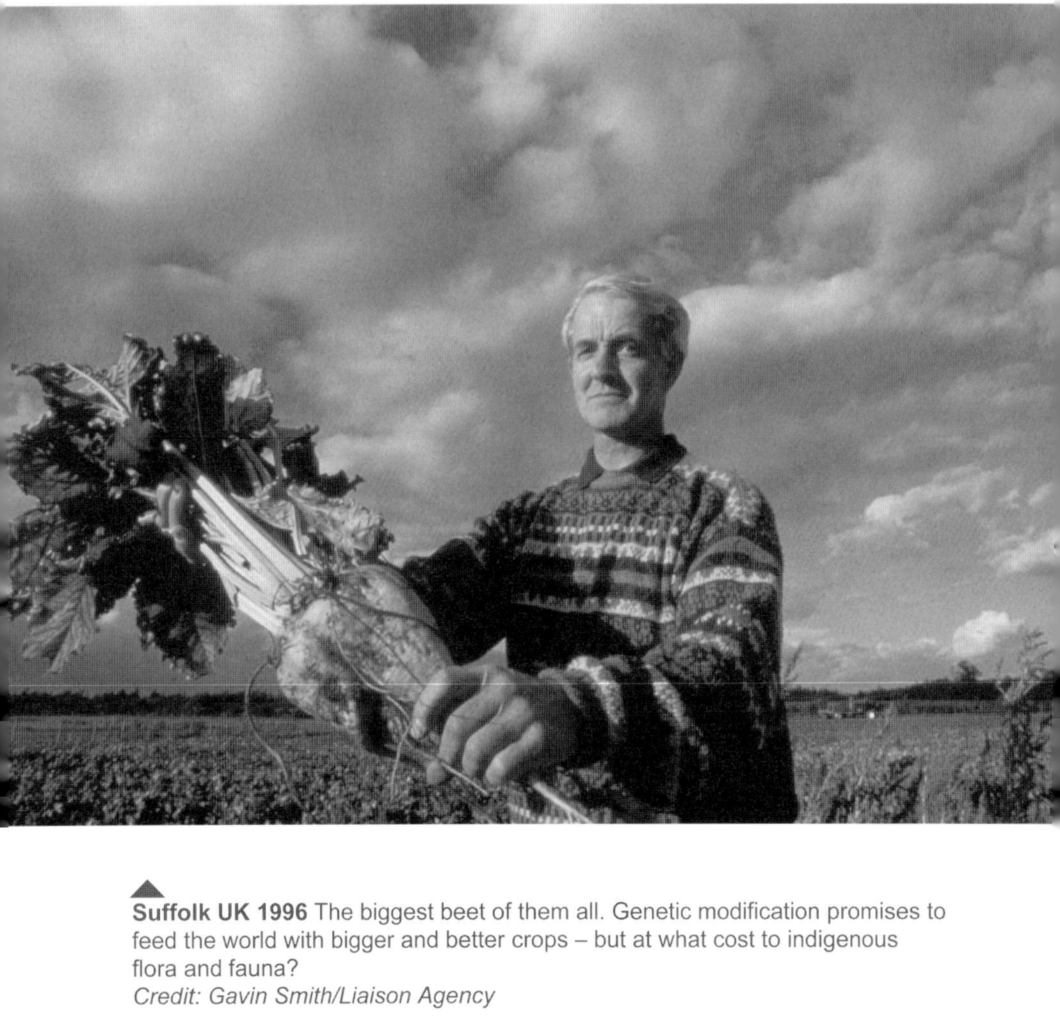

**Suffolk UK 1996** The biggest beet of them all. Genetic modification promises to feed the world with bigger and better crops – but at what cost to indigenous flora and fauna?
*Credit: Gavin Smith/Liaison Agency*

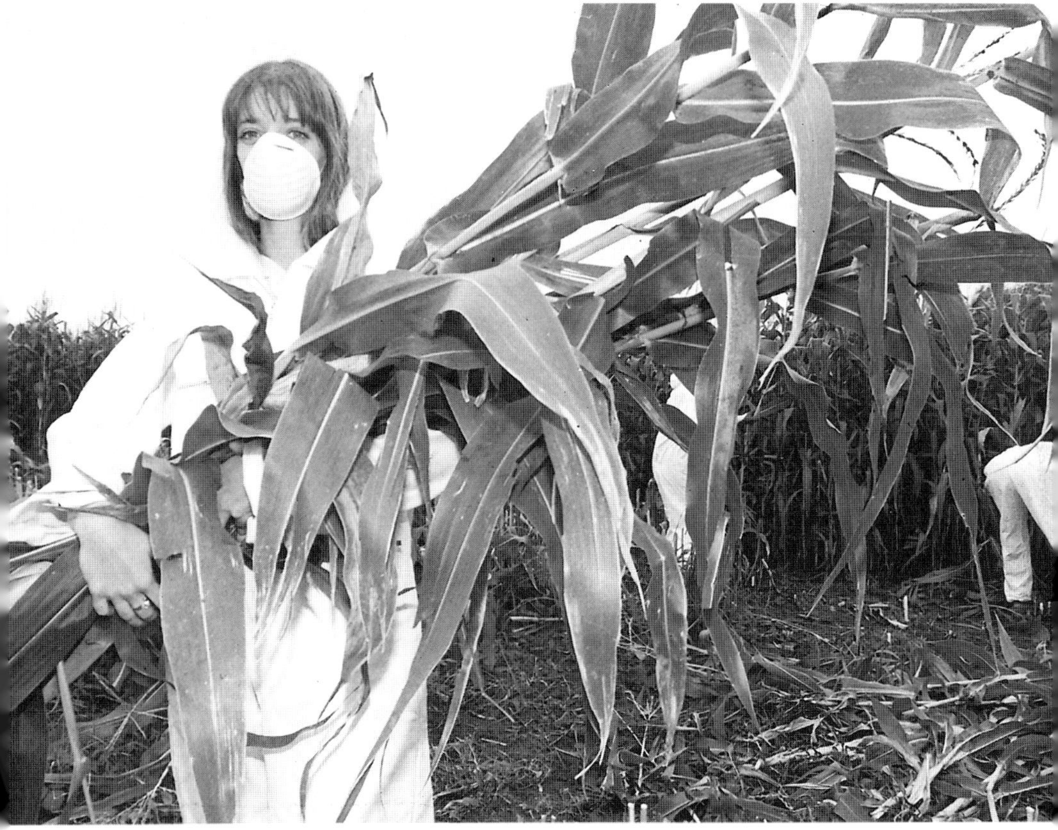

**France 1999** Meanwhile elsewhere in the European Union … Greenpeace protesters destroy genetically modified maize
*Credit: Greenpeace*

# Unfinished business

*As I progressed further with my project, it became obvious that it was really unimportant where I chose to photograph. The particular place simply provided an excuse to produce work... you can only see what you are ready to see – what mirrors your mind at that particular time.*

George Tice

**On the road from Rwanda 1995** Pursued by the victorious Rwanda Patriotic Front, Hutu refugees stream out of Rwanda after their genocidal attack on their Tutsi neighbours that left 800,000 dead
*Credit: Kevin Weaver/Hulton Getty Picture Collection*

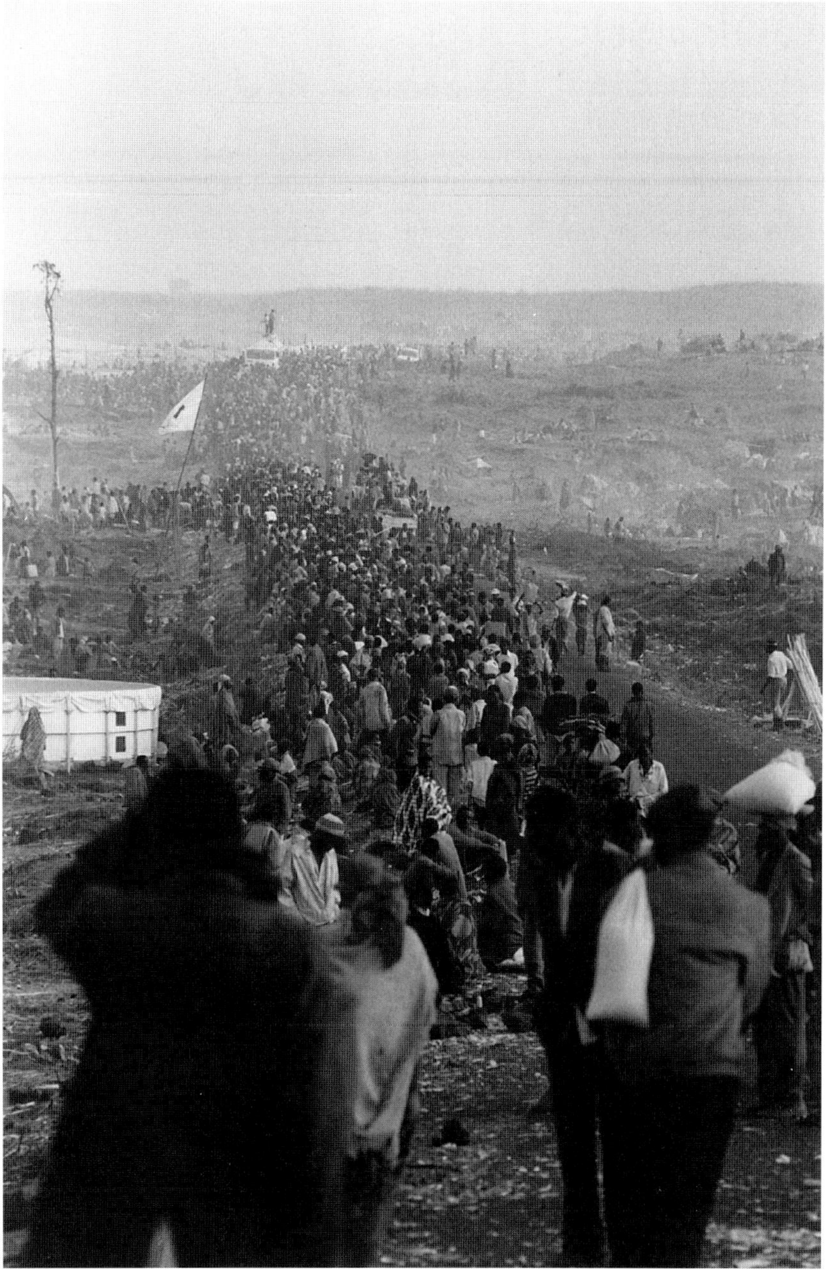

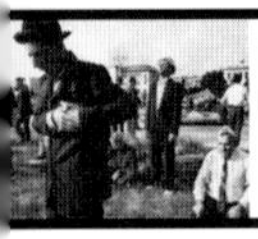

# Unfinished business

*Alex de Waal*

'The dead: are they not people too?' James Appe, refugee from Uganda, asks this question in his story 'Flight'. His use of the present tense reminds us that for those who have lived through war, massacre and flight, the dead remain present. And the unmourned dead are commonly a troubling presence.

Many African traditional religions have lavish funerary ceremonies. These refract an important truth, valid for all humankind: our relationship with a person continues even after that person has died. Mourning, properly conducted, can help conclude that relationship, resolving the grievances, tensions and anxieties that built up when the person was still living. But even long after a lavish funeral, after the construction of an appropriate permanent monument, ancestors still demand respect – or their spirits will disrupt the affairs of the living.

Ugandan refugees, fleeing the massacres of the Obote regime in the early 1980s, described the unmourned dead as though they were still alive, still exerting their demands on their living relatives. Many were suffering from profound psychological disturbances – post-traumatic stress disorder or 'survivor's syndrome' according to the pyschological literature. Time did not heal these wounds. More important was finding the bodies of the dead, or at the least the places where they had died, and paying their final respects. But the anxiety, the fear, would linger. The trauma was as if it had happened yesterday. For them, the notion of 'justice' was a means of reconciling with the dead.

In Ethiopia, during the 30-year war that ended in 1991, tens of thousands of families saw their sons taken away to the warfront in Eritrea, never to see them again. Boys and young men were simply rounded up at schools, markets or football matches, and marched to the front. Some came back whole; some lacking limbs; many were cut down by the guns of the Eritrean guerrillas, or shot by their own officers who trained their sights on any who tried to retreat. After the war was over and Eritrea achieved its independence, a few mothers sought out the places where their children had died. By that time, only anonymous bones bleached by the sun, lying scattered over the trenches, could be found.

For the victorious Eritreans it was easier to mourn. The Eritrean People's Liberation Front kept scrupulous records of their 'martyrs', their names, dates of enrolment and date and time of death. Each bereaved family was presented with a plaque bearing this information; each village and battlefield has a small memorial surrounded by a grove of trees. The new nation of three million people counted more than 60,000 dead in its 30-year struggle, and every year on 20 June it commemorates those who died.

At the moment of victory, the new government of Eritrea was instantly friendly with the new government in Ethiopia, headed by its Tigrayan allies who had themselves fought a long and bitter guerrilla war, and who also sought to commemorate their own dead and to expose the victims of the now vanquished communist regime. The true record of the Red Terror, when tens of thousands were murdered in the streets of the capital in 1977-8, was exposed. Some victims, including the Emperor Haile Selassie, were disinterred, reburied, and their families could finally grieve for them.

But for the defeated Ethiopian soldiers there was no such recognition, let alone respect. The million or more soldiers who never came home were simply forgotten by the state. Who can say whether this incomplete reconciliation with the past has contributed to the current war between Ethiopia and Eritrea?

In Rwanda, the unmourned dead are active players in the region's crisis. The million Tutsis dead from the genocide loom larger than when they were still alive. When the genocidal killers organised the flight of over a million people to neighbouring countries they were pursued by the ghosts of those they had murdered. Exiled Hutu communities in neighbouring Zaire and Tanzania were disturbed every night by loud, passionate and sometimes violent outpourings of anxiety and fear – those who had witnessed or participated in the genocide said they were disturbed by the spirits of murdered Tutsis, travelling by night like supernatural ballistic missiles, coming to demand of them, 'Why?' Killer's syndrome is a mirror of survivor's syndrome: both are disturbed by what has been done.

The presence of the dead is a metaphor for the persistence of war and mass killing in Africa, as elsewhere in the world. In many ways – material, political, military – war helps beget new war. Today's conflicts are a legacy of the previous generation of wars. The ostensible reasons may have changed, especially with the demise of apartheid and the end of the Cold War, but the fact of armed conflict is stubbornly enduring. The presence of the unmourned dead is also more than a metaphor: they are a day-by-day reality in the lives of tens of millions and, until they rest content, the continent cannot know peace. ❑

***Alex de Waal*** *is the head of Justice Africa. He has been a writer on war, famine and human rights in Africa for 15 years. He lives in London*

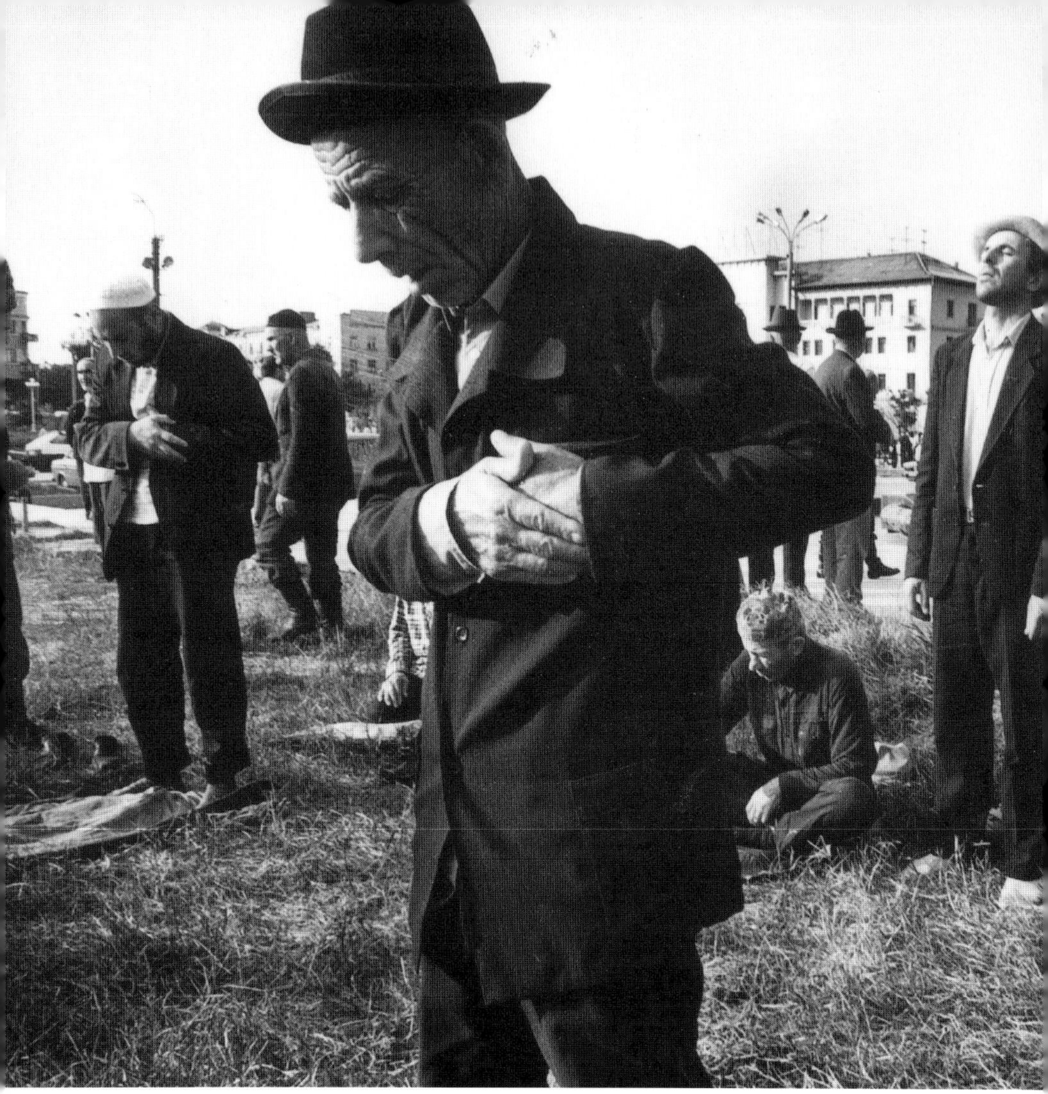

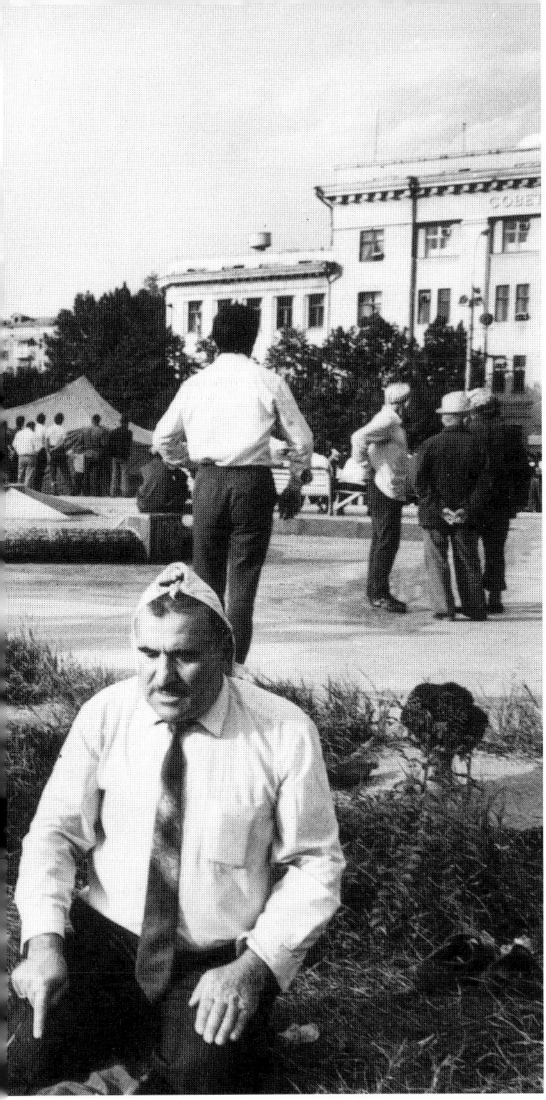

**Chechnya 1991** Chechens give thanks in Freedom Square, Grozny, at the moment of their self-declared independence from the USSR. Three years later, the city was razed by Russian troops; in 1999 they invaded again
*Credit: V Siomin/Endeavour Group UK*

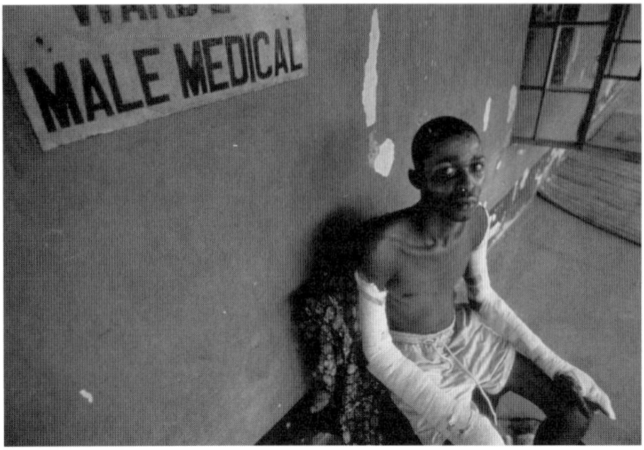


**Sierra Leone 1995** Victim of torture in one of Africa's most brutal civil wars
*Credit: Roger Job/Liaison Agency*

**Eritrea 1988** A soldier of the Eritrean People's Liberation Front, fighting for independence from Ethiopia, walks through a tank graveyard. Eritrea is independent, but again at war with Ethiopia
*Credit: Anthony Suan/Liaison Agency*

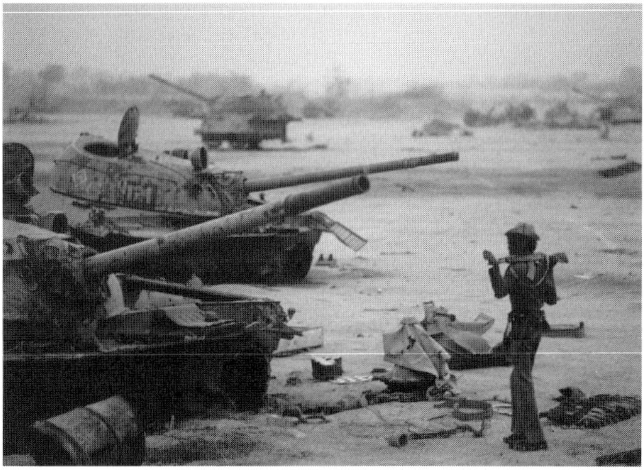

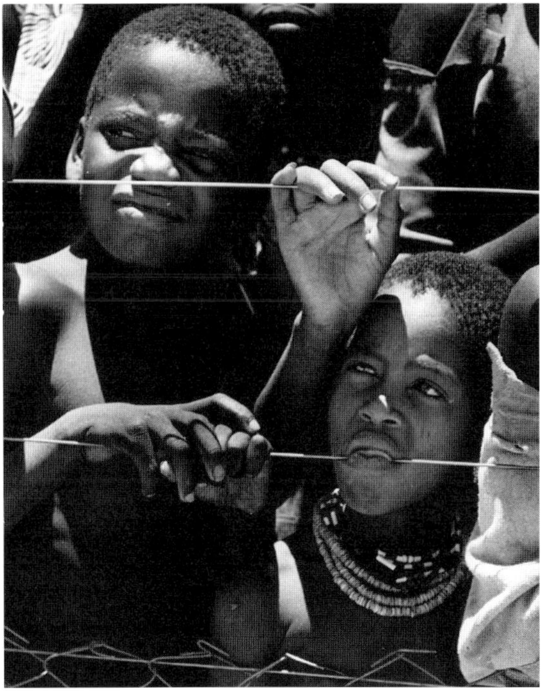

**Angola 1976** Refugee camp in Ovambo. Three decades of civil war has produced over 300,000 refugees and a crop of up to 20 million landmines strewn across the country. Peace treaties and truces are fragile and short-lived *Credit: Hulton Getty Picture Collection*

**Southern Sudan 1991** Children caught in the civil war beween the largely black Christian and Animist south and the Arab Muslim north that has plagued the country intermittently since independence in 1956 and is still short of a solution *Credit: Hulton Getty Picture Collection*

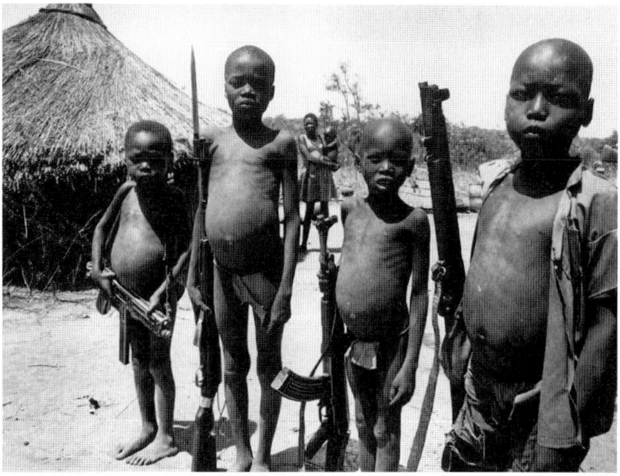

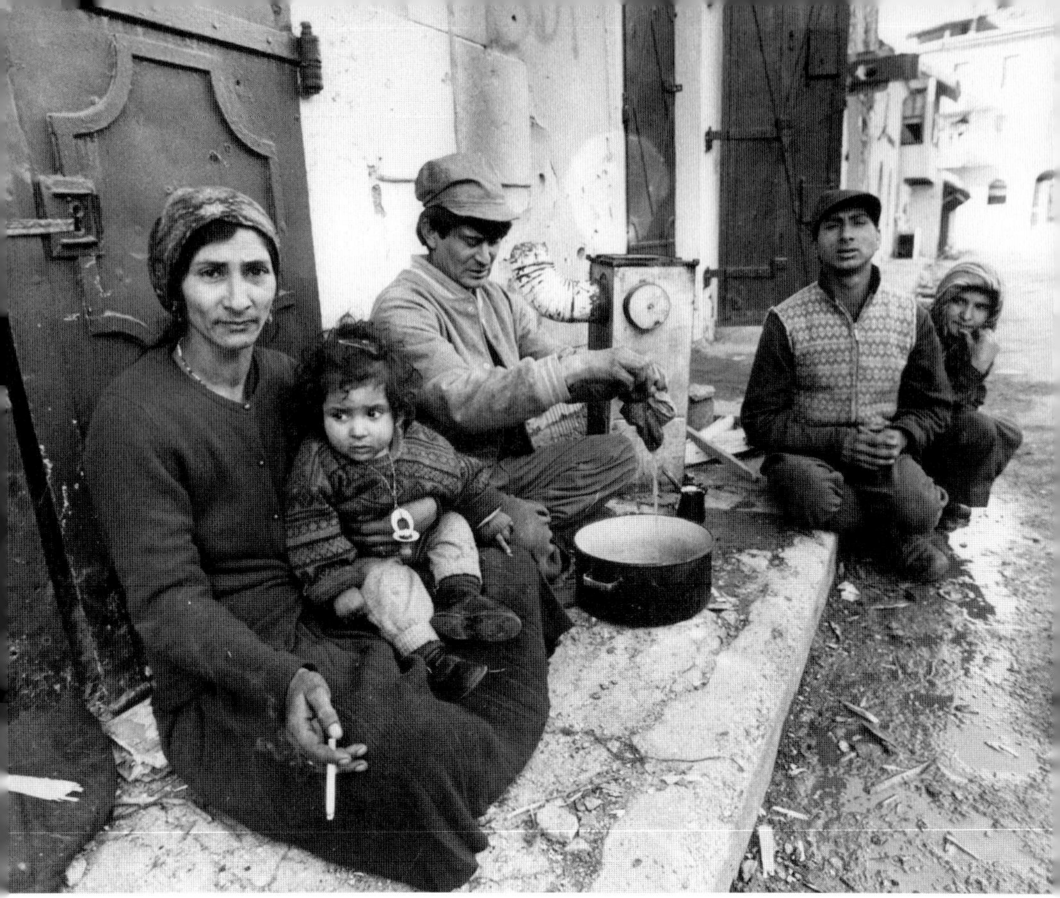

**East Timor 1979** Indonesia occupied East Timor in the wake of the Portuguese departure in 1974. Resistance was immediate and in addition to attacks by the Indonesian Army, there were attempts to starve the population into submission
*Credit: Andrew Wilson/Observer/Hulton Getty Picture Collection*

**Mostar Bosnia 1994** Caught in the crossfire of the disputed city of Mostar, Romanies sit out the war in Yugoslavia. As in Kosovo, they have largely been the forgotten 'third party' in the post-Soviet Balkan wars
*Credit: Kevin Weaver/Hulton Getty Picture Collection*

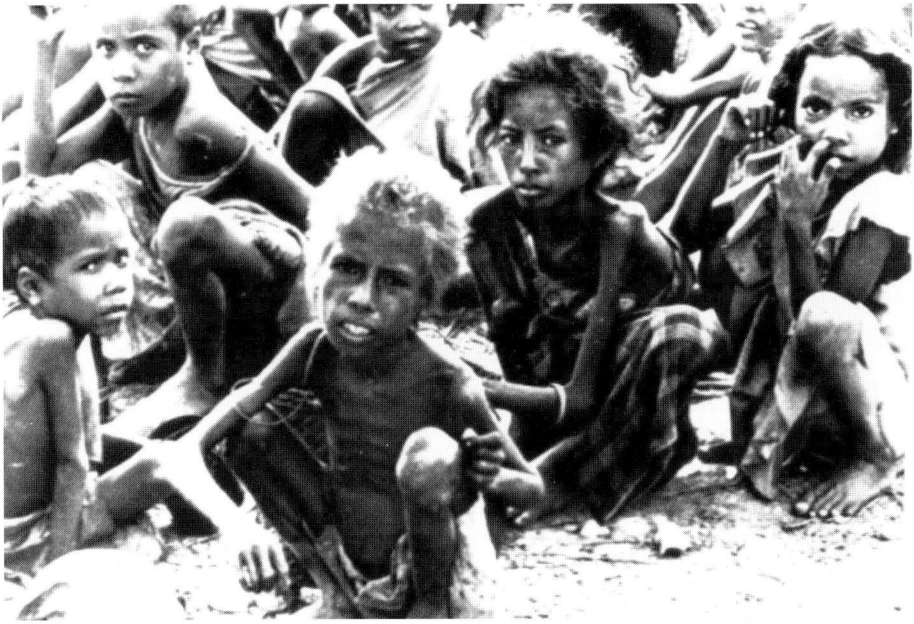

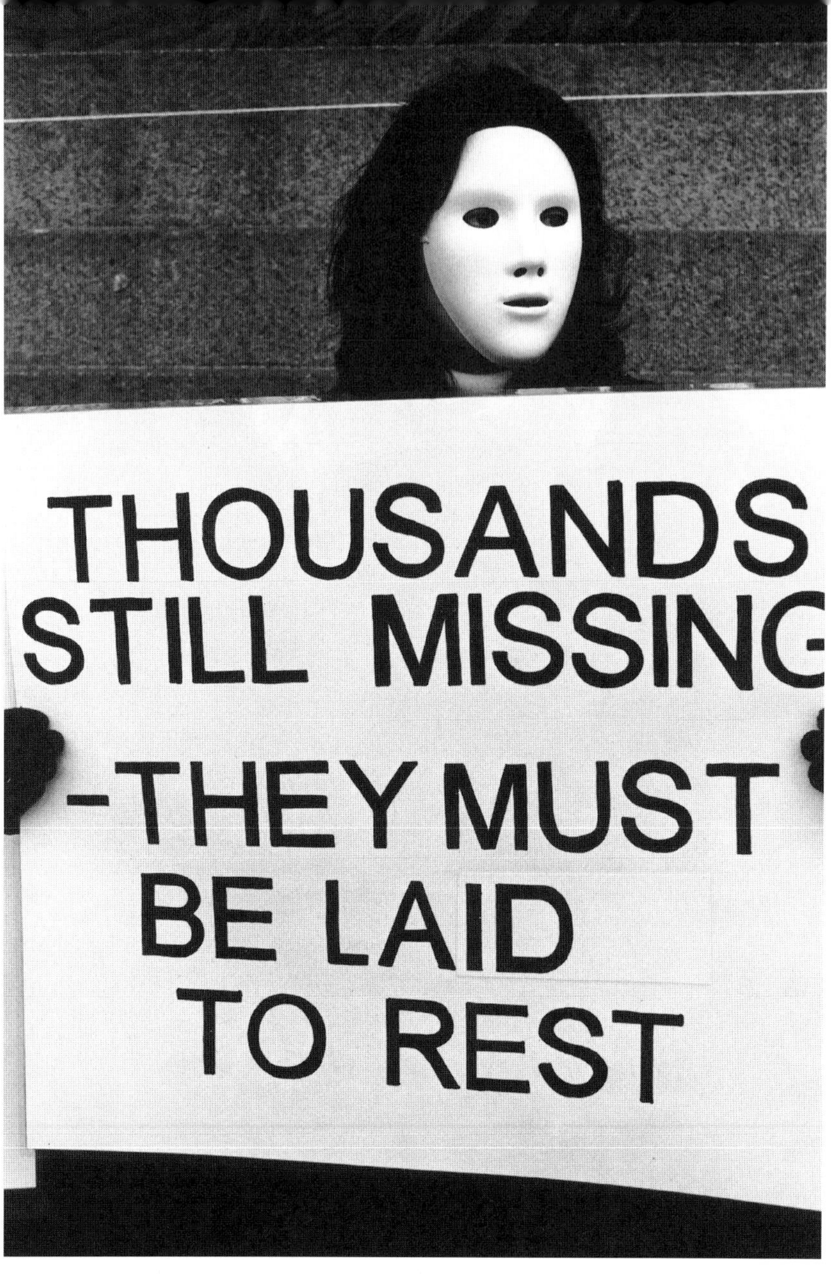


**London 1999** Thousands of Chileans commemorate the thousands of 'disappeared' as they demonstrate in London for the extradition of General Augusto Pinochet to stand trial in Spain for crimes against humanity
*Credit: Carlos Reyes/Andes Press Agency*

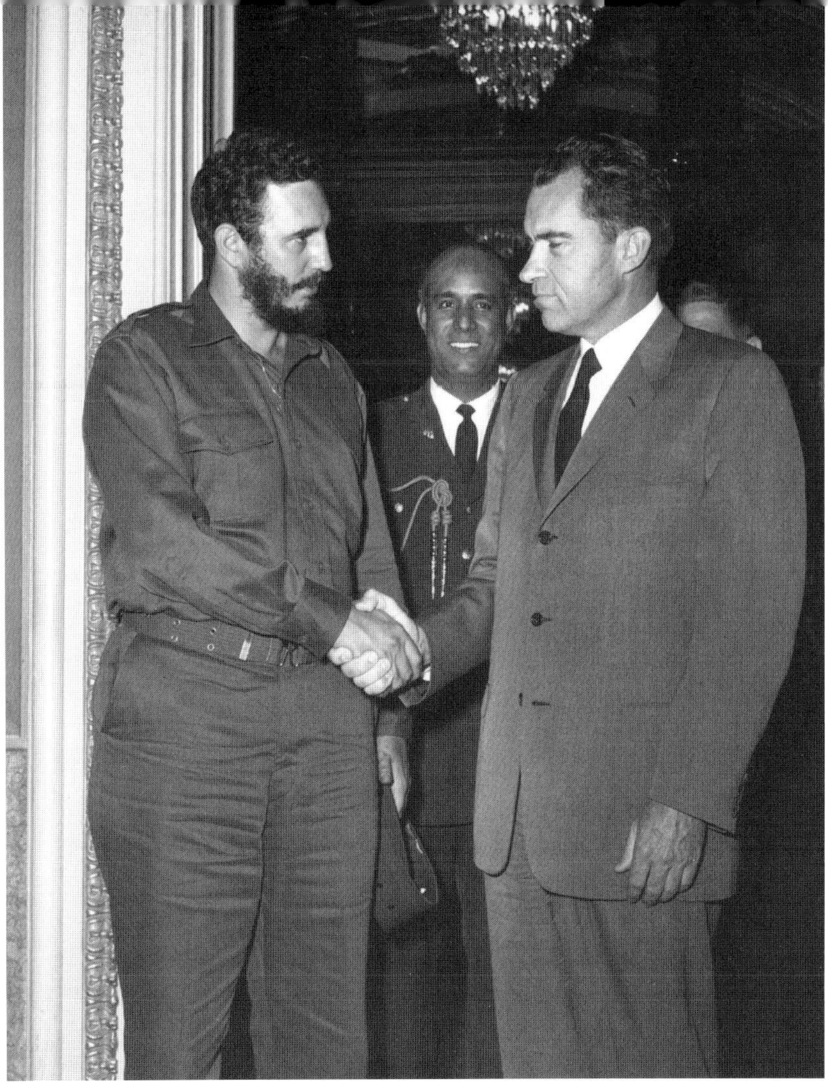

**Cuba 1959** The détente that might have been. Fidel Castro and Richard Nixon two months after the revolution
*Credit: Hulton Getty Picture Collection*

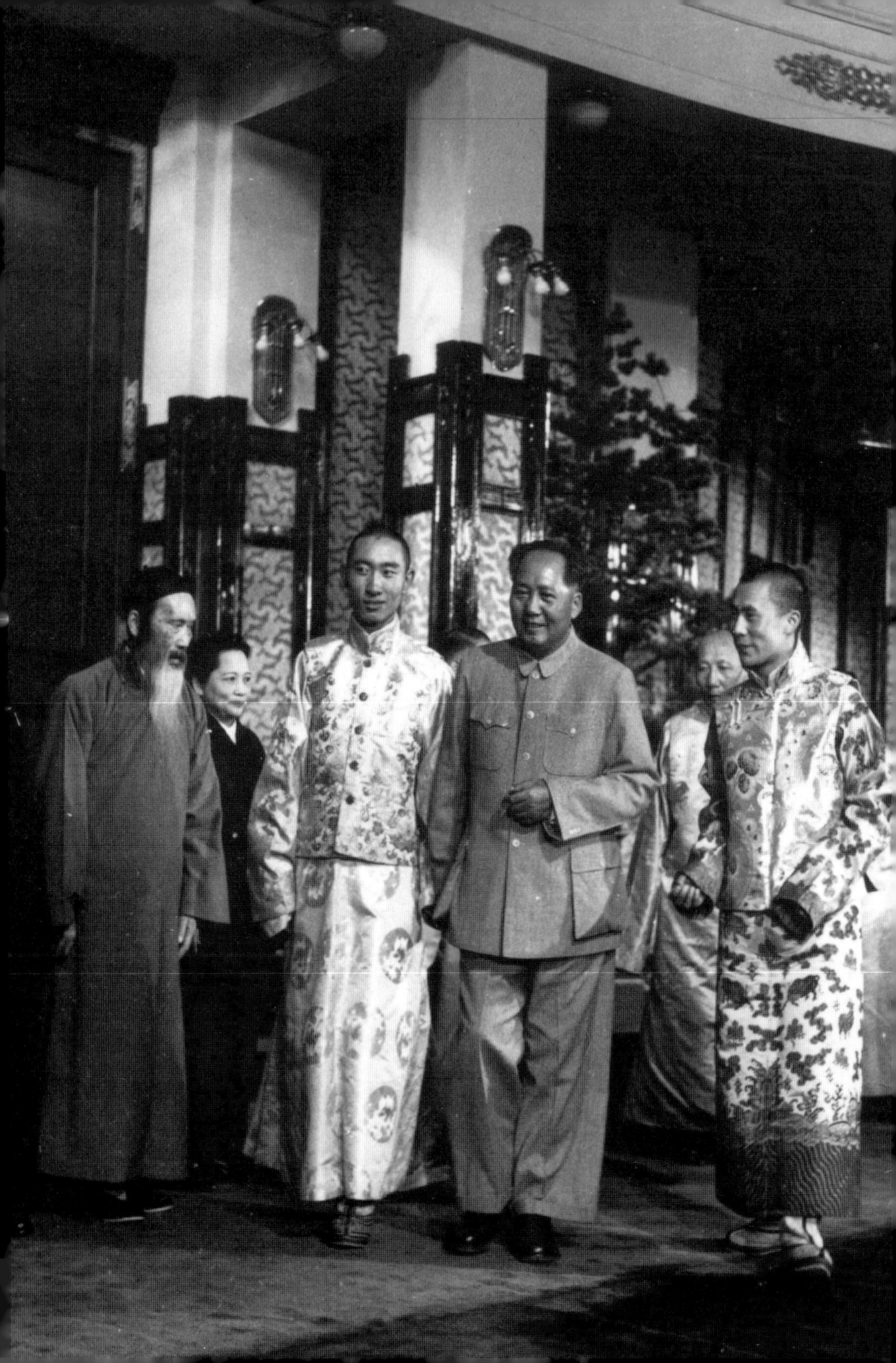

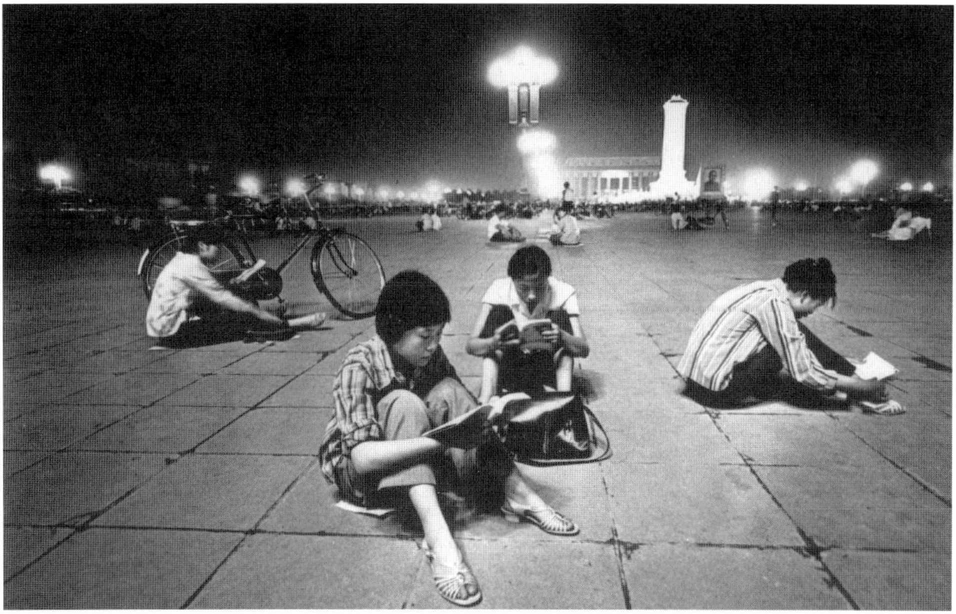

**Tiananmen Square China 1989** Women students study by the lights of the square as their elders did by the light of glow-worms. Soon after, the square showed a different face as tanks moved in to crush the students and the democracy movement
*Credit: Contact Press Images/Colorific*

**Beijing 1954** Walking the Chinese way: Mao, the Dalai Lama (right) and the Panchen Lama three years after Tibet capitulated to the 'liberating' Chinese Army
*Credit: Xinhua News Agency Beijing/Endeavour Group UK*

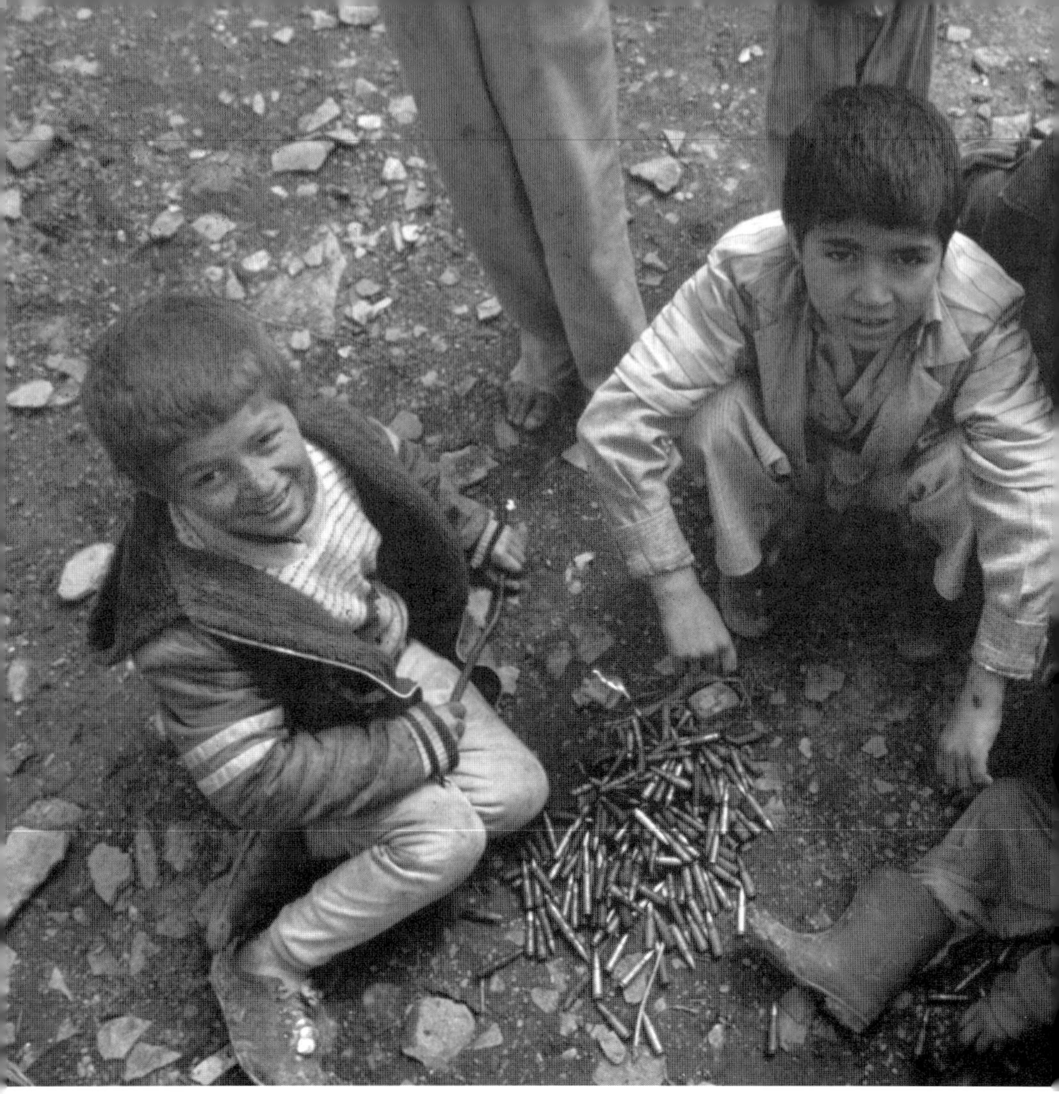

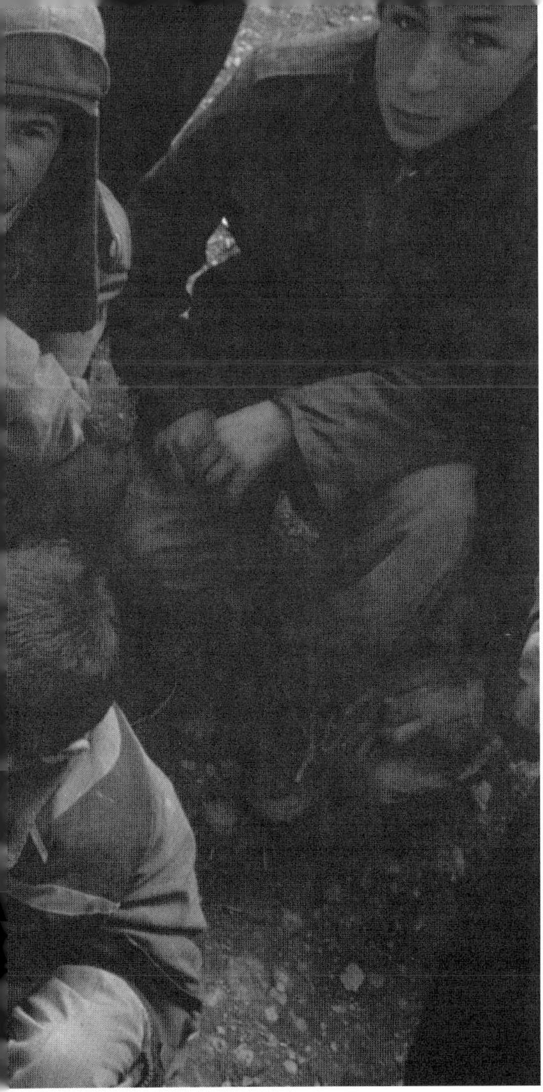

**Turkey 1990s** Spoils of war. Kurdish refugee children in a camp in SE Anatolia. Iraqi Kurds fled to Turkey to escape Saddam Hussein's post-Gulf War invasion of their territory. Not that there was anything new in this: Kurds in Turkey and Iran, as well as in Iraq are harried by their respective governments. They are the largest nation without an independent state
*Credit: Scott Peterson/Liaison Agency*

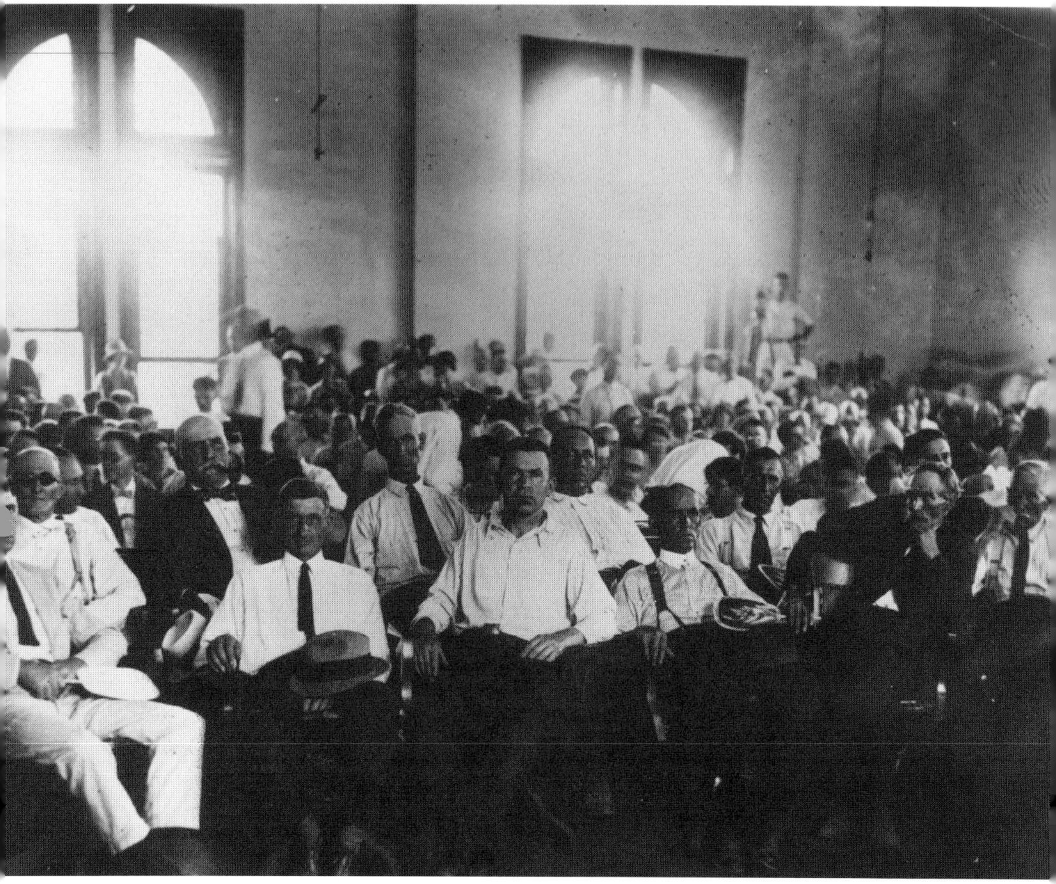

**USA 1925** Men and monkeys. The jury at the trial of professor John Scopes – known as the 'monkey trial' – in Dayton, Tennessee. He was indicted for teaching evolution. In 1999 the teaching of evolution was once again banned, this time in Kansas
*Credit: Hulton Getty Picture Collection*

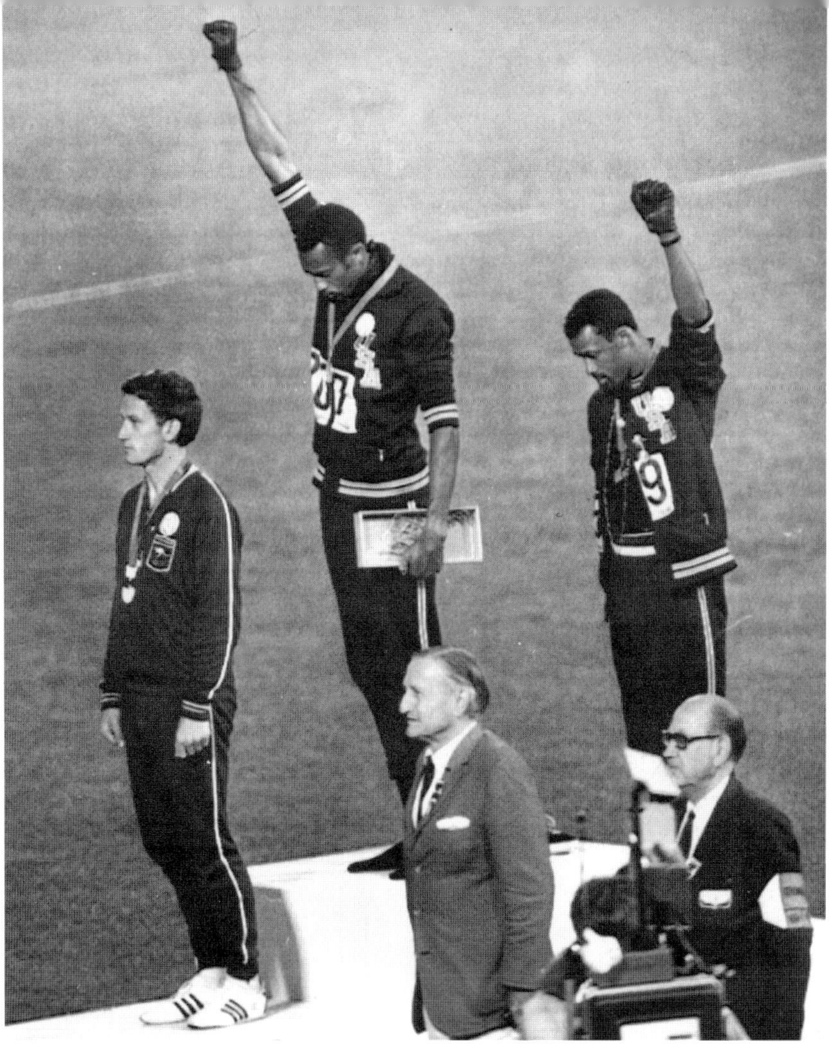

**Mexico City Olympics 1968** Gold medallist Tommy Smith (centre) and bronze winner John Carlos (right) give the Black Power salute as the US national anthem is played in honour of their victory. Their protest against the treatment of blacks in the USA ensured these athletes never ran for their country again
*Credit: Associated Press*

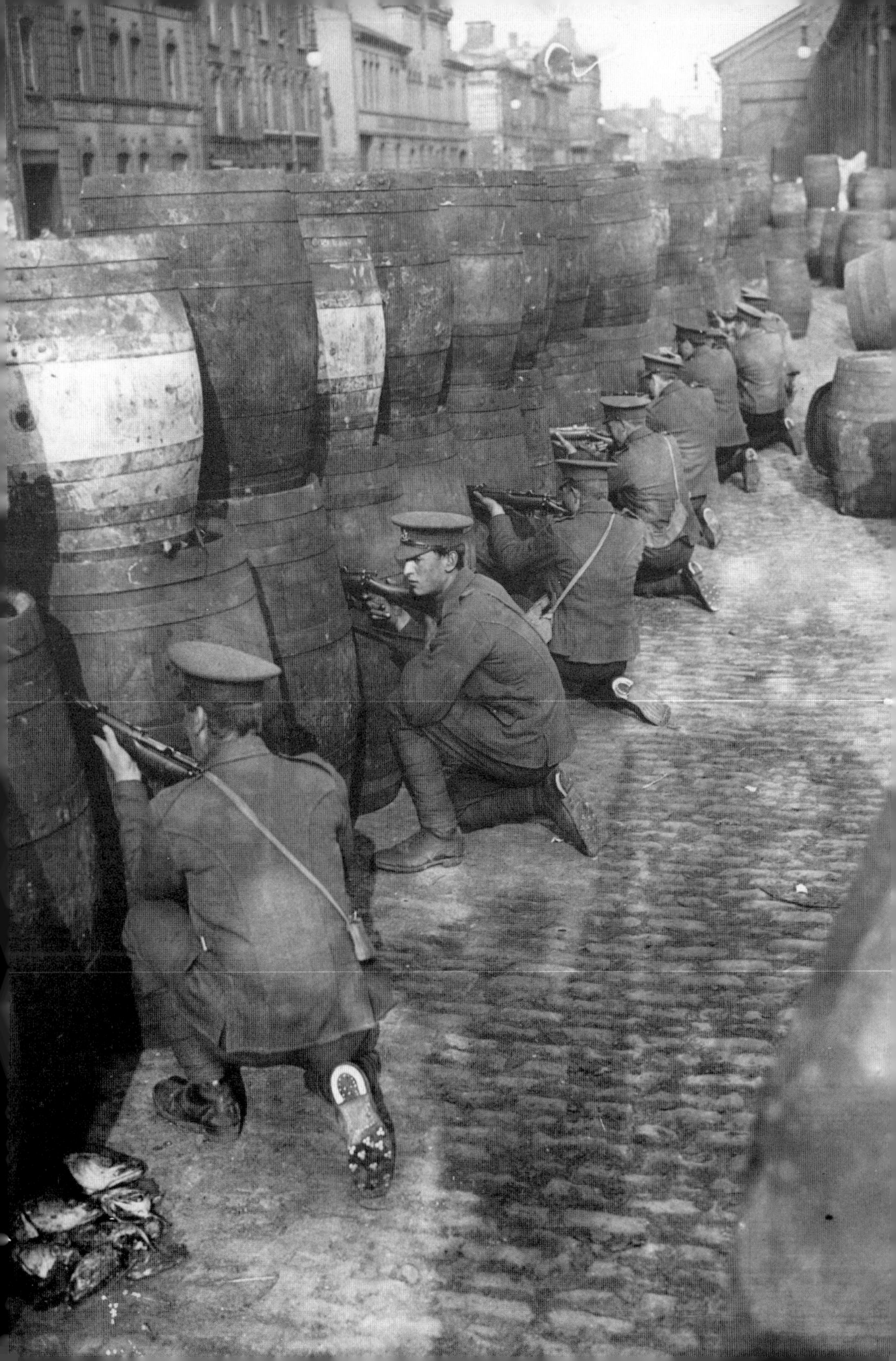

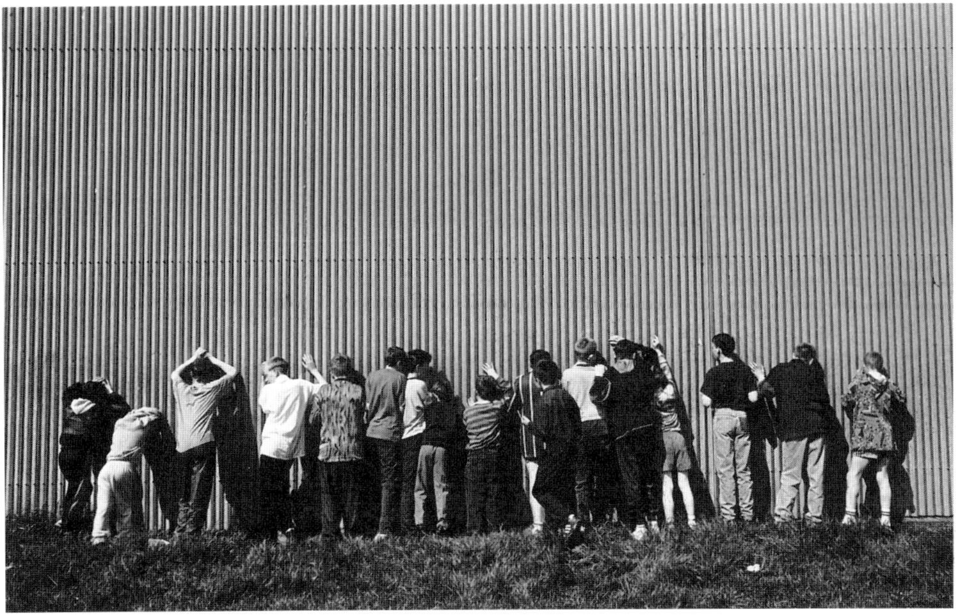

**Belfast 1994** Barricaded behind the 'Peace Lines' that still separate Belfast's Protestant and Catholic communities
*Credit: Frankie Quinn*

**Dublin 1916** British troops barricaded by fish barrels during the Easter Rising
*Credit: Hutlon Getty Picture Collection*

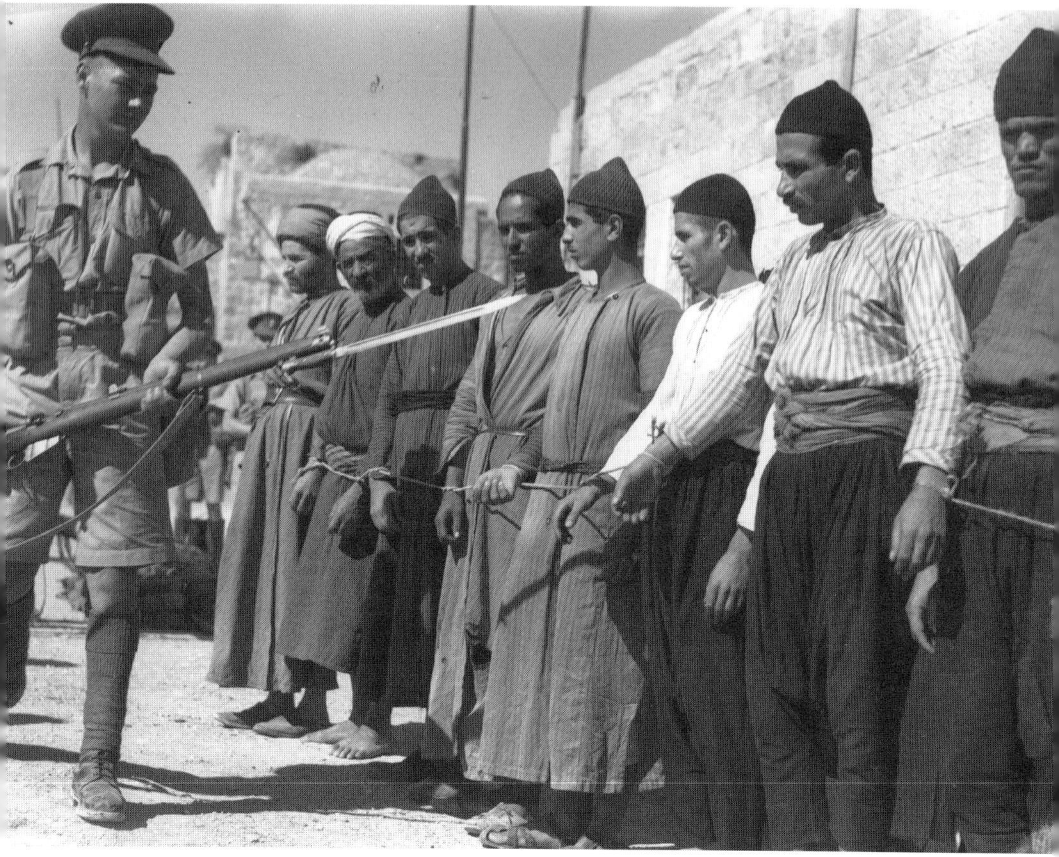

**Gaza 1993** Israeli checkpoint at Erez in occupied Gaza. Now notionally independent, not much has changed in Palestinian Gaza ... peace and prosperity have a long way to travel
*Credit: Stephen Ferry/Liaison Agency*

**Jerusalem 1938** The usual suspects. Arab prisoners under guard in the British Mandate of Palestine. Palestinians were caught up in the violence of increasingly aggressive Jewish claims to a state of Israel backed by terrorist attacks on British targets by groups like the Stern Gang
*Credit: Hulton Getty Picture Collection*

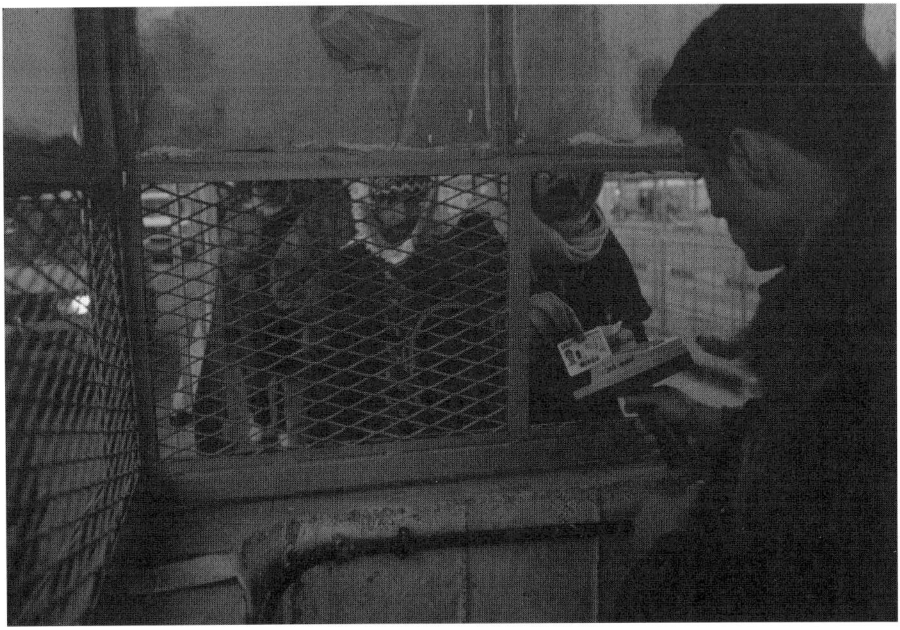

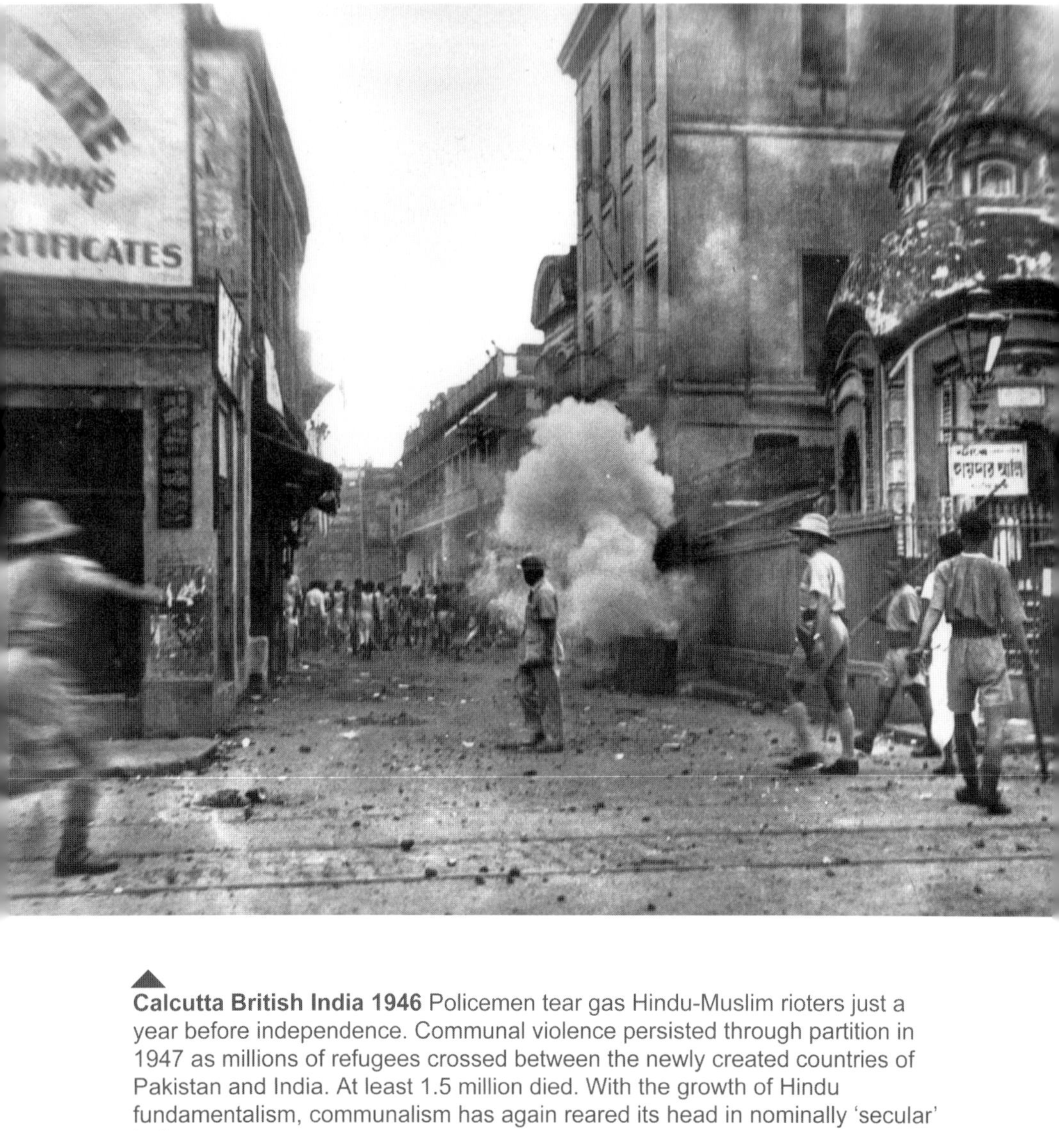


**Calcutta British India 1946** Policemen tear gas Hindu-Muslim rioters just a year before independence. Communal violence persisted through partition in 1947 as millions of refugees crossed between the newly created countries of Pakistan and India. At least 1.5 million died. With the growth of Hindu fundamentalism, communalism has again reared its head in nominally 'secular' India

*Credit: Hulton Getty Picture Collection*

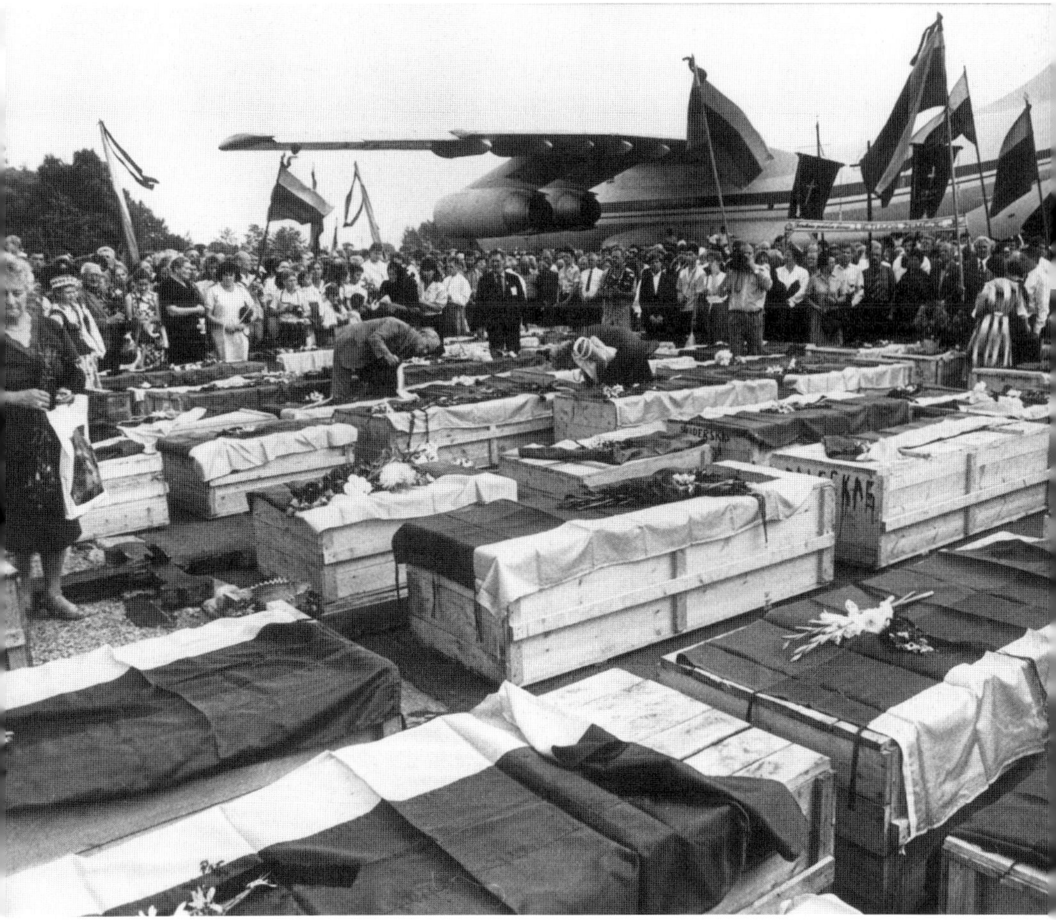

▲
**Vilnius Lithuania 1989** Business concluded as the coffins of some of the 14,693 Lithuanians deported by Stalin to Siberia during three days in June 1941 come home. It was one of the first gestures of *glasnost* by Mikhail Gorbachev
*Credit: Romaulda Pozersis/Liaison Agency*

# Death of the photographer

*Men still kill one another, they have not yet understood how they live, why they live: politicians fail to observe that the earth is an entity, yet television has been invented. Tomorrow we shall be able to look into the heart of our fellow-man, be everywhere and yet be alone... The unambiguousness of the real, the truth in the everyday situation is there for all classes.*

Laszlo Moholy-Magy

**Rome 1966** King of the paparazzi Rino Barillari gets an ice-cream come-uppance from dissatisfied victim, Yugoslav actress Sonia Romanoff
*Credit: Hulton Getty Picture Collection*

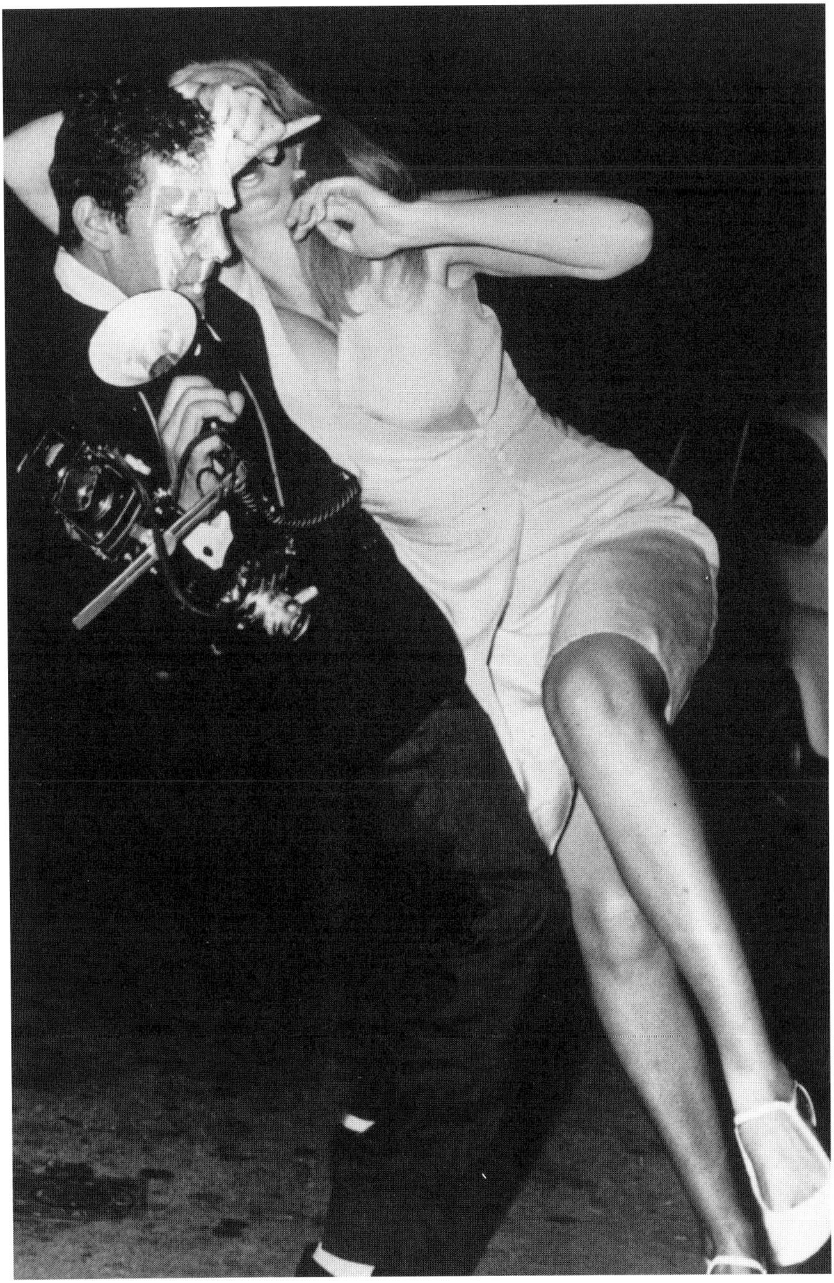

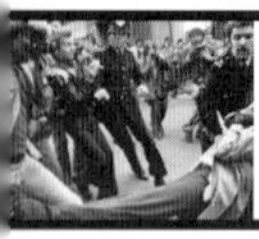

# Death of the photographer

*Philip Jones Griffiths*

Just because writing on papyrus replaced carving hieroglyphics on stone, it cannot be presumed that each new form of communication will consign the previous one to the dustbin. Today, we have a variety of media existing in a somewhat uneasy symbiosis, with the unified aim of misleading us while amusing us. TV, radio and publishing get along just fine as we, the audience, get collectively dumber.

As always the Golden Rule applies: those with the gold, rule – and, for the most part, own the means of communication. What we get to think and know about the world is firmly in the hands of a few. They exist to misinform us, whether it's *National Geographic Magazine* that can claim to have 'educated' what is now the world's largest population of parochial ignoramuses. Or US TV, whose coverage of the Gulf War meant, according to University of Detroit researchers, that the more you watched, the less you understood. Surely no-one is naive enough to believe that the great media conglomerates exist to inform us about the truth. Information is selectively gathered and packaged for our amusement and titillation, for a truly informed public is antithetical to the interests of modern consumer capitalism.

Historically, the role of photography in this structure has presented a problem. People believe photographs – it's the reason we have them, not drawings, in our passports; and why the police use a camera to record a crime scene. We need to see photographs, for they offer proof of reality. This authenticity often jars with the interests of the opulent few, so the spin meisters of obfuscation are called upon to apply their talents.

In the past, their techniques were somewhat heavy-handed. Photographs were cropped to alter their meaning, miscaptioned to mislead and retouched when necessary. In the Soviet Union, the faces of Stalin's enemies vanished from old photographs. Here in Britain, magazines such as *Picture Post* regularly 'assembled' photographs from strips taken from other pictures. Many of the great iconic images of the past have turned out to have been manipulated. Eugene Smith, heralded as America's greatest photographer, is best known for his story on life in a Spanish village. Not only did he orchestrate his pictures, using the people as models, but in one famous picture of a wake, when a woman found him more interesting than the body, out came the bleach and ink in the darkroom, redirecting her eyes towards the corpse. Not perhaps a serious occurrence, but a solid nail in the coffin of photographic veracity.

But the 'doctoring' of images was always considered a bit risky – for the original might turn up to haunt the perpetrator. The selective choice of subject matter may better illustrate the predilections of the proprietor.

My first insight into this was the coverage of a huge CND protest rally at Aldermaston by *The Times*. A plane with their photographer aboard arrived a good hour after the meeting was over and the crowds gone. Next morning's paper showed a picture of a few stragglers implying a poorly attended event.

For me, a more egregious example was that of the *Telegraph* photographer during the last day of the last pit to close in the Rhondda, who cajoled one miner into kneeling on the ground, 'So that I can get the background right.' The picture appeared the next day with the caption, 'Down, and finally out!'

Since those days, faking has enjoyed a quantum leap with the advent of computerised manipulation. Now, with digital cameras, there is no 'original' to compare with. There is nothing to stop anyone resolving the Kennedy assassination by inserting Ladybird Johnson on the grassy knoll with a smoking gun in her hand. Fraudulence is easy and detection difficult and photography will never be the same again. We are probably the last generation that will accept the integrity of the photograph.

In the meantime, television has become the dominant visual communication medium. Not because it's been embraced as the purveyor of truth, but of the pabulum we have been taught to crave. No-one expects much veracity in the world of infotainment. Truth has become superfluous.

For those of us working in the magazine world, we plod on with the usual admonishments: 'Lively pictures, everyone happy!' 'No gore, our advertisers don't like it!' And my favourite, 'Fresh colour, please!'

In a perfect world, the photographer would be handed a ticket and dispatched to some situation with the assurance that his or her interpretation would be eagerly awaited by those readers anxious for edification.

Alas, the world is far from perfect.

Today the photographer is sent off to illustrate the preconceptions, usually misconceptions, of the deskbound editor – an editor biased not by any knowledge of the subject but by the pressure to conform to the standard view ordained by the powers that be. Any deviation from the 'party line' is rejected.

The stark truth is that the media have abandoned 'stories' – the 'stories' repeated around countless campfires enrapturing mankind since the dawn of history. Today they are deemed unreliable because they stem from what we really do and think, from our real experiences, rather than the externally imposed homogenised admass culture allowed us.

Photography may be on its last legs, but those of us with cameras round our necks will still keep running. ❑

***Philip Jones Griffiths*** *is a former president of Magnum Photos. He has been a photographer since 1961.* 

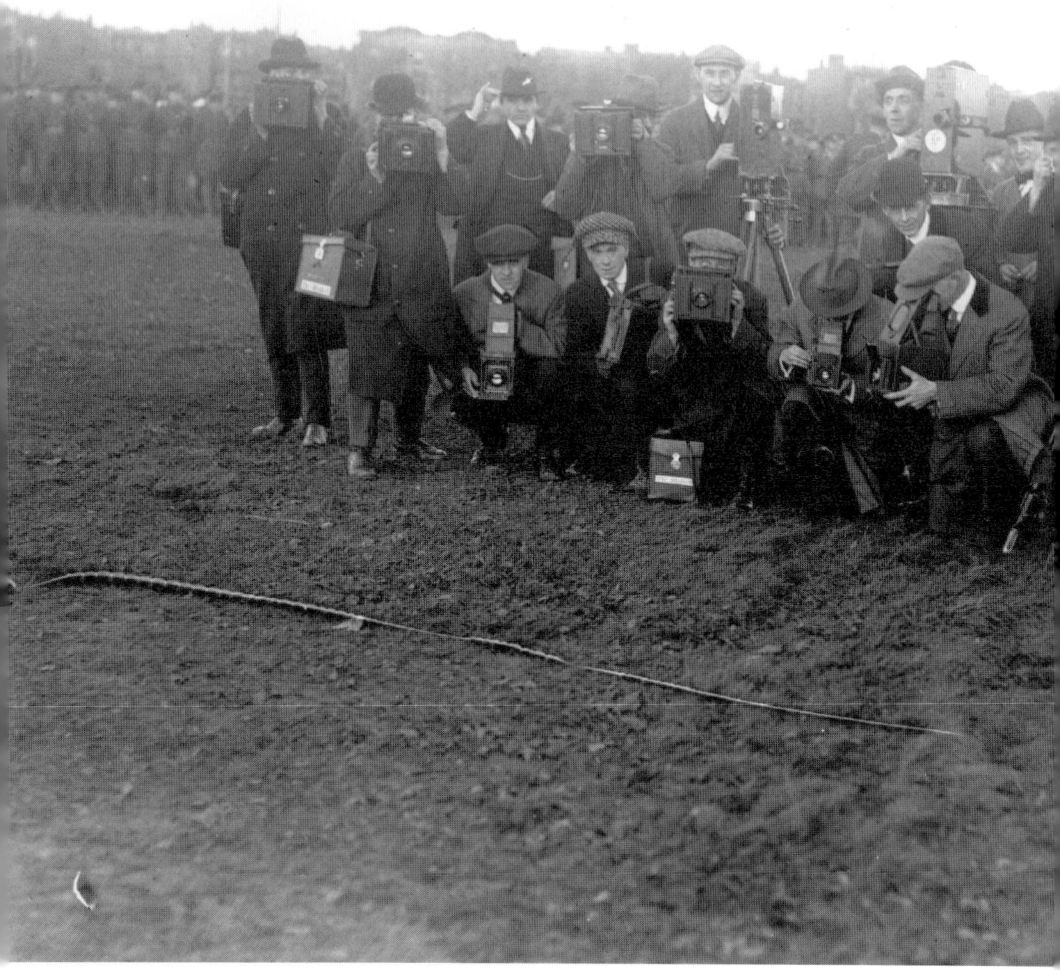

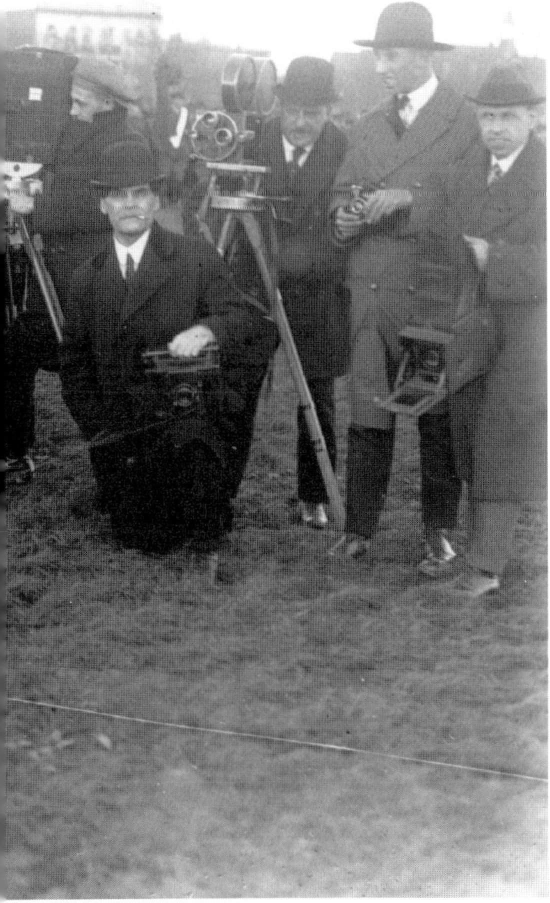

**UK 1919** Press corps follows the royal progress of Edward Prince of Wales
*Credit: Hulton Getty Picture Collection*

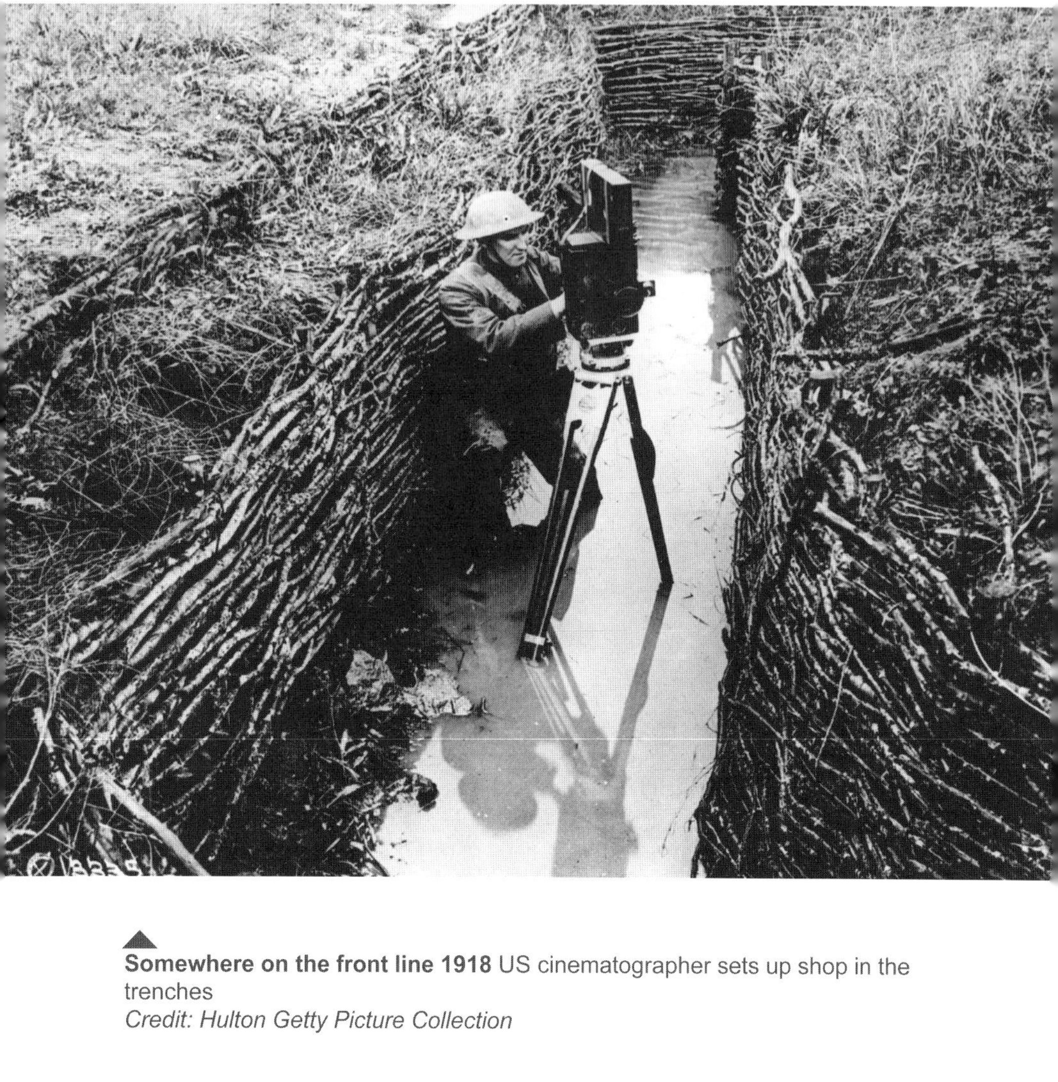

▲
**Somewhere on the front line 1918** US cinematographer sets up shop in the trenches
*Credit: Hulton Getty Picture Collection*

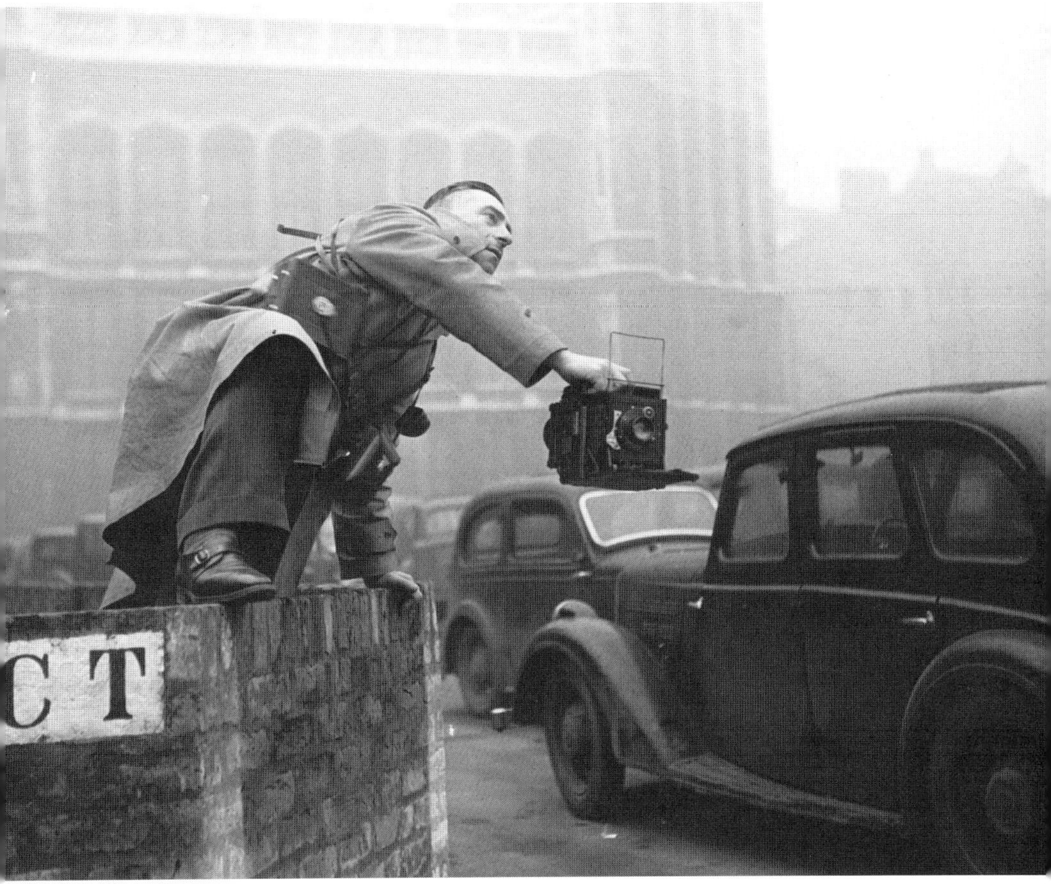


**London 1946** On the home front in the dour days after WWII, press photographer Fred Ramage
*Credit: Hulton Getty Picture Collection*

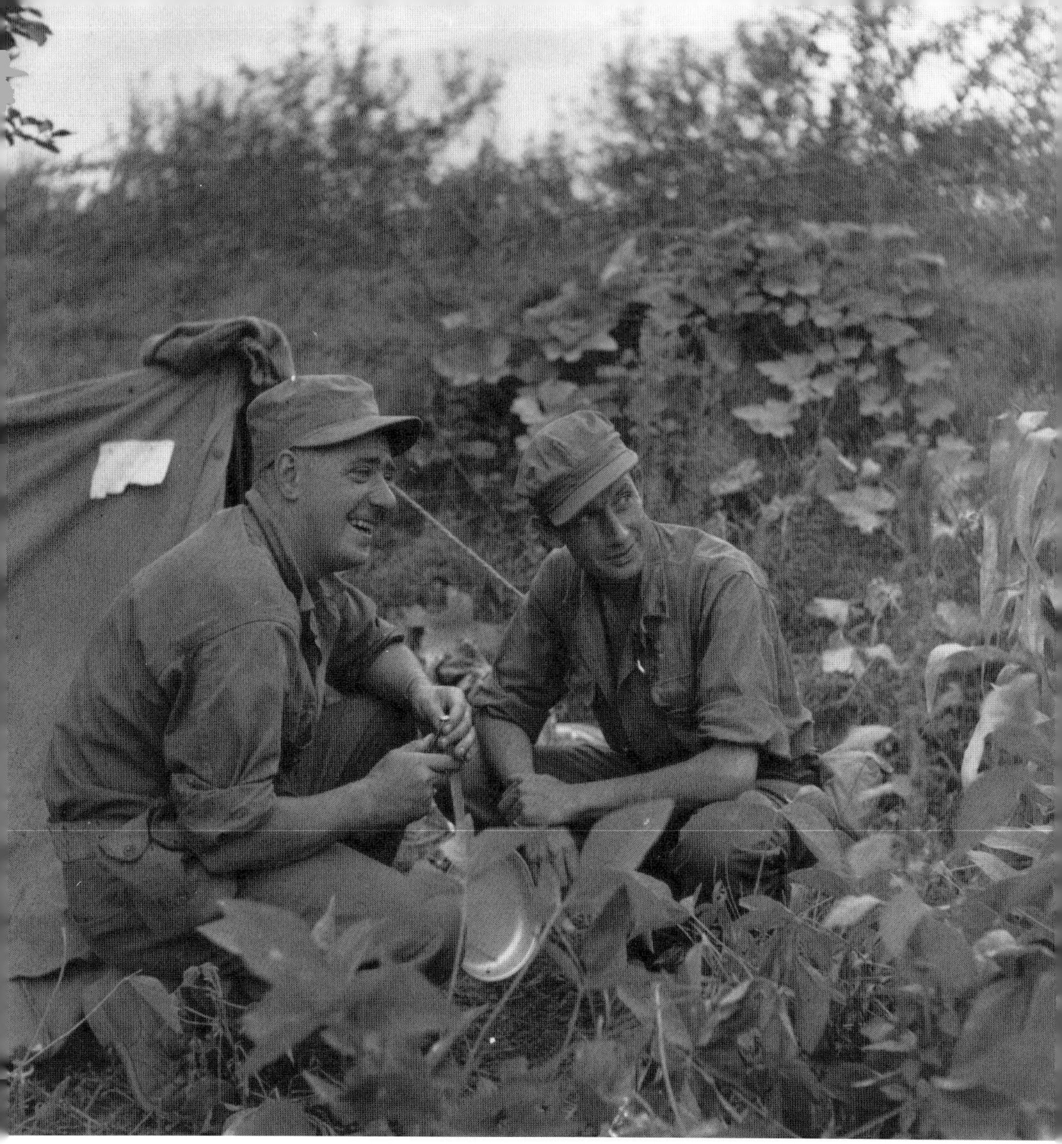

**Somewhere in Korea 1950** Picture Post photographer Bert Hardy (left) reporting from the front line with journalist James Cameron
*Credit: Hulton Getty Picture Collection*

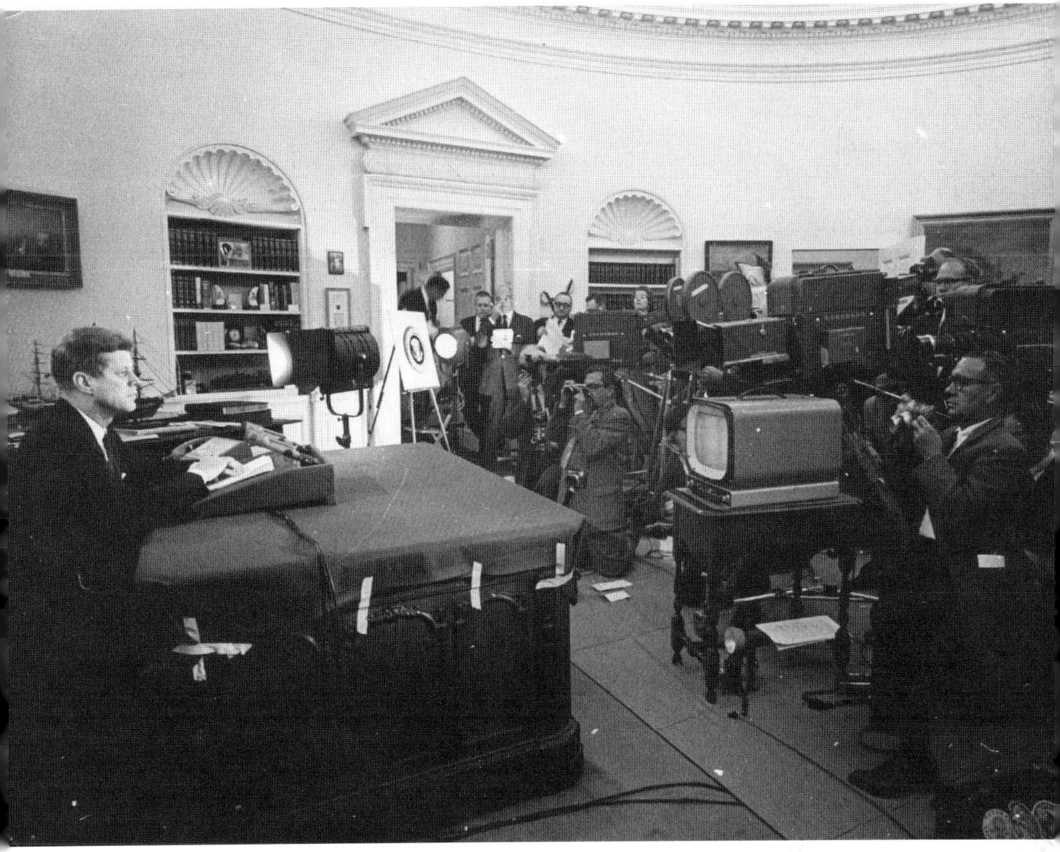

▲
**USA 1962** TV takes over. President Kennedy uses TV to announce his blockade of Cuba and challenge the USSR to remove its missiles
*Credit: Hulton Getty Picture Collection*

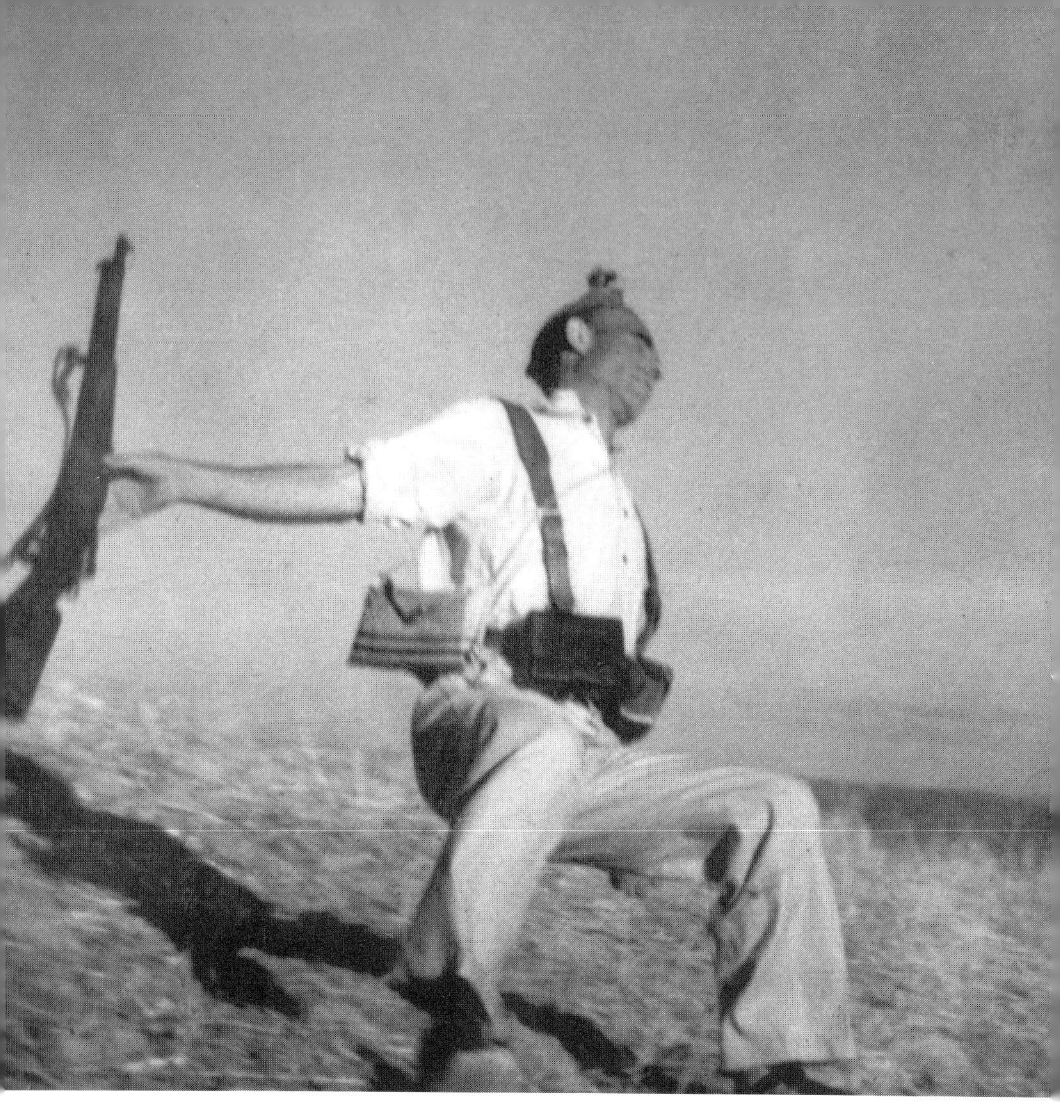

**Cerro Muriano Spain 1936**
Death of a loyalist militiaman. Robert Capa's iconic photo from the Spanish Civil War may or may not have been a 'restaging' after the event; the impact of the photo on public opinion is indisputable. After the defeat of the loyalists by Franco's fascists, Capa departed to cover the developing war in Europe, whence he moved on to cover China's Civil War and anti-colonial wars in Africa. Capa's war photography set a new standard for the genre
*Credit: Robert Capa/Magnum Photos*

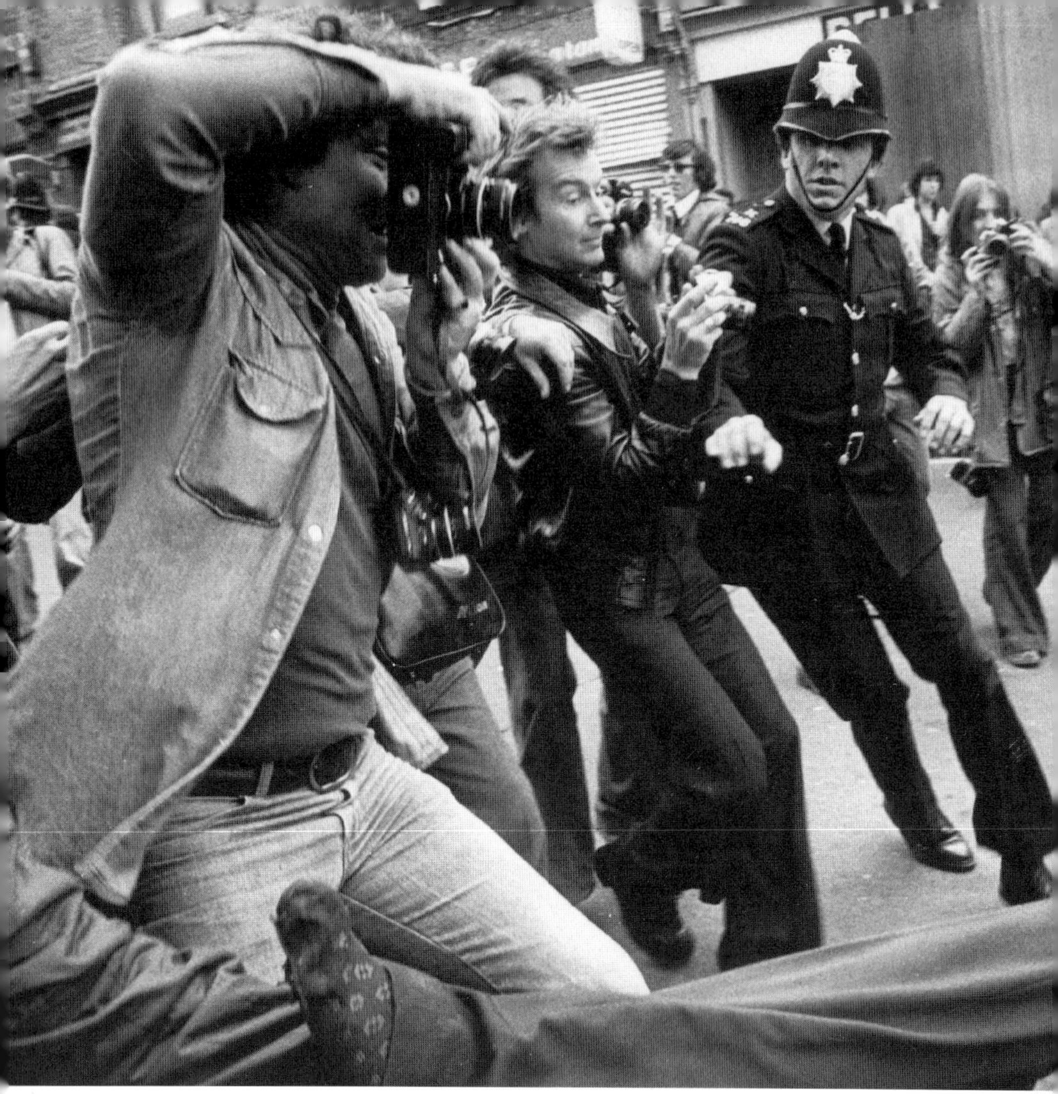

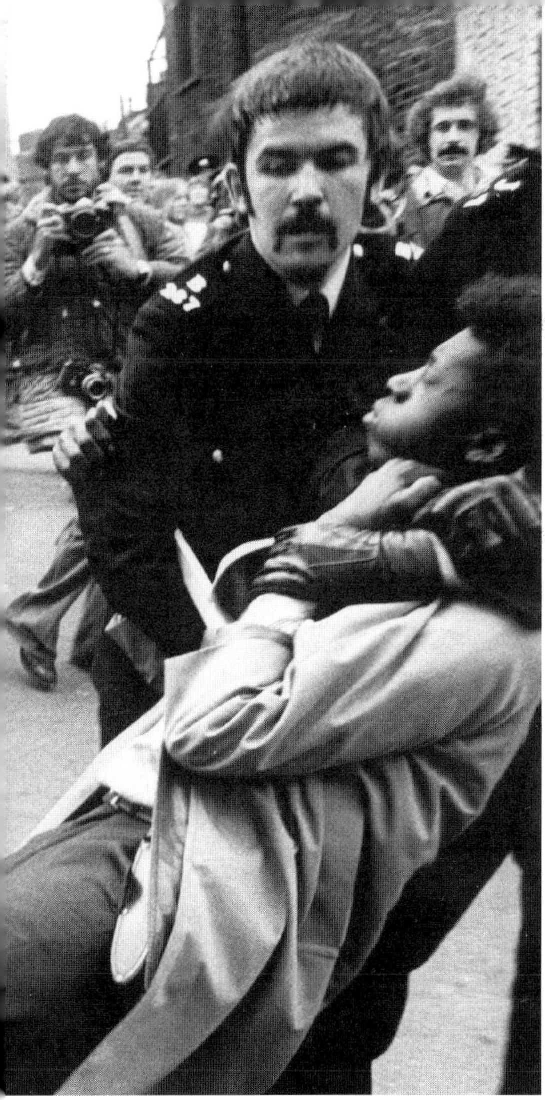

**London 1977** Caught in the frame. John Hodder gets fellow photographers on film as they surround police about to make an arrest during a National Front march
*Credit: John Hodder/Observer/Hulton Getty Picture Collection*

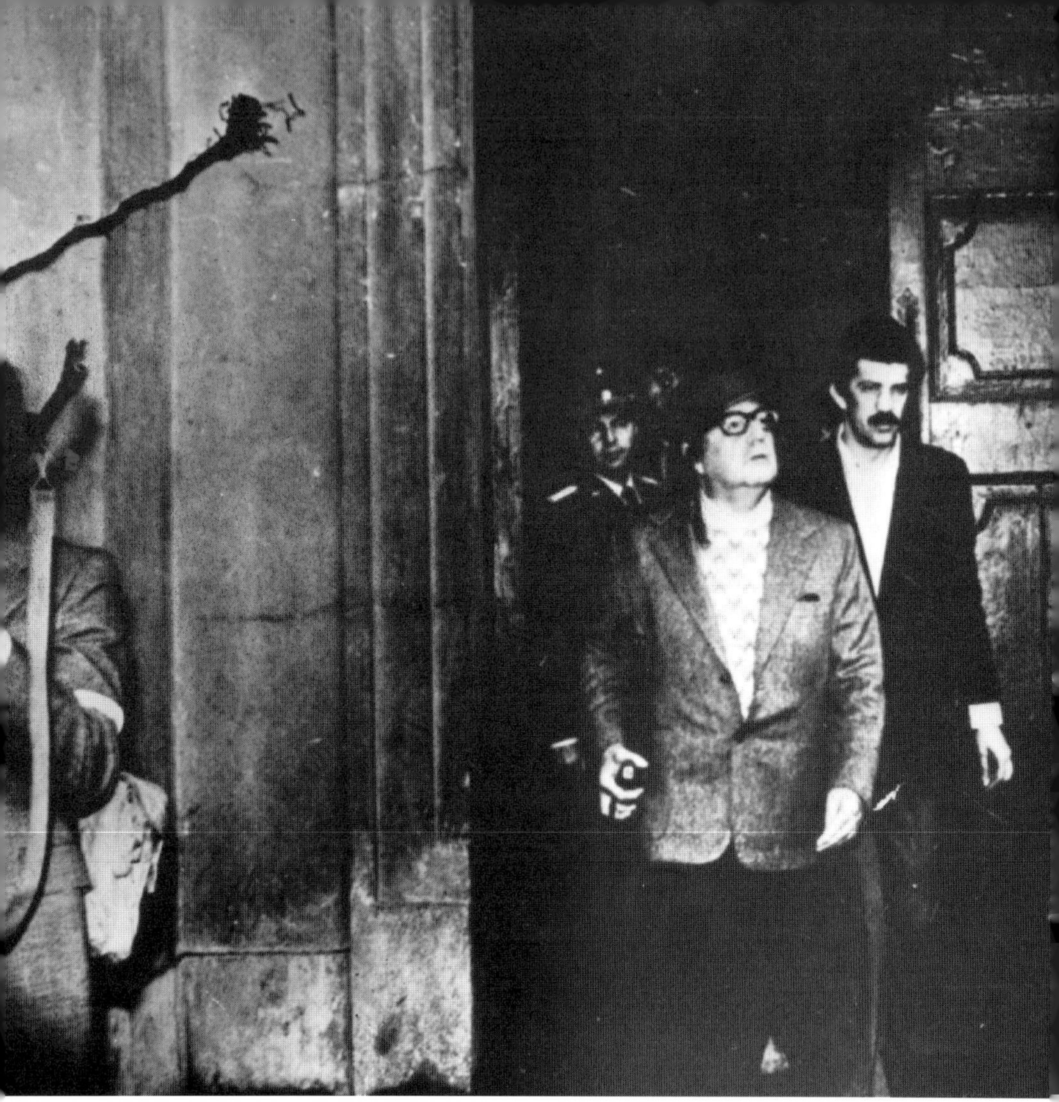

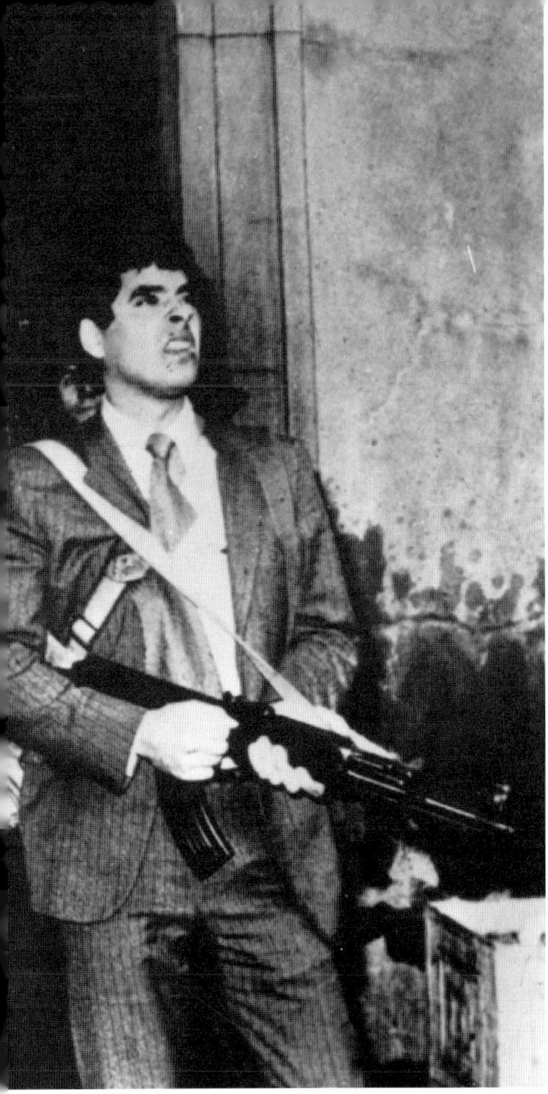

**Santiago Chile 1973** President Salvador Allende emerges from a building in the midst of the September military coup that killed him and delivered the country into the hands of the military for two decades. This photo, part of a set sent anonymously to the New York Times six weeks after the event, not only disproved accounts of his suicide in the presidential palace, it established the facts in a way that none of the thousands of column inches previously had done. It won the World Press Photo Award for that year *Credit: Hulton Getty Picture Collection*

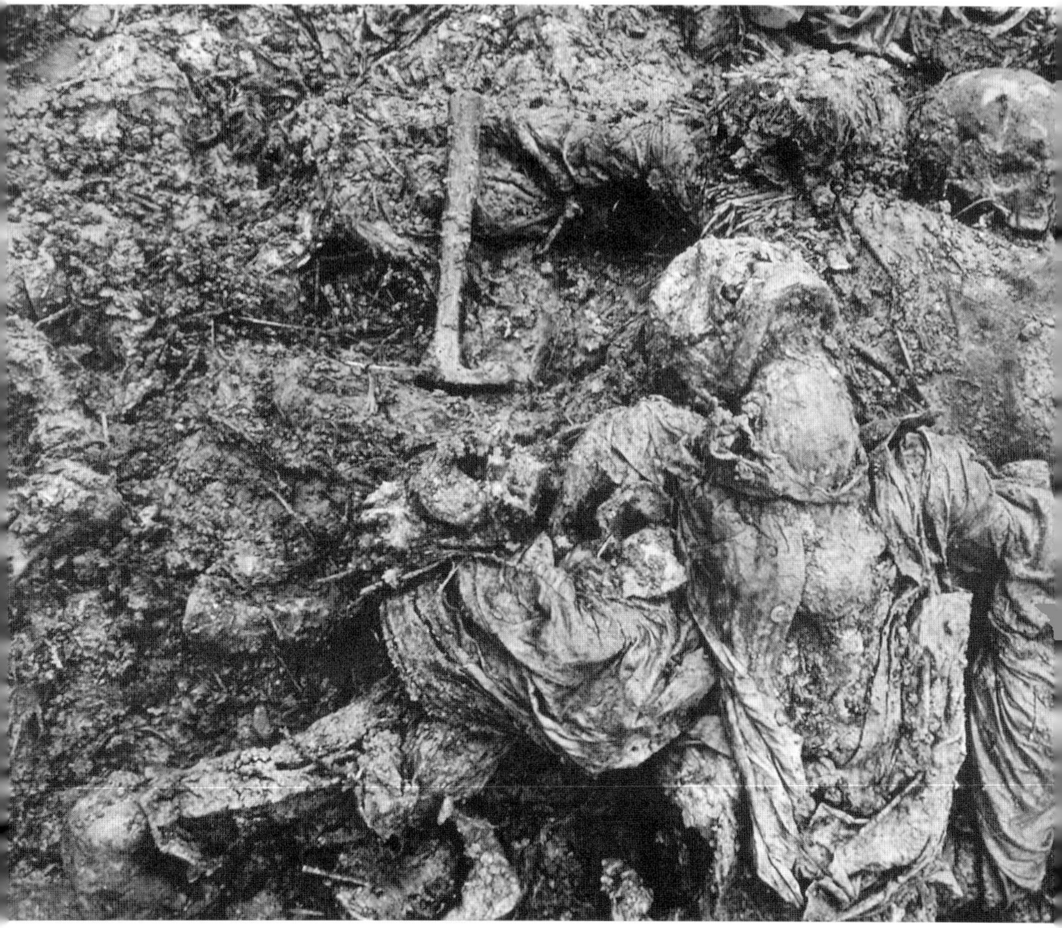

**Mass grave at Pilice near Srebrenica Bosnia 1996** Only the graves remain – and only the photojournalist remains to record the aftermath of a war exhaustively covered by real-time TV, but forgotten once the action moves elsewhere
*Gilles Peress/Magnum Photos*

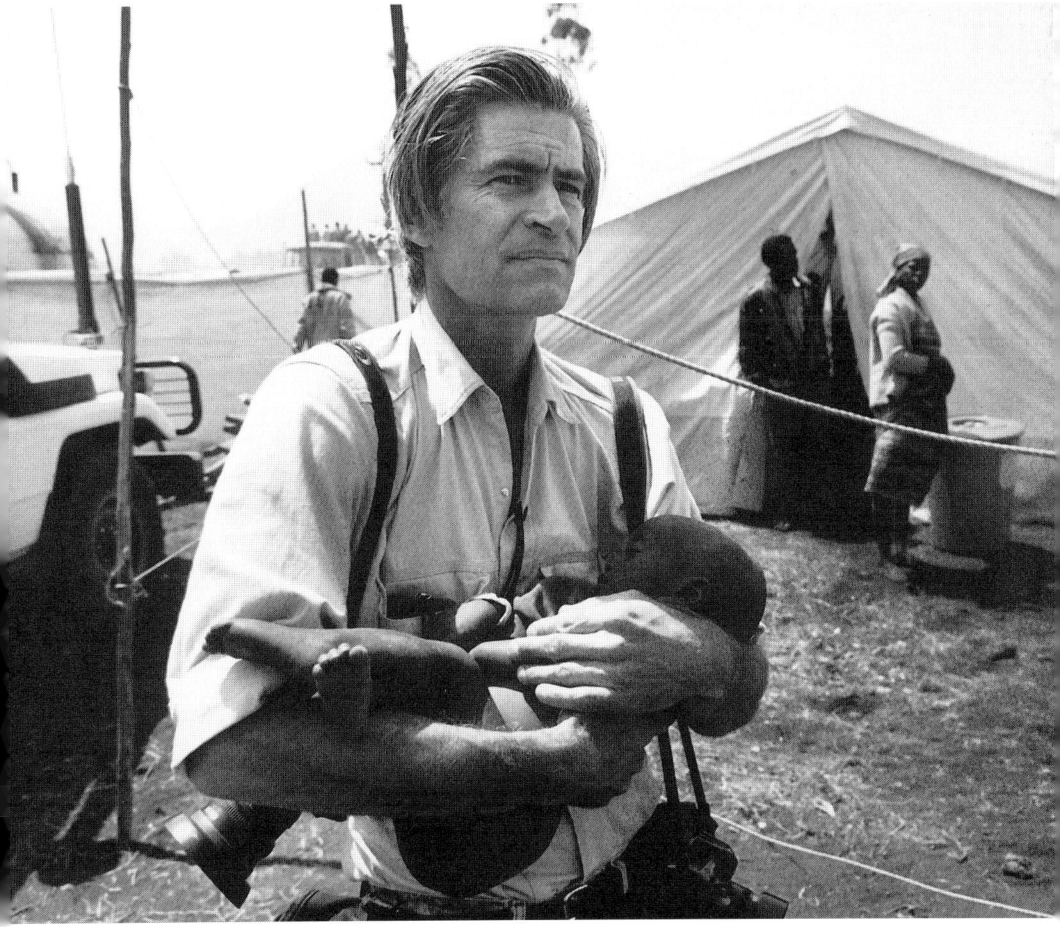

**Zaire 1994** Crossing the line. Magnum photographer James Nachtwey photographed carrying a baby girl, orphaned by the massacres in neighbouring Rwanda, to safety. Is this the 'journalism of attachment'? Nachtwey's own photos of the war in Rwanda won all three major prizes for photojournalism – the Robert Capa Gold Medal, the World Press Photo of the Year and the Magazine Photographer of the Year – in 1994
*Credit: Gilles Peress/Magnum Photos*

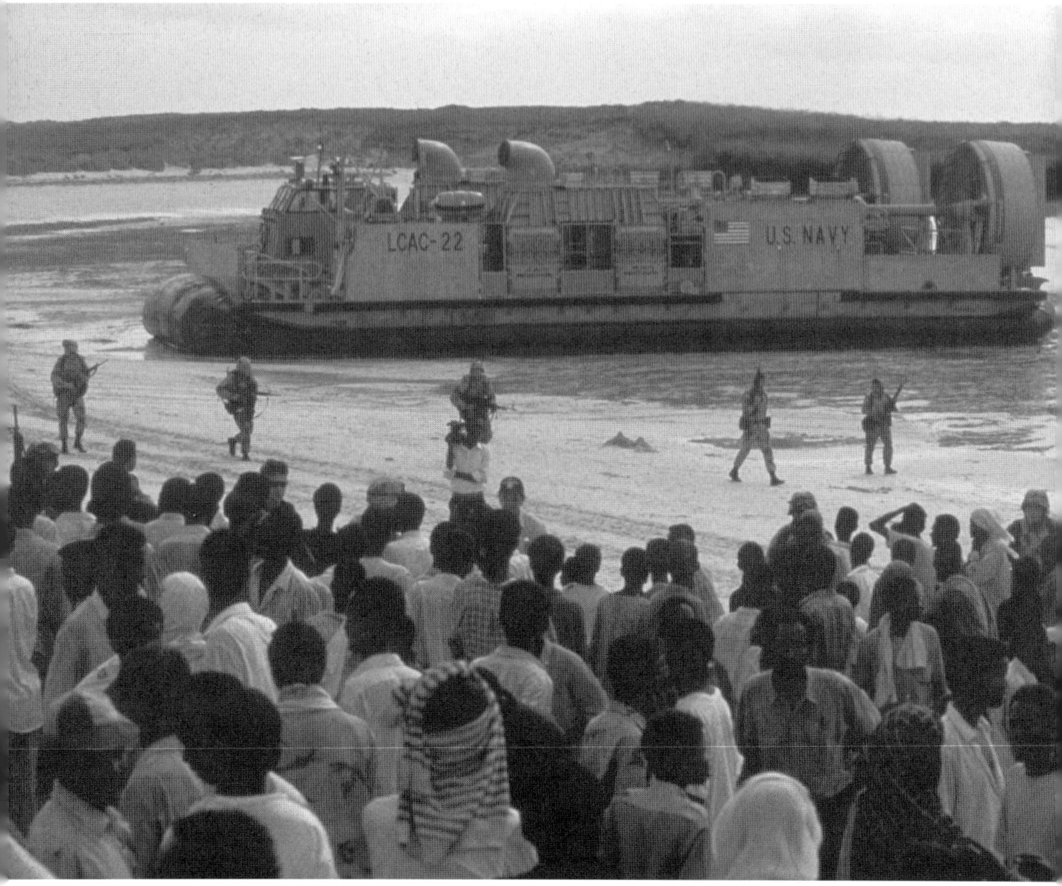


▲
**Somalia 1992** US troops of the disastrous Operation Restore Hope stage a landing for the TV cameras of CNN: 'It ain't news till it's on CNN'.
*Credit: Duclos/Van der Stockt/Liaison Agency*

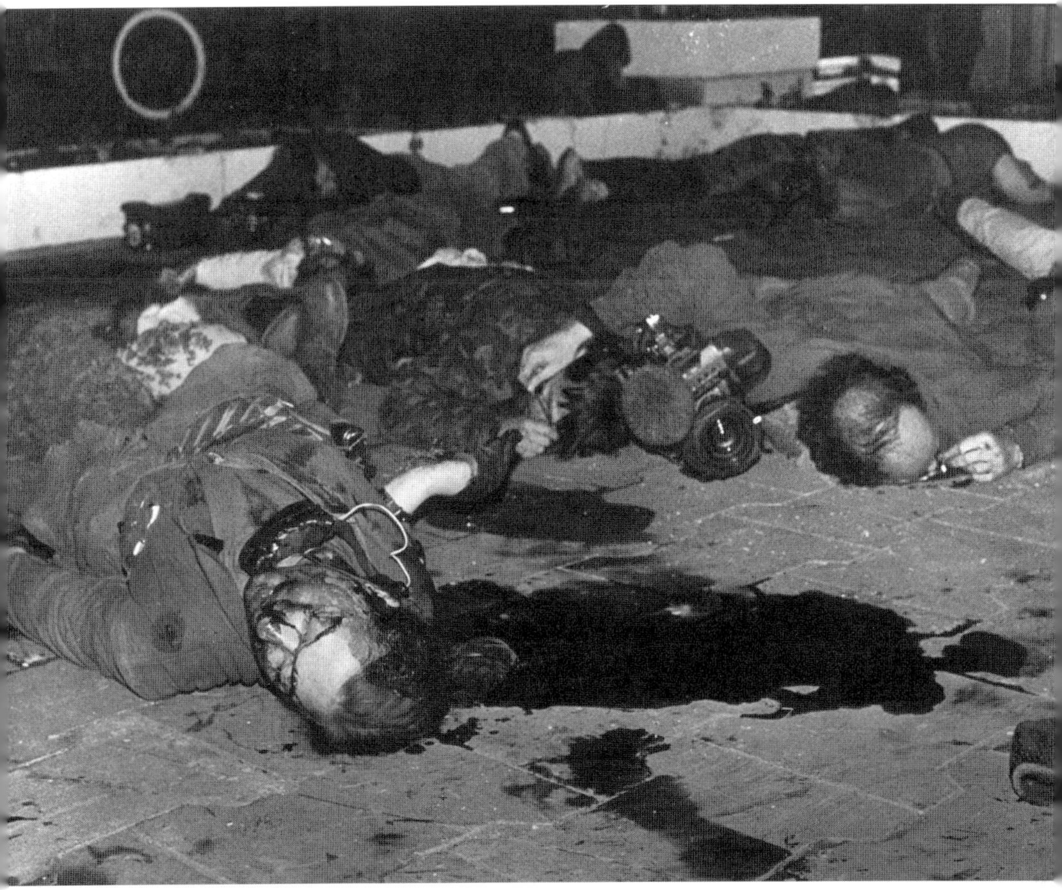

**Moscow 1993** Journalists and TV cameramen caught in the crossfire as Yeltsin fights the Duma for control of the airwaves
*Credit: A Zamakhin*

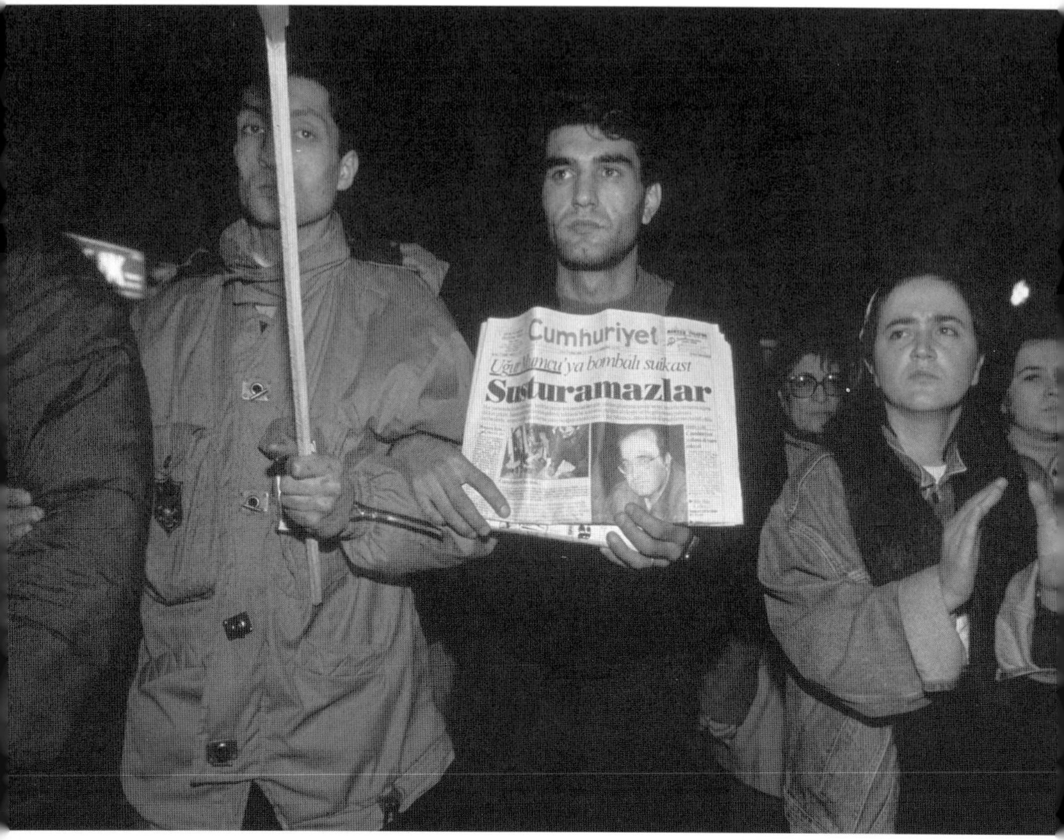


**Buenos Aires Argentina 1997**
Death of the photographer.
Funeral of Jose Luis Cabezas, killed by Argentine security forces
*Credit: Editorial Atlantida/Liaison Agency*

**Istanbul Turkey 1998**
Demonstration in support of journalists killed by Turkish security forces
*Credit: Jon Levy/ Liaison Agency*

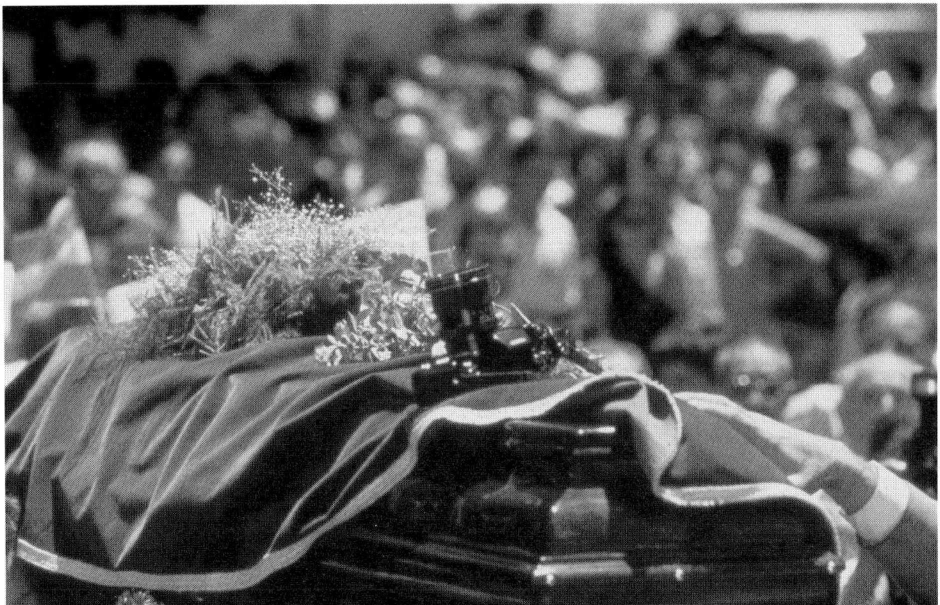

# One cheer for dictatorship

It was left to a handful of westerners to mourn the passing of Pakistani democracy on 15 October, the day after the overthrow of Prime Minister Nawaz Sharif by General Pervez Musharraf.

The *Frontier Post,* whose chief editor has been held in prison since April (*Index* 3/1999), spoke of a 'palpable sigh of relief among the citizens' and Najam Seithi, editor of the *Friday Times*, had experienced at first hand Sharif's style of vindictive autocracy (*Index* 4/1999, 5/1999). *Dawn* columnist Ayaz Amir wrote scathingly of 'the dolt … who had not the wit to understand that it is only so much incompetent audacity the furies can stand'. But the West may yet rue the dictator who has taken his place.

Disciplined, secularist and trained at Fort Bragg, Musharraf has since been cautiously welcomed as a 'safe pair of hands' for the first nuclear bomb owned by a Muslim state. On 4 November, former CIA chief Milton Bearden told a congressional committee that Musharraf represented 'the last good chance' for the US to influence Pakistan's direction in the new millennium.

Musharraf seized power because Sharif, having first emasculated the judiciary and the press, sought to extend his control to the army by replacing him with Lt General Khaiwaja Ziauddin, head of ISI intelligence. Founded by the avowedly Islamist dictator Zia ul-Haq, the ISI is best known for distributing US and Gulf military aid to the Afghan *mujahedin* during the Soviet occupation.

What is not known with any certainty is which of Pakistan's rival institutions was responsible for the May incident in Kashmir, when 400 insurgents sneaked into the snows above the Kargil road, transgressing the Line of Control which has demarcated the Indian and Pakistani sectors since 1949. Coming a year after India first came out as a nuclear power, it was an act of desperate brinkmanship.

After two months' fighting, Sharif flew to Washington to meet President Clinton on 4 July, the same day that the London *Observer* scooped the entire US intelligence complex by disclosing the whereabouts of Osama bin Ladin, the Saudi whom Washington accuses of organising the US embassy bombings in August 1998. The Clinton administration has displayed an impenetrable ambivalence about bin Ladin and the Taliban who currently protect him. On one hand, it denounces him to the skies – while lifting not a finger to bring him to justice; on the other, it has refused, since 25 August 1998, to hand over secret papers to a foreign affairs committee, which suspects US complicity in the rise of his Taliban hosts.

Three hours after meeting Clinton, Sharif signed the Washington Agreement, committing Pakistan to the immediate withdrawal of its forces from Kargil and the ratification of the Comprehensive Test Ban Treaty. Sharif had inflicted lasting damage on the nation's prestige – and his own ability to rule – by surrendering control of a deterrent that had been 20 years in the making. He flew home to an army on the verge of mutiny, but he did not come back empty-handed.

Throughout June, journalists in Kabul had reported a build-up of Pakistani troops and Arabs from bin Ladin's former training camps in readiness for the traditional summer offensive against Ahmed Shah Massoud, the last Afghan commander to withstand Taliban rule. Despite UN attempts at mediation, the Taliban launched an attack in late July which led directly to the ethnic cleansing of 250,000 Tajiks from Massoud's positions in the Shomali Plain.

Was the pledge of a free hand in Afghanistan the *quid pro quo* extracted by Sharif in a bid to placate the army for its humiliation at Kargil? Evidence suggests that it may have been. On 21 September, the US cautioned the military against a coup and, in the following week, the ISI boss was back in Washington to negotiate a further list of US demands, including the end of army support for the Taliban. In the days preceding the coup, Sharif had begun to carry them out. He denounced the Taliban's 'terrorist training camps' and passed trade restrictions on Afghanistan, both of which further offended the army. Sharif's attempt to do without his army chief altogether was the last straw.

The 'safe hands' analysis of General Musharraf, offered by the CIA's Milton Bearden, contained the following analysis of the Pakistan army. 'The once outward-looking officer corps ... whose foundations were laid at Fort Benning and Fort Bragg ... [is] being replaced by inward-looking officers who have been trained only in religious fundamentalist *madrassah* schools.' This was over-egging the pudding. But, before Sharif's overthrow, it was the fear of losing democracy which stood between Pakistan and the 'Islamist bomb'. Now it is a general of the old school, whose example has only shown his Islamist subordinates the path to follow. ❑

***Michael Griffin***

*A censorship chronicle incorporating information from the American Association for the Advancement of Science Human Rights Action Network (AAASHRAN), Amnesty International (AI), Article 19 (A19), the BBC Monitoring Service Summary of World Broadcasts (SWB), the Committee to Protect Journalists (CPJ), Canadian Journalists for Free Expression (CJFE), Glasnost Defence Foundation (GDF), Instituto de Prensa y Sociedad (IPYS), The UN's Integrated Regional Information Network (IRIN), the Inter-American Press Association (IAPA), the International Federation of Journalists (IFJ/FIP), Human Rights Watch (HRW), the Media Institute of Southern Africa (MISA), Network for the Defence of Independent Media in Africa (NDIMA), International PEN (PEN), Open Media Research Institute (OMRI), Pacific Islands News Association (PINA), Radio Free Europe/Radio Liberty (RFE/RL), Reporters Sans Frontières (RSF), the World Association of Community Broadcasters (AMARC), World Association of Newspapers (WAN), the World Organisation Against Torture (OMCT) and other sources*

## ANGOLA

Journalist **Paulo Julião** and director **Emanuel da Mata** from independent church-owned Radio Ecclesia were released on 10 August, nine hours after being arrested in connection with the station's rebroadcast of a BBC interview with the UNITA rebel leader (*Index* 4/1999). **Laurinda Tavares**, arrested in same raid by the Criminal Investigation Department (DNIC), appears also to have been released. On the same day, local BBC correspondent **Reginando Silva** and three employees of state-owned television station TPA – **Nelson Rosa**, **Manuel a Silva** and **Jose Maria** ñ were instructed to report for questioning. TPA had broadcast the same BBC interview, in contravention of Law 7/78, which proscribes 'crimes on state security'. All four were released the same day. (MISA)

**Isaias Soares**, Voice of America's correspondent in Malanje, was detained on 19 August following his report in the programme 'Linha directa, linea aberta' that the security and police forces in the city had misappropriated World Food Programme relief destined for local civilians. (RSF)

**Mauricio Cristovão**, a journalist with state-owned Radio Nacional de Angola, was shot dead in an ambush by unknown assailants on 31 August. Another employee of Radio Nacional, **Avelino Miguel**, was killed on the same day in an apparent car robbery. Eight journalists were interrogated between 31 August and 6 September and observers point to recent anti-media speeches by Information Minister Hendrik Val Neto as a possible reason for the attacks (*Index* 5/99). (MISA)

On 3 September **Gilberto Neto**, a journalist with the bi-weekly independent *Folha 8* paper, was detained in connection with his article on the raid on Radio Ecclesia, asked about his sources and assaulted before being released nine hours later (*Index* 4/1999). On 6 September *Folha 8*ìs director **William Tonet** was called in for questioning and, two days later, two of the paper's layout artists were interrogated. On 10 September, Tonet was prevented from leaving the country on a fund-raising mission for his newspaper. In an interview, he claimed that DNIC had established a 'censorship bureau' to deal specifically with *Folha 8*. He was again arrested on 2 October without any specific charge being made. Sources variously claimed it was for 'not paying fiscal duties' on imported goods, for an article alleging corruption in the Economic Crimes Unit or for publishing excerpts from a UNITA press release on conditions in the besieged cities of Andula and Balundo. He was released on bail of 2.2 billion kwanzas (US$500) on 4 October (MISA, CPJ)

On 5 September **Aguiar dos Santos**, director of the independent weekly *Agora*, was summoned to the DNIC building on four separate days to answer questions about a special edition of the paper to commemorate the 20th anniversary of President Eduardo dos Santos' term in office. Two articles concerned the DNIC: one was a summary of the president's achievements and the other a reprinted article from the French daily *Libération* about the Eduardo dos Santos Foundation, a charity set up in the president's name. (MISA)

The independent weekly *Angolense* failed to appear on 19

September following a dispute between editor **Graca Campos** and publisher Reis Da Costa, who objected to an article critical of the Eduardo dos Santos Foundation. Staff opposed Costa's moves to sack Campos who, on 20 September, took Campos to court to enforce his dismissal, citing mismanagement of the paper. The case was postponed. (MISA)

On 29 September four journalists were suspended indefinitely from the state-owned news agency ANGOP for 'clarifications' about their ties with the independent press. Editor **Antonio Picarra**, sports editor **Silva Candembo** and reporter **Antonio Campos** were suspended for alleged 'collaboration' with *Agora*, *Folha 8* and *Angolenses*. **Manuel Borges**, Angop's correspondent in Bie, was accused of also being a correspondent for Portuguese news agency LUSA. Journalists in the state media are subject to severe censorship and are unable to report on the civil war, corruption, abuse of power, human rights and maladministration. (MISA)

## ARGENTINA

Between 18 and 23 July, the assistant editor of the *Pagina 12* newspaper, **Sergio Moreno**, received seven anonymous calls from a person, identifying himself only as 'Chinese Solís', warning him to 'take care of himself'. 'Chinese Solís' appears to be a reference to Colonel Solís who, a number of years ago, began legal proceedings against Moreno for defamation. In an article published on 24 November 1994 in *La Prensa* newspaper, Moreno and his colleague **Silvia Términe** suggested that the colonel was associated with alleged anti-Semitic groups that hindered the work of the judge in charge of the investigation of an attack in July 1994 on the Jewish organisation AMIA. Moreno has been receiving calls periodically since 1995. (RSF)

The Supreme Court overturned a December 1996 ruling that cleared three *Página 12* journalists in a case for damages brought against them five years ago by President Carlos Meném, it was reported on 13 August. The court decided that the case should be re-opened by the National Court, which considers annulments. On 20 November 1994, an article by the journalist **Horacio Verbitsky** denied President Meném's claims that he had been tortured as a captive during the years of the dictatorship (*Index* 1/1995). The president brought charges against Verbitsky, *Página 12*'s director **Ernesto Tiffenberg** and editor **Fernando Sokolowicz**. (Periodistas)

On 16 August **Gabriela Vigo**, a columnist with *Clarín* newspaper, photographer **Rubén Dubrovsky** and their driver were attacked by members of the Buenos Aires Gymnasium and Fencing Club (GEBA) when they visited to check if the club had fenced a disputed piece of land. GEBA had been in conflict over an area of around eight hectares that local organisations claim were occupied illegally. The courts are investigating the case. (Periodistas)

On 9 September the vice-governor of Córdova province and mayoral candidate German Kammerath threatened legal action against local media if they published any further information on his investments. A letter in the 9 September edition of the weekly *Informe Cordova* said Kammerath owned property of far greater value than declared to the taxation department, an amount, moreover, out of proportion to the salary of a vice-governor. (Periodistas)

## ARMENIA

**Nikol Pashinian**, editor-in-chief of the opposition daily *Oragir* (Diary), was jailed for one year on 31 August for 'libel, contempt of court and refusal to publish a correction'. The conviction – the first for criminal libel in post-Soviet Armenia – is the latest of a series of attempts to punish Oragir for his articles since March alleging corrupt business dealings by Interior Minister Serge Sarkissian, Professor Norayr Ayvazian and Anush Pilizian, wife of politician Artashes Geghamian. Since early 1999, *Oragir* and Pashinian have been the target of eight civil and criminal actions. A fine in April of US$25,000 (*Index* 2/1999, 4/1999) forced the temporary closure of the paper, but it has since reappeared under the name *Haykakan Zhamanak* (Armenia's Hour). On 4 September the printers announced that they could not print it 'because of a paper shortage.' (RSF, Helsinki Association, GDF)

Recent publication: *ëRespect My Human Dignity': Imprisonment of Conscientious Objectors* (AI, September 1999, 18pp)

## AZERBAIJAN

The trial of former presidential candidate Ashraf Mehtiev, accused of 'insulting the honour and dignity' of President Aliev by alleging he had Kurdish parentage, was suspended on 6 August indefinitely. (Turan)

**Telman Didirov**, a technician with the DM television in Baku, was found stabbed to death at the station's studio in the Balaken district on 17 August. Some equipment appears to have been stolen, but it remains unclear whether Didirov was killed in the course of a robbery or because of the station's reporting. Didirov's brother was fired as president of DM TV on 6 June. (RSF, WAN, RFE/RL)

The Trade Union of Journalists (TUJo) launched an international campaign on 18 August to halt the abuse of libel laws by officials. TUJo maintains President Aliyev's much-vaunted abolition of censorship last year (*Index* 6/1998) has resulted in the government using the laws on libel and defamation to staunch press criticism. (TUJo)

On 18 August journalist **Yashar Agazade** from *Muxalifet* newspaper was reportedly beaten severely by several Baku policemen. The beating appears to have been intended to punish Agazade for reporting on police violence in Baku. (WAN)

**Khalid Kazimli**, a journalist with the newspaper *Reytinq*, was summoned to the National Security Ministry on 25 August and questioned about an article he had recently written on the Karabakh peace process. Kazimli was asked who had provided him with details of discussions within the Security Council on the possibility of ceding to Armenia part of the territory currently occupied by Karabakh Armenian forces. He refused to name his source. (TUJo, RFE/RL)

Six Jehovah's Witnesses were fired from their positions at the Azerbaijan Gas Refinery on 3 September, a week after local television aired a programme portraying their faith as 'sinister and subversive'. The late-August broadcast on local pro-government Space TV alleged the group paid Azeri Muslims who became Jehovah's Witnesses between US$100 and US$300; that it did not recognise the constitution; and that it was funded by the US and Armenia. The next day the refinery director assembled its staff and 'asked' employees to 'volunteer' their own criticisms of Jehovah's Witnesses. One man was goaded into publicly repudiating his Jehovah's Witness daughter. The factory director then told the six women to provide a written renunciation of their beliefs, or face dismissal. (Human Rights Centre of Azerbaijan)

On 9 September **Irada Husseinova**, a writer with *Bakinski Bulvar* newspaper, was given a one-year suspended jail sentence for libelling and defaming the president's brother and MP, Jalal Aliyev. The case relates to a December 1998 article in which Husseinova described Aliyev as the 'king of the oil industry' (*Index* 5/1999). (RSF)

On 25 September the Supreme Court rejected the request of nine Muslim women to be allowed to keep their hair covered for their passport photographs, overturning a 23 June District Court decision that the women could keep their heads veiled. (FAR)

On 9 October the justice minister ordered the closure of Sara TV, one of three independent stations, saying its foreign ownership contravened local law and that its schedule had veered too far from its original brief of 'entertainment and culture'. In recent weeks, the station had criticised President Haydar Aliev's son, Ilham, and broadcast opposition calls for anti-government rallies. The station's owner, **Rasul Rauf**, an ethnic Azeri from Iran, holds a British passport. (RSF)

Fifty journalists staged an unsanctioned picket outside the Justice Ministry in Baku on 13 October to protest the closure of Sara television. (Reuters, Turan)

## BANGLADESH

On 17 August a magistrate with Lalmonirhat District Court

issued arrest warrants in a defamation case aganst **K. G. Mostafa** and **Iqbal Ahmed**, the editor and managing editor of *Dainik Muktakanta*, and **Mukul Manbood**, a correspondent in Lalmonirhat. The case was filed by a local ruling Awami League leader after the newspaper published a report about a petition to the prime minister and the home minister by journalists calling for protection from harassment by local politicians. (RSF)

The BBC's Dhaka office was threatened on 25 August by an unidentified man who ordered staff to stop broadcasting news on developments in the strained relations between India and Bangladesh. He threatened that, if his order was not obeyed, the office would be the target of a bomb attack. (Media Watch)

The office of the *Daily Janakantha* was repeatedly shot at during a rally by the main opposition party, the Bangladesh National Party (BNP), on 30 August. At least 30 people were injured, two critically, in the attack. Anwar Zahid, deputy minister for information under President Ershad's regime, was subsequently arrested for being one of the ring-leaders of the incident. (Media Watch)

## BELARUS

Deputy chair of the disbanded 13th Supreme Soviet, **Victor Gonchar**, disappeared in Minsk on 16 September after calling his wife, Zinaida, that afternoon to tell her a friend would be driving him home. Zinaida Gonchar told the newspaper *Belapan* of her deep concern over his safety in the light of the disappearances of **Yuri Zakharenko** (*Index* 4/1999) and **Tamara Vinnikova**, and Gonchar's own past detention. Gonchar was due to deliver a speech on 19 September at a session of the Soviet. (International League for Human Rights)

The 'judicial harassment' of journalist **Irina Khalip** continued on 17 September when she was summoned to the Minsk public prosecutor's office for questioning over defamation cases. Khalip, editor-in-chief of the independent weekly *Imia*, is being sued for having 'violated the honour' of Ivan Titenkov, head of the presidential administration, and Oleg Bogelko, the public prosecutor (*Index* 5/1999). She was also asked by the Minsk authorities to provide justification for a trip to the US, where she was to participate in a journalism internship. (RSF)

On 24 September the thrice-weekly, independent *Navini* was ordered by a Minsk court to pay a fine of 10 billion roubles (US$50,000) to Viktor Sheiman, director of the presidential Security Council for a 14 September article by **Serguej Anisko** expressing shock at his lifestyle. Sheiman had recently had a luxurious residence built. The article's author was personally fined 5 billion roubles and the newspaper's accounts were frozen and its assets seized. The newspaper, which is unable to pay, announced that it would close and bring an appeal to the Supreme Court. It published its last edition on 29 September on borrowed funds (RSF, CPJ))

On 4 October Viktor Guretsky, director of the State Press Committee's licensing board, cancelled the registration of nine Minsk-based publications, claiming they had failed to obtain local authority approval for opening their offices. One title, *Nasha Svaboda*, had been launched that week to replace the defunct *Navini*. (CPJ)

## BENIN

Six journalists and editors were given jail sentences ranging from a six-month suspension to a year-long imprisonment and fines on 7 and 8 September. **Patrick Adjamosi** and **Basile Pchibozo**, editor and journalist with *L'Aurore* newspaper, were accused of slandering a Red Cross worker. **Vincent Folly** and **Pierre Matchoudo**, editor and editor-in-chief of *Matin* newspaper, are being sued by the former director of the Air Navigation Security Agency. **Celestin Abissi** and **Charles Tori**, editor and reporter with *L'Oeil du Peuple*, were sentenced with regard to a long-running and apparently settled case dating back several years. The punishments occurred after *L'Aurore* and *Matin* published articles criticising the former state prosecutor. (RSF)

## BOLIVIA

On 11 September ATB television studios and *La Razón* newspaper found that they had their telephone lines intercepted and bugs installed in their premises. Six microphones were located in the offices of president **Raúl Garáfulic Gutierrez** and director **Lorenzo Carri** of ATB, and another at the office of the director of *La Razón*. (RSF)

## BRAZIL

On 16 August two men in motorcycles fired four times at **Nesol Gonçalves** of the daily *O Jornal da Cidade de Bauru* and fled when a neighbour came to the rescue. Gonçalves, who was unharmed, links the incident to his articles on corruption by the Bauru mayor, Antonio Izzo Filho, currently in jail. Last March, a man arrested by police admitted that two of the mayor's former aides had offered to pay him to shoot the journalist in the legs. (RSF)

## BOSNIA-HERZIGOVINA

On 21 September Serbian editions of weekly independent *Reporte,* critical of the Belgrade regime, were seized by Serbian police at the Bosnian-Serb border. According to editor **Perica Vucinic**, the publication of an article listing the 200 richest families, entitled 'They have looted Serbia', motivated the seizure. On 9 June, the daily and weekly Serbian editions of *Nezavisne Novine*, a Banja Luka newspaper critical of Milosevic, were seized by Serbian police (*Index* 4/1999).

## BURKINA FASO

On 15 September at 8 pm the editor-in-chief of the weekly *San Finna*, **Paulin Yaméogo**, was called before the Office of State Security. Since then he has not been allowed to contact his family and noone has visited him. An official of the local press freedom organisation reported that he was blamed for a critical editorial, 'Blaise Compaoré rolls out the red carpet for the putschists', which criticised 'the Power's gangster-like administration'. (RSF)

On 22 September RSF representatives, seeking to clarify the progress made in the investigation into the death of journalist **Norbert Zongo** (*Index* 2/1999, 5/1999), were once again refused entry at Ougadougou airport and escorted onto a plane bound for Mali. An independent inquiry into the case stated in May that the motive for the killing can be found in the journalist's investigation of the murder of David Ouedraogo, chauffeur of presidential advisor François Compaoré. (RSF)

## BURMA

Briton **James Mawdsley**, 26, was sentenced to 17 years's imprisonment on 1 September for illegally entering the country and distributing pro-democracy leaflets. He was arrested on 31 August at the north-eastern town of Tachilek after crossing from Thailand, to where he was deported in 1998 after early release from another sentence for human-rights activism. A five-year suspended term from this second conviction was added to the 12-year term handed down on 1 September. (*Guardian*)

On 16 September, 28-year-old human rights worker **Rachel Goldwyn** from the UK was sentenced to seven years for tying herself to railings in Rangoon and singing a pro-democracy song and slogans deemed to be a 'threat to state security', according to the court. She was taken to the notorious Insein prison outside Rangoon where most of Burma's political prisoners are kept. She was freed on 1 November. (*The Times*)

Two employees of the state-owned newspaper *Kye mon*, **Tha Win** and **Hla Han**, allegedly died under police torture in Rangoon on September 25, after the official newspaper 'accidentally' carried a front-page photo of junta First Secretary-General Khin Nyunt with the title, 'the World Famous Crook'. The two were among 20 staff rounded up after publication, reported an opposition radio station. The junta said Tha was an alcoholic who was already in terminal coma before the event, and Hla retired from the *Kye mon* 10 years previously. (Agence France-Presse)

## BURUNDI

The government on 9 September ordered the army to treat journalists as 'legitimate military targets'. Defence Minister Colonel Alfred Nkurunziza, said in a speech on state radio that the army should 'consider all journalists as enemies' if they entered Bujumbura Rurale province where the army is fighting rebels of the Hutu ethnic group. (CPJ)

Recent publications:

Nyankanzi, L. Edward, 1998, *Genocide: Rwanda and Burundi* Schenkman Books $32.95 (hardcover); Lund, Michael and Kathi Austin, 1998: *Democratisation and Violence in Burundi: The Failure of Prevention Action* Priority PR Publications 120 pp.

## CAMBODIA

The daily newspaper *Sathearnakroath* was shut down on 15 September following the publication of articles critical of King Norodom Sihanouk. Information Minister Lu Layserang ordered the newspaper to close for 30 days while charges were brought. Police were ordered to remove all editions and the newspaper's printer was warned to discontinue publication. (Associated Press)

## CANADA

On 15 September 3,000 Quebec orphans who were sexually and physically abused in church-run institutions in the 1940s and 1950s were told they would receive no apology from the Roman Catholic church on the grounds that to do so would 'constitute a denial of the historic work accomplished under difficult conditions by the religious communitites involved', according to Monsignor Pierre Morissette, head of the Assembly of Quebec Bishops. A Quebec government offer of C$3 million (US$2.3 million) was rejected as inadequate by the orphans, some of whom were beaten, molested or raped while in the care of the institutions. (Associated Press)

## CENTRAL AFRICAN REPUBLIC

**Steven Smith**, a journalist with the French newspaper *Libération*, was barred from entering the republic on 13 September. He was due to cover the forthcoming general election but was considered 'undesirable' following a public inquiry into allegations of governmental corruption in the diamond mining industry. (RSF)

## CHINA

The prominent Uighur businesswoman **Rebiya Kadeer** was arrested on 11 August as she arrived to meet representatives of the US Congressional Research Service (CRS) at the Yingdu Hotel in Urumqi. The authorities also arrested a woman accompanying her and, later that day, two of Kadeer's sons and her secretary, **Kahriman Abdukarim**. Two other sons in Aksu were placed under house arrest. Kadeer has been accused of 'attempting to sell state secrets' to the CRS. The meeting arose from a 15 July briefing to the CRS Caucus by exiled Uighurs, Amnesty International and the US State Department. Among the speakers at that meeting was Kadeer's husband's **Sidik Rouzi**, who was granted asylum in the US in 1996. (AI, HRW)

It was reported in September that authorities had released **Tsering Dorje**, the Tibetan translator detained on 15 August along with two foreigners investigating a proposed World Bank project to resettle Chinese farmers on lands traditionally inhabited by Tibetans in Qinghai province. Beijing claimed that the US pro-Tibet activist **Daja Meston** and **Gabriel Lafitte** from Australia had engaged in illegal photography but Lafitte was released on 21 August and Meston was evacuated from China on 26 August after suffering serious injuries apparently sustained in an escape attempt. There were urgent fears for Dorje's safety as no statement had been issued concerning his arrest. It was reported that Dorje has returned to his work as a teacher, but it is not known whether he faces re-arrest, (Human Rights in China, Reuters, Tibet Information Network)

On August 20 the Law Reform Commission in Hong Kong released a consultation paper proposing the creation of a statutory press council to deal with breaches of a press code on privacy-related matters. Under the proposal, the Press Council for the Protection of Privacy will have the power to impose fines of up to HK$1 million (US$128,000) and will be appointed by a committee itself appointed directly by Hong Kong's Chief Executive. The Hong Kong Journalists' Association has expressed concern that 'the Press Council ... could very likely become a tool for the government to control the press'. (Hong Kong Journalists' Association)

A man arrested for lowering the Chinese flag in Lhasa on 26 August died in hospital in early

October. **Tashi Tsering** lowered the flag in Potala Square, attempted to raise the Tibetan flag and then tried to kill himself before being detained by police, who beat him severely. In the run-up to the 50th anniversary of the People's Republic on 1 October, Lhasans were told that wages and pensions would be cut if they failed to take part in rehearsals for celebrations of the event. On 1 September a 10-year-old Tibetan boy was detained for four months in Tingka in China for refusing to repeat the phrase 'I am a Chinese citizen'. (Associated Press, *International Herald Tribune*, Tibet Information Network, Tibetan Centre for Human Rights and Democracy, Xinhua)

On 5 September the state-run *Guangzhou Daily* reported that police in Guangdong province had arrested 31 people and demolished three churches in a campaign against the 'Cold Water Religion'. The sect, which claims that cold water is the blood of God, has been blamed for the death of five people who drank the 'divine water' instead of seeking orthodox medical treatment, an allegation similar to the one made by the government against the banned spiritual movement Falun Gong (*Index* 5/1999). *China Women's News* reported the arrest of six key members of Falun Gong in Jilin on 12 October, naming **Xu Yingquan**, a provincial leader of the movement, as one of the detained. On 24 August, the government signalled that key leaders of the group in detention – estimated at more than 50 organisers – would go on trial and 'be punished in accordance with the law'. Beijing's relentless crusade against Falun Gong is now being waged in the pages of government-backed comic books with titles like *Li Hongzhi: The Man and His Evil Deeds* demonising the movement's founder as a 'charlatan and an evil genius'. This is a new addition to the regular attacks on **Li Hongzhi** in the state media: in August the Guangzhou-based *Southern Weekend* likened him to a 'despotic tyrant like Hitler'.

(Associated Press, *New York Times*, *Washington Post*)

At the same time as President Jiang Zemin and Time-Warner President Gerald Levin launched the Fortune Global Forum business conference in Shanghai on 30 September, censors were banning the latest edition of *Time*, which ran 'China's amazing half-century' as its cover story. They also blocked the web site of *Fortune*, another Time-Warner publication. Beijing objected to articles in *Time* by the Dalai Lama and exiled dissidents **Wei Jingsheng** and **Wang Dan**. President Jiang was quoted by the official *China Daily* as saying 'the media are playing an important role in modern life and relations between countries'. (Reuters)

On the same day dissident **Wei Jinsheng** e-mailed the text of Article 19 of the Universal Declaration of Human Rights to five official addresses, including the foreign ministry, in protest at the government's control of the internet and repression of dissidents who use it. On 3 September, an activist with the China Development Union was arrested by police in Poutou, Hebei, for preparing to print and distribute *VIP Reference*, an internet newsletter on human rights (*Index* 6/1998). **Qi Yanchen** could face a prison sentence for subversion, as in the case of **Lin Hai**, a Shanghai computer programmer sentenced in January to two years for supplying *VIP Reference* with e-mail addresses (*Index* 2/1999). The government requires users to register with their local security offices and uses filters to prevent access to sites deemed subversive. (Reuters, RSF)

On 1 October police in Hangzhou arrested another member of the banned opposition China Democractic Party (CDP). **Nie Mizhi** was taken from his home and his whereabouts are not known. **Dai Xuezhong**, a Shanghai member, was arrested on 4 October for 'intentionally hurting other people', although police declined to explain to his family what he had done that would constitute the offence. On 29 September, two CDP members, **Yu Dengqiang** and **Liu Jin**, were sentenced to four and three years' imprisonment respectively for subversion by a court in Hebei which provided no witnesses. (HRW, Reuters)

On 18 October **Cheung Mann-yee** was removed from her post as director of state-owned Radio Television Hong Kong (RTHK) and named economic and trade representative to Japan. The reassignment came soon after RTHK gave air time to a senior Taiwan official seeking to explain President Lee Teng-hui's apparent shift in policy towards China. Miss Cheung, 53, had built a solid reputation as a defender of editorial autonomy at RTHK, which was founded in 1923 by the British administration. 'Cheung Man-yee made a lot of enemies in the new establishment,' said talk-show host Albert Cheng. 'Sending her to Japan is almost like putting her in exile.' (*New York Times*)

## COLOMBIA

A hired assassin shot journalist **Guzmán Quintero Torres** three times in the face on Cesar Street, in the city of Valledupar on 16 September. Quintero was editor-in-chief for the regional newspaper *El Pilón*, correspondent for the *Televista* news programme, a member of the Fundación para la Libertad de Prensa, vice-president of the Valledupar Journalists' Group and organiser of training courses for local journalists. *El Piló* is the only newspaper of Cesar department, one of the regions most affected by the political violence and economic crisis. (CJFE, IAPA).

Following the murder of **Jaime Garzon** in August (*Index* 5/1999), a pamphlet signed by the little-known Colombian Rebel Army was openly distributed in the streets of Bogotá, Cali and Medellín containing death threats against three journalists and 18 others whom it accused of being enemies of the country's peace process. The three journalists are **Alfredo Molano**, columnist with *El Espectador*, who fled the country after being threatened by Carlos Castaño, leader of the right-wing paramilitary United Self-Defence Forces (AUC) (*Index* 2/1999); **Patricia Lara**, former owner of the weekly *Cambio* who now writes occasionally for the daily *El Tiempo*; and **Arturo Alpe**, biographer of Manuel Marulanda, leader of the FARC rebels, and also a columnist for *El Espectador*. (CPJ)

## COMOROS ISLANDS

On 14 October police in the capital Moroni arrested **Aboubacar Mchangama**, editor of the independent weekly *L'Archipel* and a correspondent for Agence France-Presse, for publishing an article which examined the troubled relationship between members of the armed forces and the government. Mchangama was questioned and referred to the courts a day later. (RSF)

## CÔTE D'IVOIRE

**Abdoulaye Bakayoko**, owner and manager of the daily *Le Libéral* newspaper, was assassinated on the evening of 21 September. The killers shot him at close range and fled in a vehicle. *Le Libéral* is the newspaper of the Rassemblement des Républicains (RDR), Alassane Dramane Outtata's opposition party. According to police the killing was linked to a car theft. Less than a week later, **Lama Fofana**, manager of the daily *Libération*, escaped an assassination attempt. Two bullets were fired through his car windscreen while he was making his way to the newspaper's office in the Yopougan neighbourhood of Abidjan, but no-one was injured. Fofana is also a member of the opposition central committee of the RDR. (RSF)

## CUBA

**Ramón Colas**, co-founder of Cuba's independent library movement, was detained on 23 August and released the following day. He was arrested in his apartment for protesting against the eviction of his family and their forced relocation to a remote village on a military farm. State Security police seized papers belonging to Colas and his wife, the library's co-founder **Berta Mexidor**, but they were unable to find the collection of the independent Felix Varela Library, which had been dispersed among friends and supporters before the eviction. (Friends of Cuban Libraries)

**Angel Pablo Polanco,** a journalist working for the Independent Journalist Cooperative press agency, was arrested on 8 September by the police accused of 'participating in illegal activities'. Polanco is well known for his reports on human rights activities. Since 1 January, more than 30 independent journalists have been arrested. (RSF)

**Raúl Rivero**, founder and director of the independent news agency *CubaPress*, had his permit to travel to New York's Columbia University denied in September. Rivero was due to receive a special citation from the Graduate School of Journalism for 'Independent reporting in the face of harassment, arrests and threats from the government' on 29 September. (CPJ)

## CZECHOSLOVAKIA

The national broadcaster, Czech TV, has been accused of 'spreading Bolshevik propaganda' by rebroadcasting the popular, Soviet-era TV series *The 30 Cases of Major Zeman*. The lead character, who pursues 'bourgeois agitators', has been heavily criticised by former political prisoners and newspaper editors. But **Jakub Puchalsky**, director of Czech TV, said: 'The series will start a discussion which should have begun in 1989.' (*International Herald Tribune*)

## DEMOCRATIC REPUBLICOF CONGO

A University of Lubumbashi professor, **Kambaji wa Kambaji** was detained on 29 July for his critical analysis of the use of ethnic hate language in political discourse in Katanga. President Laurent Kabila is from Katanga. (HRW)

On 17 August **Hrvoje Hranjski**, a journalist with Associated Press, was injured in a hail of automatic weapon gunfire in Kisangani, while returning to his hotel accompanied by two Rwandan soldiers. He was shot in the right shoulder. It is not known who fired the shot, or whether the journalist was targeted. (RSF)

**Mwamba wa ba Mulamba,** editor-in-chief of the weekly *Bloc-Notes*, was arrested on 24 August by members of the National Information Agency (ANR). The motive for his arrest and location of his detention are unknown. Mulamba is secretary-general of the press freedom organisation Journalistes en Danger. (RSF)

Two freelance journalists, **Kizito Mushisi** and **Omba Kamengele** of Radio Maendeleo, were arrested on 25 August by soldiers of the Congolese Rally for Democracy as they left a meeting in rebel-held Bukavu. They were taken to the offices of the National Information Agency and transferred to an unknown location. On 21 July soldiers had seized the station's transmitter and mixing table (*Index* 5/1999). (RSF)

**Modeste Mutinga Mutuishayi**, editor-in-chief of the independent *Le Potentiel* and president for non-governmental organisation Media for Peace, had his travel documents confiscated on 12 September (*Index* 4/1999, 5/1999). Mutinga was prevented from departing to the UK where he was to attend a conference on good governance. (CJFE)

On 15 September programme directors of the private television stations TKM and Antenne A received orders from the Agence Nationale de Sécurité to cease broadcasting debates or any other programmes of a political nature. TKM had recently featured Mr Ndom, a politician who claims to represent an oppositional group, as a guest on the programme *Temps Fort*, which is broadcast on Sundays. (CJFE)

Editor **Ngov Kikungula** and publications director **Bella Mako** of the Lubumbashi-based *Le Lushois* newspaper were released on 25 September on the order of President Kabila. The president's decision followed a demand for the journalist's release by Lumbashi journalists at an American Cultural Centre-sponsored information seminar. The military court had earlier sentenced the two journalists to eight-month prison terms for defamation and 'spreading false rumours, slander, and lies'. They had served three months prior to release. (CJFE)

On 28 September **Mathieu Mpukundi**, correspondent of *La Référence Plus* newspaper in Matadi, Lower-Congo province, was told by the political advisor that the newspaper would be banned in the province if further information was published that 'incriminated local authorities'. Published in Kinshasa, *La Référence Plus* has recently accused Governor Seraphin Bavudi of embezzlement and analysed tensions between Bavudi and the ministry of public works. The journalist denied writing the articles. (RSF)

On 8 October Kinshasa-Gombé High Court sentenced

the editor of the independent *Le Peuple* newspaper, **Paulin Tusumba** (*Index* 1/1999), and **Michael Godefroid** of *La Libre Afrique* to six-month prison terms with no parole for publishing an article on 8 January which accused then lands minister Anatole Bidhikwabo Chubaka of corruption. *La Libre Afrique*'s publications director, **Freddy Loseke Lisumbu,** who was held for 15 days as part of the case, was acquitted. (RSF)

## DJIBOUTI

**Daher Ahmed Farah**, editor-in-chief of *Le Renouveau* and an RSF correspondent, was sentenced to one year in prison without parole, on 2 September, for 'dissemination of false news stories' and 'damaging the armed forces' morale'. Another journalist, **Ali Meidal Wais**, who was a former senior officer at the army and currently edits the opposition *Le Temps*, was sentenced to eight months in prison. Both were fined and their two papers banned. (RSF)

The disappearence of **Amir Adawehi**, editor-in-chief of *La République*, was reported to Foreign Minister Ali Abdi Farah on 1 October. *La République* is the mouthpiece of the opposition National Democratic Party (PND) and Adaweh is said to be a member of the PND's political office There is concern that he may be imprisoned in Harer in Eastern Ethiopia because of his activities as a journalist. The appeals court trial of 31 PND activists, including Adaweh, was due to take place on 13 October. (RSF)

**Mousa Ahmed Idriss**, editor of the monthly *Le Temps*, was arrested on 23 September and taken to Gabode prison after publishing an article which claimed that a military helicopter was destroyed by the opposition group FRUD. (RSF)

## EIRE

The High Court in Dublin overturned a six-month ban on the listings magazine *In Dublin* on 19 September (*Index* 5/1999) after the publisher promised to remove advertisements for escort agencies and health studios. (*The Times*)

## EUROPEAN UNION

The Dutch auditor, who exposed the EU corruption which led to the resignation of the entire European Commission last March, may be disciplined for his book about the affair, it was reported on 12 October (*Index* 5/1998, 3/1999). **Paul van Buitenen's** *Fight for Europe,* was published in defiance of EU vice-president Neil Kinnock's advice. Van Buitenen was suspended for four months on half pay following his initial revelations, but assigned to another EU post in April with less responsibility. Kinnock said the book constituted a 'breach of staff regulations' and contained numerous references that could be defamatory to EU staff. (*Daily Telegraph* )

## FIJI

Two newspaper editors, **Samisomi Kakaivalu** of *Fiji Times* and **Jale Moala** of *Daily Post,* face possible two-year jail sentences for reporting parliamentary questions raised by opposition leader Ratu Inoke in defiance of the House of Representatives speaker on 27 August. The questions concerned alleged misuse of public funds by a current minister when he was permanent representative to the UN in New York. They were 'expunged' under a parliamentary ruling, which Kakaivalu and Moala are alleged to have breached. (Pacific Islands News Association)

## FRANCE

Justice Minister Elisabeth Guigou has promised a full inquiry into the destruction of three tonnes of documents, including evidence for a trial of Church of Scientology officials due to start on 20 September. The officials are on trial for embezzlement, illegal practice of medicine and violence with premeditation. The destruction of the documents is the second incident of its kind relating to the Church of Scientology in the past two years. (*Daily Telegraph*, Associated Press, *Libération*)

A new law being debated in the National Assembly prevents the publication of images that 'infringe on the dignity of the individual'. The law, due for a final reading in October, has been denounced by editors and photographers alike. One revision would penalise the publication of photographs or footage showing someone in police handcuffs before conviction in court on the grounds that such an image 'tarnishes the presumption of innocence'. Opponents see the law as a veiled attack against French paparazzi, who became notorious when they were investigated for their role in the crash that killed Diana, Princess of Wales. All charges against the photographers were dropped in August. (*Washington Post*)

## GEORGIA

Members of the Protestant 'Word of Faith' congregation, who gathered on 28 August at the House of Culture in the Gldani neighbourhood of Tbilisi for a service to celebrate the Assumption, were attacked and driven away by adherents of the defrocked Orthodox priest Basil Mkalavishili. The incident was observed by 15 police, who declined to intervene, and subsequently allowed Father Basil to congratulate the attackers on their victory over 'the apostles of the Antichrist'. (*Shvidi Dge*)

## GUATEMALA

The president and general manager of *El Gráfico* newspaper, **Marta Arrivillaga de Carpio**, announced on 11 August that she had received death threats, apparently related to the publication of information from the National Security Archive (NSA). According to the NSA the former defence minister, General Mario Enriquez, is alleged to have destroyed files in an attempt to dispose of evidence incriminating the military in illegal activities. De Carpio's husband, journalist **Jorge Carpio Nicolle**, was murdered in mysterious circumstances in 1997. De Carpio was threatened and warned not to make any connection between NSA's information and the murder of her husband. (Guatemalan Journalists Association).

## HUNGARY

On 22 August Agriculture Minister Jozsef Torgyan ordered his bodyguard to seize the interview videotape of reporter **Aniko Disco**, during an interview for Budapest-based Duna TV. The journalist was asking about the problems of agriculture when the minister became angry. Torgyan denied responsibility for the incident but was contradicted by his guard's official report. (RSF)

## INDIA

**Father Arul Doss** was killed in Orissa province by unidentified attackers using bows and arrows on 1 September. As in the murder of missionary Graham Staines and his two sons last January (*Index* 2/1999), Christian activists believe that Doss was killed by a mob organised by the fundamentalist Hindu youth group Bajrang Dal. (*International Herald Tribune*, BBC World Service)

On 24 September it was reported that publisher Penguin India is planning to censor references to Mecca, the Haj and other 'religious terms' from a new version of *The Company of Women*, the latest novel by **Khushwant Singh**. The move is allegedly prompted by threats to both Penguin India and the Bangalore office of the daily *Asian Age* from Islamic fundamentalists. (*Asian Age*)

On 10 October **Lalrohlu**, editor of the local vernacular newspaper *Shan*, was shot dead by suspected militants of one of the separatist movements in the state of Manipur. Lalrohlu had published articles critical of the various guerilla groups in the region. (RSF)

Recent Publications: *India: A vital opportunity to end impunity in Punjab* (AI, August 1999, 18pp); *India: An appeal against death sentences* (AI, August 1999, 7pp).

## INDONESIA

The East Timor referendum on independence was accompanied by a massive rise in violence against objective voices in the island. ANTV's news manager, **Bachtiar**, was interrogated by police on 8 August in relation to an interview with the Free Aceh Movement (GAM) leader **Tengu Abdullah Syafie**. The interview was judged to be 'inflammatory' and 'threatened national unity'. An hour earlier ANTV editor-in-chief **Azkarmin Zaini** was interrogated on the same charge. (AIJ)*Kompas* photographer **Eddy Hasbi** was threatened on 15 August by two men who identified themselves as an 'intelligence agency unit'. They demanded Hasbi report to the nearest police station. (AJI) **Amy Goodman** of Pacifica Radio was prevented from flying from Bali to Dili on 23 August. She was told she had been blacklisted since her presence at the Santa Cruz massacre of over 200 people in 1991 (*Index* 2/1992). (RSF)On 25 August **John Stanmeyer** of *Time* and his Indonesian assistant **Heriyanto** were attacked by members of the Aitarak militia outside the group's HQ in Dili. Stanmeyer had taken photos of militiamen standing outside. Heriyanto was seriously injured. (AJI)A number of violent attacks were made on journalists of several nationalities in East Timor on 26 August. **Kornelius Kewa Ama Khayam** of *Kompas* was shot several times by militiaman but escaped death because he was wearing a bullet-proof vest, suffering only a leg wound. He was beaten and his motorbike set ablaze. **Jaka**, a reporter for the state-owned Antara news agency, was attacked and beaten nearby by militia. The same day, **Marianne Kearney** of the *Canberra Times*, **Torgier Norling** and three other journalists were surrounded as they hid in an army truck by over 100 Aitarak militiamen, who chanted 'kill all Australian journalists'. Torgier was stabbed, but saved by police. Elsewhere in Dili, **Chris Jones** of New Zealand Television and two Australian journalists were shot at and pelted with rocks. They escaped uninjured. **Tjitske Lingsma** of the *Irish Times* was kicked and threatened with a hand grenade in Dili after witnessing the execution of an unarmed man in the street. **Rien Kuntari** and **Eddy Hasbi** of *Kompas*, **Mindo** of Radio Nederland, **Decky** of RCTI and **Albert Kuhon** of SCTV were threatened by militia in Dili as police looked on. **Kornelis Ama** of *Kompas* and **Bea Wiharta** of Reuters were both shot in the leg in an incident with militia in Dili. Thirty journalists were forced out of the Hotel Dili and pursued by armed militiamen as they proceeded to attack the nearby National Council for Timorese Resistance buildings. (Digital Freedom Network, National Public Radio, Reuters)**Panca**, a journalist for East Timor's Lorosae Radio, reported a statement by the Independent Committee for Direct Ballot Monitor several times on 28 August. His house was burned down by militia on 30 August. (Digital Freedom Network) A CBS *60 Minutes* TV crew from Australia was deported from East Timor on 31 August for 'visa irregularities'. Reporter **Richard Carleton**, producer **Mark Llewellyn** and two crew were detained with an Indonesian journalist after questioning voters at a Dili polling station. (*Fiji Daily Post*)

US journalist **Allan Nairn** was deported from West Timor to Singapore on 20 September. He had been detained on arrival in East Timor on 14 September for 'not having a correct visa', then interrogated by police and the commander of military operations, Major-General Kiki Syanhakri. Officials threatened to prosecute him on two violations of immigration law, each carrying five years imprisonment. In 1991, Nairn's skull was fractured after a beating by soldiers during the Santa Cruz massacre (*Index* 2/1992); he was refused entry to East Timor with another journalist in 1994 (*Index* 1/1995); and blacklisted by police in 1998. (IFJ) Dutch journalist **Sander Thoenes** was killed by militia on 21 September in Becora, a Dili suburb. Six men wearing military uniforms opened fire on the *Financial Times* freelancer and his driver as they attempted to pass a roadblock, only hours after Thoenes's arrival in East Timor. UN troops, already in the area since 20 September, discovered his mutilated body the next day. (IFJ, *Guardian*)British journalist **Jon Swain** of the *Sunday Times* and photographer **Chip Hires** escaped an ambush on their car on 21 September as they drove through Baucau, 100km east of Dili. Swain and Hires managed to escape into the hills, where Australian troops later rescued them. The fates of their Timorese driver and translator, taken by the attackers, is unknown. (CPJ)Indonesian journalist **Agi Muliawan**, 26, of Asia Press International, was in a group of nine people massacred near Com, East Timor, on 25 September. He was travelling to Baucau with a religious group to assess humanitarian requirements. Some time after nightfall their vehicle was ambushed by army troops. Their bodies were found next day, some near the van and others dumped in the river Ramoako. Fifteen soldiers were arrested by Interfet forces in connection with the murders. (CPJ)Corruption charges against former president Suharto (*Index* 5/1998, 5/1999)

## ALI ABBAS NEMATI

# The examination

12th Imam: You shall shave your head on Friday. At eight o'clock in the morning you will go to Revolution Avenue. When I arise, you shall be recruiting followers for the final uprising.

Abbas: Friday?

What is wrong? Is it too late?

Um, er, we have the university entrance exam on Friday at eight. Let's postpone it to Saturday.

No, it cannot be. It is God's will for it to be Friday.

Look, I'm not asking to postpone it till after the exam results. I said Saturday. One thousand and three hundred and fifty four years and fifty five days you have been hiding. Why can't you wait one more day for me?

I said it can not be! The world has become filled with oppression and tyranny.

What a turn-up? Dear Lord, if you want to carry out the insurrection tomorrow, I know what will happen. You see, we've had a revolution before. I will miss the exams, your insurrection will take one to two years, then there will be a cultural revolution, universities will be closed for two to three years When they are opened again, instead of 1.5 million to 2 million participants, there will be 7 to 8 million people taking the exams. I would have forgotten my studies by then. I may as well kiss university goodbye.

But you always prayed for me to appear asap. You prayed to be one of my disciples.

And I still do my Lord. But if I become a member of your government tomorrow, I will be a minister without expertise and education. Whereas we need expert disciples. You were in hiding when our revolution happened. Same thing happened here. Take my father, I don't mean to be rude but he got suckered into becoming a revolutionary and served time in prison, so he missed higher education. Then, after the revolution, he got a high-profile position in the government because of his revolutionary activities. Pardon the expression, but he really buggered things up.

The Almighty has decided. If you refuse to become a martyr…

What? You are getting worse than these Ayatollahs. They promised us so much and look what happened. You've only just resurrected and you've already decided I should be a martyr. Lord, don't talk to me like this. Because I love you, I say nothing back to you, but if you talk like this to others, they will land a punch right on your chin and tell you that they have a wife and children.

Do you not love martyrdom ?

Me? I die for martyrdom! I love martyrdom. I wish I could be a martyr 100 times over. But I am not just me. I have responsibilities. You know, better than me, that Plato says 'Everyone has a missing half who is made to marry him'. If I become a martyr, my 'missing half' will become someone else's wife and, because they weren't supposed to wed each other, they will have arguments with each other, their kids will be brought up badly. Because of my sacrifice, their offspring will turn out wrong.

That is enough, I understand, I have to go.

[The man moves away. Abbas grabs the man's hand and shouts:] Where are you going? You think I am going to let you make me miss my exams?
[Abbas puts his hand in his pocket and draws a knife. The stage goes dark. The lights are turned on and off]

[Prayer group, late evening. Everyone is seated and holding the Quran to their heads. Abbas is also holding the Quran and chanting. Abbas punches his feet more vigorously than others and chants louder]

[Abbas is weeping loudly] ❑

*Three students at Amir Kabir Technical University were arrested in September on charges of heresy for a comic sketch published in the campus journal* Mowj (The Wave)*. The play is an argument between a student and the 12th Iman, whose return after 1,300 years in hiding is awaited by all pious Shi'ites. The 12th Imam has selected exam day as the one on which he will choose his 313 disciples and lead the 'insurrection' against injustice and tyranny.* ***Ali Abbas Nemati****, the author, and two others involved in the publication,* ***Hamed Ahangari*** *and* ***Mohammad Reza Namnamat****, face hanging if convicted in a trial which began on 20 October. (www.iran-daneshjoo.org)*

are being dropped because of 'lack of evidence', acting Attorney-General Ismudjoko stated on 11 October. Ismudjoko said investigation of Suharto-controlled charities activities uncovered some irregularities, but 'nothing where Suharto personally enriched himself'. (Reuters)

## IRAN

Five journalists – **Dijavad Emami** and **Mohamad Massoud Salamati** of the banned weekly *Hoviyat-e-Khich*, **Mehti Khaki Firose**, an independent journalist and **Ali Mehri** and **Oroudj Amiri** with the weekly *Omid Zandjani* ñ were reported to have been arrested in the 11 and 18 August editions of the independent weekly *Aban*. Their whereabouts are still unknown. (RSF)

A new bill on political activities, due to be discussed in the Majlis, drew fire on 8 August for the 'abuse that can be made of imprecise and catch-all provisions'. The judiciary has proposed allowing for the prosecution of those 'involved in the interview and collusion with foreign embassies, missions, government organisations, parties and the mass media at any level'. (RSF)

On 5 September the Press Court ordered the indefinite closure of the leading liberal newspaper *Neshat* because of an editorial calling for the abolition of the death penalty and the 'eye for an eye' principle in Islamic justice. Publisher **Latif Safari** was sentenced for a two and half year suspended prison term and banned from journalism for five years. (RSF, *Middle East International)*

On 10 October **Jaleh Oskoui**, director of the weekly *Pend-chanbeh-ha*, was arrested and the paper closed after the publication of articles 'contrary to Islam'. The ministry of culture has lodged a dozen charges against the newspaper. (RSF)

## ISRAEL

Education Minister Yossi Sarid has stepped up a controversial campaign to change the way modern history is taught in schools. Sarid has urged teachers to incorporate the 1956 Kafr Qassem massacre in the curriculum and to commemorate an event in which 50 Arab villagers were gunned down by troops. (BBC)

On 2 September security forces in South Lebanon abducted a Lebanese freelance journalist, **Cosette Elias Ibrahim**, along with her companions, **De Gaulle Butros Bou Taleb** and **Samir George Khimai**. Her family's home in Rumaish was raided and she was taken to Khiam prison in the occupied zone. (CPJ, RSF)

## ITALY

An attempt to intercept a Libyan fighter aircraft on 27 June 1980 was the cause of the crash which killed all 81 people on board a DC9 passenger flight, according to Judge Priore, who has spent nine years investigating the crash. The judge said in his report on 1 September that Italian generals had withheld information that a US fighter was in the area. He spoke of a 'conspiracy of silence' and said that the decisions taken by the Italian military were of such consequence that they must have been decided at a higher, and possibly, international level. (*Daily Telegraph*)

## JORDAN

**Abdel Karim Al-Barghouti**, editor-in-chief of the weekly *Al-Bilad*, was arrested on 23 August and ordered detained by the Amman general prosecutor after Prime Minister Rawabda's eldest son, Issam, filed a libel suit. *Al-Bilad* had published a letter from **Ali Hawamda**, director of the Islamic Hospital, to the prime minister complaining that Issam had harassed nurses in a hospital bus and pulled a gun on the driver. Barghuthi was released five days later on bail. (RSF)

**Azzam Younis,** editor-in-chief of the daily *Al-Al-ArabYaoum,* was sentenced to 14 days in jail on 29 September by the Amman prosecutor general for an article in the 27 September edition about Abdel Moneim Abou Zanat, a Hamas leader and former member of parliament. (RSF)

## KAZAKSTAN

Journalist **Armial Tasymbekov** was found dead at his Almaty apartment in mid-August. Earlier this year, he had been briefly incarcerated in a mental hospital after he was accused of writing graffiti criticising President Nursultan Nazarbeyev and promoting former premier Akezhan Kazhegeldin. (*Index* 3/1999, 4/1999). (RFE/RL)

Following the government's decision in August (*Index* 5/1999) to suspend financing for most official newspapers, the state publishing house in Almaty has refused to print some local newspapers, it was reported on 2 September. Although newspapers have secured alternative funding, they cannot find another printing house. (RFE/RL)

## KENYA

On 20 August **Tony Gachoka** (*Index* 3/1999, 5/1999), editor of the *Post on Sunday*, was sentenced to six months' imprisonment without the option of a fine after he was found guilty of contempt of court. His company, Post Limited, was fined US$13,500 and ordered to cease publication of the paper or any other title until the fine is paid. Gachoka was charged with publishing 'sub-judicial comments' relating to the Goldenberg scandal in which the government lost millions of dollars in shady mineral exports. (Media Institute, NDIMA).

Three editors of the *Weekly Citizen*, **Tom Oscar Alwaka**, **Joseph Omyanje Amusala** and **John Wafula Nangole**, were arrested in Nairobi on 18 August and charged with publishing without 'executing a printer's board'. The contentious issue contained a report that a nominated MP, Zipporah Kittony, and her husband were blaming each other for the break-up of their marriage. (Ndima)

## KUWAIT

On 4 October the Court of Appeal sentenced **Dr al-Baghdadi**, professor and chair of Kuwait University's political science department, to one month in prison for an article he wrote for the student magazine *Al-Shoula* (The Flame) in 1996. Al-Baghdadi had contended that the Prophet had failed to convert the non-believers during his time in Mecca, an argument that angered local clerics. In May, he was given a six-month suspended sentence for blasphemy, in accordance with the 1961 Press and Publications Law. A frequent contributor to the daily *al-Siyassa*, Dr al-Baghdadi was forcibly taken from his home to Taha prison on 5 October where he immediately went on hunger strike to protest his conviction. (HRW)

## KYRGYZSTAN

Staff at the *Vecherny Bishkek* newspaper were the subject of a detailed investigation by the Organised Crime Department in mid-September, after a rash of tax inspections and criminal prosecutions instigated by the state in late August. Editor-in-chief **Alexander Kim** narrowly escaped arrest when the interior ministry, tax authorities and local police laid siege to the building housing the newspaper. The investigation has been denounced as unfounded even by the head of the government's own press service. A front-page editorial on 16 September commented: 'If the fiscal and law-enforcement agencies were to pursue their normal duties with such zeal, tax revenues would swell and organised crime would plummet.' (CPJ, *Vecherny Bishkek*)

## LEBANON

In the first week of October Beirut's investigating judge issued an indictment against **Marcel Khalife**, one of the country's best known singer-composers, for 'offending Islam' in his musical adaptation of a poem by the revered Palestinian poet **Mahmoud Darwaish**. Khalife could face trial and imprisonment of up to three years. (*Independent*, HRW)

## MALAYSIA

Prime Minister Mahatir's government cracked down on web-sites supportive of disgraced former minister **Anwar Ibrahim** (*Index* 6/1998, 1/1999/, 2/1999, 3/1999, 4/1999) throughout August. Ibrahim Ali, Anwar's replacement, said 'the slanderous accusations made on these sites are threats to national security'. Up to 48 sites were identified as making 'defamatory accusations'. (*Index* 3/1996, 1/1998). (freeMalaysia.com, *New Straits Times*)Opposition leader **Lim Guan Eng** was released from prison in Kuala Lumpur on 25 August to cheering crowds. He was jailed a year earlier for 'sedition' and 'publishing false news' in a pamphlet criticising the government's handling of a statutory rape case against a former minister, where the alleged victim was jailed and presented as the criminal. Lim, no longer an MP, is barred from standing in the country's forthcoming elections. (*Economist*)**Anwar Ibrahim**ís US$26m defamation suit against Prime Minister Mahatir was dismissed on 30 August by Judge R.K. Nathan as a 'frivolous and vexatious' abuse of the court process (*Index* 6/1998, 1/1999/, 2/1999, 3/1999, 4/1999). (Associated Press)On 11 September **Anwar Ibrahim** was admitted to Unversiti Kebangsaan Malaysia Hospital after urine samples showed a high level of arsenic poisoning. Doubts about his welfare in custody were first raised in September 1998 when he was violently assaulted in prison. Doctors declared on 5 October that there was no evidence of poisoning. (Digital Freedom Network)Canadian journalist **Murray Hiebert** was jailed for six weeks in Sungai Buloh prison on 11 September for 'scandalising the court'. The charge stemmed from a 1997 article in the *Far Eastern Economic Review* concerning increasing ligitiousness in the country and which cited a case involving a prominent judge, Gopal Sri Ram. Hiebert was freed on bail, but forbidden to leave the country. (*Guardian,* CPJ)

## NEW CALEDONIA

The national radio and television services, Réseau France-Outremer (RFO), went off air for three days up to 7 October after a strike by union activists. They were supporting colleagues who had been punished for halting a current affairs programme in which a business leader gave his views about a series of strikes. The Union Syndicale des Travailleurs Kanak Exploités began the strike against the wishes of 90% of RFO staff. (PINA)`

## PAKISTAN

In mid-August three reporters were attacked in separate incidents in Sindh province. Unidentified armed men snatched the camera of **Muhammad Ali**, a photographer for the daily *Ibrat.* On 17 August, **Ghulam Hussain Hajjano**, a reporter with *Ibrat*, was beaten by two uniformed and one plainclothes policemen after he refused to go with them to see the local police chief. Then, on 18 August, **Shabir Baidar Buttho**, Sukkur bureau chief of the daily *Kawish*, was shot at by three unidentified men in his office. Buttho is well known for his exposés of local corruption. (RSF)

In a letter disclosed by his son on 30 August, **Rehmat Shah Afridi**, the imprisoned editor-in-chief of the Peshawar-based dailies *Frontier Post* and *Maidan* (*Index* 3/1999), expressed fears for his life as a result of a 'police encounter' or other 'extra-judicial means'. In a separate incident that day, **M. Ziauddin**, the Islamabad bureau chief of the daily *Dawn*, was asked by an unnamed official to reveal the source of a report he had filed on the federal finance ministry's approval of a supplementary budget for the prime minister's office in the first quarter of the current financial year. Ziauddin was threatened with the 'same treatment' **Najam Sethi** (*Index* 4/19 99, 5/1999) and **Hussain Haqqini** (*Index* 4/1999) received if he did not comply. (RSF)

Photographers **Saeed Iqbal** of the Sindhi-language *Hilal-Pakistan* and **Mohammed Farooq** of the Associated Press were beaten by police while covering an opposition rally in Karachi on 1 September. (Pakistan Press Foundation)

**Anwarullah Khan**, a correspondent in Banjaur Agency for the daily *Nation*, was arrested on 16 September under Article 40 of the Frontier Crime Regulations (40 FCR). His arrest followed the publication of an article criticising the authorities' inefficiency and incompetence in solving people's problems. The 40 FCR cannot be challenged in court and the accused can be jailed for years without trial. (RSF)

Three weeks after the US State Department publicly expressed concern about a possible military overthrow, the army took over state-run television and radio during a 12 October coup d'etat against the government of Prime Minister Nawaz Sharif, led by by General Pervez Musharraf. After five days of speculation, General Musharraf told the nation that the armed forces would only stay in power for as long as it took to renew the organs of 'real democracy', which he argued had been made sick by corrupt and power-hungry politicians. He also promised fiscal probity and said that he would publicly disclose all of his assets. (BBC World Service, *Financial Times*, CPJ, *Guardian*)

## PALESTINE

On 15 September security service agents arrested **Maher Al-Desssouki**, a journalist for the private Al-Quds Educational channel, in a raid on the Arab Cultural centre in Ramallah. He was accused of 'possessing material inciting against the Palestinian National Authority'. The arrest followed the 12 September edition of his weekly programme which included interviews with Palestinians whose family members were not included in the prisoner release a week earlier. One mother interviewed sharply criticised President Yasser Arafat. (CPJ)

**Saleh al-Naameh**, of the weekly *Rissala*, and **Rizq**, a journalist with the daily *Al-Hayat Al-Jadida*, were arrested on 28 September, apparently for giving information to the London-based daily *Al-Hayat*. The day after, they were charged with 'spreading false news harmful to the Palestinian National authority'. (WAN)

## PERU

On 21 July journalist **Manuel Jesús Silva Ruíz** received a three-year suspended sentence and a fine of 20,000 soles (US$6,055) in damages in a slander case filed by former provincial mayor Manuel Vasquez Valera. The court's decision did not take into account the evidence that the journalist presented in his defence. (IPYS)

**Cesar Hildelbrant** no longer faces charges for treason, violation of state secrets and espionage (*Index* 2/1998, 4/1998, 4/1999). On 10 August Attorney Jose Ochoa Lamas shelved the case after he failed to prove that the journalist had distributed confidential information regarding the deployment of Ecuadorian troops on Peruvian territory. Attorney Ochoa Lamas argued that there was insufficient proof of the supposed risk to national security as there was no confirmation that the information he gave on the programme was the same as that discussed in congress. (IPYS)

On 12 August the political and military headquarters of Huancavelica locality sent out an official letter ordering the media to submit copies of all their news reports immediately after being broadcast. The same order was received by several television stations. The document was signed by Captain A. Delgado R. and bore the stamp of the Secretary of the Huancavelica Political and Military Command. (IPYS)

A sentence prohibiting **Ricardo Bullón Mateos**, news director of Radio Señorial, from carrying out any journalistic work for two years was passed on 16 August. He received two years' suspended prison sentence and has to pay 15,000 soles (US$4,500) for defamation and insult. Bullón had reported on an auditor's report revealing irregularities by the president of the city's welfare society, Janina Soria de Veliz. (IPYS)

An intimidating letter was sent to **Jesús Raimundo** at ATV Noticias TV station on 23 August, reminding the journalist of the threats directed against him in 1998, when he worked for *El Comercio*ís Sunday sister-paper, *El Dominical*. Raimundo had received threats after publishing an investigation about vice-minister Fredy Moreno on 9 August 1998 in which he denounced his abuse of authority. Moreno was then president of Chavin region and prefect of Huaraz. (IPYS)

**Eduardo Cenepo Eljarrat**, editor of the regional weekly magazine *El Clarín* in Pucallpa, was summoned by Lieutenant Colonel Jorge Martinez Fernández, regional military chief, to clarify and substantiate information published in the magazine on 19 August. The inquiry refers to an interview with the mayor of the district of Yurua, Fidel Soria Rodriguez, and with the municipal director, Hecer Cardenas. During the interview, the two officials had accused Major Luis Muñoz Loarte of having 'committed irregularities'. In the opinion of Jorge Martinez the article 'damages the army's institutional image and deserves to be investigated'. (IPYS)

The Military Justice Supreme Council (CSJM), the judicial body of the armed forces, accused journalists at the Prensa Libre Association (PLA) of having used false documents for their accusation that the Military Intelligence Service had played a role in political espionage. PLA claimed that intelligence agents followed and spied on presidential candidates Alberto Andrade and Luís Castañeda. On 25 August the press association presented documents and films proving that the politicians had been followed. (IPYS)

Journalist **Kela León** and photographer **Paul Vallejo**, working for *Caretas* magazine, were attacked in Talara province on 3 September and had their credentials and equipment stolen. (IPYS)

On 5 September journalist **Marco Villanueva Escobar** received a fractured left hand and injuries to the back and legs when a security guard at a local hospital in Chimbote threw him out of the premises. The guard was trying to prevent Villanueva taking photographs of a elderly patient he was interviewing. (IPYS)

Another underground tabloid, ridiculing the critical daily *La República*, began publication in September under the title of the *Repútica del Gran Sur*. This publication, as well as the previously published *La Repúdica* and *Repudio*, aim to defame journalists critical of the government (*Index* 4/1998, 1/1999, 4/1999). (IPYS)

Journalist **Angel Durán** announced on 16 September that he would begin an indefinite hunger strike until guarantees for his safety are provided by the authorities. Durán has been the target of death threats, attempted bribery and a campaign to discredit him. On 13

September he was refused protection by the police who argued that an investigation into his case had been carried out the previous year. Duran's problems started when he accused Vice-Minister Fredy Moreno of unlawful appropriation of over 10m soles (US$2,9m). (IPYS)

**Pedro Anccori**, priest at the San Juan Bautista parish which owns Radio La Voz de Allinccapac in the Macusani district, was summoned by local police on 20 September. He was asked to provide 'documentation' after the radio station denounced the assassination of a young man by the police. (IPYS)

On 22 September a tabloid was distributed in the city of Huaraz insulting, defaming and threatening journalist **Juan Sánchez Oliva**, director of the radio news programme 'Quassar en la Noticia' on Radio Quassar. Sánchez had revealed earlier on air that he and his family had been receiving threats and intimidation for the previous six months. Sánchez's show reports the abuses and irregularities committed in smaller towns that are often at the mercy of mining company executives. On 27 August Sánchez's brother was stopped on the street by six masked individuals, dressed in military clothing and carrying heavy weapons. He was brutally beaten and had to be taken to hospital. (IPYS)

## ROMANIA

On 24 September a group of construction workers assaulted **Lorena Boros** and **Dorina Tataran**, both reporters with the *Gazeta de Nord-Vest* daily in Satu Mare, as they were investigating accusations that the SC IMA SA Baia Mare construction firm had won the municipal contract in a rigged auction. The journalists' equipment was also seized and destroyed in front of them. The workers told the police, who arrived over an hour later, that they had acted in self-defence after the journalists had attacked them. The previous day, a reporter with the daily *Jurnalul de Constanta*, **Marian Tudor**, was assaulted by two unidentified assailants aboard a train from Constanta to Bucharest while delivering edited manuscripts for that day's edition to printers in the capital. Tudor was thrown from the moving train after the documents were seized. (CPJ)

## RUSSIA

On 31 August Radio Lemma was served a warning by the Federal TV and Radio Service that its licence would be revoked if it did not broadcast 24 hours a day. At present, the station broadcasts from 7am to midnight. The move follows attacks on correspondents, which started when the station began an investigation into Vostoktranslot, the largest refrigerated shipping line in the region. (CPJ)

**Dimitri Balbourov**, a correspondent with the weekly *Moskovskie Novosti*, went missing on 3 October near Nazran in the Ingushia Republic, which borders Chechnya. **Said Issayev**, a correspondent with the Itar-Tass press agency in Grozny, disappeared on 15 October and is reported to have been kidnapped. Issayev was previously kidnapped on 28 March and held for three months before being released in late June. Four journalists have been kidnapped in the Caucasus region in 1999 and 17 in the the last two years. (RSF)

Defence Minister Igor Sergeyev claimed reports that a Russian tank attacked a busload of Chechen refugees on 7 October were 'disinformation', despite the recordings of an amateur cameraman which were smuggled out of Chechnya. The footage was not broadcast on Russian television. (*Guardian*)

## RWANDA

**Amiel Nkuriza**, editor-in-chief of the newspaper *Le Partisan*, left Kinironko prison on 18 August, two weeks after the official release date. He had been detained without trial since May 1997 following the publication of articles critical of the government. (AI)

## SERBIA-MONTENEGRO

On 16 September, journalists **Radmila Ognjenovic** and **Sonja Curic**, and editor **Vukota Corovic**, were interrogated for several hours at police headquarters in Belgrade over an article in the independent *Novosti*, entitled 'Rise of the black market' on the street exchange rate for the Deutschmark. **Slavko Curuvija**, editor at the *Dnevni Telegraf*, had also been summoned to police headquarters for interrogation on a similar article prior to the Kosovo conflict and his own murder (*Index* 3/1999). (RSF)

The offices of the Belgrade-based Radio Globus were broken into in the early hours of 26 September, when equipment loaned to the station to allow it to continue broadcasting was stolen. The equipment had been loaned to Globus following a break-in on 11 September, when more than DM5,000 worth of equipment was stolen. Globus staff have criticised the theft, which they believe was intended to hinder the independent station. The offices of Plus Radio, based in the same premises but with no political remit, were untouched. The break-in came soon after the launch of a media campaign by local NGOs demanding that the manager of the government-controlled Radio Kraljevo be replaced. (ANEM, RSF)

On the evenings of 29 and 30 September, a number of journalists were attacked by security officers while covering demonstrations of the opposition Alliance for Change party in Belgrade's city centre. Two cameramen working for Sky News and CNN International were injured and their equipment was destroyed. **Slavisa Lekic** and **Aleksandra Rankovic**, journalists with the Beta independent press agency, were also injured after anti-riot police moved in. The rallies had attracted over 20,000 protesters. (RSF)

## SIERRA LEONE

Reuters' **Christo Johnson** (*Index* 5/1999) was released on 6 August after being taken hostage by military junta rebels during the handover of 200 abducted children. (CPJ)

On 20 August **Jonathan Leigh**, managing editor of the *Independent Observer*, received a death threat by telephone from an ECOMOG officer following a satirical article on ECOMOG's peacekeeping abilities. (*Index* 4/1999, 5/1999). (CPJ)

On 20 August **Paul Kamara**, publisher of *For Di People* was assaulted by three Revolutionary United Front (RUF) commanders following an article alleging laziness and corruption by RUF commanders based in Freetown. An ECOMOG officer declined to intervene while the attack took place. (CPJ, RSF)

Journalist **Emmanual Sanossi** of the *Reporter* was arrested by CID officers on 27 August, released, rearrested and detained on 29 and, finally, on 3 September, served with a deportation order back to his native Cameroon. The actions follow the publication of an article by Sanossi accusing the government of trying to derail the peace process. (RSF, CPJ)

## SOUTH KOREA

**Seok Hyun Hong**, publisher of the highly critical, pro-opposition *Joong Ang Ilbo* newspaper, was arrested on 30 September on multiple charges of tax evasion and subsequently jailed, although he has no legal liability in the Bokwang business group, which is under investigation. Though chief shareholder Dr Hong was not involved in the group's management, never held a post there and legally has no liability for any alleged tax evasion. (WAN)

On 1 October the Korean Federation of Broadcasting Unions launched the country's biggest ever media solidarity campaign together with 325 Korean NGOs to call for long-awaited democratic reform of broadcasting legislation. The campaign was launched following news that six union leaders, arrested for leading a 12-day strike at major television stations in Seoul, face jail terms under legislation against unofficial strikes. **Hyun Sang-Yoon**, **Park Young-Chun**, **Park Jin Hae**, **Choi Eun**, **Kim Soo-Tae** and **Han Myung-By** led a walk-out of staff at the Korean Broadcasting System (KBS) and the Munwha Broadcasting Corporation (MBC) in support of demands for parliamentary supervision of top appointments, new rules guaranteeing editorial independence and laws to prevent excessive concentration of ownership. Although the management of KBS and MBC have agreed to petition for the release of the union leaders, prosecutors are expected to press for the maximum sentence of four years. (IFJ)

## SRI LANKA

On 21 August unidentified attackers threw two hand grenades at the office of New Uthayan Publications, publishers of the Tamil-language daily *Uthayan* and the weekly *Sanjeavy*, the only newspapers in the government-controlled city of Jaffna. Noone claimed responsibility for the attack but **Vellipurum Kaanamylnathan**, editor of the group, believes that pro-government militias – which his papers regularly criticise – are responsible for the attack. (RSF)

**Rohan Kumara**, editor of the pro-opposition tabloid *Satana* (Battle), was shot dead on 7 September by unknown attackers while travelling home from his office in a taxi. Opposition leaders have demanded a quick investigation into the murder, claiming that 'certain powerful people' who were embarrassed by Kumara's exposes of government corruption were behind the killing. (International Press Institute, CPJ, Free Media Movement)

In early October **Victor Ivan**, editor of the Sinhalese-language weekly *Ravaya*, expressed fear for his life to *Index* after he was followed on several occasions and his lawyers received threats over the telephone. Ivan believes the intimidation is related to his allegations of moral turpitude against the chief justice of the supreme court, Sarath Silva. Ivan has written numerous articles in which he accuses Silva of supressing evidence in a case where magistrate Lenin Ratnayake, a relative of his, faced allegations of rape and misappropriation of funds. (*Colombo Sunday Times*)

## SUDAN

Temporary suspension is the chief censorship tool of the National Press and Publications Council (NPPC). On 22 July, the daily *Alwan* was supended for two days for an article that criticised the authorities for seizing farmers' wheat harvest in eastern Sudan. On 26 July, the NPPC ordered an unspecified period of suspension of the daily *Al-Raï Al-Akbar* for articles 'critical of government policies' (*Index* 5/1999). On 10 August, the daily *Al Bayan* was suspended for three days because of an article, written by an unaccredited journalist, that was critical of the ruling National Congress Party. On 18 August the National Press Council announced another suspension of the *Al-Raï Al-Akbar*, this time for seven days following the publication of articles critical of governmental policy. On 1 September the *Al-Raï Al-Akhar*t was suspended for a further week, *Al Rai Al-A'am* for two days (*Index* 3/1999) and the government-owned daily *Al-Anba'a* for one day for reporting 'inaccurate and harmful' economic information. On 17 September the independent daily *Al-Rai Al-Akbar* was suspended indefinitely. This seventh suspension since the beginning of the year was for printing a story that was found to be 'sceptical of the Jihad' for its suggestion that 'rebel leader John Garang deserved a monument in central Khartoum for sending Sudan's young men to heaven as martyrs'. (RSF, Agence France Presse)

## SWAZILAND

**Bheki Makhubu**, editor of the *Times Sunday*, was reportedly forced to resign following the publication of an article on 12 September alleging that King Mswati's new bride, the Liphovela Senteni Masango, was a 'high school drop-out'. Makhubu was arrested on 26 September and charged with defamatory libel under a law dating back to the colonial era. The *Times Sunday* did not appear on that day. Makhubu was later released on bail of around US$500. It is reported that the authorities are seeking a court order forcing Makhubu to 'reveal his sources'. The government also tabled a Certificate of Urgency legislation addressing defamation of character by the media on 20 September. (MISA)

## SYRIA

Journalist and democracy advocate **Nizar Nayouf** is nearing death in a military prison following years of torture and lack of suitable treatment for cancer and other related diseases. Nayouf was sentenced to hard labour for being a member of an unauthorised organisation – the Committee for the Defence of Democratic Freedom. He was also the editor of the CDF monthly journal *Democracy*. (RSF, WAN)

## TAJIKISTAN

Ibrohim Usmonov, who heads parliament's committee on culture and international relations, berated editors at a 19 August meeting for producing papers 'full of violence, cruelty and war,' and failing to promote 'higher human values' and to 'protect the dignity of the Tajik people'. Ten of the nation's 30 weeklies are owned by the state and there is no daily. (RFE/RL)

## THAILAND

The daily *Thai Post's* office was invaded on 13 July by armed men sent by Deputy Prime Minister Trairong Suwnkhiri, demanding to see the reporter who wrote about Trairong's 'fear in the face of protesting fishermen'. The gang leader Chalie Noppawong na Ayuthaya said the story was untrue and, if another unflattering story were published, he would come back, but 'in a different manner'. (CPJ)**William Stevensonís** biography of King Bhumibol Adulydej will be banned from sale and print, the foreign ministry announced on 26 August. Despite royal co-operation, spokesman Don Pramudwinai – who didn't read the book – said factual errors and a 'lack of reverential treatment' led to the ban. Some copies have already entered the country and are being photocopied and circulated. (*International Herald Tribune*)

## TURKEY

The privately owned national TV channel Kanal 6 was ordered shut down for a week from 30 August for its critical coverage of the government's reaction to the country's worst-ever earthquake, which struck on 17 August, killing an estimated 40,000 people. In the days following, there was an unprecedented barrage of criticism of the authorities' inept and uncaring response to the thousands buried under jerry-built housing erected on what was a well-known faultline. Health Minister Osman Durmus became the main target after he rejected foreign aid but the army was also castigated for not mobilising its 500,000 troops to assist with the rescue and clean-up operations . On 25 August Durmus urged the High Board of Radio and Television (RTUK), the broadcasting watchdog, to take action against six national channels which he accused of 'directing grave insults' against him. On 26 August, the RTUK singled out Kanal 6, which had been been particularly scathing, and accused it of 'encouraging violence, terror and ethnic discrimination and allowing broadcasting that could create feelings of hatred among the people'. Prime Minister Bulent Ecevit distanced himself from the decision to ban Kanal 6 but said that the media should help 'boost morale' and not put out reports that 'upset people'. (Reuters, BBC, IPI, RSF)

On 28 August parliament adopted an amnesty bill which will release some 25,000

## ED MOLONEY

# No deal

For much of the last 30 years the media in Ireland has been on the defensive against official and unofficial acts of censorship and the abuse of undemocratic politicians. The sordid affair of William Stobie and the murder of Pat Finucane has given journalists an opportunity to make a significant fight back on an issue most of them have immediately recognised as having grave implications for the practice of their profession.

One thing has to be said about my decision not to hand over notes or to give evidence against William Stobie, a former Loyalist paramilitary and my source for the story on allegations of collusion in the murder of Pat Finucane. I am not doing this to protect a murderer. I would not make a deal, and I know of no journalist who would make a deal, to protect a murderer.

I made a deal with Stobie because of his very serious allegations that, as an Royal Ulster Constabulary agent, he had informed his handlers both before and after the murder of Pat Finucane, but to no avail. He believed his life was in danger, or that he might be framed on false charges, because he fell out with the Special Branch afterwards.

He spoke to me because he wanted someone to be able to tell his story if the worst happened. Events unfolded in such a way as to give considerable credence to his allegations. In those circumstances I had no difficulty making a deal with him.

This stand is not about protecting the identity of a source. It is about protecting a source. When I sat down with Stobie nine years ago there was an unwritten contract between us. First, I would not write the story without his say so. He was a spy for the police. If the story got out in an uncontrolled fashion he could be killed.

Secondly, there was an implicit understanding that I would act only as a journalist – I would confine my activities to disseminating his story in the media. If I had told Stobie I would also hand over my notes to the police and give evidence against him he would never have spoken to me and the serious allegations about the Finucane killing would never have surfaced.

If I were now to renege on that contract, none of my media colleagues would thank me – indeed many would revile me – and I would be telling the world that journalists are not to be trusted. In a worst case and admittedly extreme scenario, sources everywhere would think twice before speaking to reporters. The vital role of the watchdog played by the media would be gravely, irreparably damaged.

On a personal level I would be unable to work again as a journalist in

Ireland. No source could ever trust me again and who could blame them? Equally this action could put my life in danger. There will be those in the paramilitary world who would see my handing over this material as the thin end of a dangerous wedge. They may decide to teach me and other journalists a lesson.

If we lose this case it will be a setback for journalism in Ireland. But worse would be if I were to hand these notes over. ❑

***Ed Moloney**, Northern Ireland editor of the Dublin-based* Sunday Tribune, *faced up to five years in jail and unlimited fines for refusing to comply with a court order on 23 September to hand over interview notes to police. Scotland Yard had asked the courts to compel Moloney to do so after he published a story in which he reported that Alfred Stobie, the man charged with the 1989 murder of Belfast lawyer Patrick Finucane, was a double agent for the Royal Ulster Constabulary. This edited extract was published in the winter edition of the* Irish Journalist. *On 27 October Northern Ireland's senior judge ruled that Moloney did not have to comply with the order*

prisoners and reduce the sentences of a further 32,000. In response to widespread criticism that the bill would release mafia chiefs, corrupt politicians and thieves, but not journalists and other victims of censorship regulations, President Suleyman Demirel on 2 September signed into law an amendment which the Turkish Press Council said would release or pardon some 60 journalists and writers. Among those expected to benefit were **Oral Calislar**, **Yilmaz Odabasi** and **Ismael Besikci**, but others convicted for 'speech crimes' about the Kurdish problem, such as the blind lawyer and short-story writer **Esber Yagmurdereli**, MP **Leyla Zana** (*Index* 1/1997, 6/1998, 5/1998, 1/1999, 4/1999, 5/1999) and **Akin Birdal**, former head of the Human Rights Association (*Index* 4/1998, 5/1998, 1/1999, 4/1999) will remain in prison. Responding to public anger over the 17 August earthquake, the amnesty bill excludes contractors convicted of negligence or corruption. (CPJ, *Info-Turk*, WiPC)

**Nadire Mater**, a reporter with Inter Press Service, was formally charged with 'insulting' the military in *Mehmed's Book*, her collection of interviews with veterans of the Kurdish conflict, it was learned in the week of 13 September (*Index* 5/1999). Although *Mehmed's Book* had already sold 20,000 copies in four editions, an Istanbul court banned its distribution on 23 June. Mater and **Semih Sokmen**, of Metis publishing house, were formally indicted on 29 September when the case was postponed to 26 November. If convicted, Mater faces one to six years in prison. (CPJ, WiPC)

On 27 September an Istanbul State Security Court banned distribution of the 27 September edition of the Islamist daily *Akit*, because of an 'Open Letter' from columnist **Abdurrahman Dilipak** to Prime Minister Bulent Ecevit on the occasion of his first visit to Washington. Dilipak asks: 'Could you tell me how you will defend yourself against the questions about hundreds of teachers and students that you threw away from their schools just because they were wearing headscarves...?' The court charged that the column constituted an 'incitement of the people against the state'. (CPJ)

## UK

DJ **Steve Jackson** of London's *Kiss FM* radio station told an industrial tribunal on 18 August that he was dismissed as part of a policy of 'ethnic cleansing' aimed at making the station more mainstream. Jackson was sacked in December 1998 along with 19 other staff in a 'restructuring' move by owners Emap Radio.(*Daily Telegraph*)

In late August, Scarborough Borough Council banned the September edition of the Yorkshire-wide listings magazine *Panic* from its tourism information centre. The five-year-old free magazine had published the word 'fuck' and reviewed a feminist book, entitled *Cunt,* in recent issues. A representative told editor/publisher **Richard Rouska** that the office would not longer stock *Panic* on its display shelves, but would still sell it 'under the counter'. (*Panic*)

The Labour government is spending £1 million of taxpayers' money each month on private polling but only releases a third of the data collected, according to figures released by the Liberal Democrat Party on 3 September. Surveys that ministers have felt unwilling to publish include research into attitudes towards the Millennium Dome, the new British Library and electoral reform. (*Daily Telegraph*)

Greater secrecy for future genetically modified crop trials is being planned by the government after another farmer withdrew from the environmental tests, it was reported on 11 September (*Index* 3/1999). The ministry of the environment has stopped short of imposing a German-style blanket ban of naming sites. One option is to name the general geographic location based on the council area or parish, instead of publishing a grid reference of the test area in local newspapers. (*Daily Telegraph*)

Journalist **Tony Geraghty** has been charged under the Official Secrets Act, it was reported on 19 September (*Index* 2/1999). The charge concerns his latest book, *The Irish War,* published by HarperCollins. Geraghty refused to show his manuscript in advance of publication to the D-Notice committee, part of a voluntary system whereby authors can check their books don't 'offend' under the Act. The offending part of the book concerned computerised methods of surveillance in Northern Ireland. In December last year Ministry of Defence police raided his house and confiscated all his files and computer equipment. (A19)

The Home Office has refused to release the names of scientists who have broken regulations in experiments on animals, it was reported on 22 September. The request for details of these infringements was made by the *Guardian* under the open government code introduced in 1996 by the previous administration. The Home Office replied that identities of the researchers concerned had to be protected to prevent possible attacks by animal rights extremists. (*Guardian*)

On 24 September it was reported that Public Record Office files of a covert propaganda unit in 1953 show the existence of pressure on broadcasters and the widespread use of psychological warfare. Programmes were allegedly uncritical of the Soviet regime; failed to make comparisons between life in Britain and the USSR that would have been unfavourable to the Soviet Union; and attacked western politicians, such as anti-communist Senator Joe McCarthy. An official of the Information Research Department (IRD) of the Foreign Office at the time met BBC officials and asked them to monitor broadcasts. (*Guardian*)

On 28 September the European Court of Human Rights declared that the UK ban on homosexuals in the armed forces violated the basic human right to privacy. (*International Herald Tribune*)

Following the Paddington rail crash on 5 October, it was reported that safety warnings that could have alerted the public that trains had overrun signals outside the station are protected by Whitehall's secrecy laws. Railtrack, which is responsible for safety on the railways, is outside of the scope of the 'open government' code introduced by the previous government. (*Guardian*)

*Guardian* journalist **David Hencke** was questioned by Scotland Yard's organised crime squad in early October, for revealing that a leaked district auditor's report was about to condemn the former Conservative leader of the City of Westminister council, Dame Shirley Porter. His alleged crime was 'aiding and abetting' the person who leaked the report. After refusing to name his source, Hencke's file was passed on to the Crown Prosecution Service for a decision on whether to prosecute. (*Guardian*)

Pro-democracy demonstrators protesting during President Jiang Zemin of China's state visit to the UK were met with a policy of 'zero tolerance' by the police, it was reported on 20 October. One demonstrator was arrested for throwing confetti, while others had pro-democracy banners and Tibetan flags confiscated by the police. (*The Times, Guardian*)

## USA

In mid-July, journalists **James** and **Elizabeth Sanders** were given probation and community service sentences for stealing seat material from the re-assembled wreckage of TWA Flight 800, which crashed into the sea off Long Island in 1996. The material was to be used to prove Sanders' theory that a US navy missile was to blame for the accident, a theory he put forward in his 1997 book, *The downing of TWA flight 800*. Three years on, the cause of the accident remains unknown. (*News Media and the Law*)

Thirteen-year-old Daniel Shellhammer of Toledo, Ohio, was ordered to remove his T-shirt, decorated with publicity for the rap group 'Insane Clown Posse', or face arrest, it was reported on 9 August. The T-shirt was confiscated from the youth by three police officers who made it clear to him that 'if I didn't take off the shirt I was going to jail.*í*(*Toledo Blade*)

Mayor Rudolph W. Giuliani threatened on 22 September to cut off all city funding to the Brooklyn Museum after seeing the catalogue for a British exhibition, 'Sensation: Young British Artists From the Saatchi Collection', and condemning it as 'sick stuff'. His main objection was to a portrait of the Virgin Mary by Chris Ofili which used elephant dung and was deemed to be deeply offensive to catholics. Ofili is a Roman Catholic. Giuliani's actions have been condemned as 'an unconstitutional attempt to censor ideas you personally oppose' in a letter from the American Civil Liberties Union. A survey by the *Daily News* showed that New Yorkers supported the museum over Giuliani by a majority of two to one. (*New York Times*, ACLU)

In the last week of August the FBI issued a statement admitting it had fired two inflammable tear-gas grenades at a bunker within the Waco compound during the 1993 siege, having vigorously denied any use of such weapons. The FBI offices were raided by US marshals from the Justice Department who were looking for video recordings of the siege. Attorney General Janet Reno claimed that she had not seen a single document on the subject until early September. (*Daily Telegraph*, *International Herald Tribune*)

It was reported on 3 September that 67,000 government workers with access to defence secrets have been ordered to report any sexual or romantic relations they have had with foreigners – unless it was a 'one-night stand'. (*Guardian*)

A teenager who typed 'the end is near' on his computer screen has been convicted of 'communicating threats' and given a 45-day suspended sentence, 18 months' probation and 48 hours' community service, it was reported on 30 September. Joshua Mortimer from Wilmington, North Carolina, spent three nights in prison following the remark. (Associated Press)

George Washington's fob watch has had to be censored from a nineteenth century portrait in a school text-book because it risked being mistaken for his genitals. The watch, hanging down the president's thigh, was painted out by hand from over 2,000 copies of the book *United States in Modern Times*, it was reported on 8 October. (BBC Online)

## UZBEKISTAN

Six men were sentenced on 18 August to terms of between eight and 15 years for possessing copies of a banned newspaper and for their affiliation with the banned political party Erk (Freedom). All six alleged they suffered torture in detention, including electric shocks, burns, beatings with batons and water-filled plastic bottles, and near suffocation with plastic bags. The six convicted men were **Mamadali Mahmudov**, author of nationalist novel, *The Immortal Cliffs*; **Muhammad** and **Rashid Bekjanov**, brothers of exiled opposition leader Muhammad Solih; and **Kobil Dierov**, **Ne'mat Sharipov** and **Iusuf Ruzimuradov**. The prosecution case centred on the defendants' alleged possession of the *Erk* newspaper, which the state claimed contained slanderous criticisms of President Islam Karimov. The eight-year sentence against businessman Ne'mat Sharipov, who is not an Erk member, rested solely on his having imported from Ukraine several copies of a book by Solih. (AI, HRW)

## VANUATU

The editor and desk editor of the Vanuatu Broadcasting and Television Corporation (VBTC) were suspended on 18 September after revealing details of government interference in the reporting of news. **Moses Stevens** and **Hilare Bule** told a meeting of the journalists group Pres Klab blong Vanuatu that they had been ordered not to report the defection of a government backbencher to the opposition. They were reinstated on 29 September 'with a strong warning'. (PINA)

## VIETNAM

The Unified Buddhist Church of Vietnam (UBVC), effectively outlawed since 1975, has been under increasing pressure of late with the arrest and persecution of several prominent persons. **Thich Tue Sy**, monk and dissident, was interrogated by Saigon police on 14 September. Thich, who is secretary-general of the UBVC, was accused of 'seeking to overthrow the government'. Police claimed the proof was contained in his computer, but Thich said it held only translations of Buddhist Sutras and internal UBVC documents. Thich was charged with the same offence in 1984 and condemned to death in 1988 (*Index* 1/1989, 2/1989), though he served a prison sentence totalling 14 years instead. (AI)Two days later, UBVC activist **Thich Khong Tanh** was arrested in Saigon and interrogated, his documents were confiscated and he was accused of 'seeking to turn Vietnam into another Kosovo'. Next day, he was again arrested, interrogated and released. It is reported the police tried to force Tanh to sign a confession of 'attempting to overthrow the government' and 'belonging to an illegal organisation'. (AI)The UBVC's number two, **Thich Quang Do**, applied to the communist authorities on 22 September for permission to publish a magazine so as to 'correct the distortions of Buddhism' as portrayed in the official media. Do stated from his Saigon house that the application was made on 22 September, but he doubted its success, citing the refusal earlier this year of dissident and former top ideologue **General Tran Do**ís application to publish a newspaper (*Index* 2/1999, 5/1999). (AI)

## YEMEN

On 11 September **Hisham Basharaheel**, editor-in chief of the thrice weekly *Al-Ayyam*, was summoned to the prosecutor's office for questioning about an interview with the London-based Muslim cleric Abu-Hamza Al-Masri that appeared in the paper in August. During interrogation Hisam was accused of publishing information from 'unreliable sources'. Seven days later, on 18 September, he was summoned to answer charges about a news item that apparently misquoted passages from the Quran. (CPJ)

On 16 September the appellate court ordered the closure of the opposition weekly *Al-Shoura*. The court's decision stemmed from an incident in February, when two separate versions of the paper were published under the same name, thus violating provisions of the press law. But according to the journalists from *Al-Shoura*, security authorities had published the second version as a subterfuge. (CPJ)

On 9 October the weekly *Al-Haq* was ordered closed for one month by San court. Its editor-in-chief, **Abdul Latif Kutubi Omar**, was fined 40,000 riyals. The newspaper was sued last May after it published an article accusing local officials of corruption and abuse of authority. (RSF)

## ZIMBABWE

In the week beginning 6 September lawyers representing *Standard* journalists Mark **Chavunduka** and **Ray Choto** (*Index* 3/1999, 4/1999) filed an application in the Supreme Court forcing the commissioner of police to investigate their arrest and torture by state police. On 4 October the two journalists were charged under the Law and Order Maintenance Act of 1960 with a remand hearing set for 4 January. The two were also recipients of the Canadian Journalists for Free Expression International Press Freedom Awards. (CFJ)

The media group Public Eye Publishing (PEP) filed for liquidation on 4 October, citing financial and viability problems. The group, publishers of the popular and influential political magazine *Horizon*, claimed escalating printing costs had forced them into the decision. (MISA)

*Compiled by: Jake Barnes, John Kamau, Shifa Rahman, Daniel Rogers (Africa); Rupert Clayton, Andrew Kendle, Jon Parr, Robin Tudge (Asia); Alex Lockwood (Eastern Europe); Dolores Cortés, Daniel Rogers (south and central America); Arif Azad (Middle East); Humfrey Hunter (north America and Pacific); Steve Donachie (UK and western Europe)*

Support for

# INDEX ON CENSORSHIP

*Index on Censorship* and the *Writers and Scholars Educational Trust (WSET)* were founded to protect and promote freedom of expression, which is not self-perpetuating but has to be maintained by constant vigilance.

The work of *Index* and *WSET* is made possible thanks to the generosity and support of our many friends and subscribers worldwide. We depend on donations to guarantee our independence, to fund research and to support projects which promote free expression.

The Trustees and Directors would like to thank the many individuals and organisations who support *Index on Censorship* and *Writers and Scholars Educational Trust*, including:

Anonymous
The Ajahma Charitable Trust
The Arts Council of England
The Bromley Trust
The John S Cohen Foundation
DANIDA
Demokratifonden
The European Commission
The Ford Foundation
The Goldberg Family Trust
The Golsoncot Foundation
The Calouste Gulbenkian Foundation
Institusjonen Fritt Ord
The JM Kaplan Fund
The Open Society Institute
The Onaway Trust
Pearson plc Charity Trust
CA Rodewald Charitable Settlement
The Royal Literary Fund
The Royal Ministry of Foreign Affairs, Norway
Scottish Media Group plc
Stephen Spender Memorial Fund
Tom Stoppard
Swedish International Development Co-operation Agency
United News and Media plc
UNESCO

If you would like more information about *Index on Censorship* or would like to support our work, please contact Hugo Grieve, Fundraising Manager, on (44) 171 278 2313 or e-mail hugo@indexoncensorship.org